The Selected Poetry and Prose of VITTORIO SERENI

The Selected Poetry and Prose of
VITTORIO SERENI

A BILINGUAL EDITION

Edited and Translated by
PETER ROBINSON
AND MARCUS PERRYMAN

with an Introduction by
PETER ROBINSON

The University of Chicago Press :: *Chicago and London*

Vittorio Sereni (1913–1983), widely regarded as among the most important Italian poets of the last century, was also an essayist and a translator.

Peter Robinson is professor of English literature at Kyoto Women's University. He has published over thirty books of poetry, translations, and literary criticism including *Selected Poems* (2003), *The Greener Meadow: Selected Poems of Luciano Erba* (2006) and *Twentieth Century Poetry: Selves and Situations* (2005).

Marcus Perryman is a freelance translator and consultant, among whose most recent publications are versions of two Renaissance Italian works by Andriano Banchieri, *The Folly of Old Age* and *The Wisdom of Youth*. With Peter Robinson, he has translated and published poetry by Giuseppe Ungaretti, Franco Fortini, and Maurizio Cucchi, as well as an earlier selection of poems by Sereni.

The University of Chicago Press, Chicago 60637
The University of Chicago Press, Ltd., London
© 2006 by The University of Chicago
All rights reserved. Published 2006
Printed in the United States of America

15 14 13 12 11 10 09 08 07 06   1 2 3 4 5

ISBN-13: 978-0-226-74878-8 (cloth)
ISBN-10: 0-226-74878-2 (cloth)

Italian poetry © Copyright the Estate of Vittorio Sereni. All rights reserved.

This publication was made possible thanks to the support of the Italian Ministry of Foreign Affairs, the Istituto Italiano di Cultura of Chicago, Director Tina Cervone, and the Istituto Italiano di Cultura of Los Angeles, Director Francesca Valente.

The University of Chicago Press gratefully acknowledges the generous support of Kyoto Women's University toward the publication of this book.

Library of Congress Cataloging-in-Publication Data

Sereni, Vittorio.
 [Selections. English & Italian. 2006]
 The selected poetry and prose of Vittorio Sereni : a bilingual edition / edited and translated by Peter Robinson and Marcus Perryman ; with an introduction by Peter Robinson.
  p. cm.
 Includes bibliographical references and index.
 ISBN: 0-226-74878-2 (cloth : alk. paper)
 I. Robinson, Peter, 1953– II. Perryman, Marcus. III. Title.
 PQ4879.E74A27 2006
 851'.914—dc22

2006019212

⊚ The paper used in this publication meets the minimum requirements of the American National Standard for Information Sciences—Permanence of Paper for Printed Library Materials, ANSI Z39.48-1992.

CONTENTS

Illustrations xiii
Preface xv
Acknowledgments xix
Introduction 1
Chronology 31

Selected Poetry

da FRONTIERA / *from* FRONTIER

Concerto in giardino / Garden Concert   42
    Inverno / Winter   42
    Concerto in giardino / Garden Concert   42
    Domenica sportiva / Sport on Sunday   44
    Memoria d'America / Recalling America   46
    Canzone lombarda / Lombard Song   46
    Compleanno / Birthday   48
    Nebbia / Fog   48
    Temporale a Salsomaggiore / Storm at Salsomaggiore   50
    A M. L. sorvolando in rapido la sua città / To M. L. Passing Above
        Her Town in an Express Train   52
    Diana / Diana   54
    Soldati a Urbino / Soldiers in Urbino   54

  3 dicembre / 3 December 56
  Poesia militare / Military Poem 58
  Piazza / Piazza 58
  Alla giovinezza / To Youth 58

Frontiera / Frontier 60
  Inverno a Luino / Winter in Luino 60
  Terrazza / Terrace 62
  Strada di Zenna / Zenna Road 62
  Settembre / September 64
  Un'altra estate / Another Summer 66
  Immagine / Image 66
  In me il tuo ricordo / Your Memory in Me 68
  Strada di Creva / Creva Road 68

Ecco le voci cadono / See How the Voices Fall 72
  "Ecco le voci cadono e gli amici" / "See how the voices
    fall and friends" 72

DIARIO D'ALGERIA / ALGERIAN DIARY

La ragazza d'Atene / The Athenian Girl 76
  Periferia 1940 / Outskirts 1940 76
  Città di notte / City at Night 76
  Diario bolognese / Bolognese Diary 76
  Belgrado / Belgrade 78
  Italiano in Grecia / Italian in Greece 80
  Dimitrios / Dimitrios 80
  La ragazza d'Atene / The Athenian Girl 82
  Risalendo l'Arno da Pisa / Up the Arno from Pisa 86
  Villa Paradiso / Villa Paradiso 86
  Pin-up Girl / Pin-up Girl 86

Diario d'Algeria / Algerian Diary 88
  "Lassù dove di torre" / "Over there where from tower" 88
  "Un improvviso vuoto del cuore" / "An unexpected
    vacancy of heart" 88
  "Rinascono la valentia" / "Valor and grace" 90
  "Non sa più nulla, è alto sulle ali" / "He knows nothing anymore,
    is borne up on wings" 90

"Ahimè come ritorna" / "Alas how what returns"   92
"Non sanno d'essere morti" / "They don't know they're dead"   92
"Solo vera è l'estate e questa sua" / "Only the summer is
   true and this"   94
"È ancora in sogno d'una tenda s'agita" / "And again in a dream
   the tent's edge"   94
"Spesso per viottoli tortuosi" / "Often through tortuous alleys"   96
"Troppo il tempo ha tardato" / "Too late has the time come"   96
"Se la febbre di te più non mi porta" / "If fever for you no more
   sustains me"   98
"Nel bicchiere di frodo" / "In the smuggled glass"   100
Algeria / Algeria   100

Il male d'Africa / The African Sickness   102
   Frammenti di una sconfitta / Fragments of a Defeat   102
   Il male d'Africa / The African Sickness   106
   Appunti da un sogno / Notes from a Dream   112
   L'otto settembre / September the Eighth   114

da GLI STRUMENTI UMANI /
from THE HUMAN IMPLEMENTS

Uno sguardo di rimando / A Backward Glance   118
   Via Scarlatti / Via Scarlatti   118
   Comunicazione interrotta / Interrupted Communication   118
   Il tempo provvisorio / The Provisional Time   120
   Viaggio all'alba / Journey at Dawn   120
   Un ritorno / A Return   122
   Nella neve / In the Snow   122
   Viaggio di andata e ritorno / Journey There and Back   122
   L'equivoco / The Misapprehension   124
   Ancora sulla strada di Zenna / On the Zenna Road Again   124
   Finestra / Window   126
   Gli squali / The Sharks   128
   Mille Miglia / Mille Miglia   128
   Anni dopo / Years After   130
   Le ceneri / The Ashes   132
   Le sei del mattino / Six in the Morning   132

Una visita in fabbrica / A Factory Visit   134

Appuntamento a ora insolita / Appointment at an Unusual Hour   140
    Il grande amico / The Great Friend   140
    Scoperta dell'odio / Discovery of Hatred   142
    Un incubo / A Nightmare   142
    Quei bambini che giocano / Those Children Playing   144
    Saba / Saba   144
    Di passaggio / Passing   146
    Situazione / Situation   146
    Gli amici / The Friends   148
    Appuntamento a ora insolita / Appointment at an Unusual Hour   148

Il centro abitato / The Inhabited Center   152
    Nel sonno / In Sleep   152
    I versi / The Lines   158
    Corso Lodi / Corso Lodi   158
    L'alibi e il beneficio / The Alibi and the Benefit   160
    La poesia è una passione? / Poetry Is a Passion?   160

Apparizioni o incontri / Apparitions or Encounters   166
    Un sogno / A Dream   166
    Ancora sulla strada di Creva / On the Creva Road Again   168
    Intervista a un suicida / Interview with a Suicide   170
    Il piatto piange / Il Piatto Piange   174
    Sopra un'immagine sepolcrale / On a Cemetery Photograph   176
    A un compagno d'infanzia / To a Childhood Companion   178
    Dall'Olanda / From Holland   180
    La pietà ingiusta / The Unjust Pity   184
    Nel vero anno zero / In the True Year Zero   186
    La speranza / The Hope   188
    Metropoli / Metropolis   190
    Il muro / The Wall   192
    Pantomima terrestre / Earthly Pantomime   194
    I ricongiunti / The Reunited   196
    La spiaggia / The Beach   198

da STELLA VARIABILE / *from* VARIABLE STAR

I   202
    Quei tuoi pensieri di calamità / Your Thoughts of Calamity   202
    In una casa vuota / In an Empty House   202

Toronto sabato sera / Toronto Saturday Night 204
Posto di lavoro / Place of Work 204
Lavori in corso / Works in Progress 206
Addio Lugano bella / Beautiful Lugano Goodbye 210
Interno / Interior 212
Crescita / Growth 214

II 214
Di taglio e cucito / Of Cuts and Stitches 214
Poeta in nero / Poet in Black 216
Revival / Revival 216
Sarà la noia / It Will Be the Boredom 218
Festival / Festival 220
Esterno rivisto in sogno / Exterior Seen Again in Dream 220
Giovanna e i Beatles / Giovanna and the Beatles 222
Ogni volta che quasi / Each Time That Almost 224

III 226
Un posto di vacanza / A Holiday Place 226
Niccolò / Niccolò 244
Fissità / Fixity 246

IV 248
Traducevo Char / Translating Char 248
  I "A modo mio, René Char" / "In my way, René Char" 248
  II Muezzìn / Muezzin 248
  III Un tempio laico / A Lay Temple 250
  IV Villaggio verticale / Vertical village 250
  V Martellata lentezza / Hammered Slowness 252
  VI Notturno / Nocturne 252
  VII Madrigale a Nefertiti / Madrigal to Nefertiti 254
  VIII "Bastava un niente" / "A nothing sufficed" 254

V 256
Verano e solstizio / Verano and the Solstice 256
Requiem / Requiem 256
Paura prima / First Fear 258
Paura seconda / Second Fear 258
Altro posto di lavoro / Other Place of Work 260
La malattia dell'olmo / The Disease of the Elm 260
In salita / Uphill 262

Il poggio / The Knoll   264
Nell'estate padana / Summer in the Po Valley   264
A Parma con A. B. / In Parma with A. B.   266
Autostrada della Cisa / Autostrada della Cisa   268
Rimbaud / Rimbaud   270
Luino-Luvino / Luino-Luvino   272
Progresso / Progress   274
Altro compleanno / Another Birthday   274

Selected Prose

from THE IMMEDIATE SURROUNDINGS

Prewar Letter   281
Bologna '42   282
Ljubliana   283
Sicily '43   285
Algeria '44   289
Barbed-Wire Fever   292
That Film of Billy Wilder's   296
Airs of '53–'55   300
The Title of Poet   306
You Began   308
On the Back of a Piece of Paper   309
Two Old Flames   310
Creative Silence   313
The Year '43   315
The Year '45   322
The Reunited   329
On the Death of Ungaretti   330
Self-Portrait   331
Port Stanley Like Trapani   334
Infatuations   338

from CROSSING MILAN
The Capture   341
The Option   348
Twenty-Six   375

Commentary   389
Bibliography   427
Index of Titles and First Lines   433

ILLUSTRATIONS

- ii   Sereni (1935)
- 7   Manuscript of "Compleanno"
- 17   Sereni in via Scarlatti (1940)
- 21   Typescript of "L'alibi e il beneficio"
- 30   Sereni as a child with family members
- 41   Manuscript of "Inverno a Luino"
- 74   Sereni at Garessio (1940)
- 75   Manuscript of "Non sa più nulla"
- 116   Sereni with Vladimir Nabokov (1959)
- 117   Cover of the 1965 edition of *Gli strumenti umani*
- 200   Sereni with his wife and Piero Bigongiari in the Vaucluse (1968)
- 201   Manuscript of "Notturno" from *Stella variabile*
- 278   Sereni with Franco Fortini (1982)
- 279   Corrected proof of "I ricongiunti"
- 339   Cover of *L'Opzione e allegati*
- 388   Sereni in his study in via Paravia (1980)

PREFACE

Vittorio Sereni visited Verona for a night in late June 1981 — and it was, in a manner of speaking, thanks to Ungaretti that we came to meet him. During the previous year, we'd been polishing a few of our collaborations on the older man's poems for a limited edition to be published in Verona by the Plain Wrapper Press, run by Richard-Gabriel Rummonds and Alessandro Zanella. Some time earlier, we'd both been intrigued by Franco Fortini's epigram "To Vittorio Sereni," which includes the lines: "Once you told me I was a destiny. / But we are two destinies." Eugenio Montale's review of Sereni's 1965 book, *Gli strumenti umani,* come across at about the same moment, offered further reasons for finding out more about a sympathetic-sounding poet evidently admired by seniors and contemporaries. We began to read as widely as possible, made four draft translations, and sent them to Sereni at Mondadori in Milan. We received a kind reply saying he would give the translations to his eldest daughter to look over. As chance would have it, the Plain Wrapper Press printed a limited edition of Sereni's *Stella variabile* in 1979. So it was at the press's offices that we first met just a few months before Montale's death. We talked over some of the translations we'd already made and had dinner together. There was further discussion at the press the following day. A second meeting was arranged at the Mondadori offices in Segrate, Milan, during April 1982. Through the rest of that year and into the next, arrangements were being made for a series of Italian poetry events at the Cambridge International Poetry Festival where Sereni was to read. His sudden death, on 10 February 1983, turned that reading into a memorial.

During the second of our meetings we were discussing an ambiguous word with no equivalent ambiguity in English. Knowledgeable about the difficulties involved from his own experiences of translating poetry, Sereni suggested we render the most apparent meaning. We have done our best to take his advice. Whether by means of an apparently literal or an equivalent rendition, we have aimed to be faithful to his original poem. Wishing to pay homage to Sereni's verse, we have kept as close to the number of lines, the syntax, and the layout of the Italian as has been possible in another language. The rhymes, meters, and textures of a poem will usually be lost in translating the sense. In compensation, we have sought comparable devices and textures, composing our versions to supply the loss and give a sense of Sereni's originality. In translating his prose, we have aimed for fluidly readable texts that nevertheless preserve their intimate relationship with his poetry and its shared sources of inspiration. We have wanted to convey Sereni's distinctiveness in Italian and have not over-naturalized his sensibility in our language.

In presenting a bilingual *en regard* edition of a substantial selection from Sereni's authorized poems, we hope to be useful for a range of readers. To those who have little or no Italian, we offer accurately faithful translations that are, to the best of our ability, poems in their own right. We believe that reading our versions gives a clear impression of the poetic achievement, stylistic development, and themes of a major poet whose work has been crucial to the evolution of the art in Italy throughout the middle of the twentieth century. For those who have some working knowledge of Italian, our versions—which closely resemble Sereni's in their form and shape—can be used as guides to the intricacies of his complex originals. For those who are fluent in both languages we offer an edition of most of Sereni's poetry and the occasion to consider our solutions to the problems that rendering his works in English will inevitably raise. In the interests of illuminating his poetry and underlining the range of his concerns we have added a selection of key texts from his extensive prose writings. These mostly concern his wartime and postwar experiences and his—not unrelated—examinations of poetry's function and the poet's role in the second half of the twentieth century. *The Option* is included as a major short story in its own right, illuminating Sereni's unease during the postwar reconstruction of Europe and his lingering sense of complicity in the period's nightmares. The introduction offers a critical account of his work, its sources, development, and influences. Further introductory information about Sereni's times, his life, and oeuvre can be found in the chronology and the commentary sections.

The translations collected here are the result of many years of illuminating, educative, and pleasurable collaboration. Conversations with many people in Parma, Verona, and elsewhere have been invaluable. We would especially like to remember those with Luciano and Mimia Erba, Franco Fortini, Gilberto Lonardi, and P. V. Mengaldo. We consulted the French version of *Stella variabile* by Philippe Renard and the late Bernard Simeone. We have also compared our translations with English versions by Luigi Bonaffini, Gavin Ewart, Ruth Feldman and Brian Swann, Robin Fulton, Anthony Oldcorn, Tom Paulin, Sonia Raiziss and Glauco Cambon, John Sanders, Eric Sellin, G. Singh, and Paul Vangelisti. Barbara Colli at the Sereni Archive in Luino has helped with clarifying details and with photographic materials. Dante Isella provided invaluable elucidation of some key passages. Yoko Funasaka, Eiichi Hara, and Haruhide Mori helped with material support for the book at a crucial moment. Those who reported on our manuscripts provided many useful prompts for revision; and Randolph Petilos, our editor, has been invaluably helpful, patient, and encouraging throughout. We would also like to thank Cristina Matteoni and Ornella Trevisan for detailed advice and personal support.

We thank Silvia Sereni, Giovanna Sereni, and Laura Chiari-Sereni for permission to publish the texts of Vittorio Sereni's poetry, and for agreeing to the publication of our translations. We also gratefully acknowledge their permission to publish material from the Sereni archives, as well as the permission of the Lombardy Regional Authority and the Luino Town Council. Giovanna Sereni kindly helped us locate and prepare the illustrations for this edition. After the poet's death, we visited his eldest daughter, Maria Teresa Sereni (1941–1991), on numerous occasions to ask for elucidation, suggestions, and criticism. She devoted a great deal of her time to the proofs of our 1990 *Selected Poems*. Maria Teresa was her father's daughter in her patient, painstaking approach to the art of translation and in her scrupulous sensitivity to nuance. We would especially like to remember her invaluable assistance, and to recall the hospitality that she and her family always showed in Viale Rustici, Parma.

Above all, for his friendly encouragement, guidance and understanding, we owe a deep debt of gratitude to Vittorio Sereni.

P. R. and M. P.
31 October 2005

ACKNOWLEDGMENTS

Grateful acknowledgement is made to the editors of the following publications where many of these translations, or their earlier versions, first appeared:

"Fog," Poetry Ireland Translations, no. 7, *Poetry Ireland Newsletter* (1983); "Soldiers in Urbino," *Siting Fires* 2 (1983), *London Magazine* 27, nos. 1–2 (1986), *Poetry Ireland Review* 80 (2004); "Terrace," *Siting Fires* 2 (1983), *Poetry Ireland Review* 80 (2004); "September," *Molly Bloom* 1 (1980); "Image," *Modern Poetry in Translation* 5 (1994); "Your Memory in Me," *Siting Fires* 2 (1983); "City at Night," *Argo* 5, no. 1 (1983); "Belgrade," *Siting Fires* 2 (1983), *Poetry Ireland Review* 80 (2004); "Italian in Greece," *Argo* 5, no. 1 (1983), *London Magazine* 27, nos. 1–2 (1986); "Algerian Diary," *PN Review* 32, 9/6 (1983); "Over there where from tower," *Faber Book of Twentieth-Century Italian Poems,* ed. J. McKendrick (London: Faber & Faber, 2004); "He knows nothing any more, is borne up on wings," *London Magazine* 27, nos. 1–2 (1986); "They don't know they're dead," *Faber Book of Twentieth-Century Italian Poems;* "Fragments of a Defeat, 2," *London Magazine* 36, nos. 5–6 (1996); "The Great Friend," *Poetry Kanto* 13 (1997); "Saba," *Molly Bloom* 1 (1980), *Siting Fires* 2 (1983), *Faber Book of Twentieth-Century Italian Poems;* "Passing," *Molly Bloom* 1 (1980); "Appointment at an Unusual Hour," *London Magazine* 27, nos. 1–2 (1986); "In Sleep," *Siting Fires* 2 (1983); "A Dream," *Faber Book of Twentieth-Century Italian Poems;* "Interview with a Suicide," *Scripsi* 9, no. 2 (1994); "Il Piatto Piange," *Poetry Ireland Review* 80 (2004); "From Holland," *Poetry Ireland Review* 80 (2004); "In the True Year Zero," *London Magazine* 36, nos. 5–6 (1996); "Earthly Pantomime," *Poetry Ireland Review* 80 (2004);

"The Reunited," *New Grains* 2 (1998); "Toronto Saturday Night," *Writing: A Literary Review* 1 (2005); "Works in Progress," *New Directions* 47 (1983); "Interior," *New Directions* 47 (1983); "Revival," *New Directions* 47 (1983); "It Will Be the Boredom," *Modern Poetry in Translation* 5 (1994), *London Magazine* 36, nos. 5–6 (1996); "Festival," *New Directions* 47 (1983); "A Holiday Place," I: *Translation and Literature* 12, no. 1 (2003), III: *Poetry Ireland Review* 80 (2004), VI: *Agenda* 40, no. 4 (2004); "Niccolò," *New Directions* 47 (1983), *Numbers* 3 (1987); "Translating Char," *Translation and Literature* 12, no. 1 (2003); "The Disease of the Elm," *New Directions* 47 (1983); "Uphill," *New Directions* 47 (1983); "Summer in the Po Valley," *New Grains* 2 (1998); "In Parma with A. B.," *New Directions* 47 (1983), *PN Review* 46, no. 12/2 (1985); "Autostrada della Cisa," *New Directions* 47 (1983), *London Magazine* 27, nos. 1–2 (1986); "Rimbaud," *New Directions* 47 (1983); "Luino-Luvino," *Testo a Fronte* 9 (1993); "Self-Portrait," *Poetry Ireland Review* 80 (2004); "Port Stanley like Trapani," *London Magazine* 36, nos. 5–6 (1996); "Twenty-six," *Numbers* 1 (1986).

From Vittorio Sereni, *The Disease of the Elm and Other Poems* (London: Many Press, 1983): "On the Zenna Road Again," "Six in the Morning," "Passing," "Situation," "A Dream," "To a Childhood Companion," "The Wall," "Place of Work," "Of Cuts and Stitches," "Each time that almost," "Niccolò," "Fixity," "Requiem," "Another Place of Work," "The Disease of the Elm," "In Parma with A. B.," "Autostrada della Cisa," and "Another Birthday."

From *Selected Poems of Vittorio Sereni* (London: Anvil Press, 1990): "Lombard Song," "Birthday," "Fog," "Storm at Salsomaggiore," "To M. L. Passing above Her Town in an Express Train," "Diana," "Soldiers in Urbino," "3 December," "To Youth," "Winter in Luino," "Terrace," "Zenna Road," "September," "Your Memory in Me," "Creva Road," "See how the voices fall and friends," "Outskirts 1940," "City at Night," "Bolognese Diary," "Belgrade," "Italian in Greece," "Dimitrios," "The Athenian Girl," "Algerian Diary," "The African Sickness," "September the Eighth," "Via Scarlatti," "Journey There and Back," "The Misapprehension," "On the Zenna Road Again," "Window," "The Sharks," "Years After," "Six in the Morning," "Discovery of Hatred," "Those Children Playing," "Saba," "Passing," "Situation," "The Friends," "Appointment at an Unusual Hour," "In Sleep," "The Lines," "The Alibi and the Benefit," "Poetry Is a Passion?" "A Dream," "On the Creva Road

Again," "On a Cemetery Photograph," "To a Childhood Companion," "From Holland," "The Wall," "The Beach," "Those Thoughts of Yours of Calamity," "In an Empty House," "Place of Work," "Works in Progress," "Interior," "Of Cuts and Stitches," "Revival," "Giovanna and the Beatles," "Each Time that Almost," "Niccolò," "Nocturne," "Madrigal to Nephertiti," "Requiem," "First Fear," "Second Fear," "Other Place of Work," "The Disease of the Elm," "Uphill," "In Parma with A. B.," "Autostrada della Cisa," "Rimbaud," "Progress," and "Another Birthday."

From Peter Robinson, *The Great Friend and Other Translated Poems* (Tonbridge, Kent: Worple Press, 2002): "The Great Friend," "On the Creva Road Again," "In the True Year Zero," "Festival," "Niccolò," and "The Disease of the Elm."

The introduction includes passages adapted and revised from the following publications: "A Thread of Faith," *London Magazine* 27, nos. 1–2 (1987); introduction, *Selected Poems of Vittorio Sereni;* "Envy, Gratitude, and Translation," *In the Circumstances: About Poems and Poets* (Oxford: Oxford University Press, 1992); "The Music of Milan," *Times Literary Supplement* 4868 (1996); "'Una fitta di rimorso': Dante in Sereni," *Dante's Modern Afterlife: Reception and Response from Blake to Heaney,* ed. N. Havely (London: Macmillan, 1998); and "Vittorio Sereni's Escape from Capture," *Poetry Ireland Review* 80 (August 2004).

INTRODUCTION

I

Vittorio Sereni's first real encounter with America occurred between eleven o'clock and midnight on 24 July 1943—just three days before his thirtieth birthday and one before Mussolini's fall from power in Rome. Even in early 1943, Sereni and his fellow soldiers expected to be sent to support the retreating forces on the other Mediterranean shore. By April, having narrowly missed becoming air reinforcements for the North Africa campaign when the runway at Castelvetrano was bombed, Sereni's Pistoia Division was sent to the defense of Sicily, preparing for anticipated Allied landings in the west of the island near Trapani. However, on 10 July the invasion of Sicily began in the east at Gela and Syracuse. This effectively meant Sereni and his fellow soldiers were trapped in a pocket that, during the following two weeks, tightened around them.

Sereni's prose accounts of these events make it clear that there was little will to resist. The Sicilians, far from sympathetic to the fascist regime, were encouraging the soldiers to surrender or desert. The chain of military command was in tatters even at the highest levels with morale, understandably, not good. There was desertion, but also a prevalent air of fatalistic passivity. Writing twenty-six years later, Sereni describes a sense of culpability in that state of mind: "[F]ate, we say, or else chance; on the contrary, it's the point at which a lengthy inertia unconscious of itself is released and becomes a precipitous slide."[1] When the American

---

1. See p. 381 below.

82nd Airborne Division arrived at Paceco, the remnants of Sereni's division, with little reason left to save face, surrendered with barely a shot being fired.

They were first imprisoned in the sports stadium at Trapani, then, on 15 August, shipped across the Mediterranean to near Bizerta. The first plan was to send these POWs to camps in the United States, and Sereni was aboard ship at Oran when news of the Italian armistice arrived. On 8 September General Badoglio's government signed a separate peace with the Allies. As a result of his changed status (from enemy prisoner of war to captured soldier of a cobelligerent) the poet didn't cross the Atlantic, but spent one-and-a-half years in various lightly guarded American-run camps in Algeria. Though the first year of captivity under canvas had its hardships, including food shortages and—in Sereni's case—a period of illness that required hospitalization, the final six months were spent at the relatively comfortable Fedala Camp in French Morocco on the Atlantic coast near Casablanca.[2]

In two prose pieces written many years later, "The Capture" and "Twenty-Six," Sereni contemplates an alternative fate for himself. The former, first published in 1963, is a fictionalized account of an incident that may have happened between his capture and the voyage to Africa. Returning from a small island where he has acted as interpreter for an American platoon effecting the surrender of an Italian garrison, Franchi—the Sereni figure—is sitting on a crate of grenades:

> [I]t would have been sufficient to glance meaningfully at the soldiers captured with him, to make a circle around the crates of grenades the enemy had imprudently put aboard as trophies of war. He was himself sitting on one of those crates. It wouldn't have been difficult to lift the latch, to get up swiftly, open the lid . . .[3]

Sereni describes how a glance at George, the American officer, whose company Franchi enjoys, effectively ends this fantasy of es-

---

2. For further details, see the following prose pieces translated in this volume: "Sicily '43," "Algeria '44," "Barbed-Wire Fever," "The Year '43," and "The Year '45," pp. 285–96 and 315–29.
3. See p. 344 below.

cape: "Not because a farcical tenderness had intervened; no, his very way of looking at that face made it clear that he, personally, was not made for such deeds of daring-do." The story presents a captured soldier who can find in himself no reason to act any of the parts that the regime under which he grew had assigned him. Even such a violent escape would have been false to Franchi's sense of himself. Yet his passivity implies a deeper resistance and a wholly different means for escaping capture.

In "Twenty-Six," written during 1969, he imagines how the remnants of his trapped regiment might have taken the corporate decision to filter through the Allied lines, to cross the Straits of Messina, and perhaps form one of the first partisan units. Such an alternative fate has some support in historical fact. The Allies captured Messina on 17 August after over 62,000 Italian troops (according to Sereni's "The Sands of Algeria") had been evacuated.[4] The poet imagines how he and his companions would

> slip away through the opposing ranks no longer men in arms but swarms of pilgrims—by dry fords, skirting riverbeds, within sight of metropolises which are rubble against the light—scattered, reunited by prearranged routes and rendezvous, filtering, breaking through: overflowing finally, motley and bare, but already rich in other resources, deftnesses and crafts, unanimous in the furrow of one of the possible futures—which is what I was in search of down there . . .[5]

"Twenty-Six" is both a memoir of his revisiting the sites of his surrender and a meditation on the relationship between those events and a life of writing. It is as if his fate as a man and his destiny as a writer divide and turn upon each other with the events of that night in July 1943. The loss of such freedom as was allowed in fascist Italy for his first thirty years would release his imagination to contemplate possible futures. His art would eventually come to flourish in the division between the endured and the imaginable, in the conflict between what can be conceived as possible and what turns out apparently to be inevitable.

4. See "Le sabbie dell'Algeria," in Vittorio Sereni, *La tentazione della prosa,* ed. G. Raboni (Milan: Mondadori, 1998), p. 249.
5. See p. 381 below.

Vittorio Sereni was born on 27 July 1913 in Luino, a small town on the edge of Lago Maggiore and on a railway line crossing the border with Switzerland.[6] The title of his first book, *Frontiera,* has a distinctly 1930s ring.[7] Sereni, just seventeen at the start of that decade, only began publishing in its second and increasingly tragic half. The use of such a title for his 1941 collection of early poems, a book published in an Italy already at war, points to a number of interlocking concerns. It refers to the geographical border between Italy and Switzerland, to the boundary marking the end of youth and, as in Joseph Conrad's novella *The Shadow-Line*—to which Sereni's early poems have been compared, the border that separates the living from the dead.[8] It is also the line about to be crossed between the precarious peace of the 1930s and another devastating world war. The presence of such frontiers adds a thematic density to what the poet and critic Franco Fortini called Sereni's tendency to "reduce as much as he can his own visual field."[9]

It is in the nature of a frontier both to focus tension and to be on the periphery. A frontier also marks the point where an "elsewhere" beckons and threatens. It can equally be the line across which fidelity to the poet's inner impulse and fidelity to the objects of vision must be negotiated. Writing in 1940, Sereni praised Montale's second book, *Le occasioni* (1939), for a distinctive type of poem "faithful to its actual earthly origins, to the difficulties that shaped it, to the occasions that have favored it." Later in the same piece, he describes the space of the text as "an enchanted limit within which things may truly exist."[10] The acknowledgment of

6. For more detail concerning the poet's life and times, see the chronology.
7. See, for example, W. H. Auden and Christopher Isherwood's play, *On the Frontier* (London: Faber and Faber, 1938).
8. Carlo Muscetta, "Vittorio Sereni: *Diario d'Algeria,*" in *Rinascita* 4, nos. 11–12 (Nov.–Dec. 1947), p. 351.
9. Franco Fortini, *Saggi italiani,* 2 vols. (Milan: Garzanti, 1987), vol. 1, p. 125.
10. Vittorio Sereni, "In margine alle *Occasioni,*" *Letture preliminari* (Padua: Liviana Editrice, 1973), pp. 9, 11; *Sentieri di gloria: Noti e ragionamenti sulla letteratura,* ed. G. Strazzeri (Milan: Mondadori, 1996), pp. 59, 60.

limits and the danger involved in crossing them give to Sereni's early poetry a quietly voiced political dimension, implicitly opposed, like Montale's, to the self-aggrandizing rhetoric of either a d'Annunzio or a Marinetti. Yet his frontiers are also alluring in these poems, and their idyllic tones transform ambivalent circumstances into a romance of fleeting attachment, an attempted evasion of the entrapping circumstances into which he and his generation had been born. Their resistance may be no more than a form of perplexity, yet their perplexity *is* a tacitly understood resistance.

Sereni's poetry and subsequent prose might at first seem to be for the Second World War what Giuseppe Ungaretti's were for the first. The Milanese poet calls himself the older man's "son" in a 1970 piece prompted by Ungaretti's death. Yet this affinity conceals innumerable ironies. "Italia" from *L'allegria* ("But your people are borne / from the same earth / that bears me / Italy"[11]) is enough to underline how war service would unite Ungaretti with the country from which his parents emigrated to Egypt in 1878. He had not lived in his native land for any length of time until he was serving with its armed forces.[12] When Mussolini, who had been an interventionist in 1915, used the idea of a national humiliation at the battle of Caporetto as a means to gain power in 1922, Ungaretti's war service made him a convenient symbol for national heroism and culture. Sereni notes in the same piece that "I've felt I'm his son and as a son lived and endured his lightning perceptions and his wrath, his peering into the future and his mistakes: rather like Italy itself, because Ungaretti was—and how— also Italy."[13]

Understandably Sereni, some fifteen years younger, was not able to identify with his country and its 1930s neo-imperialism. Among his earliest poems is "Garden Concert," first published in 1935, the year the League of Nations introduced sanctions in protest against Mussolini's Abyssinian adventure. Here the young poet projects himself into "gardens all over Europe" where the heat is being counteracted by jets of water:

11. "Ma il tuo popolo è portato / dalla stessa terra / che mi porta / Italia," Giuseppe Ungaretti, *L'allegria* (1942; Milan: Mondadori, 1973), p. 71.
12. See *Album Ungaretti,* ed. P. Montefoschi (Milan: Mondadori, 1989).
13. See p. 330 below.

> On the children at war in the borders
> it fans out, makes vortices;
> sound suspended in droplets
> instantaneous
> you mirror yourself in the shadowy green;
> red and white torpedoes
> beat on the asphalt of Avus,
> trains head southeast
> through fields of roses.[14]

Avus is a racing circuit in Berlin where the "torpedoes," Alfa and Auto Union cars, are battling it out while, elsewhere, the Orient Express trundles towards Venice. Sereni's poem signals by means of the tacit sensitivities available to one living under a dictatorship a passive resistance—one that the poet would, nevertheless, come to accuse himself of in his postwar writings. So it was Sereni's fate to be on the wrong side during the 1930s and the war—and to find himself enduring those years, passively once more, and imagining that he could live them as the author of *L'allegria* had done. Yet just as Ungaretti was soon in conflict with the regime, so Sereni's father (a customs officer in Luino) left the fascist party in 1924 in protest against the murder of Matteotti.[15] Sereni's wartime predicament points to the difficulties encompassing the virtues of patriotism and loyalty for those living under oppressive governments. However, if it was Sereni's fate to find himself on the wrong side during his first thirty years, it was his destiny as a writer to witness and then explore that fate.

Other poems from the book's first section express aspects of the predicament felt by young people in those ominous years. "Birthday" is still a poem about the attractions of the countryside in summer for city people with rural roots, one in which a young man's attraction to a woman and its coming to nothing makes the summer a "bitter" one. Yet the close of the poem, "youth that finds no release," points beyond the ordinary difficulties of the young to a more insidious constraint, a literal frontier, across which the poet and his generation will not be able to escape.

14. See pp. 43 and 45 below.
15. See *Album Ungaretti* and chronology, p. 31.

Another poem, "Diana," has a painfully subtextual connection with "3 December." A handwritten copy of this poem was found on the body of the poet and scholar Antonia Pozzi. She had committed suicide on 3 December 1938 at the age of twenty-six for reasons that have never been made entirely clear.[16] From 1933 to her death, Pozzi and Sereni were literary friends and colleagues, and her ambiguous note scribbled on the poem ("Goodbye, Vittorio dear—my dear brother. You'll remember me together with Maria")[17] expresses the desire to live posthumously through the poet's feelings for his future wife Maria Luisa Bonfanti. Placed between "Diana" and "3 dicembre" is a poem from the time of

---

16. See Antonia Pozzi, *La vita sognata e altre poesie inedite,* ed. A. Cenni and O. Dino (Milan: Scheiwiller, 1986), p. 155.
17. Antonia Pozzi and Vittorio Sereni, *La giovinezza che non trova scampo: Poesie e lettere degli anni trenta,* ed. A. Cenni (Milan: Scheiwiller, 1995), p. 45.

Sereni's prewar military service, "Soldiers in Urbino," which concludes with a sudden shock delivered to the soldiers by the distant rumble of lorries. Its position in his book would suggest that the "peace" and "death" in the elegy for Antonia Pozzi are not just those of an individual friend but of an entire generation.

The volume's second part, which has the same title as the entire book, carries these prewar conditions nearer to the disaster of the early 1940s. It also focuses more closely on the poet's sense of his roots in Luino. In "Terrace" a torpedo boat on Lago Maggiore looking for contraband, but ominously warlike, catches the poet and his companions in its searchlight. When the vessel disappears at the poem's close, it leaves behind feelings both of relief and abandonment. Such fleeting encounters in these poems foreshadow a more harrowing scrutiny, as in "September," the month of the Munich Crisis:

> In already certain death
> we will walk with more courage,
> slowly forward with the dogs we'll wade
> into the tiny rolling wave.[18]

Frontiera is a book composed of landscape studies in a violently threatened context pierced by glimpses of transitory beauty, friendship, and love. The poet appears to be emerging into his own amid an idyllic scenery, but these are portrayals of moments doomed to come to grief—and the poet's own culpability in that nemesis awaits his future creative attention. In his note to the definitive 1966 edition, Sereni called it "my prewar book, but with one foot already in the war—as can be seen, I believe, not only from the dates."[19]

III

Diario d'Algeria appeared, published by Vallecchi, in 1947. The previous year, Sereni had been awarded a Libera Stampa Prize

18. See pp. 64–67 below.
19. See p. 391 below.

ex acqueo with Umberto Bellintani for the then-unpublished work. His second book of poems—most of which was written while on active service, as a POW, or immediately on repatriation—bears witness to the wartime experiences of combat deferral and enforced absence from home. In the first section of the book, Sereni constructs a tenuous counterweight against his experience of Europe's disintegration into violence and mutual destruction between 1940 and 1943. He personifies the continent in "Italian in Greece," calling upon a Europe watching over him as he descends "unarmed and absorbed / in my slender myth within the ranks of brutes." Fortini took issue with these lines in an epigram, "Sereni slender myth," written in 1954: "You beg pardon from the 'ranks of brutes' / if you want to leave them. Give up the tired / and bloody game, of modesty and pride."[20] A politicized criticism of Sereni's sensibility, its absence of overt commitment, finds a pointed form—to which the poet responded almost two decades later in the first part of his masterpiece, "A Holiday Place." Fortini's epigrammatic jibe might equally be deflected by Leonardo Sciascia's suggestion that "[t]here is evidently still in Sereni the sense of Europe's fragility . . . but also an idea of Europe as *other* than the war, the violence, the Nazi-fascism. An idea, a myth, a utopia."[21]

When the idea of Europe returns in the fourth part of "Algerian Diary," it invokes both the political map of the D-Day landings and that utopia of peace and culture to which Sciascia referred. Giacomo Debenedetti has written of how, with the dialogue between the first Allied soldier fallen on the Normandy beaches and the poet in Camp Hospital 127, "history entered into Sereni's poetry."[22] However, Giovanni Raboni, introducing a 1998 edition of *Diario d'Algeria,* has sought to qualify this declaration. After all, as he notes, what Sereni says to the dead soldier is not promising as an indication of someone acknowledging the role of history for his art. In the poem's first verse a hand has touched him on the

20. Franco Fortini, "Sereni esile mito," *L'ospite ingrato,* 2nd ed. (Casale Monferrato: Marietti, 1985), p. 16.
21. Leonardo Sciascia in an interview cited by Marco Forti on the back cover of *Diario d'Algeria* (Milan: Mondadori, 1965).
22. Giacomo Debenedetti, "Il poeta da giovane," *Poesie,* pp. xxiii–xxiv.

shoulder, murmuring "pray for Europe / as the New Armada / drew on the coast of France":

> But if you truly were
> the first fallen splayed on the Normandy beaches,
> you pray if you can, I am dead
> to war and to peace.
> This, the music now:
> of the tents that flap against the poles.
> It's not the music of angels, it's my own
> music only and enough—.[23]

The idea of praying "for Europe" at such a moment could be considered thoroughly ambiguous. The opening of a second front in northern France was to bring a year of fighting and terrible suffering to armed forces and civilians alike. Equally, it could be taken to mean that Europe is about to be saved from the horrors of the fascist regimes, and he should pray that the Allies are successful. Sereni, in the poem, finds himself in no position to commit to either form of prayer. He is metaphorically, while the Allied soldier is literally, "dead / to war and to peace." All the poet has is his marginal music, that of the poem. These lines turn the move towards an aesthetic realm in which history can be resisted upon itself. In Sereni's verse the aesthetic does not transcend history; but neither does history bully the poet into opportune pieties.

Asked what he had intended by counterposing the music of the angels and his own, Sereni said he wanted to underline his "estrangement, marginalization, and lack."[24] His isolation in the prisoner of war camps of North Africa leaves him apparently unable to respond. Yet, by means of this appeal and admission, Sereni registers his vitality, his being alive to the continent's fate, notwithstanding the location of the poem, Camp Hospital 127. The music of the tents is composed into the bitter harmonies of Sereni's lines, offering a truth to immediate surroundings where there had been distraction or illusion. It looks forward to his work of the 1950s and 1960s when he was able to find his own motifs in the Milan of the so-called economic miracle. It also contributed to

23. See pp. 90–93 below.
24. Sereni, cited in *Poesie*, ed. D. Isella (Milan: Mondadori, 1995), p. 444.

Montale's more colloquial style, as in "La mia Musa" of 1971, which closes with his muse conducting "her quartet / of drinking straws. It's the only music I can hear."[25]

Continuing to obey orders after his regiment had been isolated in western Sicily by the Allied landings on the Syracuse side, Sereni failed to take whatever opportunity there might have been to cross the Straits of Messina. He was thus excluded from Italy's crucial years of German occupation and partisan resistance. So a further shadow of a self-betrayal hangs over much of his wartime and postwar verse. The twelve poems of "Algerian Diary" shape the period of a year into a purgatorial expiation for passive complicity. The aggravated inner divisions of Sereni's position are expressed, as Fortini again noted, in "an anger without object, beneath the appearance of perplexity and stupefaction."[26] Yet also audible in these poems of such unpropitious circumstances is a mitigating, a sustaining tenderness toward loved ones at a distance and a celebration of the gifts and talents, the resourcefulness of fellow prisoners. The sequence's tone nurtures by example virtues opposed to the conditions it must face. By a persistent and, as it was to prove, a consistent fidelity to the given occasions, Sereni's work rejects simplifying certainties and, glimpsing possibilities of personal and cultural gladness, refuses to be overwhelmed.

The fifth poem in the sequence takes place on a purgatorial Algerian hillside. Climbing the path, Sereni addresses the object of a schoolboy romance in Brescia. The POWs, like dead spirits in the *Inferno* and *Purgatorio*, need to recount past lives, reminding themselves of a world beyond the wire fences or before the Beyond. In the next two poems, Dantean echoes reinforce this implicit parallel, echoes in which attempted expiation declines into infernal stasis. This "girone" assumes in its verbal echo the context of Dante's poem: the prisoners are now compared directly with the dead inhabitants of a grim elsewhere, ghosts who repeat their lives in emblematic punishment, trying to keep cheerful. At this moment of flickering hope a North African starlit night is evoked like a landscape of the *Purgatorio*. Sereni's note explains that on limpid nights someone had taught him to tell the time by

25. Eugenio Montale, *L'opera in versi*, ed. R. Bettarini and G. Contini (Turin: Einaudi, 1980), p. 429.
26. Fortini, *Saggi italiani*, vol. 1, p. 192.

the positions of certain stars. The movement of prisoners from one camp to another, all in the surroundings of Oran, recalls not only a Dantean circle but also a constellation of barbed wire. If the stars might signal an exit from Hell, Sereni's poem quickly reasserts the fix in which the POWs have found themselves.

In the seventh poem a promise of release is again offered, this time by the summer, only to be darkened once more and withdrawn. The Italian prisoners are enjoying the season. However, their promise of cooling shade, or beatific cleansing, and release from the boredom of captivity is clouded over by a reminder of past error. This hedge or bush functions like the opening of Leopardi's "L'infinito": "Always dear to me was this lone hill, / And this hedge, which closes off / The gaze from so much of the far horizon." In Sereni's poem, the hedge and the halo promise infinite spaces where, as Leopardi has it and Ungaretti knew, "shipwreck is sweet to me in this sea."[27] Yet even that release is banished by the anachronistic present of captured German troops still singing their martial hymns. Sereni calls them "una torma," Dante's word to describe the damned of *Inferno*.[28] When silence is restored, it's not like the "otherworldly silences, and profoundest quiet" of Leopardi's poem but rather a return to enclosure and isolation: "Now every frond is silent / oblivion's shell compacted / the circle perfect."[29] Nevertheless, the memory of Dante has given form and significance to the fates of these isolated men. It is, perhaps, more bearable to be guilty than to be nothing, and this context of judgment offers a meaning to these POWs made marginal to the historical events into which they had been swept.

P. V. Mengaldo has drawn attention to the "at first sight contradictory character of Sereni's syntax: at once soft on the inside, and entirely intent on the transitions, hard at the joints. Everyone recalls his peremptory *but, now*."[30] Such a "but" and a "now" appear in the seventh poem, counteracting at the compositional level

---

27. Giacomo Leopardi, *Canti,* ed. J. H. Whitfield (Manchester: Manchester University Press, 1967), p. 63.
28. Dante Alighieri, *Inferno,* 16, ll. 4–6.
29. See pp. 94–95 below.
30. Pier Vincenzo Mengaldo, "Ricordo di Vittorio Sereni," *Sei poeti all'insegna del pesce d'oro* (Milan: Scheiwiller, 1987), p. 116.

the prisoners' predicament that the words also articulate. The POWs fall from an expiatory or redemptive captivity back toward a perpetual exclusion by means of the contradicting "but" in "but like the grave the German crowd's / song" and the eternal "now" in "Now every frond is silent." Thus they dramatize disillusion or unpredictable change, leaving the men in a fix; yet having articulated this contrast between the Italians hoping for "blissful purifying water" and the song of the Germans means that their fate has been taken to heart and morally interpreted. Through its use of conjunctions, the poem represents an act of lay conscience and intelligence in crisis. Excluded from the experience of the resistance by his capture and imprisonment, Sereni, like his fellow prisoners of war, was left on the edge of a decisive historical moment; yet this condition itself constituted a part of Italy's history. Added to the frontier in Sereni's first book, this historical periphery further confirms Raboni's observation that "The centrality of Sereni's poetry significantly derives from an initial marginality."[31]

IV

Among the many creative strands that began with Sereni's imprisonment was his involvement with poetic translation. *Il musicante di Saint-Merry* (1981) is a selection of his work in the field, and contains a brief account of involvement with the art. Sereni states that he had "never thought of translating the work of others until a fellow prisoner, who read English much better than I did, but who had no experience in writing poetry, gave me his literal version of a poem by E. A. Poe, and asked me to make an Italian poem of it."[32] He then quotes from memory the first two lines from his lost translation of "The Conqueror Worm" ("Lo! 'tis a gala night / Within the lonesome latter years!"), and notes that they, and only they, seemed to "be in accord with the particular situation and

31. "Vittorio Sereni," *Poesia italiana: Il Novecento,* ed. P. Gelli and G. Lagorio, 2 vols. (Milan: Garzanti, 1980), vol. 2, p. 643.
32. Vittorio Sereni, "Premessa," *Il musicante di Saint-Merry* (Turin: Einaudi, 1981), p. v.

state of mind in which we found ourselves then."³³ Nevertheless, comparison of "The Conqueror Worm" with Sereni's "Algerian Diary" sequence reveals a number of parallels in references to theatrical performance, the music of angels, a circle fixed to a single spot, and a ghostly image that writhes as the light goes.³⁴

Sereni recalls the lost Italian version to imply something of his own compulsion in translating, a desire to overcome isolation, to discover our own true limits in relation to others. In the same introductory piece, Sereni cites a passage by Sergio Solmi to describe how the inspiration to translate may arise:

> The translation is born, in contact with the foreign text, with the power, the irresistibility of the original inspiration. At its birth there presides something like a surge of envy, a regret at having missed this irrecoverable lyric occasion, at having lost it to a more fortunate confrère in another language.³⁵

In his versions of Ezra Pound's early poems from 1955 and of William Carlos Williams from 1957–1961, he addressed himself to the freshness and openness of American modernist experiment. Sereni's contemporaneous translations of longer works by William Carlos Williams, such as "Dedication for a Plot of Land," "Adam," "A Unison," or "Desert Music" were instrumental in helping him evolve his mature style. The last of these works in particular helped him evolve the more extended and inclusive style of *Gli strumenti umani* (1965) and *Stella variabile* (1981). The influence is acknowledged through echo and citation. "Penny please! Give me penny please, mister" from "The Desert Music" may have prompted a memory of Algerian children calling to a trainload of prisoners *"give me bonbon good American please"* in "The African Sickness."³⁶ "Works in Progress" quotes Sereni's translation of the lines "the beds lying empty, the couches / damp, the chairs un-

---

33. Ibid. Sereni's version of Poe's opening two lines reads: "Ecco si spiega una notturna danza / in cuore ai solitari ultimi anni."
34. See Edgar Allan Poe, *The Complete Poems*, ed. T. O. Mabbott (Urbana: University of Illinois Press, 2000), pp. 325–26, and pp. 88–101 below.
35. Sergio Solmi cited in Sereni, "Premessa," p. vii.
36. See *Il musicante di Saint-Merry*, p. 68, and p. 107 below.

used" from "These."[37] When, in the 1950s, Sereni began to write longer poems of memory and encounter, poems such as "The African Sickness," Williams's poems suggested how he might combine an eloquent speaking out with a resistance to rhetorically forged connections.

He also translated all of René Char's *Feuillets d'Hypnos* during 1958, and a selection of later work appeared as *Ritorno sopramonte* in 1974. With these renderings, the Italian poet was enabled imaginatively to involve himself in the partisan conflict that his imprisonment in North Africa has rendered impossible. In "The Sands of Algeria," Sereni describes how hearing about the resistance movements "tormented us."[38] Section 138 of Char's wartime aphorisms has the French poet assisting "one hundred meters away, at the execution of B." One of Captain Alexandre's companions, about to be shot by the SS, could have been saved if Char had given the order to open fire:

> I didn't give the signal because this village had to be saved at *all costs*. What's a village? A village like any other? Perhaps he understood, he himself, at that final moment?[39]

Reading Sereni's version on the facing page to the French original we can sense the translator's exclusion from the occasion, and his imaginative involvement, his assistance in this horrible day. The accuracy and restraint of Sereni's rendering, the inclusion of the translator in the process of remembrance and transformation, converts the "surge of envy" into a living gratitude. In translating American and French poetry he lives out in imagination his other fate (the one unlived) in support of the side he was truly—at a cultural and human level—always on.

Concluding his review of *Il musicante di Saint-Merry* (1981), Fortini cited lines from René Char's prose poem "Remanence" [Retentivity] "—What do you suffer from? / From the unreal intact within the devastated real . . . —I believe poems are written, and are translated, as an irrevocable response, as much to that

---

37. See *Il musicante di Saint-Merry*, p. 50, and p. 207 below.
38. Sereni, "Le sabbie dell'Algeria," p. 255.
39. René Char, *Fueillets d'Hypnos*, no. 138 in Sereni, *Il musicante di Saint-Merry*, pp. 24–25.

question as to its reply."[40] While envy can be creatively inhibiting, it may also, through translation, impel a writer to counteract its influence by finding, in the irreducibly different experiences of other poets' lyric occasions, analogous solutions to comparable predicaments.[41] Rendering these prose poems related to Char's experience in the Resistance helped Sereni to address the wound that is revealed in later poems such as "In Sleep" and "Appointment at an Unusual Hour."

V

Sereni did not publish a third book of poetry until 1965. *Gli strumenti umani* covers thus a period of twenty years, spanning the postwar reconstruction of Italy as well as its industrial and consumer transformation, the miracle of the 1950s and 60s, under various coalitions of the center-left, excluding the Communists. "Via Scarlatti," written towards the end of 1945 (Sereni had been repatriated in August), was originally the final piece in *Diario d'Algeria,* only to become the opening poem to his subsequent book twenty years after its composition. Via Scarlatti 27, near Milan railway station, was home for Sereni, his parents, wife and children, until 1953. Their living together, Giosue Bonfanti notes, was "not always easy, given the acute straits—economic and social—of the moment, and the differences of mentality and character."[42] He implies that two lines ("But the faces, the faces I can't say: / shadow on shadow of exhaustion and rage") allude to these difficulties. The poem's debt to Umberto Saba's "Città vecchia" would suggest that the faces were those of people in the street. Yet an intimate significance also sharpens its closing lines:

> Clicking heels of teenagers
> mock at that pain,

40. Fortini, *Nuovi saggi italiani,* 2 vols. (Milan: Garzanti, 1987), vol. 2, p. 169.
41. For more on this theme, see Peter Robinson, "Envy, Gratitude, and Translation," *In the Circumstances: About Poems and Poets* (Oxford: Oxford University Press, 1992), pp. 149–52.
42. Giosue Bonfanti, "Cronologia," in Vittorio Sereni, *Poesie,* ed. D. Isella (Milan: Mondadori, 1995), p. cxiii.

the improvised strain of an opera duet
at a small crowd converging.

And here for you I wait.⁴³

These young, this snatch of singing, and even the street's name taunt them. Yet, just as the poem's "you" may be Sereni's wife, Maria Luisa, but equally any reader, so too the faces marked by the postwar can be both those of his immediate family and anyone of a certain age passing through Via Scarlatti.

Sereni's accurate music evokes the precise timbre of experience, the heart of things as he senses them. The difficult evolution of his poems shows the poet searching for what occasions in a life had meant, and for possibilities implicit within them, unlived or to come. An interviewer asked, "Does writing poetry make up part of the love of life?" Sereni answered, "Undoubtedly, indeed it is the most authentic mode, at least for me, to express this love even when one says 'I don't love my times.'"⁴⁴ In "The Misunderstanding," he describes the near recognition of himself and a

---

43. See pp. 118–19 below. Sereni lyrically praises the close of "Città vecchia" in his back cover note for the 1980 fourth edition of Umberto Saba, *Trieste e una donna* (Milan: Mondadori, 1950).
44. Sereni, *Poesie,* ed. D. Isella, pp. 582–83. He is quoting his poem "Nel sonno."

stranger: "Between us was my glancing back / and, audible barely, a voice: / *love*—it was singing—*and beauty reborn.*"[45] In a letter of 7 May 1958 to Fortini, he calls this moment of attraction, reminiscent of Baudelaire's "A une passante." It is, he writes, "the Proustian vendetta of love which fatally recognizes itself as valid only in as much as the subject has suffered, has rejoiced, while the object lays itself bare, grows sorry, and loses consistency."[46] The poem closes with a memory of his imprisonment in which such an attraction to life has seemed both to dazzle and delude.

That intertwining of Sereni's intermittently elaborated responses to life with his country's history is a clue to his crucial role in Italian poetry's exit from hermeticism, the dominant mode of the interwar years. After completing *Diario d'Algeria*, Sereni suffered a period of almost total "creative silence" that lasted until the early 1950s.[47] It is as if the poet, like the subject of "Interview with a Suicide," also "*came back to life . . . years later.*"[48] In 1982, the poet gave an equivocal account of his "meager vein": "In a positive sense, this signifies the necessary maturation of a motif; in a negative, slowness, laziness, impotence, psychological blockage, fear."[49] These difficulties may be partly attributed to his POW experiences, and to the fact that Sereni, in allowing himself to be captured, had acted in the belief that devotion to duty was the correct course to take—a belief which concealed within it an evasion of responsibility, an inertia.

Nevertheless, the publication of *Gli strumenti umani* was to remove any doubts that might have lingered about Sereni's long "creative silence." The book was recognized as among the most significant single volumes of poetry published in Italy during the 1960s. Many of today's senior poets, such as Giovanni Giudici and Maurizio Cucchi, have declared its importance for their development, showing how a definitively new direction had been taken. "In Sleep," completed in 1963 but exploring the atmosphere of 1948–53, gives specific contexts in work, sport, music

---

45. See p. 125 below.
46. Sereni, *Poesie*, ed. D. Isella, pp. 530–31.
47. See "Creative Silence," pp. 313–15 below.
48. See p. 173 below.
49. Sereni, *Poesie*, ed. D. Isella, p. 582.

and love for Sereni's thoughts of guilt, his suspicion that the course of life has been "deviated down false tracks," as he puts it in "Those Children Playing."[50] The hidden wound in the last part of "In Sleep," in "Appointment at an Unusual Hour," and expressed at the conclusion to "Saba" rebukes the contemporary scene—which Sereni's continuing commitment to poetry of occasions and objects obliges him stubbornly to record. Once more, the poet's only acceptable weapon is a sense of joy, a gift for friendship and the need to foster love. "Years After" concludes: "Then don't turn away love I beg you / and friendship remain and defend us."[51] Similarly, "The Friends" exemplifies the reassurance and help that "Years After" calls for. In "On the Back of a Piece of Paper," Sereni writes of this poem that "The people called by name in that poem, by their actual names, are alive and real."[52] He fears that even thanking them by name in a poem may have "reduced them to a literary pretext." Much of his work is similarly situated on the difficult and shifting territory where each composition is simultaneously an aesthetic fact, and also a contextually located utterance.

Massimo Grillandi has noted that the years in which Sereni's third book was patiently composed were characterized by the call for a poetry determined to express and advance its position in relation to the individual and society.[53] The neorealism of the '40s and '50s gave way in the 1960s to a new wave of avant-garde experimentation. Poems such as "The Lines," "Poetry is a Passion?" and "A Dream" exemplify Sereni's disinclination to supply a poetry of overt political commitment, or, equally, a poetry written to fit any form of ideological or aesthetic program. The influence of Benedetto Croce's concept of intuition as the foundation of art can be detected here. Sereni makes reference to the philosopher in a published letter to Charles Tomlinson, another poet crucially influenced by William Carlos Williams. There he praises the English poet's being free of "any preconstituted understanding" and continues "In you understanding is an outcome,

---

50. See p. 145 below.
51. See p. 131 below.
52. See p. 309 below.
53. Massimo Grillandi, *Vittorio Sereni* (Florence: il Castoro, 1972), p. 3.

a crowning of the specific experiment, it forms with the formation of the poem."[54]

Gli strumenti umani is a book with a deep and wide cultural allusiveness, from the quoted snatches of a popular song in the final part of "In Sleep" to the enigmatic citation of a statement by Leonardo da Vinci in "On a Cemetery Photograph." Sereni's work demonstrates an embattled sense of the naturalness of poetic composition, a defense of his own creative impulse against the dangers of distortion presented by literary, economic and political currents in the intellectual life of his immediate surroundings. Giuliano Dego, however, thought at the time that the "loud, empty call of some of the avant-garde had distracted Sereni from his true nature."[55] There is decisive development in the poet's language and style. He moves from the stunned and piercing postwar lyrics, such as "The Return" and "Journey There and Back," to "The Alibi and the Benefit," "On the Creva Road Again," or "The Wall," longer reflective monologues or colloquies which draw upon narrative qualities and Dantean encounters with rebarbative voices.

Montale catches a distinctive paradox of reluctance and persistence in Sereni's work when he observes that the poet, accepting "the necessity of camouflaging oneself beneath the *modus vivendi* of the man on the street," achieved a style that, while it "should logically lead to silence, is nevertheless obliged to be eloquent."[56] He remained faithful to his inner impulse and prevented it from drying up by absorbing something of its accuser, the literary and sociopolitical criticisms of that tender lyricism, of "his true nature."

The poet writes of himself as recently dead and returned to haunt his own house in "Six in the Morning." Writing to Fortini on

---

54. "A Letter from Vittorio Sereni," *PN Review* 5 vol. 2, no. 1 (1977), p. 42. For Sereni and Croce, see Laura Barile, *Sereni* (Palermo: Palumbo, 1994), p. 14; and for his relations to the school of Antonio Banfi, ibid., pp. 12–14. For Sereni's debt to Banfi, see his essay "Per Banfi," in Francesca D'Alessandro, *L'opera poetica di Vittorio Sereni* (Milan: Vita e Pensiero, 2001), pp. 213–26.
55. Giuliano Dego, "A Poet of Frontiers," *London Magazine* 9, no. 7 (October 1969), p. 31.
56. Eugenio Montale, "Vittorio Sereni," *Sulla poesia*, ed. G. Zampa (Milan: Mondadori, 1976), p. 331.

2 March 1958, Sereni observes that he "has doubts about the last line" which seems "a bit empty, a bit for effect, and hiding an inability to say more."[57] The removal of "ancorata" erases the arresting image of Milan like a ship at anchor in a gale, and replaces it with a plainer sense bound together by the music of the line. This makes for less of a flourish and more of a close. His nagging doubt and inability to do more than change a preposition for eight years— from composition to correction of proofs for the book—suggest a poet acutely sensitive to how the music of words may touch, or evade, the heart of things. In "Passing," he asks: "Am I already dead and come back here?" Sereni appears a ghostly revenant in postwar Italy; his early preoccupation with the presence of the dead among the living is refocused to define the survival of wounding experience into a world that has not shared, or has too soon

57. Vittorio Sereni, *Scritture private: Con Fortini e con Giudici* (Bocca di Magra: Edizioni Capannina, 1995), p. 15.

forgotten, or actively concealed the suffering endured by others. The final poem of *Gli strumenti umani,* "The Beach," ends with an affirmation:

> What's being wasted from day to day
> is not the dead, but it's those
> patches of the nonexistent, lime or ashes
> ready to become light and movement.
>   Don't
> be in doubt,—the sea's strength assails me —
> speak they will.[58]

Sereni had said of himself in 1944 that he was dead to war and to peace. Nevertheless, despite an ever more continuous preoccupation with mortality, his later works form extended meditations upon and prophylactics against the dangers of becoming dead to life.

VI

In the interview with Dego, Sereni observed that "I find myself falling into ways of thought like those which perplexed me during the war, and even more frantic, more confused. I feel the same sense of emptiness, of despair as I felt then, not knowing what to do with myself."[59] Perhaps most significant of his journeys was the 1969 return to Sicily on holiday with his wife and youngest daughter which produced "Twenty-Six." Here Sereni attempts to bring himself through his debilitating memories and recurrent images of war, to dissociate himself from irrational fears and gnawing desires for an experience unlived. By living the events again, transformed in writing, he seeks to resolve his self-division, his isolation from others, and even to put his impulse to write behind him:

> Why besides having a body, a gaze, and a voice, are we not
> endowed with a special transparency allowing those close

58. See p. 199 below.
59. Dego, "A Poet of Frontiers," p. 31.

to us to live with us fully, without recourse to that distorted emanation of ourselves which writing is, and to which we regularly refer them?[60]

It is the confrontation of this wish in writing, a self-perpetuating contradiction, which provides one of the impulses for Sereni's final poetic phase.

Numerous echoes of "Twenty-Six" occur in the poems of Sereni's fourth book, *Stella variabile*. The emblematic "trees we'll leave to die" of the prose are intensified and concentrated in "The Disease of the Elm." Similarly, the narrative concludes: "There stands before me a wood, the words, to travel through following a line that gradually forms as you walk, forward (or back) towards the transparency, if that is the right word for the future."[61] This "transparency" also figures in the "horror of that emptiness" in the poem "In Parma with A. B." (addressed to the Parmese poet Attilio Bertolucci), and in the "color of nothingness," the final line of "Autostrada della Cisa."[62] The conclusion of "Twenty-Six" also reaffirms Sereni's impulse, present too in these last poems, always to move by transforming the material of memory towards experiencing the world afresh. Yet this transparency, emptiness and nothingness indicate how, while the moral basis for social and political analysis in *Gli strumenti umani* remains, the grounds of the encounter have shifted to a more metaphysical trajectory. The occasions of friendship in Sereni's earlier work have become, with *Stella variabile,* encounters with absent, because now dead, friends. No longer simply a time-honored literary motif, the presence of the dead among the living has become a matter of personal and intimate experience. In "Niccolò," set in Bocca di Magra, Sereni calls upon the literary critic Niccolò Gallo (with whom he had coedited the literary magazine *Questo e altro*) to "stay with me, you like it here, / and heed me, you know how."[63]

The first part of Sereni's masterpiece, "A Holiday Place," contains two snatches of quotation in italics. The poet's few notes for his book had indicated that the second is from his translation of

60. See p. 384 below.
61. See pp. 260–63 and p. 387 below.
62. See p. 269 and p. 271 below.
63. See p. 247 below.

"Ton oeuvre" by Jean-Joseph Rabéarivelo. He had seen no need to point out that the first was of lines from the epigram by Fortini, "Sereni slender myth," which had in turn cited his own war poem "Italian in Greece" to criticize its "perplexed music" and attack his belief in youth: "Youth's not always truth," Fortini writes.[64] The holiday place is again Bocca di Magra, on the Ligurian coast south of La Spezia. It had become a regular haunt for Italian literati in the postwar period, and by 1951 both poets were renting houses there. The first letter (dated 27 May 1952) in *Scritture private* is Sereni's justification of his interrupting Fortini's serious debate one evening. "Look, when you talk of certain things, I seem in front of you like that negro-french poet ... which you, Franco, know." "This must be a betrayal, but let's go on," Fortini replied. Sereni then mumbled, "A betrayal of myself, if anything."[65] As this exchange with Fortini shows, Sereni continued to bear a sense of "culpable inferiority" and "incompleteness as a man"—the result of his POW experiences and consequent exclusion from the partisan war in which Fortini had taken part. This exchange occurred at a time when Sereni had published little new poetry since *Diario d'Algeria*. In that 1952 letter, he distinguishes himself from his most searching critic: "now and then the Sereni horse tears towards song, while the Fortini horse more eagerly tears towards books."[66] His verb picks up the final sentence of Fortini's epigram: "Tear it up, that blank paper / you're holding in your hand."[67]

Sereni's later work often contains a brief quotation, indicating a need for some verbal mediation alongside the lived moment from which the poem grew. Rabéarivelo's lines translated from the *Orphée Noir* are inseparable from the sponsoring occasion of "A Holiday Place":

> ["]Have you sung, not spoken, not put questions to the heart of
>   things: how can you know them?" laughing say
>   the scribes and orators when you magnify
>   the everyday miracle of sea and sky.[68]

64. Fortini, "Sereni esile mito," *L'ospite ingrato*, p. 16.
65. Sereni, *Scritture private*, p. 11.
66. Ibid., p. 14.
67. Fortini, "Sereni esile mito," *L'ospite ingrato*, p. 16.
68. Sereni, "Cinque poeti negri," *La tentazione della prosa*, p. 33.

Remembering these words, he challenges Fortini's assurance that committed cultural analysis is necessary for poetry's contact with its times. Sereni's emphasis on song and the heart makes a plea for qualities not usually to the fore in analytical critique, but he also raises a doubt about his own gift: if inspired to sing of life's beauty, are you in touch with the nature of existence, or dazzled by it? At the end of "A Holiday Place," he seems to grant the point to Fortini, echoing his epigram with "To love is not always to understand." Yet the opening section of "A Holiday Place" includes allusions to two songs. In one, political debates are being conducted at tables beside others who "danced barefoot *el pueblo del alma mia.*" The other is a disc played on the other bank of the river which "returns to tempt me" with its "throat offered to the wound of love"—but Sereni adds "I won't write this story."[69] Fortini had seemed like someone who would accuse him of losing his way by listening to such voices, but his poetry (under the guise of perplexity and astonishment) reaffirms that though "To love is not always to understand," it can be.[70]

If the resilience of Sereni's work derives from his ear for the music of words, the sounds that frequently spurred him into composing were other's lyrics or tunes. In *Frontiera,* "Lombard Song" and "Diana" both contain allusions to music. Later, these strains tend to be painfully evocative. With "In Sleep," the quotations from a song of the moment, "In cerca di te" [In search of you], convey the hurt of a youth wasted by the Fascist period and its aftermath. "In an Empty House" remembers "the swastikas / under the rain one September," the revised version of lines directly alluding to a song title in English: "september in the rain tra le svastiche."[71] Similarly, "Toronto Saturday Night" begins with a white jazz musician playing "Tipperary," while "Revival" evokes the early Cold War context of his evocative story "The Option"—its narrative voice addressing a survivor of the concentration camps— to the tune of "The Third Man Theme." In "Giovanna and the Beatles," one of Sereni's last poems, completed at Bocca di Magra on the 25 and 26 August 1981, other people's music evokes his own once more. He is startled into memory by suddenly hearing the

---

69. See p. 229 below.
70. See p. 243 below.
71. Sereni, *Poesie,* p. 668.

sound of a record played by his youngest daughter Giovanna (b. 1956). Isella's edition indicates the poem's development, including lines in which Sereni pictures the music as "echoes, / memories of escapades in a vacant club."[72] He wonders about the speed that a particular generation's moment passes, and to this end, had at one point attempted but crossed out a line pointing out how the "oh so loveable Beetles" were supplanted: "And at the first turn Bob Dylan."[73]

A variable star is one whose brightness varies periodically and does not maintain the same apparent size in the sky. It is, as it were, the opposite of Keats's "Bright star! would I were steadfast as thou art —."[74] The alternating intensity of the light signifies the poet's movement between creative "impotence and potentiality," between what Sereni called his "difficulties in understanding the world and the continuing impulse to discover new and hidden significances."[75] He calls upon this very symbol of his creativity in "The Disease of the Elm": "Lead me, variable star, as long as you're able . . ."[76] Yet a further significance of the changing degrees of brightness is a wavering between the enchanting and flattering appearances of life and the alluring transparency, the emptiness which is death.

In the interview with Grillandi, Sereni noted that "There's an age at which we begin to know with certainty that one day we will die. Before this, whoever writes poetry is only paying court to death. I include myself, you understand. When one enters into that certainty, one tends to name death much less."[77] In *Ventisei* and *Stella variabile* the presence of death, albeit unnamed, dominates the concluding pages. Talking to Ferdinando Camon, Sereni said about his position regarding the conflicting claims of aesthetic styles and political attitudes: "Above all I believe in dialogue."[78] In his last book the conversation is, as Cucchi review-

---

72. Ibid., p. 731.
73. Ibid.
74. John Keats, *The Complete Poems*, ed. J. Barnard, 3rd ed. (Harmondsworth: Penguin Books, 1988), p. 452.
75. See also the preliminary note on *Stella variabile*, p. 411 below.
76. See p. 261 below.
77. Grillandi, *Vittorio Sereni*, p. 3.
78. Ferdinando Camon, *Il mestiere di poeta* (Milan: Garzanti, 1982), p. 127.

ing *Stella variabile* wrote, a "no longer interrupted colloquy with death."[79] The attempt to come into relation with another presence in Sereni's poetry enacts its search for truth. The words of others in the poems set their existence at risk. Sereni's work achieves self-definition, in turn, through its attentively skeptical relation to the voices opposed to it.

"Autostrada della Cisa" invokes Petronius's sibyl, the one who "more and more wishes to die" and also appears in the epigraph to T. S. Eliot's *The Waste Land*.[80] Sereni attempts in his poem once more to initiate a meeting. Driving through the alternating brightness and darkness of tunnels on the motorway from the Ligurian coast towards Parma, he writes "I extend a hand. It returns to me empty. / I reach out an arm, embrace a shoulder of air."[81] Yet by a familiar paradox, the resignation to approaching death, the realization that you are about to leave and not return gives a sudden final vividness to the apprehended world of that car journey through the Apennines.

VII

Not least of the ironies associated with his life and work is that Vittorio Sereni's should have been so caught up, not with serene victory but humiliating defeat. His poetry and imaginative prose never forget that he is assisting the cause of European humanism as its defeated enemy, always at the border of the imagined fate sketched in "Twenty-Six." Near that memoir's close he evokes a few lines from C. P. Cavafy's "Comes to Rest": "twenty-six years / your phantom's crossed over / now to remain in these lines."[82] With their help, Sereni writes, he had "played out the conflict" in his name and "established a reciprocity by which we found ourselves over and over again imploring forgiveness of each other for the

---

79. Maurizio Cucchi, "Poeta, scaccia da me la memoria," *Rinascita*, no. 32 (27 August 1982), p. 23.
80. See T. S. Eliot, *Collected Poems, 1909–1962* (London: Faber and Faber, 1963), p. 61.
81. See p. 271 below.
82. "Comes to Rest," C. P. Cavafy, *Collected Poems*, trans. by E. Keeley and P. Sherrard (Princeton: Princeton University Press, 1975), p. 183.

time that had passed unopposed by us."⁸³ Thus, unlike Italy in September 1943, he can never switch to the winning side.

His fate was always to believe himself in the wrong, as he makes clear, recalling the Munich agreement of September 1938, at the close of "In an Empty House" from May 1967. Yet it was his destiny to witness and then, with an unflinching memory of his own, to express that sense of culpability and its consequences:

> Provided there were a story anyway
> —and meanwhile in the papers Munich at first light
> ah thank goodness: there'd been an agreement—
> provided there were a story, exquisite among the swastikas
> one September in the rain.
>
> Today *we are*—and anyway we're bad,
> part of the evil you yourself should sun and lawn turn overcast or no.⁸⁴

And it is this fidelity to reconsidered experience, achieved through the wedding of the technical and the spiritual in his evolving style, which gives his work its overwhelming cultural importance. It shows how with sustained effort goodness can be born from error and self-betrayal. What's more, its historical memory prevents the slightest righteousness or triumphalism in the representation of the lyrical protagonist. Thus located, Sereni could produce the astonishing counter-factual possibility that concludes his prose piece "Port Stanley like Trapani," written in June 1982, only eight months before his death. He imagines how the opposed British and Argentinian soldiers might "break out of the circle dividing them and run towards each other . . . slap each other on the backs or treat themselves to festive kicks up the rear, and embrace." The piece ends poised upon the border of a "a victory over absurdity by means of the unthinkable."⁸⁵ Yes, thinking the unthinkable: that's how Sereni's art is a sustained and sustaining escape from capture.

Sereni's oeuvre is inextricably intertwined with the history of his century, from the rise of fascism to the Falklands War. In this

83. See p. 386 below.
84. See p. 203 below.
85. See pp. 337 and 338 below.

it imaginatively explores concerns that are still very much current ones—the Balkan states, the unity of Europe, postcolonialism in North Africa and the Middle East, the recurrence of extreme right-wing politics in the civilized world, the acknowledgement of culpability, and the urge to make amends. Yet, as the intimate and metaphysical dimensions of his work imply, he is not only a poet tied to historical circumstance, but one who can act in relation to it by means of artistic responsibility, remorse, and regret. Further, and perhaps most important, reading his poems invites and fosters a reinvigorated and refreshed relationship to existence itself. In "Self-Portrait" the poet notes of his creative impulse that "It lives, if it lives, on a contradiction from which filters, on and off, a primary (call it deluded, call it unfulfilled, call it unrequited) love of life."[86] Vittorio Sereni is above all among the great love poets of what it means to be thoroughly alive.

Peter Robinson

86. See p. 334 below.

CHRONOLOGY

VITTORIO SERENI

1913   *27 July:* The only child of Enrico (1879–1953) and Maria Michelina Colombi (1884–1958), Vittorio Sereni is born in Luino, a small town on Lago Maggiore near the Swiss frontier.

1915   *May:* The poet's earliest memory, recalled in an interview from 1969, was the news that Italy had entered the First World War.

1917   *October:* Sereni also said he clearly remembered word reaching Luino of the defeat at Caporetto, this defeat and subsequent sense of national shame significantly contributing to the rise of fascism.

1922   The March on Rome. Benito Mussolini achieves power.

1924   Sereni's father, a customs official, leaves the Luino fascist party in protest at the murder of Matteotti. The Sereni family moves to Brescia, where the poet's father had been transferred. The move may have been made to allow their son to attend middle and high schools that did not then exist in Luino.

1929   Begins to write love poetry about a girl at school, a relationship important enough to be recalled in the fifth part of "Diario d'Algeria" fifteen years later.

1932   The family moves again, this time to Milan, where they live at Via Mario Pagano 42. The move may have again been for the son's continuing education.

      29 October: Enrolls at the university in the faculty of law.

1933 *22 March:* Transfers to the faculty of literature and philosophy.

1934 Ties for second place with Giosue Bonfanti behind Leonardo Sinisgalli in the Littorali della Cultura contest that year. His poetic vocation is already well known among his university friends, and he becomes a member of the circle formed around the anti-fascist philosophy professor Antonio Banfi. This group includes Antonia Pozzi and Daria Mendicanti. He also begins to frequent the cafés of literary Milan and becomes acquainted with poets such as Sergio Solmi, Salvatore Quasimodo, Leonardo Sinisgalli, and Roberto Rebora.

1935 *May:* Gian Luigi Manzi, a friend of Sereni and Pozzi, commits suicide.

October: Pozzi graduates with a thesis on Flaubert, published posthumously by Garzanti in 1940. The invasion of Abyssinia leads to sanctions against Italy led by Great Britain and the League of Nations.

1936 Meets Maria Luisa Bonfanti, a first-year student of literature, from Felino near Parma. They are together in the summer during a visit to Salsomaggiore with her mother; however, at the end of the stay, when she does not keep an appointment, Sereni fears that their relationship is over (cf. "Temporale a Salsomaggiore"). At this point she becomes engaged to a doctor from Parma ten years older. Her relationship with Sereni is only taken up again in 1938.

10 November: He graduates with a thesis on Guido Gozzano (1883–1916), but there is a disagreement between the examining professors, and he is awarded a pass mark only.

13 December: "Terre rosse" is published in the *Meridiano di Roma*, his first poem to appear in print. He makes a brief visit to Luino, where the poet rediscovers a sense of his roots.

1937 *February:* Temporary teaching post in lower-level literary subjects at the Istituto Tecnico "Schiapparelli" in Milan.

July: On holiday in Luino, meets Bianca B., a fifteen-year-old girl who inspires poems in his first book.

October: temporary teaching post in Italian and history at the Istituto Magistrale "Carlo Tenca," Milan, a girl's high school. Works as Antonio Banfi's voluntary assistant at the university. Begins to attract critical attention when the poet Carlo Betocchi publishes and introduces two of his poems in *Frontespizio*.

1938 *March:* Becomes coeditor of *Corrente* and begins to contribute to numerous literary magazines. Mussolini signs the Pact of Steel with Hitler's Germany.

15 July–30 October: Military training at Fano and Urbino. Sereni returns to Luino on leave in September and becomes friendly once more with Bianca B. Also in contact with Maria Luisa Bonfanti.

30 September: The Munich Agreement is signed, and presented in Italy as a triumph of diplomacy for Mussolini. Sereni finds another temporary teaching post, this time in Italian and Latin at the liceo "Manzoni," Milan.

3 December: Antonia Pozzi commits suicide at the age of twenty-six.

6 December: Sereni writes to Maria Luisa Bonfanti, and they disappear together for ten days.

1939 *30 June:* End of teaching post at the liceo "Manzoni."

1 July: At Brescia as a lieutenant with the 77th Infantry Regiment, "Lupi di Toscana" Division.

28 July: Passes the state exam and takes up a permanent post as a teacher of Italian, Latin, and history.

1 September: German armies invade Poland; Britain and France declare war two days later. Italy announces its "nonbelligerent" status. After a summer training camp at Vezza d'Oglio, Sereni spends the winter in barracks at Brescia, making brief visits to see Maria Luisa.

1940 *March:* Demobilized, takes up a school teaching post in Modena. Further visits to Maria Luisa in Felino, and sees Attilio Bertolucci at the Baccanelli on the outskirts of Parma.

10 June: Mussolini declares war on Britain and France.

13 June: Maria Luisa Bonfanti graduates from Milan University.

14 June: Sereni is called up again.

19 June: On short leave, wearing his lieutenant's uniform, Sereni marries Maria Luisa. They spend a few days' honeymoon at the Hotel Berzieri in Salsomaggiore.

July: Posted to the southern French front, but his regiment does not arrive in time to see action and is stationed at Mondovì, and Garessio (Cuneo) in Piedmont. There he and his wife meet secretly.

September: Allowed to return to his teaching post at Modena, he is not involved in the disastrous Greek campaign. Lives with his wife at Piazza Mazzini 43, experiences a prolific return of poetic inspiration.

1941 *20 February:* First book, *Frontiera,* published in an edition of three hundred copies by Corrente in Milan.

24 July: Maria Teresa, the Serenis' first daughter, is born.

October: Recalled to arms, Sereni, a lieutenant in the Pistoia Division of motorized infantry, becomes part of a draft intended to reinforce the armies in North Africa.

1942 *Autumn:* Enlarged second edition of *Frontiera,* entitled *Poesie,* is published in Florence. Spends the winter and spring of 1941–42 in Bologna. To avoid the danger of sailing too near the British bases on Malta, Sereni is sent by troop train through the Balkans to Greece in preparation for a posting to North Africa. The Pistoia Division spends four months encamped on the coast at Piraeus near Athens.

October: After the defeat of Rommel's Afrika Corps at El Alamein, the division returns to Italy, still expecting a posting to the North African front.

1943 *6 April:* Castelvetrano airbase is bombed, making the transport of Sereni's division by air to Tunisia impossible. After the fall of Tunis, it forms part of the defense of Sicily preparing for anticipated Allied landings from the sea in the western part of the island near Trapani.

10 July: The invasion of Sicily begins in the east of the island.

24 July: American forces arrive at Paceco from the landward side, and the trapped Italians surrender with little resistance. Sereni is taken prisoner by the American 82nd Airborne Division.

25 July: Mussolini falls from power.

15 August: Shipped across the Mediterranean and arrives with other prisoners of war near Bizerta. Plan to send him and his fellow POWs to camps in the United States.

8 September: He is aboard ship at Oran on when General Badoglio's government signs a separate armistice with the Allies. As a result of his changed status (from enemy prisoner to captured soldier of a cobelligerent) Sereni spends one-and-a-half years in various POW camps in Algeria near Oran and six months at the Fedala Camp in French Morrocco on the Atlantic coast near Casablanca.

1944 *6 June:* D-Day landings in Normandy.

1945 *25 April:* End of the war in Italy.

28 July: Leaves North Africa.

August: Sereni arrives in Italy and takes up teaching again at a high school in Milan.

1946 The Italian monarchy is voted into exile by referendum, and a republic formed. The Libera Stampa Prize is awarded *ex acqueo* to Sereni and Umberto Bellintani for as yet unpublished work.

1947 *May:* Second book, *Diario d'Algeria,* is published by Vallecchi in Florence.

12 June: Second daughter, Silvia, is born.

1948 *18 April:* The Christian Democrats defeat the Communists and Socialists in the first elections for the new republic. Secures a position as a high school teacher of Italian and Latin at the liceo classico "Carducci" in Milan.

1951 Begins to spend summer vacations at Bocca di Magra on the Ligurian coast, where the family is to rent a number of different houses over the coming years.

1952 Leaves teaching and joins Pirelli, working for the next six years as chief editor of the literary magazine *Pirelli* and in the advertising and press departments.

1953 *September:* Moves to Via Mauro Macchi 35. Some years later they move again, this time to Via Benedetto Marcello 67. The poet's grandparents remain in Via Scarlatti.

9 December: Death of the poet's father.

1956 Makes a first visit to Paris on a business trip. Receives the Libera Stampa Prize at Lugano for an unpublished collection with the provisional title *Un lungo sonno* [A Long Sleep], which evolves into his 1965 collection, *Gli strumenti umani.*

22 June: Third daughter, Giovanna, is born.

1957 Scheiwiller publishes *Frammenti di una sconfitta*. Italy is a founder member of the European Community with the signing of the Treaty of Rome.

1958 *7 January:* Death of the poet's mother. Becomes chief literary editor at Mondadori with special responsibility for poetry and begins to make the annual visit to the Frankfurt Book Fair from which his story *L'Opzione* draws its inspiration. Sereni had first been offered work with Mondadori as early as 1941 and advised the firm during the 1950s before taking up the post. Elio Vittorini is appointed director of international literature. With Giancarlo Buzzi completes a screenplay on the life of Apollinaire. It is not made into a film.

1962 Publishes a volume of occasional writings, *Gli immediati dintorni*. Spring, begins to coedit with Niccolò Gallo, Dante Isella, Geno Pampaloni and others the literary magazine *Questo e altro*.

1964 Publishes *L'Opzione* first in the eighth and final issue of *Questo e altro* then in *L'Opzione e allegati* (Scheiwiller).

1965 Visits Holland. Third book of poetry, *Gli strumenti umani*, appears from Einaudi and is awarded the Montefeltro Prize at Urbino. New edition of *Diario d'Algeria* published by Mondadori.

1966 *January:* Gives readings and talks in the United States and Canada, visiting New York, Chicago, Toronto, Boston, Philadelphia, and returning to Italy via London. New edition of *Frontiera* appears from Scheiwiller.

1967 Visits Prague.

October: The family moves into their own apartment in a house constructed with friends in Via P. A. Paravia.

1968 Visits the Vaucluse with Piero Bigongiari.

1969 Mondadori launches the prestigious Meridiani series at the instigation of Sereni, who chooses the name and appoints Giansiro Ferrata as director. Under Sereni the series includes volumes of Kafka, Ungaretti, Goethe, Quasimodo, Poe, Fitzgerald, Baudelaire, Buzzati, Melville, Hemingway, Cervantes, Joyce, Vittorini, and Hardy. Revisits Sicily on holiday and begins to write *Ventisei*, a prose evocation and analysis of the months leading up to his capture in 1943.

26 October: Maria Teresa Sereni marries Domenico Chiari at Parma. They have one daughter, Laura, referred to in "Sarà la noia."

1970–71 Composes "Un posto di vacanza."

1972 "Un posto di vacanza" published in *Almanacco dello Specchio,* no. 1 (1972). The Accademia Nazionale dei Lincei awards him the Antonio Feltrinelli Prize for poetry.

1973 Publishes *Poesie scelte 1935–1965,* edited by Lanfranco Caretti, and *Letture preliminari,* a collection of essays and reviews written between 1940 and 1971, including pieces on Montale, Attilio Bertolucci, Prevert, Solmi, W. C. Williams, Primo Levi, Apollinaire, Char, and Seferis.

1974 Visits Mexico.

1976 Receives the Monselice Prize for his translations of René Char: *Ritorno sopramonte e altre poesie* published in 1974.

1978 Retires from publishing but continues to act as an advisor for Mondadori. Visit to Provence and the Vaucluse. Meeting with René Char. First visit to Egypt.

1979 Second visit to Egypt.

1980 Visit to China in November with other Italian writers including Mario Luzi. *Il sabato tedesco* appears, containing "L'Opzione" and another prose work that gives the book its name.

1981 *Il musicante di Saint-Merry,* selected translations from the Orphée Noir, Pound, Char, Williams, Frenaud, Apollinaire, Camus, Bandini, and Corneille, appears.

December: Fourth book of poetry, *Stella variabile,* is published.

1982 Awarded the Viareggio Prize for *Stella variabile.* Visits Char for the last time with Feruccio Benzoni and Stefano Simoncelli.

1983 *10 February:* Sereni dies of an aneurysm. He is buried in Luino the following day.

Selected Poetry

da *Frontiera* / from *Frontier*

CONCERTO IN GIARDINO

Inverno

. . . .
ma se ti volgi e guardi
nubi nel grigio
esprimono le fonti dietro te,
le montagne nel ghiaccio s'inazzurrano.
Opaca un'onda mormorò
chiamandoti: ma ferma—ora
nel ghiaccio s'increspò
poi che ti volgi
e guardi
la svelata bellezza dell'inverno.

Armoniosi aspetti sorgono
in fissità, nel gelo: ed hai
un gesto vago
come di fronte a chi ti sorridesse
di sotto un lago di calma,
mentre ulula il tuo battello lontano
laggiù, dove s'addensano le nebbie.

Concerto in giardino

A quest'ora
innaffiano i giardini in tutta Europa.
Tromba di spruzzi roca
raduna bambini guerrieri,
echeggia in suono d'acque
sino a quest'ombra di panca.

Ai bambini in guerra sulle aiole
sventaglia, si fa vortice;
suono sospeso in gocce

GARDEN CONCERT

Winter

. . . .
but if you turn and watch
fountains behind you exhale
clouds against the gray,
mountains in the ice turn blue.
Opaque, a wave murmured
calling you: but stilled—now
in the ice it rippled
just as you turn
and watch
the beauty of winter unveiled.

Harmonious features rise
in fixity, in the freeze: and you
make the vaguest gesture
as if to someone who'd smile at you
from beneath a lake of calm
while your distant boat laments
down here, where the fogs grow dense.

Garden Concert

At this hour
they're watering gardens all over Europe.
Hoarse trumpet of the spray
gathers warlike children,
echoes in sounds of water
far as this bench's shade.

On the children at war in the borders
it fans out, makes vortices;
sound suspended in droplets

istante
ti specchi in verde ombrato;
siluri bianchi e rossi
battono gli asfalti dell'Avus,
filano treni a sud-est
tra campi di rose.

Da quest'ombra di panca
ascolto i ringhi della tromba d'acqua:
a ritmi di gocce
il mio tempo s'accorda.

Ma fischiano treni d'arrivi.

S'è strozzato nel caldo
il concerto della vita che svaria
in estreme girandole d'acqua.

Domenica sportiva

Il verde è sommerso in neroazzurri.
Ma le zebre venute di Piemonte
sormontano riscosse a un hallalì
squillato dietro barriere di folla.
Ne fanno un reame bianconero.
La passione fiorisce fazzoletti
di colore sui petti delle donne.

Giro di meriggio canoro,
ti spezza un trillo estremo.
A porte chiuse sei silenzio d'echi
nella pioggia che tutto cancella.

instantaneous
you mirror yourself in the shadowy green;
red and white torpedoes
beat on the asphalt of Avus,
trains head southeast
through fields of roses.

From this bench's shade
I hear the water trumpet's snarl:
to the droplets' rhythm
my time accords.

But trains are whistling arrivals.

It's choked in the heat,
life's concert that quavers
in outermost swirlings of water.

Sport on Sunday

The green's submerged in blue-and-blacks.
But the zebras come from Piedmont
overwhelm attacks to a halloo
blared behind barriers of crowd.
They form a black-and-white realm.
Passion blossoms handkerchiefs
of color on women's breasts.

Turn of the singing afternoon,
a last trill shatters you.
At closed gates you are silent echoes
in rain that obliterates all.

Memoria d'America

Starmene solo nel ranch.

Ieri a uno schiantarsi di vetri
si disperavano le bestie;
adesso antelucani colombi
vibrano il capo
a un tremito d'ore minute.
La luna sta nella finestra—ferma
su quel paese di venti notturni.

Abbandonato nel ranch.

Ma palpita arancio colore
dalla barriera di nuvole
che fanno nevaio sul lago.
Quattro zoccoli;
e sento nitrire
di ritorno
la cavalla che ieri ho perduto
in quell'ultimo temporale d'estate.

Canzone lombarda

Sui tavoli le bevande si fanno più chiare
l'inverno sta per andare di qua.

Nell'ampio respiro dell'acqua
ch'è sgorgata col verde delle piazze
vanno ragazze in lucenti vestiti.
Noi dietro vetri in agguato.
Ma quelle su uno svolto strette a sciami
un canto fanno d'angeli
e trascorrono:
      —Digradante a cerchi
      in libertà di prati, città,
      a primavera.

Recalling America

Stay by myself on the ranch.

Yesterday at a shattering of glass
the animals panicked;
now before dawn doves
quiver their heads
in a tremor of tiny hours.
The moon's at the window—fixed
above that town of nighttime winds.

Left alone on the ranch.

But orange color palpitates
from the cloud barrier
making a snowfield on the lake.
Four hooves;
and I hear
neighing her return
the mare I lost a day ago
in that final summer storm.

Lombard Song

On the tables the drinks grow clearer
winter's ready to go from here.

In the ample breath of water
disgorged with the piazza's green
girls go out in gleaming clothes.
We behind glass panes in ambush.
But those at a turning tightened in swarms
make an angel's song
and go on by:
> —*Diminishing in circles*
> *with the freedom of meadows, cities,*
> *in springtime.*

E noi ci si sente lombardi
e noi si pensa
a migrazioni per campi
nell'ombra dei sottopassaggi.

Compleanno

Un altro ponte
sotto il passo m'incurvi
ove a bandiere e culmini di case
è sospeso il tuo fiato,
città grave.
Ancora al sonno
canti di uccelli sento
lontanissimi unirsi
e del pallido verde
mi rinnovi il tempo,
d'una donna agli sguardi serena
mi ritorni memoria,
amara estate.

Ma dove t'apri
e tra l'erba orme di carri
e piazze e strade in polvere spaési
senso d'acque mi spiri
e di ridenti vetri una calma.
Maturità di foglie, arco di lago
altro evo mi spieghi lucente,
in una strada senza vento inoltri
la giovinezza che non trova scampo.

Nebbia

Qui il traffico oscilla
sospeso alla luce

And we feel we are from Lombardy
and it's us who think
of migrations through fields
in the underpasses' shadows.

Birthday

Another bridge
beneath my feet you lead me
where from flags
and house heights
our breath hangs,
grave city.
Again I hear
the birdsong merging
distant into sleep
and of the pallid green
you renew me the time,
return me the memory
of a woman who to glances is serene,
bitter summer.

But where you open
and among grasses, cart tracks
and squares and streets disperse in dust,
you breathe me a sense of waters
and of smiling windows a calm.
Leaves' timeliness, lake's curve
you unfold me another age gleaming,
in a windless road extend
youth that finds no release.

Fog

Here the traffic wavers
held up at the light

dei semafori quieti.
Io vengo in parte
ove s'infolta la città
e un fiato d'alti forni la trafuga.
Chiedo al cuore una voce, mi sovrasta
un assiduo rumore
di fabbriche fonde, di magli.

E il tempo piega all'inverno.
Io batto le strade
che ai giorni delle volpi gentili
autunno di feltri verdi fioriva,
i viali celesti al dopopioggia.
Al segno di luce si libera il passo
e indugia l'anno, su queste contrade.

S'illumina a uno svolto un effimero sole,
un cespo di mimose
nella bianchissima nebbia.

Temporale a Salsomaggiore

Questa notte sei densa e minacciosa.
Dalla pianura balenano città
nell'ora finale dei convogli e il vento
nemico preme alle porte,
nelle piazze s'ingolfa e appanna i globi
della strada elegante.
                        S'oscura
la tua grazia e la memoria
dei parasoli brillanti per le vie
sotto le nubi tiepide, d'oro.

Né più verrà
nelle placide ore del sonno
il raccolto battito dei pozzi
che misurava le notti. I passanti
tutti hanno un volto di morte,

of the still signals.
I come to a place
where the city condenses
and a breath from blast furnaces spirits it away.
I ask the heart for a voice, above me looms
a persistent clamor
of distant factories, of forges.

And the weather tends towards winter.
I tramp the streets
which autumn adorned with green felts
in the days of delicate foxes,
the avenues azure after rain.
At the light's sign the way is made clear
and over these lands the year lingers.

At a turning, an ephemeral sun,
a cluster of mimosa
flares within the whitest fog.

Storm at Salsomaggiore

Tonight you are close and threatening.
From the plain cities flare
in the last hour of convoys and the enemy
wind presses at the gates,
engulfs the squares and mists the globes
of the elegant street.
                      Along roads
your grace and the memory
of dazzling parasols dims
under warm, golden clouds.

Nor will it return
in tranquil hours of sleep,
the wells' muffled tapping
which measured nights. The passersby
all have a face of death,

Emilia, nei viali
dove impazzano le foglie.
Si spegne il tempo e anche tu sei morta.

Mi riafferri coll'aria dei giardini.
Gelsomini stillanti si riaprono
a lenire la notte, si ripopola
il paese all'uscita d'un teatro.
Torna il tuo volto,
vuoi punire le torve fantasie.

Nel rombo che s'allontana
degli ultimi tuoni sorvolanti le case,
sorrido alla tua gente
sotto tettoie sonanti, in ascolto.

A M. L. sorvolando in rapido la sua città

Non ti turbi il frastuono
che irrompe con me nel tuo quieto mattino
se un poco io mi sporgo a ravvisarti,
mentre tu forse cammini
con la tua gente
nelle plaghe del sole;
non ti turbi quest'ansia che ti sfiora
e dietro un breve vento si lascia
di festuche in un vortice di suoni.

Come ti schiari,
come consenti al fuggitivo amore
dai balconi dagli orti dalle torri
. . . .

Emilia, on avenues
where leaves are frenzied.
The weather spends itself and you too are dead.

You grasp me again in the gardens' air.
Dripping jasmine are reopening
to soothe the night, the town's repopulated
once more at a theatre's exit.
Your face is returning,
you want to smite the sullen fantasies.

In the rumble that grows distant
of final thunderclaps flying over houses,
I smile at your people
under resonant roofs, listening.

To M. L. Passing Above Her Town in an Express Train

Be untroubled by the roar
which bursts with me into your peaceful morning
if I lean out a little to recognize you,
while you perhaps are walking
with your people
across the beaming lands;
be untroubled by this fretfulness which touches you
and behind itself leaves a brief wind
of motes in a swirl of sounds.

How you brighten,
how you consent to the fugitive love
from the balconies, from gardens, from towers
. . . .

Diana

Torna il tuo cielo d'un tempo
sulle altane lombarde,
in nuvole d'afa s'addensa
e nei tuoi occhi esula ogni azzurro,
si raccoglie e riposa.

Anche l'ora verrà della frescura
col vento che si leva sulle darsene
dei Navigli e il cielo
che per le rive s'allontana.

Torni anche tu, Diana,
tra i tavoli schierati all'aperto
e la gente intenta alle bevande
sotto la luna distante?

Ronza un'orchestra in sordina;
all'aria che qui ne sobbalza
ravviso il tuo ondulato passare,
s'addolce nella sera il fiero nome
se qualcuno lo mormora
sulla tua traccia.

Presto vien giugno
e l'arido fiore del sonno
cresciuto ai più tristi sobborghi

e il canto che avevi, amica, sulla sera
torna a dolere qui dentro,
alita sulla memoria
a rimproverarti la morte.

Soldati a Urbino

Queste torri alte sulla memoria
nell'ora dolce dei bastioni

Diana

Your sky of those days returns
above the Lombard lofts,
thickens in clouds of heat
and every blue, an exile in your eyes,
gathers and reposes.

Also the freshening hour will come
with the wind which lifts on the wharves
of the Navigli and the sky
that grows distant along their banks.

Diana, do you also return
amid tables paraded in the open
and people intent on their drinks
under the faraway moon?

Muted, an orchestra hums;
here with the bouncy air
I recognize your swaying walk,
the proud name sweetens in the evening
should somebody murmur it
across your wake.

June comes quickly
and the parched flower of sleep
grown in the saddest suburbs

and the song you had in the evening
returns to ache within here,
breathes on the memory
to reprove you for dying.

Soldiers in Urbino

These towers high in the memory
when the ramparts are at peace

e la nebbia che appena
approssima l'autunno a queste terre,
a noi
due, girovaghi soldati. Dici:
—*purtroppo*—e taci
un nome se una foglia chissà
di dove distolta ti sfiora,
poi parli d'una stella
che ancora un giorno
sulla tua strada forse spunterà.

Forse da oggi soltanto
avvertiremo l'impeto dell'ore
a mezzo il nostro secolo volgenti,
mentre al vento oscillano le lampade
bisbiglia un portico in ombra
e tu trasali al rombo
degli autocarri che mordono la montagna.

3 dicembre

All'ultimo tumulto dei binari
hai la tua pace, dove la città
in un volo di ponti e di viali
si getta alla campagna
e chi passa non sa
di te come tu non sai
degli echi delle cacce che ti sfiorano.

Pace forse è davvero la tua
e gli occhi che noi richiudemmo
per sempre ora riaperti
stupiscono
che ancora per noi
tu muoia un poco ogni anno
in questo giorno.

and the fog is barely
drawing autumn onto these lands,
onto us
two, wandering soldiers. You say,
—*unhappily*—and choke back
a name if a leaf torn from who knows
where brushes against you,
then you speak of a star
which one day once more
over your path will perhaps appear.

Perhaps only from today
will we feel the hour's surge
curving halfway through our century,
even as the wind rocks the lamps
a portico whispers in shadow
and you start at the rumble
of lorries gnawing the mountain.

3 December

At the final tumult of the lines
peace comes to you, where the city
in a flight of bridges and avenues
hurls itself into the country
and those who pass don't know
about you just as you don't know
about the echoes of the hunts touching you.

Peace perhaps is truly yours
and the eyes we closed
forever now reopened
are astonished
that still for us
you die a little every year
on this particular day.

Poesia militare

Mezzanotte fu sui cancelli
fresca d'acqua nel vento
la voce dolente di sonno.
Arretrava nell'ora
un paese d'azzurri santuari
perduto tra le perse primavere.

Ma salvo nelle voci degli addii
sommesso presentiva il mare
al passo dei notturni battaglioni.

Piazza

Assorto nell'ombra che approssima e fa vana
questa che mi chiude d'una sera,
anche più vano
di questi specchi già ciechi,
io non so, giovinezza, sopportare
il tuo sguardo d'addio.

Ma della piazza, a mezza sera,
vince i deboli lumi
la falce d'aprile in ascesa.

Sei salva e già lunare?
Che trepida grazia,
la tua figura che va.

Alla giovinezza

È cominciata una canzone losca
di rane tra le colline
e da un'estate mortale
—forse l'ultima tua—

Military Poem

Midnight on the gates was
fresh with water in the wind
sleep's plaintive voice.
A village of blue sanctuaries
was retreating with the hour
gone among the springs gone by.

But safe in the farewell voices
submerged it prefigured the sea
to the tread of nocturnal battalions.

Piazza

Absorbed in shadow that nears and makes vain
this closing for me with evening,
even more vain
than these mirrors blind already,
I don't know, youth, how to endure
your gaze of farewell.

But April's scythe in ascent
defeats the weak lights
of the piazza, midevening.

You're already safe and moonlike?
What timorous grace
your figure has leaving.

To Youth

Among the hills a raucous song
of frogs has begun
and from a mortal summer
—perhaps the last for you—

s'avventano rondini in volo
perdutamente, come tu cammini
verso un'aria fondissima, brumale.

E delle voci che da me
si dilungano, quale
potrà volgere il tuo e il mio cammino
a una marcia d'insonni girasoli?
Ma non sanno altro bene o altro male
che un lago azzurro o grigio
i tuoi occhi dall'ombra d'un viale.

FRONTIERA

Inverno a Luino

Ti distendi e respiri nei colori.
Nel golfo irrequieto,
nei cumuli di carbone irti al sole
sfavilla e s'abbandona
l'estremità del borgo.
Colgo il tuo cuore
se nell'alto silenzio mi commuove
un bisbiglio di gente per le strade.
Morto in tramonti nebbiosi d'altri cieli
sopravvivo alle tue sere celesti,
ai radi battelli del tardi
di luminarie fioriti.
Quando pieghi al sonno
e dài suoni di zoccoli e canzoni
e m'attardo smarrito ai tuoi bivi
m'accendi nel buio d'una piazza
una luce di calma, una vetrina.

swallows hurl themselves headlong
in flight, like you walking
towards a most dense, wintry air.

And, of the voices that stray
far from me, which one
will be able to turn your journey and mine
into a march of sleepless sunflowers?
But no other good or other evil do they know
than a lake of blue or gray,
your eyes from an avenue's shadow.

FRONTIER

Winter in Luino

You stretch out and breathe in the colors.
Along the restless bay,
in coal heaps jagged in the sun
the outskirts of the town
glitter and abandon themselves.
I gather your heart
if in deep silence I'm moved
by a murmur of people through streets.
Dead in foggy dusks of other skies
I survive your celestial evenings,
the occasional late boats
speckled with lights.
When you tend towards sleep
and sound with clogs and singing
and I'm lingering bewildered at your crossroads
you kindle for me in the dark of a square
a light of calm, a window pane.

Fuggirò quando il vento
investirà le tue rive;
sa la gente del porto quant'è vana
la difesa dei limpidi giorni.
Di notte il paese è frugato dai fari,
lo borda un'insonnia di fuochi
vaganti nella campagna,
un fioco tumulto di lontane
locomotive verso la frontiera.

Terrazza

Improvvisa ci coglie la sera.
                        Più non sai
dove il lago finisca;
un murmure soltanto
sfiora la nostra vita
sotto una pensile terrazza.

Siamo tutti sospesi
a un tacito evento questa sera
entro quel raggio di torpediniera
che ci scruta poi gira se ne va.

Strada di Zenna

Ci desteremo sul lago a un'infinita
navigazione. Ma ora
nell'estate impaziente
s'allontana la morte.
E pure con labile passo
c'incamminiamo su cinerei prati
per strade che rasentano l'Eliso.

I'll flee when the wind
assails your shores;
the harbor people know how vain
is the limpid days' defense.
At night the town is searched by rays,
sleepless fires edge round it
straying in the countryside,
a faint rumble of distant
locomotives towards the frontier.

Terrace

Suddenly the evening seizes us.
                              You no longer know
where the lake finishes;
only a murmur
skims over our life
beneath a suspended terrace.

We're all hanging
on a mute event this evening
in that torpedoboat's searchlight
which scrutinizes us then turning vanishes.

Zenna Road

We will arise on the lakeside
to infinite crossings. But now
in listless summer
death grows more remote.
Yet still with traceless steps
we're setting out over ashen fields
through streets that border Elysium.

Si muta
l'innumerevole riso;
è un broncio teso tra l'acqua
e le rive nel lagno
del vento tra le stuoie tintinnanti.
Questa misura ha il silenzio
stupito a una nube di fumo
rimasta di qua dall'impeto
che poco fa spezzava la frontiera.

Vedi sulla spiaggia abbandonata
turbinare la rena,
ci travolge la cenere dei giorni.
E attorno è l'esteso strazio
delle sirene salutanti nei porti
per chi resta nei sogni
di pallidi volti feroci,
nel rombo dell'acquazzone
che flagella le case.
Ma torneremo taciti a ogni approdo.
Non saremo che un suono
di volubili ore noi due
o forse brevi tonfi di remi
di malinconiche barche.

Voi morti non ci date mai quiete
e forse è vostro
il gemito che va tra le foglie
nell'ora che s'annuvola il Signore.

Settembre

Già l'òlea fragrante nei giardini
d'amarezza ci punge: il lago un poco
si ritira da noi, scopre una spiaggia
d'aride cose,
di remi infranti, di reti strappate.
E il vento che illumina le vigne

It alters,
the incalculable smile;
it's a scowl stretched between water
and shores in a wailing
of wind through the tinkling fencework.
The silence has this cadence,
dumbfounded to a cloud of smoke
left behind here from the surge
which just now divided the frontier.

You see on the deserted beach
the sand's whirling,
day's ashes overwhelm us.
And all around is the extended torment
of the sirens' farewells in the ports
for whoever remains in dreams
of fierce pallid faces,
in the rumble of the cloud burst
that thrashes the houses.
But we'll return silent at each approach to shore,
be no more than a sound,
you and I, of voluble hours
or perhaps short thuds of oars
from disconsolate boats.

You, the dead, never give us any peace
and it may be the wail
going through the leaves is yours
in the hour that the Lord clouds over.

September

Already in the gardens the fragrant olea
stings us with bitterness: the lake withdraws
from us somewhat, reveals a beach
of dried-up things,
of shattered oars, of shredded nets.
And the wind that brightens the vineyards

già volge ai giorni fermi queste plaghe
da una dubbiosa brulicante estate.

Nella morte già certa
cammineremo con più coraggio,
andremo a lento guado coi cani
nell'onda che rotola minuta.

Un'altra estate

Lunga furente estate.
La solca ora un brivido sottile
alle foci del Tresa
sì che alcuno ne trema
dei volti già ridenti,
ora presaghi.
Ma tutto quanto non soggiacque all'afa
s'appunta al volo
degli uccelli lentissimi del largo
avventurati negli oscuri golfi
di un'Italia infinita.

Immagine

La finestra ti reggeva nella sera
alta sulle canzoni della strada.
Così nel buio degli anni indecisi
resterai . . . —frequente
il tuono ti fingeva gli orrori
d'una guerra lontana.

Ancora a volte ti ritrovo a un suono
d'ore oltre la pioggia, curvo
sul primo tizzo autunnale.
O fu il lampo d'un viso

is already turning into firm days these lands
from a doubtful swarming summer.

In already certain death
we will walk with more courage,
slowly forward with the dogs we'll wade
into the tiny rolling wave.

Another Summer

Long raging summer.
Now a slight shudder furrows it
at the Tresa's mouths
so that one of them trembles,
the faces just then laughing
foreboding now.
But all that hasn't succumbed to the heat
follows the flight
of the slowest birds in the offing
ventured among dark gulfs
of an infinite Italy.

Image

The window lifted you one evening
high above songs of the street.
Just so in the dark of indecisive years
you will remain—the frequent thunder
would feign for you
horrors of a distant war.

Still I regain you at times in a sound
of chimes beyond the rain, inclined
on the first autumnal ember.
Or it was the flare of a face

tra campi arsi e mietuti
a Garessio, d'estate, in Val d'Inferno.

Siamo usciti sui colli a mezzanotte
al vago appello remoto
d'una veranda occulta: — *Santa,
Santa mia.*
C'è chi sorride placido, distante
e cammina sul gorgo degli anni
gridati dal fiume
stanotte, nel più chiaro plenilunio.

In me il tuo ricordo

In me il tuo ricordo è un fruscìo
solo di velocipedi che vanno
quietamente là dove l'altezza
del meriggio discende
al più fiammante vespero
tra cancelli e case
e sospirosi declivi
di finestre riaperte sull'estate.
Solo, di me, distante
dura un lamento di treni,
d'anime che se ne vanno.

E là leggera te ne vai sul vento,
ti perdi nella sera.

Strada di Creva

I

Presto la vela freschissima di maggio
ritornerà sulle acque
dove infinita trema Luino

between reaped and charred fields
at Garessio, summer, in Val d'Inferno.

We went out on the hills at midnight
to the vague remote call
of a hidden veranda: — *Santa,*
Santa mia.
Some placidly smile, faraway
and walk upon the whirlpool of years
howled from the river
tonight, in the clearest of full moons.

Your Memory in Me

Your memory in me is a solitary
whirring of pedal-bikes that go
peaceably where the height
of noon descends
to the more blazing sunset
amongst gates and houses
and wistful inclines
of windows reopened onto summer.
What's left of me, only
a faraway wail of steam trains lingers,
of souls that are departing.

And light on the wind there you leave,
lose yourself in the evening.

Creva Road

I

Soon May's freshest sail
will return across the waters
where infinite Luino trembles

e il canto spunterà remoto
del cucco affacciato alle valli
dopo l'ultima pioggia:
      ora
d'un pazzo inverno nei giorni
dei Santi votati alla neve
lucerte vanno per siepi,
fumano i boschi intorno
e una coppia attardata sui clivi
ha voci per me di saluto
come a volte sui monti
la gente che si chiama tra le valli.

II

Questo trepido vivere nei morti.

Ma dove ci conduce questo cielo
che azzurro sempre più azzurro si spalanca
ove, a guardarli, ai lontani
paesi decade ogni colore.
Tu sai che la strada se discende
ci protende altri prati, altri paesi,
altre vele sui laghi:
      il vento ancora
turba i golfi, li oscura.
Si rientra d'un passo nell'inverno.
E nei tetri abituri si rientra,
a un convito d'ospiti leggiadri
si riattizzano i fuochi moribondi.

E nei bicchieri muoiono altri giorni.

Salvaci allora dai notturni orrori
dei lumi nelle case silenziose.

and far away the song will appear
of the cuckoo looking out towards valleys
after the most recent rain:
                              now
one mad winter in the Saints' days
devoted to the snows
lizards move through hedgerows,
all around the forests steam
and a couple lingering on the slopes
has voices of greeting for me
as on the mountains sometimes
people calling to each other across valleys.

   II

This timorous living among the dead.

But where this bluer, always bluer
sky opens wide and leads us
to the distant villages,
gazing, every color decays.
You know that if the road descends
to us it extends other fields, other villages,
other sails on the lakes:
                           again the wind
disturbs the bays, obscures them.
We go back a step into winter.
And to the gloomy dwellings we go back,
at a banquet of enchanting guests
dying fires are rekindled.

And other days die in the glasses.

Then save us from the horrors of night,
the lights in silent houses.

ECCO LE VOCI CADONO

Ecco le voci cadono e gli amici
sono così distanti
che un grido è meno
che un murmure a chiamarli.
Ma sugli anni ritorna
il tuo sorriso limpido e funesto
simile al lago
che rapisce uomini e barche
ma colora le nostre mattine.

SEE HOW THE VOICES FALL

See how the voices fall and friends
are so far distant
that a cry is less
than a murmur calling them.
But on the years' returns
your transparent fatal smile
similar to the lake
that carries boats and men away
but brings color to our mornings.

*
  *   *

Non sa più nulla, è alto sulle ali
il primo caduto bocconi sulla spiaggia normanna.
Per questo qualcuno stanotte
mi toccava la spalla mormorando
di pregar per l'Europa
mentre la Nuova Armada
si presentava alla costa di Francia.

Ho risposto nel sonno: – È il vento,
il vento che fa musiche bizzarre.
Ma se tu fossi davvero
il primo caduto bocconi sulla spiaggia normanna
prega tu se lo puoi, io sono morto
alla guerra e alla pace.
Questa è la musica ora:
delle tende che sbattono sui pali.
Non è musica d'angeli, è la mia
sola musica e mi basta. —

Campo-Ospedale 127
    giugno 1944

Diario d'Algeria / Algerian Diary

LA RAGAZZA D'ATENE

Periferia 1940

La giovinezza è tutta nella luce
d'una città al tramonto
dove straziato ed esule ogni suono
si spicca dal brusio.

E tu mia vita salvati se puoi
serba te stessa al futuro
passante e quelle parvenze sui ponti
nel baleno dei fari.

Città di notte

Inquieto nella tradotta
che ti sfiora così lentamente
mi tendo alle tue luci sinistre
nel sospiro degli alberi.

Mentre tu dormi e forse
qualcuno muore nelle alte stanze
e tu giri via con un volto
dietro ogni finestra—tu stessa
un volto, un volto solo
che per sempre si chiude.

Diario bolognese

Io non so come sempre
un disperato murmure m'opprima
nell'aria del tuo mezzogiorno
tanto diffusa ai colli dentro il sole

THE ATHENIAN GIRL

Outskirts 1940

Youth is all in the light
of a city at sunset
where tormented and exiled each sound
stands out from the hum.

And my life save yourself if you can
spare yourself for who's to come
passing and those semblances on bridges
in the headlamps' glare.

City at Night

Uneasy in the troop train
brushing against you so slowly
I lean to your ominous lights
in the sighing of the trees.

Meanwhile you sleep and perhaps
someone's dying in the upper rooms
and you turn away with a face
behind each window—yourself
a face, a face only
that forever closes.

Bolognese Diary

I don't know how always
a desperate murmur oppresses me
in your midday air
so spread out on the hills in sunlight

tanto quaggiù gremita e fumicosa.
E non è fiore in te che non m'esprima
il male che presto lo morde,
non per finestra musica s'inoltra
che amara non ricada sull'estate.
Invano sotto San Luca ogni strada
voluttuosa rallenta, alla tua gioia
sono cieco ed inerme.
E l'ombra dorata trabocca nel rogo serale,
l'amore sui volti s'imbestia,
fugge oltre i borghi il tempo irreparabile
della nostra viltà.

Belgrado
A GIOSUE BONFANTI

— ... Donau? —
Nein Donau, Sava — come in sogno
dice la sentinella e rulla un ponte
sotto il convoglio che s'attarda.
E non so che profondità remota
di lavoro e di voci dai tuoi spalti
celebra una tranquilla ora d'Europa
nata con te tra due chimere
— il Danubio! la Sava! —
azzurre di un mattino
perduto, di là da venire:
sogno improvviso di memorie, come
le sentinelle sognano
dai ponti della Sava
qualche figura tra le piante a caso,
un intravisto romanzo d'amore.

Tradotta Mestre-Atene, agosto 1942

so crowded and smoke-filled down here.
And there's no flower of yours fails to express
for me the evil quickly gnawing it,
and no music at windows advancing
that doesn't fall bitterly back onto summer.
In vain beneath San Luca every road
voluptuously eases, I'm blind
and defenseless to your joy.
And gilded shadow brims in evening's pyre,
love grows brutal on the faces,
beyond townships the irreparable time of our
cowardice is fleeing.

Belgrade
TO GIOSUE BONFANTI

        — . . . Donau? —
Nein Donau, Sava — as in a dream
the sentry says and a bridge
drums beneath the lingering convoy.
And I don't know what remote depth
of labor and voices from your parapets
celebrates a peaceful hour in Europe
born with you between two chimeras
— the Danube! the Sava! —
azure in a morning lost,
to come to pass:
unforeseen dream of memories, as
the sentries dream
from the bridges of the Sava
some figure among the trees at random,
a love romance just caught sight of.

Mestre-Athens troop train, August 1942

Italiano in Grecia

Prima sera d'Atene, esteso addio
dei convogli che filano ai tuoi lembi
colmi di strazio nel lungo semibuio.
Come un cordoglio
ho lasciato l'estate sulle curve
e mare e deserto è il domani
senza più stagioni.
Europa Europa che mi guardi
scendere inerme e assorto in un mio
esile mito tra le schiere dei bruti,
sono un tuo figlio in fuga che non sa
nemico se non la propria tristezza
o qualche rediviva tenerezza
di laghi di fronde dietro i passi
perduti,
sono vestito di polvere e sole,
vado a dannarmi a insabbiarmi per anni.

Pireo, agosto 1942

Dimitrios
A MIA FIGLIA

Alla tenda s'accosta
il piccolo nemico
Dimitrios e mi sorprende,
d'uccello tenue strido
sul vetro del meriggio.
Non torce la bocca pura
la grazia che chiede pane,
non si vela di pianto
lo sguardo che fame e paura
stempera nel cielo d'infanzia.

È già lontano,
arguto mulinello

Italian in Greece

First Athens evening, drawn-out goodbye
of the convoys that file off at your margins
crammed with agony in the long half-dark.
Like an affliction
I've left summer on the curves
and sea and desert's my tomorrow
with no more seasons.
Europe, Europe who watch me
descending unarmed and absorbed
in my slender myth within the ranks of brutes,
I'm one of your sons in flight who knows
no enemy if not his own sorrow
or some reawakened tenderness
of lakes, of fronds behind the steps
that are lost,
I'm clothed in sun and dust,
go to damn and bury myself in sand for years.

Piraeus, August 1942

Dimitrios
TO MY DAUGHTER

To the tent approaches
the little enemy,
Dimitrios, and takes me unawares,
scrawny bird's cry
on the glass of midday sun.
The pure mouth's not twisted
by the grace that asks for bread,
not veiled in tears
the glance dissolving fear
and hunger in childhood's sky.

He's already far,
sharp will-o'-the-wisp

che s'annulla nell'afa,
Dimitrios—su lande avare
appena credibile, appena
vivo sussulto
di me, della mia vita
esitante sul mare.

Pireo, agosto 1942

La ragazza d'Atene

Ora il giorno è un sospiro
e tutta l'Attica un'ombra.
E come un guizzo illumina gli opachi
vetri volgenti in fuga
è il tuo volto che sprizza laggiù
dal cerchio del lume che accendi
all'icona serale.
               Ma qui
dove via via più rade s'abbattono
dell'ultima caccia le prede
tra le piante che seguono il confine,
ahimè che il puro
segno delle tue sillabe si guasta,
in contorto cirillico si muta.
E tu: come t'oscuri a poco a poco.
Ecco non puoi restare, sei perduta
nel fragore dell'ultimo viadotto.

               *

Presto sarò il viandante stupefatto
avventurato nel tempo nebbioso.

Deboli voli, nomi inerti ormai
ad una ad una si sgranano note
per staccarsi dal coro, oscuri scorci

diminishing in heat haze,
Dimitrios—on grasping lands
barely believable, barely
living tremor
in me, in my own life
hesitant on the sea.

Piraeus, August 1942

The Athenian Girl

Now the day's a sigh
and all of Attica a shade.
And as a flash illumines the opaque
windows turning in flight
so your face sparkles down there
from the ring of light you kindle
to the evening icon.
                     But here
where more and more scarce
the last hunt's prey falls to earth
among trees that follow the border,
alas, the pure
sign of your syllables is rotten,
alters to twisted Cyrillic.
And you: how you darken little by little.
See how you can't remain, are lost
within the last viaduct's roar.

*

Soon I'll be the bewildered traveler
hazarded out in foggy weather.

Weak flights, by now inert names
one by one notes fall away
tearing themselves from the chorus,

d'un perduto soggiorno: Kaidari,
una conca dolceamara d'ulivi
nel mio pigro rammentare—o quelle
navi perplesse al vento del Pireo.

E tutto che si prese sguardo e ascolto
confitto nella bruma è già passato.

*

Perché di tanto la ruota ha girato
oggi una flotta amica incrocia al largo,
tardi matura il frutto d'ansietà
primizia ad altri che non te,
despinís.
Chi dorme dorme nell'alta
neve lassù tra i cari morti.
Tu coi morti ti levi e in loro parli:
— Io voglio una bandiera
del mio strazio sonora
smagliante del mio pianto,
io voglio una contrada ove sia canto
lieve dagli anni verdi
l'inno che m'opprimeva,
ove l'allarme che solcò le notti
torni mutato in eco
di pietà di speranze di timore—.

*

Così, distanti, ci veniamo incontro.
E a volte sembra
d'incamminarci, despinís, nel sole
lieto anche ai vinti
nei giardini dell'Attica vivaci.

E ancora il tuo ricordo ne verdeggia.

Tradotta Atene-Mestre, autunno 1942
Africa del Nord, autunno 1944

dark glimpses of a lost sojourn: Kaidari,
a bittersweet vale of olives
in my idle recall—or those
boats perplexed in the wind of Piraeus.

And all that took the eye and ear
nailed into the mist is already passed.

*

Because the wheel's revolved so far
a friendly fleet cruises offshore today,
anxiety's fruit ripens late
first harvest to others than you,
despinís.
Whoever sleeps sleeps in the high snows
up there among the dear dead ones.
With the dead you arise and in them speak:
—I want a banner
with my torment resounding
radiant with my lament,
I want a land where it'll be song
light from the green years,
the hymn weighing on me
where the alarm that furrowed nights
returns changed to an echo
of mercy of hope of fear—.

*

So, distant, we converge.
And at times it seems
we step out, despinís, in sunlight
kindly to the defeated also
in the vivid gardens of Attica.

And still with them your memory grows verdant.

Athens-Mestre troop train, autumn 1942
North Africa, autumn 1944

Risalendo l'Arno da Pisa

O mia vita mia vita ancora ansiosa
d'un urbano decoro...
Se case e campi diventano vacui
se assurde si fanno le voci
e il velo sollevare non sai più,
è tua quella bruma, tristezza
foriera a ritroso dalle foci
d'una sua grigia bellezza.

Poi venne una zazzera d'oro
su un volto nebbioso.

Fu un giorno di fine d'anno
nel torvo tempo di guerra
a Santa Croce sull'Arno.

dicembre 1942

Villa Paradiso

Avvilite delizie, non meglio del filo
di brezza che nel mattino
di glicine
s'inoltra sulla costa bombardata.

Paceco, 1943

Pin-up Girl

Guarda il ritaglio triste che s'affloscia
nell'aria abbacinata:
ha cenni di maltempo,
rade voci d'allarme
il meriggio di luglio.

Up the Arno from Pisa

O my life my life still anxious
for an urban decorum . . .
If houses and fields become empty
if voices grow absurd
and you no longer know how to raise the veil,
that mist is yours, sorrow
foreshadowing up from the mouths
its one gray beauty.

Then came a mane of golden hair
upon a foggy face.

A day at the end of the year
it was, in grim wartime,
at Santa Croce sull'Arno.

December 1942

Villa Paradiso

Disheartened delights, no better than the thread
of breeze that in the morning
of wisteria
infiltrates on the bombarded coastline.

Paceco, 1943

Pin-up Girl

Look at the sorry cutting grown limp
in the dazzling air:
the July afternoon
has hints of bad weather,
stray voices of alarm.

E per poco la sete
si placa alle tue labbra
umide ancora nel vento.

Fronte di Trapani, luglio 1943

DIARIO D'ALGERIA

A REMO VALIANTI

Lassù dove di torre
in torre balza e si rimanda
ormai vano un consenso,
il chivalà dell'ora,
—come quaggiù di torretta in torretta
dai vertici del campo nei richiami
tra loro le scolte marocchine—
chi va nella tetra mezzanotte
dei fiocchi veloci, chi l'ultimo
brindisi manca su nere
soglie di vento sinistre
d'attesa, chi va...
È un'immagine nostra
stravolta, non giunta
alla luce. E d'oblio
solo un'azzurra vena abbandona
tra due epoche morte dentro noi.

Sainte-Barbe du Thélat, Capodanno 1944

Un improvviso vuoto del cuore
tra i giacigli di Sainte-Barbe.

And for a while the thirst
is quenched on your lips
still moistened in the wind.

Trapani front, July 1943

ALGERIAN DIARY

TO REMO VALIANTI

Over there where from tower
to tower agreement
leaps in vain now and is thrown back,
the who-goes-there of the hour,
—just as down here from turret to turret
from the heights of the compound
Moroccan guards call to each other—
who goes in the gloomy midnight's
quick snowflakes, who misses
the final toast on the wind's
black thresholds, sinister
with waiting, who goes . . .
It's an image of ours
distorted, not come
to light. It abandons
a blue vein of oblivion only
between two eras dead in us.

Sainte-Barbe du Thélat, New Year's Day 1944

An unexpected vacancy of heart
among the camp beds of Sainte-Barbe.

Sfumano i volti diletti, io resto solo
con un gorgo di voci faticose.

E la voce più chiara non è più
che un trepestio di pioggia sulle tende,
un'ultima fronda sonora
su queste paludi del sonno
corse a volte da un sogno.

Sainte-Barbe du Thélat, inverno 1944

Rinascono la valentia
e la grazia.
Non importa in che forme — una partita
di calcio tra prigionieri:
                             specie in quello
laggiù che gioca all'ala.
O tu così leggera e rapida sui prati
ombra che si dilunga
nel tramonto tenace.
Si torce, fiamma a lungo sul finire
un incolore giorno. E come sfuma
chimerica ormai la tua corsa
grandeggia in me
amaro nella scia.

Sainte-Barbe du Thélat, maggio 1944

Non sa più nulla, è alto sulle ali
il primo caduto bocconi sulla spiaggia normanna.
Per questo qualcuno stanotte
mi toccava la spalla mormorando
di pregar per l'Europa
mentre la Nuova Armada
si presentava alla costa di Francia.

The heartfelt faces fade, I remain alone
with a swirl of wearisome voices.

And the clearest voice is no more
than a pummeling of rain on the tents,
one final sonorous frond
on these sleep's marshes
coursed at times by a dream.

Sainte-Barbe du Thélat, winter 1944

Valor and grace
are born again.
No matter in what form — a game
of football between prisoners:
                                especially in him
down there playing on the wing.
O you so light and quick across fields
shadow that extends
in tenacious sunset.
It contorts, flames at length on the end
of a colorless day. And as it blurs
chimerical now your run
grows great within me
bitter in the wake.

Sainte-Barbe du Thélat, May 1944

He knows nothing anymore, is borne up on wings
the first fallen splayed on the Normandy beaches.
That's why someone tonight
touched my shoulder murmuring
pray for Europe
while the New Armada
drew on the coast of France.

Ho risposto nel sonno: —È il vento,
il vento che fa musiche bizzarre.
Ma se tu fossi davvero
il primo caduto bocconi sulla spiaggia normanna
prega tu se lo puoi, io sono morto
alla guerra e alla pace.
Questa è la musica ora:
delle tende che sbattono sui pali.
Non è musica d'angeli, è la mia
sola musica e mi basta—.

Campo Ospedale 127, giugno 1944

Ahimè come ritorna
sulla frondosa a mezzo luglio
collina d'Algeria
di te nell'alta erba riversa
non ingenua la voce
e nemmeno perversa
che l'afa lamenta
e la bocca feroce

ma rauca un poco e tenera soltanto...

Saint-Cloud, luglio 1944

Non sanno d'essere morti
i morti come noi,
non hanno pace.
Ostinati ripetono la vita
si dicono parole di bontà
rileggono nel cielo i vecchi segni.
Corre un girone grigio in Algeria
nello scherno dei mesi
ma immoto è il perno a un caldo nome: ORAN.

Saint-Cloud, agosto 1944

I replied in my sleep: —It's the wind,
the wind which makes strange music.
But if you truly were
the first fallen splayed on the Normandy beaches,
you pray if you can, I am dead
to war and to peace.
This, the music now:
of the tents that flap against the poles.
It's not the music of angels, it's my own
music only and enough—.

Camp Hospital 127, June 1944

Alas how what returns
on the leafy mid-July
Algerian hillside
of you in the tall grass lain down
is the voice not ingenuous
nor even perverse
bewailing the heat
and the untamed mouth

but hoarse a little and tender only . . .

Saint-Cloud, July 1944

They don't know they're dead
the dead like us,
they have no peace.
Stubbornly they repeat life
speak words of goodness to each other
reread the old signs in the sky.
A gray circle runs in Algeria
through the month's derision
but the axis is fixed to a scorched name: ORAN.

Saint-Cloud, August 1944

Solo vera è l'estate e questa sua
luce che vi livella.
E ciascuno si trovi il sempreverde
albero, il cono d'ombra,
la lustrale acqua beata
e il ragnatelo tessuto di noia
sugli stagni malvagi
resti un sudario d'iridi. Laggiù
è la siepe labile, un alone
di rossa polvere,
ma sepolcrale il canto d'una torma
tedesca alla forza perduta.

Ora ogni fronda è muta
compatto il guscio d'oblio
perfetto il cerchio.

Saint-Cloud, agosto 1944

E ancora in sogno d'una tenda s'agita
il lembo.
Campo d'un anno fa
cui ritorno tentoni
ma qui nessuno più
a ginocchi soffre
solo la terra soffre
che nessuno più
soffra d'essere qui
e tutto è pronto per l'eternità
il breve lago diventato palude
la mala erba cresciuta alle soglie
né fisarmonica geme
di perdute domeniche
tra cortesi comitive
di disperati meno disperati
più disperati. Io dico:
—Dov'è il lume
che il giovane Walter vigilava

Only the summer is true and this
its light which evens you out.
And may everyone discover the evergreen
tree, the cone of shade,
blissful purifying water
and spider's web woven with tedium
on the evil ponds
remain a vernicle of rainbows. Down there
is the frail hedgerow, a halo
of red powder,
but like the grave the German crowd's
song to their lost power.

Now every frond is silent
oblivion's shell compacted
the circle perfect.

Saint-Cloud, August 1944

And again in a dream the tent's edge
is flapping.
Camp of a year ago
I drag myself back to
but no one any longer
suffers here on their knees
only earth suffers
that people no longer
suffer being here
and all's made ready for eternity
the brief lake become marshes
evil weeds grown to the thresholds
nor does accordion groan
of lost Sundays
amongst fond gatherings
of the desperate less desperate
more desperate. I say:
—Where is the lamp
young Walter watched over

fiammante nell'ora tarda
all'insonne compagnia... —.

   Sidi-Chami, ottobre 1944

Spesso per viottoli tortuosi
quelque part en Algérie
del luogo incerto
che il vento morde,
la tua pioggia il tuo sole
tutti in un punto
tra sterpi amari del più amaro filo
di ferro, spina senza rosa...
ma già un anno è passato,
è appena un sogno:
siamo tutti sommessi a ricordarlo.

Ride una larva chiara
dov'era la sentinella
e la collina
dei nostri spiriti assenti
deserta e immemorabile si vela.

   Sidi-Chami, novembre 1944

Troppo il tempo ha tardato
per te d'essere detta
pena degli anni giovani.

Illividiva la città nel vento
o un'iride cadeva nella danza
dei riflessi beati:
eri nel ticchettio meditabondo
d'una sfera al mio polso
tra le pagine sfogliate

flaming in the small hours
to the wakeful company . . . — .

Sidi-Chami, October 1944

Often through tortuous alleys
quelque part en Algérie
of the indefinite place
that the wind gusts bite,
your rainfall your sunlight
all at one point
amongst bitter briars of the more
bitter iron wire, thorn with no rose . . .
but already a year's gone by,
it is barely a dream:
we're all subdued to remember.

A clear phantom laughs
where the sentry was
and the hillside
of our absent spirits
deserted and beyond recall veils over.

Sidi-Chami, November 1944

Too late has the time come
for you to be spoken
pain of my young years.

The city grew pallid in the wind
or a rainbow fell into the dance
of graced reflections:
you were in the meditative ticking
of a dial at my wrist
among pages leafed over

una marea di sole,
un'indolenza di sobborghi chiari
presto assunta in un volto
così a fondo scrutato,
ma un occhio lustro ma un tatto febbrile.

Venivano ombre leggere: —che porti
tu, che offri? . . . — . Sorridevo
agli amici, svanivano
essi, svaniva
in tristezza la curva d'un viale.
Dietro ruote fuggite
smorzava i papaveri sui prati
una cinerea estate.

Ma se tu manchi
e anche il cielo è vinto
sono un barlume stento,
una voce superflua nel coro.

Sidi-Chami, novembre 1944

Se la febbre di te più non mi porta

come ogni gesto si muta in carezza
ove indugia un addio
foglia che di prima estate
si spicca.

Fatto è il mio sguardo più tenero e lento
d'essere altrove e qui non è più teso.

Strade fontane piazze
un giorno corse a volo
nel lume del tuo corpo
in ognuna m'attardo in un groviglio
di volti amati

a flooding of sunlight,
clear suburb's idleness
quickly assumed on a face
scrutinized so deeply,
but a glittering eye but a feverish touch.

Faint shadows came: —what do you
bring, what offer? . . . — . I smiled
at my friends, they vanished,
the curve of the avenue
vanished in sadness.
Behind wheels in flight
poppies over fields were
smothered in an ashen summer.

But if you're missing
and even the sky's defeated
I'm a stunted glimmer,
a superfluous voice in the choir.

Sidi-Chami, November 1944

If fever for you no more sustains me

how each gesture's changed to a caress
where a goodbye wavers,
leaf that in early summer's
torn away.

My gaze is made more tender and slow
no longer stretched to be elsewhere and here.

Streets fountains squares
flown through one day
in the lamp of your body
at each I linger in a tangle
of loved faces

nel poco verde tra gli anditi bui
nel vecchio cielo diventato mite.

Sidi-Chami, dicembre 1944

Nel bicchiere di frodo
tocca presto il suo fondo
quest'allegria che vela la tristezza
in cresta dei tizzi sopiti
sbalzati a noi dal più lontano fuoco.
E sii tu oggi il Dio che si fa carne
lontananza per noi nell'ora oscura.

Sidi-Chami, Natale 1944

Algeria

Eri prima una pena
che potevo guardarmi nelle mani
sempre dalla tua polvere più arse
per non sapere più d'altro soffrire.
Come mi frughi riaffiorata febbre
che mi mancavi e nel perenne specchio
ora di me baleni
quali nel nero porto fanno il giorno
indicibili segni dalle navi
. . . .

in the little green between dark ways
beneath the old sky grown mild.

Sidi-Chami, December 1944

In the smuggled glass
it soon touches the dregs
this gaiety veiling sadness
in the plume of quenched brands
reaching us from the most distant fire.
And let the God made flesh today
be distance for us in the darkest hour.

Sidi-Chami, Christmas 1944

Algeria

You were first a hurt
I could look at in my hands
ever more scorched from your dust
not knowing how to suffer any other.
How you rifle through me reawakened fever
that I lacked and in the perennial mirror
of me now flashes
what in the black port makes the day
unutterable signs from the ships

. . . .

IL MALE D'AFRICA

Frammenti di una sconfitta

Tra il brusio di una folla
nel latrato del mare
tra gli ordini e i richiami
mancavo, morivo
sotto il peso delle armi.
Ed ecco stranamente simultanee
le ragazze d'un tempo
tutte le mie ragazze tra loro per mano
in semicerchio incontro a me venire
non so se soccorrevoli od ostili.

*

istruzione e allarme

Dicevano i generali:
mimetizzarsi sparire
confondersi amalgamarsi al suolo,
farsi una vita di fronda
e mai ingiallire.
Ma l'anima di quali foglie
si vestirà per sfuggire
alla muta non vista osservazione
dell'occhio che scopre in ognuno
baleni di rimorso e nostalgia?
Se passa la rombante distruzione
siamo appiattiti corpi,
volti protesi all'alto senza onore.

*

Così una donna amata e passata ad altri: si muove e parla, o tace, e ancora si sa che cosa c'è dietro quei moti e quei silenzi, ma non è il sapere che tutto ciò è per altri che ti dà pena—o non è solo

THE AFRICAN SICKNESS

Fragments of a Defeat

With the rustling of a crowd
in the howl of the sea
amidst the orders and appeals
I was missing, I was dying
under the burden of arms.
And strangely in one instant here they are,
the girls of before
all my girls among them hand in hand
coming towards me in a half-circle
and I don't know whether tenderly or hostile.

*

training and alarm

Said the generals:
camouflage, conceal yourselves,
blend into, mingle with the earth,
prepare yourselves a life of foliage
and don't ever yellow.
But the spirit, with what leaves
will it clothe itself to escape
the silent unseen observation
of the eye that discovers in everyone
glints of nostalgia and remorse?
If the rumbling destruction passes
we are flattened bodies,
honor-less faces prostrate to the sky.

*

Just so a loved woman gone on to others: she moves and speaks, or is silent, and still you know what's behind these motions and silences, but it's not the knowledge that all this is for others which pains you — or not only this — it's the feeling others are taking plea-

questo—, è il sentire che altri ne prova delizia e ci legge e ci scopre, quasi fosse lui il primo, quanto già tu vi hai letto e scoperto; o, peggio, ci vede altro da ciò che tu vi avevi visto e cancella i tuoi segni, per sostituirvi i propri, dalla lavagna che è lei.

*

Il nostro tempo d'allora:
i soldati dentro i fossi
mascherati dalle fronde
e come ridenti d'amore.
Non fu mai così viva la campagna
né mai così straziante d'abbandoni.
Maggio portò, come sempre, tedeschi...
Ma si udiva compitare l'alato
dialogo dei piloti distanti
nella quotidiana regata:
struggente ne avemmo una voglia
di margini d'ombra
e come stille dal remo volante in cadenza
giungevano a noi quelle parole,
era l'umida vela del mattino
la guizzante vacanza sugli stagni.

(E come il cielo avrebbe potuto non essere
una tesa freschissima bandiera
a stelle e strisce?
Fu così che ci presero).

*

Accadeva come dopo certi sogni. Un amore perduto o un altro ritenuto impossibile o funesto appaiono. Oppure si tratta dell'immagine di persona estranea che d'un tratto, nel sogno, si scioglie in gesti e parole che la fanno amare. Non che al risveglio si corra in cerca di lei o che qualcosa muti, della vita, per questo, ma dal sogno un'acuta dolcezza si prolunga nel giorno e di essa si è vivi...

Fronte di Trapani, 1943

sure in them, reading and discovering there, almost as if the first, all you already read and found; or worse, they see other things than you saw and rub out your signs, to replace them with their own, on the blackboard that she is.

*

Our time, those days:
the soldiers in the ditches
camouflaged with branches
and as if laughing with love.
The landscape was never so alive
nor so heartrending with abandon.
May, as ever, brought the Germans . . .
But you heard the spelled-out lofty
dialogue of far-off pilots
in the daily regatta:
agonizing we would long for
the margins of shade
and like droplets from the cadenced flying oar
those words reached down to us,
it was the dampened sail of morning,
the shimmering holiday upon the waters.

(And how could the sky not have been
a tensed clean banner
of stars and stripes?
That's how we were taken.)

*

It happened as after certain dreams. A lost love or another you thought impossible or grievous appears. Or else it's the image of someone unknown that suddenly, within the dream, dissolves to gestures and words so you can't help but love her. Not that at waking you run in search of her or anything changes in life because of this, yet from the dream a piercing sweetness persists the length of the day and through it we're alive . . .

Trapani front, 1943

Il male d'Africa
A GIANSIRO CHE VA IN ALGERIA (1958)

Una motocicletta solitaria.
Nei tunnel, lungo i tristi
cavalcavia di Milano
un'anima attardata. Mah!
È passata, e ora fa la sua strada
e un'eco a noi appena ne ritorna,
col borbottìo della pentola familiare
nei tempi che si vanno quietando.
Diversa da Orano cantava
la corsa del treno sul finire della guerra
e che bel sole sul viaggio e a sciami
bimbetti, moretti sempre più neri
di stazione in stazione
già con tutta alle spalle l'Algeria.
Pensa—dicevo—la guerra è sul finire
e ponente ponente mezzogiorno
guarda che giro per rimandarci a casa.
E dei bimbi moretti sempre più neri
di stazione in stazione
give me bonbon good American please
la litania implorante. Rimbombava
la eco tra viadotti e ponti lungo
un febbraio di fiori intempestivi
ritornava a un sussulto di marmitte
che al sole fumavano allegre
e a quel febbrile poi sempre più fioco
ritmo di ramadàn
che giorni e giorni ci durò negli orecchi
ci fermammo e fu,
calcinata nel verbo
sperare nel verbo desiderare,
Casablanca.
        E poi?
Ho visto uomini stravolti
nelle membra—o bidonville!—
barracani gonfiarsi all'uragano
altri petali accendersi—«*sono astri*

The African Sickness
FOR GIANSIRO GOING TO ALGERIA (1958)

A lone motorcycle.
In tunnels, along miserable
elevated sections of Milan,
a soul delayed. What of it?
It's gone, and makes its way now
and an echo barely returns to us,
with the family pot's bubbling
in these times that quiet down.
Different from Oran,
the train's roll sang at the war's end
and what fine sun on the journey and swarms
of little black kids, darker and darker,
station after station,
already with all Algeria behind us.
To think—I said—the war's ending
and west-southwest,
what a roundabout way to send us home.
And from the black kids, darker and darker,
station after station,
give me bonbon good American please,
the beseeching litany. Between viaducts
and bridges the echo rebounded
through a February of untimely flowers,
returned to spitting stewpots
steaming gaily in the sun
and to that feverish, then ever fainter
rhythm of Ramadan
persisting day after day in our ears,
we halted and there,
chalked within the verb
to hope, the verb to desire,
was Casablanca.
                And then?
I saw men with twisted
limbs—O bidonville!—
baracans swell in the gale,
other petals flare—*"they're perennial asters,*

perenni», *«no, sono fiori caduchi»*, discorsi
di cattività—
farsi di estiva cenere,
e quando più non si aspettava quasi
fummo sul flutto sonoro
diretti a una vacanza
di volti di là dal mare, da una
nereggiante distanza, in famiglia
coi gabbiani che fidenti
si abbandonavano all'onda.
Ma caduta ogni brezza, navigando
oltre Marocco all'isola dei Sardi
una febbre fu in me:
non più quel folle
ritmo di ramadàn
      ma un'ansia
una fretta d'arrivare
quanto più nella sera
d'acque stagnanti e basse
l'onda s'ottenebrava
rotta da luci fiacche—e
      Gibilterra! un latrato,
il muso erto d'Europa, della cagna
che accucciata lì sta sulle zampe davanti:
Tardi, troppo tardi alla festa
—scherniva la turpe gola—
troppo tardi! e altro di più confuso
sul male appreso verbo
della bianca Casablanca.

     *

Questa ciarla non so se di rincorsa o fuga
vecchia di dieci o più anni
di un viaggio tra tanti...—s'inquietano i tuoi occhi—
e nessuna notizia d'Algeria.
No, nessuna—rispondo. O appena qualche groppo
convulso di ricordo: un giorno mai finito, sempre
al tramonto—e sbrindellato, scalzo
in groppa a un ciuco, ma col casco

no, flowers doomed to die," the speeches
of captivity—
turn to summer dust,
and when we'd stopped expecting it almost
we were on resounding swell,
heading for a holiday
of faces over there beyond the sea,
from a blackish distance, in the family
with seagulls that trustful
gave themselves up to the wave.
But every breeze dropped, past
Morocco sailing for the isle of Sards
a fever grew in me:
no longer that maddening
rhythm of Ramadan
                         but an eagerness,
a fretting to arrive
the more so on evenings
of stagnant low water
when the wave darkened,
broken by feeble glimmers—and
                         Gibraltar! a howl,
the raised snout of Europe,
from the bitch crouched there on front paws:
Late, too late for the feast
—the foul throat taunted—
too late! and another thing more confused
about the ill-comprehended
verb of white Casablanca.

               *

This chit-chat, catch up or flight I don't know,
now ten or more years old
about one journey among many . . . —your eyes grow troubled—
and no news of Algeria.
No, none—I reply. Or barely some convulsive
chokings of memory: a day never ended,
always at sunset—and barefoot, in rags
on the back of a donkey, but with the helmet

d'Africa ancora in capo
un prigioniero come me
presto fuori vista di dietro la collina.
Quanto restava dell'impero...
                    e il piffero
ramingo tra le tende a colmare la noia
e, non appena zitto, quel vuoto di radura
dove il fuoco passò e gli zingari...
Trafitture del mondo che uno porta su sé
e di cui fa racconto a Milano
tra i vetri azzurri a Natale di un inverno di sole
mentre—*Symphonie* nelle case, *Symphonie*
d'amour per le nebbiose strade—la nuova
gioventù s'industria a rianimare il ballo.

Siamo noi, vuoi capirlo, la nuova
gioventù—quasi mi gridi in faccia—in credito
sull'anagrafe di almeno dieci anni...

Portami tu notizie d'Algeria
—quasi grido a mia volta—di quanto
passò di noi fuori dal reticolato,
dimmi che non furono soltanto
fantasmi espressi dall'afa,
di noi sempre in ritardo sulla guerra
ma sempre nei dintorni
di una vera nostra guerra... se quanto
proliferò la nostra febbre d'allora
è solo eccidio tortura reclusione
o popolo che santamente uccide.

Questo avevo da dire
questo groppo da sciogliere
nell'ultimo sussulto di gioventù
questo rospo da sputare,
ma a te fortuna e buon viaggio
borbotta borbotta la pentola familiare.

of Africa on his head still,
a prisoner like me
quickly out of sight behind the hill.
What was left of the empire . . .
                          and the penny whistle
roaming between tents to stave off boredom
and, no sooner silent, that empty clearing
where the fire went past and the gypsies . . .
Wounds of the world you bear
and recount them in Milan
between blue windows of a sunny winter
at Christmas, while—*Symphonie* in houses,
through foggy streets *Symphonie d'amour*—the younger
generation striving to revive the dance.

It's us, don't you realize, we're the younger
generation—you almost shout in my face—
with at least ten years owed us on the civil register . . .

Bring me news of Algeria
—I almost shout in return—about
what of us passed beyond the barbed wire,
tell me they weren't only
ghosts pressed from the heat haze,
of us always late for the war
but always on the outskirts
of a real war of our own . . . if what
our fever of that time was spreading
is only slaughter, torture, isolation,
or a people that religiously kill.

This is what I had to say,
this tangle to unravel
in the last spasm of youth,
this toad to spit out,
but to you good luck and *bon voyage,*
the family pot's bubbling, bubbling.

Appunti da un sogno

I due cunicoli, con feritoie, ne farebbero in pratica uno solo se in mezzo non ci fosse uno slargo, una piazzuola circolare.

Nello slargo, al centro dell'unico labirinto che i due cunicoli formerebbero, ci sono io.

Vivo simultaneamente la vita che si svolge nei due cunicoli. A ogni feritoia, di profilo, mica guarda dalla feritoia, c'è un uomo, soldato o graduato. Ognuno veste la divisa cachi, più chiara quasi bianca quelli di là, inglesi o americani, insomma nemici, indiscutibilmente nemici.

Dalla parte di quest'altro cunicolo si apre una botola, no: una porta, una botola messa verticalmente.

Ne esce un maggiore (italiano), con un paio di baffi a cespuglio, è piuttosto tozzo, in una divisa che sarebbe cachi se non fosse propriamente verde oliva. Viene dalla gavetta. Come ho fatto a capirlo? Mah! Questo non ha importanza, ma viene dalla gavetta e io l'ho capito.

Sento che è finita e mettendomi sull'attenti saluto e gli dico che abbiamo perso. Come se gli presentassi il battaglione schierato, si mette sull'attenti anche lui e risponde al saluto. Ha la faccia come la divisa, diventa sempre più oliva, poi grigiastra, infine nera. Mi si carbonizza sotto gli occhi o mi si mummifica? Si mummifica.

Nei due cunicoli ci sono due gesti quasi ritmici, simultanei alla luce delle feritoie con lo stesso scatto istantaneo. Da una parte presentano le armi, dall'altra le depongono appoggiandole alle rispettive feritoie.

Uno solo fa un gesto diverso ma senza rompere il ritmo, anzi! sottolineandolo—come se tenesse lui il bandolo di tutto. Fa una specie di oplà, di piroetta su se stesso di gioia acrobatica nell'appoggiare l'arma a sua volta.

È un soldato biondo, più giovane degli altri. Italiano, s'intende. Ma si direbbe piuttosto inglese. Per la sua biondezza? Per la piroetta di gioia? Solo adesso capisco veramente che è finita, che la guerra è perduta.

Quanti dispiaceri la gioventù (degli altri) ci darà d'ora in poi.

Notes from a Dream

The two tunnels, with gratings, would in effect be just one if it weren't for a bulge in the middle, a circular pit.

In the bulge, at the center of the one labyrinth the two tunnels would form, there am I.

I live simultaneously the life unfolding in the two tunnels. At each grating, in profile, not looking through, is a man, a soldier or NCO. Each wears a khaki uniform, lighter almost white the ones over there, English or American, enemies in short, unquestionably enemies.

From the side of this other tunnel a trapdoor opens, no: a door, a trapdoor put in vertically.

Up comes a major (Italian), with bushy moustaches, rather stocky, in a uniform that would be khaki if it weren't actually olive-green. He's risen through the ranks. How do I know? No idea! That's not important, but he's risen through the ranks and I know.

I feel it's all over and, standing to attention, salute and tell him we've lost. As if I were presenting him the battalion on parade, he too stands to attention, and responds to the salute. His face is like his uniform. It becomes more and more olive, then a sickly gray, and finally black. Is he turning to ashes or mummifying before my eyes? He's mummifying.

In the two tunnels there are two almost rhythmic actions, simultaneous in the gratings' light, with the same instantaneous start. On one side they present arms, on the other lay them down, lean them against the respective gratings.

One only performs a different action but without breaking the rhythm, quite the reverse! emphasizing it—as if he had everybody's fate in his hands. He does a sort of skip, a pirouette upon himself from acrobatic joy when he in turn lays down his rifle.

He's a fair-haired soldier, younger than the others. Italian, of course. But English, rather, you could say. From the fair hair? The joyful pirouette? Only now do I truly comprehend that it's over, that the war is lost.

What disappointments the youth (of others) will give us from now on.

L'otto settembre
'43 / '63

Sale macaroni piove sulla memoria
lo scalpore della solfa ingiuriosa

ma scorporata, volata via dal suo senso

quale forse poté
per tutto un pomeriggio spiovere
vivere come ritmo come ciarla d'amore
dentro una stanza d'Orano sul viluppo
di una coppia in affanno, di una copula
negro-francese
franco-americana
occupata di tutt'altro
—noialtri in cenci là fuori sulle banchine e

sale macaroni la pioggia
sale macaroni le foglie
sale macaroni le navi dentro il porto
sale macaroni de mon amour
la guerra girata altrove.

September the Eighth
'43 / '63

Sale macaroni rains on the memory
the refrain's clamor taunting

but disembodied, flown from its sense

such as for a whole afternoon
could perhaps drain away
to live as rhythm as pillow talk
inside an Oran room over the tangle
of a panting couple, of a copula
Negro-french
franco-american
occupied with something quite other
—us others in rags outside there on the wharves and

sale macaroni the rain
sale macaroni the leaves
sale macaroni the ships in the harbour
sale macaroni de mon amour
the war rolled on elsewhere.

da *Gli strumenti umani*
from *The Human Implements*

UNO SGUARDO DI RIMANDO

Via Scarlatti

Con non altri che te
è il colloquio.

Non lunga tra due golfi di clamore
va, tutta case, la via;
ma l'apre d'un tratto uno squarcio
ove irrompono sparuti
monelli e forse il sole a primavera.
Adesso dentro lei par sempre sera.
Oltre anche più s'abbuia,
è cenere e fumo la via.
Ma i volti i volti non so dire:
ombra più ombra di fatica e d'ira.
A quella pena irride
uno scatto di tacchi adolescenti,
l'improvviso sgolarsi d'un duetto
d'opera a un accorso capannello.

E qui t'aspetto.

Comunicazione interrotta

                  Il telefono
tace da giorni e giorni.
Ma l'altro nel quartiere più lontano
ha chiamato a perdifiato, a vuoto
per intere settimane.
Lascialo dunque per sempre tacere
ridicola conchiglia appesa al muro
e altrove scafi sussultino fuggiaschi,

A BACKWARD GLANCE

Via Scarlatti

With none other than you
is the word.

Not long between two gulfs of cries
the street, all houses, runs;
but of a sudden a breach opens it
where gaunt kids break through
and perhaps the sun in spring.
Now, within, it seems always evening.
Beyond, it grows still darker,
the street is ashes and smoke.
But the faces, the faces I can't say:
shadow on shadow of exhaustion and rage.
Clicking heels of teenagers
mock at that pain,
the improvised strain of an opera duet
at a small crowd converging.

And here for you I wait.

Interrupted Communication

                      The telephone
has not rung for days and days.
But in the further districts someone's
been wasting their breath, in vain
for whole weeks on end.
Then let it not ring forever
ridiculous conch stuck on the wall
and elsewhere let escaping boats leap up,

sovrani rompano esuli il flutto amaro:
che via si tolgano almeno loro.

'45-'46

Il tempo provvisorio

Qui il tarlo nei legni,
una sete che oscena si rinnova
e dove fu amore la lebbra
delle mura smozzicate delle case dissestate:
un dirotto orizzonte di città.
Perché non vengono i saldatori
perché ritardano gli aggiustatori?
Ma non è disservizio cittadino,
è morto tempo da spalare al più presto.
E tu, quanti anni per capirlo:
troppi per esserne certo.

Viaggio all'alba

Quanti anni che mesi che stagioni
nel giro di una notte:
una notte di passi e di rintocchi.
Ma come tarda la luce a ferirmi.
Voldomino, volto di Dio.
Un volto brullo ho scelto per specchiarmi
nel risveglio del mondo.
Ma dimmi una sola parola
e serena sarà l'anima mia.

exiled royalty break the bitter wave:
that at least they get out of the way.

'45–'46

The Provisional Time

Here the moth in the timber,
an obscene thirst renews
and where love was, the leprosy
of pitted walls, dilapidated houses:
a crumbling city horizon.
Why don't the welders come,
why are the fitters late?
But it's no disservice to the city,
it's dead time to shovel away with all haste.
And you, how many years to grasp it:
too many to be certain.

Journey at Dawn

How many years, what months, what seasons
in the course of a single night:
a night of footsteps and tolling bells.
But how the sun comes late to wound me.
Voldomino, God's own face.
A blank face I've chosen to mirror me
at the world's reawakening.
But say to me a single word
and my soul will be serene.

Un ritorno

Sul lago le vele facevano un bianco e compatto poema
ma pari più non gli era il mio respiro
e non era più un lago ma un attonito
specchio di me una lacuna del cuore.

Nella neve

Edere? stelle imperfette? cuori obliqui?
Dove portavano, quali messaggi
accennavano, lievi?
Non tanto banali quei segni.
E fosse pure uno zampettìo di galline —
se chiaro cantava l'invito
di una bava celeste nel giorno fioco.
Ma già pioveva sulla neve,
duro si rifaceva il caro enigma.
Per una traccia certa e confortevole
sbandavo, tradivo ancora una volta.

Mendrisio, '48

Viaggio di andata e ritorno

Andrò a ritroso della nostra corsa
di poco fa
che tanto bella mai ti sorprese la luna.
Mi resta una città prossima al sonno
di prima primavera.
O fuoco che ora tu sei
dileguante, o ceneri confuse
di campagna che annotta e si sfa,
o strido che sgretola l'aria
e insieme divide il mio cuore.

A Return

On the lake the sails made a white and compact poem
but my breath was no longer equal to it
and it was no longer a lake but an astonished
mirror of me a lacuna of the heart.

In the Snow

Ivy? imperfect stars? oblique hearts?
Where were they leading, what messages
hinting at, tenuous?
Not so trivial those signs.
And what if they were a scatter of hens —
so long as it sang out clear, the invitation
of a sky-blue slaver in the weak daylight.
But already it rained on the snow,
the cherished enigma hardening again.
For a sure and comfortable trace
I strayed, betraying once more.

Mendrisio, '48

Journey There and Back

I'll go back down the way we came
a while ago
when never more beautiful the moon startled you.
There remains to me a city close to sleep
in earliest springtime.
O fire that now you are
fading, O confused ashes
of countryside that darkens and smolders,
O screech that shivers the air
and with it splits my heart in two.

L'equivoco

Di là da un garrulo schermo di bambini
pareva a un tempo piangere e sorridermi.
Ma che mai voleva col suo sguardo
la bionda e luttuosa passeggera?
C'era tra noi il mio sguardo di rimando
e, appena sensibile, una voce:
amore—cantava—*e risorta bellezza* . . .
Così, divagando, la voce asseriva
e si smarriva su quelle
amare e dolci allèe di primavera.
Fu il lento barlume che a volte
vedemmo lambire il confine dei visi
e, nato appena, in povertà sfiorire.

Ancora sulla strada di Zenna

Perché quelle piante turbate m'inteneriscono?
Forse perché ridicono che il verde si rinnova
a ogni primavera, ma non rifiorisce la gioia?
Ma non è questa volta un mio lamento
e non è primavera, è un'estate,
l'estate dei miei anni.
Sotto i miei occhi portata dalla corsa
la costa va formandosi immutata
da sempre e non la muta il mio rumore
né, più fondo, quel repentino vento che la turba
e alla prossima svolta, forse, finirà.
E io potrò per ciò che muta disperarmi
portare attorno il capo bruciante di dolore . . .
ma l'opaca trafila delle cose
che là dietro indovino: la carrucola nel pozzo,
la spola della teleferica nei boschi,
i minimi atti, i poveri
strumenti umani avvinti alla catena
della necessità, la lenza
buttata a vuoto nei secoli,

The Misapprehension

From beyond a chattering barrier of children
she seemed both to cry and smile at me.
But whatever did she want with her glance,
the blonde and mournful passerby?
Between us was my glancing back
and, barely audible, a voice:
love — it was singing — *and beauty reborn* . . .
So, straying, the voice affirmed
and lost itself upon those
bitter and sweet spring avenues.
It was the gradual glimmer we sometimes
saw lap the faces' margin
and, barely kindled, in weakness shrink away.

On the Zenna Road Again

Why do these troubled branches touch me?
Maybe because they repeat the green renews
each spring, but joy doesn't flourish afresh?
But this time it's not my lament
and it's not spring, it's summer,
the summer of my years.
Under my eyes the coastline brought on
by the road is forming itself
always unchanged and not changed by my motor
nor, lower, that sudden wind which troubles it
and at the next bend will, perhaps, die down.
And I'll be able to despair for what changes,
carry round a burning head of sorrow . . .
but the obscure threading of things
I suppose back there, the pulley in the well,
the wheels of cable ways through woods,
the least acts, the poor
human implements bound to the chain
of necessity, the fishing line
cast for nothing through centuries,

le scarse vite che all'occhio di chi torna
e trova che nulla nulla è veramente mutato
si ripetono identiche,
quelle agitate braccia che presto ricadranno,
quelle inutilmente fresche mani
che si tendono a me e il privilegio
del moto mi rinfacciano . . .
Dunque pietà per le turbate piante
evocate per poco nella spirale del vento
che presto da me arretreranno via via
salutando salutando.
Ed ecco già mutato il mio rumore
s'impunta un attimo e poi si sfrena
fuori da sonni enormi
e un altro paesaggio gira e passa.

Finestra

Di colpo—osservi—è venuta,
è venuta di colpo la primavera
che si aspettava da anni.

Ti guardo offerta a quel verde
al vivo alito al vento,
ad altro che ignoro e pavento
—e sto nascosto—
e toccasse il mio cuore ne morrei.
Ma lo so troppo bene se sul grido
dei viali mi sporgo,
troppo dal verde dissimile io
che sui terrazzi un vivo alito muove,
dall'incredibile grillo che quest'anno
spunta a sera tra i tetti di città
—e chiuso sto in me, fasciato di ribrezzo.

Pure, un giorno è bastato.
In quante per una che venne
si sono mosse le nuvole

the meager lives that for the eye of one returning
who finds nothing, not a thing has really altered
repeat themselves identically,
those flurrying arms that will soon fall back,
those hands pointlessly fresh
stretching towards me and the privilege
of motion they reproach me . . .
So pity then for the troubled branches
called forth a moment in the spiral of wind
that will soon drop away from me
waving goodbye goodbye.
And now already changed the motor
checks an instant and then is released
from immense sleep
and another landscape turns and goes by.

Window

Suddenly—you notice—it's come
the spring's come suddenly
we were waiting years for.

I watch you offered to that green
to the living breath to the wind,
to what other I don't know and fear
—and stay in hiding—
and were my heart touched I would die.
But I know too well if I lean
out on the avenue's cry,
I'm too unlike that green
that on the balconies moves a living breath,
from the incredible cricket that this year
appears at dusk among roofs of the city
—and closed in me I stay, sealed in disgust.

Even so, a day was enough.
How many clouds for one that came
have set themselves in motion

che strette corrono strette sul verde,
spengono canto e domani
e torvo vogliono il nostro cielo.
Dillo tu allora se ancora lo sai
che sempre sono il tuo canto,
il vivo alito, il tuo
verde perenne, la voce che amò e cantò —
che in gara ora, l'ascolti?,
scova sui tetti quel po' di primavera
e cerca e tenta e ancora si rassegna.

Gli squali

Di noi che cosa fugge sul filo della corrente?
Oh, di una storia che non ebbe un seguito
stracci di luce, smorti volti, sperse
lampàre che un attimo ravviva
e lo sbrecciato cappello di paglia
che questa ultima estate ci abbandona.
Le nostre estati, lo vedi,
memoria che ancora hai desideri:
in te l'arco si tende dalla marina
ma non vola la punta più al mio cuore.
Odi nel mezzo sonno l'eguale
veglia del mare e dietro quella
certe voci di festa.

E presto delusi dalla preda
gli squali che laggiù solcano il golfo
presto tra loro si faranno a brani.

Mille Miglia

Per fare il bacio che oggi era nell'aria
quelli non bastano di tutta una vita.

that closer run closer over the green,
smother song and tomorrow
and want our sky menacing.
Tell me then if you still know
I'm you're song forever,
the living breath, your own
perennial green, the voice that loved and sang—
which competing now, you listen to?,
over roofs it flushes out that bit of spring
and searches and strains and resigns itself again.

The Sharks

What escapes of us on the line of the current?
Oh, of a story that didn't have a sequel
shreds of sun, wan faces, random
fishing lamps a moment revives
and the holed straw hat
this last summer abandons to us.
Our summers, you see,
memory you still have desires:
in you the bow is drawn from the seafront
but the point flies to my heart no more.
Half-asleep you hear the sea's
smooth vigil and behind it
certain festive voices.

And soon frustrated by the prey
down there sharks furrowing the gulf
they'll soon rip each other to pieces.

Mille Miglia

To make the kiss that was in the air today
those of a lifetime aren't enough.

Voci del dopocorsa, di furore
sul danno e sulla sorte.
Un malumore sfiora la città
per Orlando impigliato a mezza strada
e alla finestra invano
ancor giovane d'anni e bella ancora
Angelica si fa.
Voci di dopo la corsa, voci amare:
si portano su un'onda di rimorso
a brani una futile passione.
Folta di nuvole chiare
viene una bella sera e mi bacia
avvinta a me con fresco di colline.

Ma nulla senza l'amore è l'aria pura
l'amore è nulla senza la gioventù.

Brescia, primavera '55

Anni dopo

La splendida la delirante pioggia s'è quietata,
con le rade ci bacia ultime stille.
Ritornati all'aperto
amore m'è accanto e amicizia.
E quello, che fino a poco fa quasi implorava,
dall'abbuiato portico brusìo
romba alle spalle ora, rompe dal mio passato:
volti non mutati saranno, risaputi,
di vecchia aria in essi oggi rappresa.
Anche i nostri, fra quelli, di una volta?
Dunque ti prego non voltarti amore
e tu resta e difendici amicizia.

After-race voices, of madness
at the harm and fate.
An ill humor grazes the city
for Orlando ensnared at half distance
and at the window in vain
still young in years and beautiful still
Angelica appears.
Voices of after the race, bitter voices:
with them they bear on a wave of remorse
a futile passion in shreds.
Thick with limpid clouds
a fine evening comes and kisses me
clasped to me with the freshness of hills.

But without love the pure air is nothing,
love's nothing without youth.

Brescia, spring '55

Years After

The splendid the delirious rain has eased,
kisses us with rare final droplets.
Outside again
love is close by me and friendship.
And that murmur, till just then almost imploring,
from the darkened portico
rumbles at my back now, breaks from my past:
faces unaltered they'll be, same as ever,
with an old air congealed in them today.
Even our own, amongst those, of that time?
Then don't turn away love I beg you
and friendship remain and defend us.

Le ceneri

Che aspetto io qui girandomi per casa,
che s'alzi un qualche vento
di novità a muovermi la penna
e m'apra a una speranza?

Nasce invece una pena senza pianto
né oggetto, che una luce
per sé di verità da sé presume
—e appena è un bianco giorno e mite di fine inverno.

Che spero io più smarrito tra le cose.
Troppe ceneri sparge attorno a sé la noia,
la gioia quando c'è basta a sé sola.

Le sei del mattino

Tutto, si sa, la morte dissigilla.
E infatti, tornavo,
malchiusa era la porta
appena accostato il battente.
E spento infatti ero da poco,
disfatto in poche ore.
Ma quello vidi che certo
non vedono i defunti:
la casa visitata dalla mia fresca morte,
solo un poco smarrita
calda ancora di me che più non ero,
spezzata la sbarra
inane il chiavistello
e grande un'aria e popolosa attorno
a me piccino nella morte,
i corsi l'uno dopo l'altro desti
di Milano dentro tutto quel vento.

The Ashes

What am I waiting for turning round the house,
for some breath of fresh air
to lift then set my pen in motion
and open me up to a hope?

Instead a pain without lament
or object's born, which a light
of truth in itself from itself presumes
—and it's barely a mild white day at winter's end.

What do I hope for more lost among things.
Too much ash scatters boredom round itself,
joy when it's here in itself is enough.

Six in the Morning

Death breaks the seal, just so, of everything.
And in fact, I came back,
the door wasn't properly shut
the panel barely ajar.
And in fact I'd been dead a short while,
done for in not many hours.
But what I saw plainly
the dead don't see:
visited by my recent death, the house
only barely disturbed
still warm with me who no longer existed,
the bar snapped
purposeless the bolt
and a great and peopled atmosphere
about me, tiny in death,
one after another the avenues
of Milan awakened in all that wind.

UNA VISITA IN FABBRICA

(1952-1958)

I

Lietamente nell'aria di settembre più sibilo che grido
lontanissima una sirena di fabbrica.
Non dunque tutte spente erano le sirene?
Volevano i padroni un tempo tutto muto
sui quartieri di pena:
ne hanno ora vanto dalla pubblica quiete.
Col silenzio che in breve va chiudendo questa calma mattina
prorompe in te tumultuando
quel fuoco di un dovere sul gioco interrotto,
la sirena che udivi da ragazzo
tra due ore di scuola. Riecheggia nell'ora di oggi
quel rigoglio ruggente dei pionieri:
                                            sul secolo giovane,
ingordo di futuro dentro il suono in ascesa
la guglia del loro ardimento...
ma è voce degli altri, operaia, nella fase calante
stravolta in un rancore che minaccia abbuiandosi,
di sordo malumore che s'inquieta ogni giorno
e ogni giorno è quietato — fino a quando?
O voce ora abolita, già divisa, o anima bilingue
tra vibrante avvenire e tempo dissipato
o spenta musica già torreggiante e triste.
Ma questa di ora, petulante e beffarda
è una sirena artigiana, d'officina con speranze:
stenta paghe e lavoro nei dintorni.
Nell'aria amara e vuota una larva del suono
delle sirene spente, non una voce più
ma in corti fremiti in onde sempre più lente
un aroma di mescole un sentore di sangue e fatica.

A FACTORY VISIT

(1952–1958)

I

Pleasingly in September air, more hiss than howl,
a factory siren somewhere far away.
Then not all the sirens were silenced?
The bosses wanted a time completely mute
over the suffering districts:
and pride themselves now on the public quiet.
With the silence that soon ends this calm morning,
there pierces and riots in you
that fire of a duty on the interrupted game,
the siren you heard as a boy
between two hours of school. It re-echoes in today's hour,
that roaring exuberance of the pioneers:
                              at the century's start,
the greed for a future on the rising sound,
the spire of their fiery ambition
but it's the voice of others, workers, in the downturn
overwhelmed in a threatening rancor growing dark
by a deafened discontent that disquiets each day
and every day's quieted—until when?
O voice now banned, already split, O two-tongued spirit
between vibrant days-to-come and wasted time,
O silenced music towering and sad already.
But this, now, petulant and mocking,
is a craftsman's siren, a workshop's with hopes:
barely pay and jobs for the surroundings.
In the bitter and empty air a ghost of sound
from the stopped sirens, no more a voice
but in brief shudders in ever slower waves
a smell of rubber compounds, a trace of blood and toil.

II

La potenza di che inviti si cerchia
che lusinghe: di piste di campi di gioco
di molli prati di stillanti aiuole
e persino fiorirvi, cuore estivo, può superba la rosa.
Sfiora torrette, ora, passerelle
la visita da poco cominciata: s'imbuca in un fragore
come di sottoterra, che pure ha regola e centro
e qualcuno t'illustra. Che cos'è
un ciclo di lavorazione? Un cottimo
cos'è? Quel fragore. E le macchine, le trafile e calandre,
questi nomi per me presto di solo suono nel buio della mente,
rumore che si somma a rumore e presto spavento per me
straniero al grande moto e da questo agganciato.
Eccoli al loro posto quelli che sciamavano là fuori
qualche momento fa: che sai di loro
che ne sappiamo tu e io, ignari dell'arte loro...
Chiusi in un ordine, compassati e svelti,
relegati a un filo di benessere
senza perdere un colpo—e su tutto implacabile
e ipnotico il ballo dei pezzi dall'una all'altra sala.

III

Dove più dice i suoi anni la fabbrica,
di vite trascorse qui la brezza
è loquace per te?
     Quello che precipitò
nel pozzo d'infortunio e di oblio:
quella che tra scali e depositi in sé accolse
e in sé crebbe il germe d'amore
e tra scali e depositi lo sperse:
l'altro che prematuro dileguò
nel fuoco dell'oppressore.
Lavorarono qui, qui penarono.
(E oggi il tuo pianto sulla fossa comune.)

II

Power circles itself with what invitations,
what blandishments: with playing fields, tracks,
sweet meadows, dripping flowerbeds,
and even, summer's heart, the rose may flourish here.
The visit grazes towers, now, gangways,
and only just begun: it descends in an uproar
as if underground, which still has rule and center
and somebody shows you. What's that?
A work cycle? Piecework,
what is it? That uproar. And machines, wire drawers and presses,
these names soon for me just sound in the mind's dark,
noise piled on noise and soon fearful for me
to the great motion foreign and held in its grip.
Here at their posts are those swarming outside
a few moments ago: what do you know of them,
what do we know you and I, of their skill unaware . . .
Closed in an order, deliberate and quick,
condemned to a line of well-being
not missing a beat—and above it all the implacable
and hypnotic dance of pieces from one room to another.

III

Where the factory tells most of its years,
of lives spent here, the breeze
is loquacious for you?
                        That one who plunged
into misfortune and oblivion's well:
that one who among stores and depots
gathered and nurtured in herself love's seed
and among stores and depots dispersed it:
that other prematurely consumed
within the oppressor's fire.
They worked here, here they suffered.
(And today your weeping on the common tomb).

IV

«Non ce l'ho—dice—coi padroni. Loro almeno
sanno quello che vogliono. Non è questo,
non è più questo il punto.»
                           E raffrontando e

rammemorando:
                    «. . . la sacca era chiusa per sempre
e nessun moto di staffette, solo un coro
di rondini a distesa sulla scelta tra cattura
e morte . . .»
              Ma qui, non è peggio? Accerchiati da gran tempo
e ancora per anni e poi anni ben sapendo che non
più duramente (non occorre) si stringerà la morsa.
C'è vita, sembra, e animazione dentro
quest'altra sacca, uomini in grembiuli neri
che si passano plichi
uniformati al passo delle teleferiche
di trasporto giù in fabbrica.
                              Salta su
il più buono e il più inerme, cita:
E di me si spendea la miglior parte
tra spasso e proteste degli altri—*ma va là*—scatenati.

V

La parte migliore? Non esiste. O è un senso
di sé sempre in regresso sul lavoro
o spento in esso, lieto dell'altrui pane
che solo a mente sveglia sa d'amaro.
Ecco. E si fa strada sul filo
cui si affida il tuo cuore, ti rigetta
alla città selvosa:
                   —Chiamo da fuori porta.
Dimmi subito che mi pensi e ami.
Ti richiamo sul tardi—.
Ma beffarda e febbrile tuttavia
ad altro esorta la sirena artigiana.
Insiste che conta più della speranza l'ira

IV

"I don't"—says he—"have it in for the bosses.
They at least know what they want. This isn't,
it's no longer the point."
                        And comparing and

remembering:
                "...the pocket was closed forever
and from dispatch riders no motion, just an endless
chorus of swallows on the choice between capture
and death..."
                    But here, it's not worse? Encircled so long
and for years still and still more knowing for sure
the vice won't be (no need) tightened harder.
There's life, it seems, and bustle inside
this other pocket, men in black aprons
who pass each other orders
dictated by the speed of the transport cables
down on the factory floor.
                    Up leaps
the kindest, most defenseless, quotes:
And the best part of me has been squandered
let out, among others' laughs and protests—*come off it.*

V

The best part? Doesn't exist. Or it's a sense
of self forever in retreat at work,
or squandered there, glad of others' bread
that only tastes bitter to the mind alert.
Exactly. And headway is made on the line
your heart's entrusted to, casting you back
to the wooded city:
                      —I'm calling from outside.
Quick, tell me you think of and love me,
I'll call you again late on—.
But no less feverish and mocking
the craftsman's siren calls for something else.
It insists anger counts for more than hope

e più dell'ira la chiarezza,
fila per noi proverbi di pazienza
dell'occhiuta pazienza di addentrarsi
a fondo, sempre più a fondo
sin quando il nodo spezzerà di squallore e rigurgito
un grido troppo tempo in noi represso
dal fondo di questi asettici inferni.

APPUNTAMENTO A ORA INSOLITA

Il grande amico

Un grande amico che sorga alto su me
e tutto porti me nella sua luce,
che largo rida ove io sorrida appena
e forte ami ove io accenni a invaghirmi...

Ma volano gli anni, e solo calmo è l'occhio che antivede
perdente al suo riapparire
lo scafo che passava primo al ponte.
Conosce i messaggeri della sorte,
può chiamarli per nome. È il soldato presago.
Non pareva il mattino nato ad altro?
E l'ala dei tigli
e l'erta che improvvisa in verde ombrìa si smarriva
non portavano ad altro?
Ma in terra di colpo nemica al punto atteso
si arroventa la quota.
Come lo scolaro attardato
—né più dalla minaccia della porta
sbarrata fiori e ali lo divagano—
io lo seguo, sono nella sua ombra.

and clarity more than anger,
it draws out proverbs of patience for us,
the clear-eyed patience to go down further
and further still into the depths,
till the knot of squalor and nausea's broken
by a cry too long repressed in us
from the depths of these sterilized hells.

APPOINTMENT AT AN UNUSUAL HOUR

The Great Friend

A great friend towering above me
and everything casting me into his light,
laughing broadly where I hardly smile
and loving strongly where I try to show affection . . .

But the years fly, and the only calm eye is the one that foresees
the boat first past the bridge
beaten when it reappears.
He's acquainted with the messengers of fate,
can call them by name. The prophetic soldier.
Didn't the morning seem born to something else?
And the flank of limes
and unexpectedly the slope lost in green shadow,
didn't they lead to somewhere else?
But at the point expected on suddenly hostile terrain
the heights become red-hot.
Just like the dallying schoolboy
—no longer distracted from the barred door's threat
by flowers and wings—
I follow him, I'm in his shade.

Un disincantato soldato.
Uno spaurito scolaro.

Scoperta dell'odio

Qui stava il torto, qui l'inveterato errore:
credere che d'altro non vi fosse acquisto che d'amore.
Oh le frotte di maschere giulive
oh le comitive musicanti nei quartieri gentili...
Alla notte altre musiche rimanda
la terrazza più alta e di nuovo fiorita
si dilunga la strada fuori porta?
Ma venga, a ora tarda, venga un'ora
di vero fuoco un'ora tra me e voi,
ma scoppi infine la sacrosanta rissa,
maschere, e i vostri fini giochi
di deturpato amore: nell'esatto
modo mio di non dovuto
amore e dissipato, gente, vi brucerò.

Un incubo

Certo si piacciono, certo
l'uno dell'altra ha gioia, a giudicare
dal cigolio del letto che si fa
ritmo d'un brutto sogno oppure
sussulto in dormiveglia, quasi vero.
Ma non è che si burlino di te,
hanno ben altro in corpo. Questo è certo.
Dunque dov'è l'offesa? Ma non è
offesa, è strazio. E poi, sappilo, nulla
più turba dell'altrui piacersi
ilare e atroce
infinitamente dolce se non trova
limite in altri—e tanto mento in te
che ne muori.

Disenchanted soldier.
Schoolboy terrified.

Discovery of Hatred

Here was the wrong, here the inveterate error:
to believe that nothing could be gained but love.
Oh the swarms of festive masks
oh the music-making parties in genteel districts . . .
The highest balcony gives back other music
to the night and beyond city gates
the road leads blossoming once more?
Then come, late on, come a time
of real fire between you and me,
let the bloody brawl blaze out at last,
you masks, with your subtle games
of ravaged love: in just my way
of unindebted and dissipated
love, you people, I'll put you to the flames.

A Nightmare

For sure they please each other, for sure
each has joy from the other, to judge
by the bed's creaks which become
rhythm of a bad dream or
starting on the edge of sleep, quite real.
But it's not that they're mocking you,
the bodies are at something else. That's for sure.
So what's the harm? But it's not harm
it's torture. Then understand
nothing disturbs more than other people's pleasure,
merry and atrocious,
infinitely sweet if it doesn't discover
limits in others — and so much less in you
who are dying of it.

Quei bambini che giocano

un giorno perdoneranno
se presto ci togliamo di mezzo.
Perdoneranno. Un giorno.
Ma la distorsione del tempo
il corso della vita deviato su false piste
l'emorragia dei giorni
dal varco del corrotto intendimento:
questo no, non lo perdoneranno.
Non si perdona a una donna un amore bugiardo,
l'ameno paesaggio d'acque e foglie
che si squarcia svelando
radici putrefatte, melma nera.
«D'amore non esistono peccati,
s'infuriava un poeta ai tardi anni,
esistono soltanto peccati contro l'amore».
E questi no, non li perdoneranno.

Saba

Berretto pipa bastone, gli spenti
oggetti di un ricordo.
Ma io li vidi animati indosso a uno
ramingo in un'Italia di macerie e di polvere.
Sempre di sé parlava ma come lui nessuno
ho conosciuto che di sé parlando
e ad altri vita chiedendo nel parlare
altrettanta e tanta più ne desse
a chi stava ad ascoltarlo.
E un giorno, un giorno o due dopo il 18 aprile,
lo vidi errare da una piazza all'altra
dall'uno all'altro caffè di Milano
inseguito dalla radio.
«Porca—vociferando—porca». Lo guardava
stupefatta la gente.
Lo diceva all'Italia. Di schianto, come a una donna
che ignara o no a morte ci ha ferito.

Those Children Playing

will one day forgive
if we stop interfering now.
They'll forgive. One day.
But the times' twistedness,
life's course deviated down false tracks,
the hemorrhage of days
from the pass of corrupted awareness:
this, no, they won't forgive.
You don't forgive a woman for deceitful love,
the smiling land of waters and leaves
torn apart revealing
putrefied roots, black slime.
"There are no sins of love,"
a poet raged in his last years,
"only sins against love."
And these, no, they'll not forgive.

Saba

Beret pipe stick, the lifeless
objects of a memory.
But I saw them brought to life on one
roaming in an Italy of dust and rubble.
Always he talked of himself
but like no one I've known who talking of themselves
and demanding life of others in his talk
gave as much and so much more
to anyone who'd stay and listen.
And one day, a day or two after the 18th of April,
I saw him wandering from square to square
from one Milan café to another
hounded by the radio.
"Bitch"—he was railing—"bitch." In amazement
people looked at him.
It was Italy he meant. Abrupt, as to a woman
who knowingly or not has wounded us to death.

Di passaggio

Un solo giorno, nemmeno. Poche ore.
Una luce mai vista.
Fiori che in agosto nemmeno te li sogni.
Sangue a chiazze sui prati,
non ancora oleandri dalla parte del mare.
Caldo, ma poca voglia di bagnarsi.
Ventilata domenica tirrena.
Sono già morto e qui torno?
O sono il solo vivo nella vivida e ferma
nullità di un ricordo?

Situazione

La forza del luogo comune,
dolorosa.
Lo zampillo della pompa nell'erba
sospiro inavvertito.
Il giardino all'imbrunire.
Seggiole in tondo, sdrai.
Sguardi noti s'incrociano: uno solo evasivo.
Generalmente calmi.

Sul rovescio del luogo comune
le campane del vespero. Inascoltate.
Da secoli e secoli a quest'ora
una spoglia ancora calda
di sangue e senso.
E attorno le rondini a migliaia.

Sono io tutto questo, il luogo
comune e il suo rovescio
sotto la volta che più e più s'imbruna.
Ma non può nulla contro un solo sguardo
di altri, sicuro di sé che si accende
dello sguardo mio stesso

Passing

A single day, not that. An hour or two.
Light you never see.
Flowers you'd not dream of for an August.
On the fields spots of blood,
towards the sea no oleanders yet.
Hot, but no real wish to go swimming.
Wafted Tyrrhenian Sunday.
Am I already dead and come back here?
Or the only one living in the vivid and still
nothing of a memory?

Situation

The force of the commonplace,
grievous.
The sprinkler jet in the grasses,
unnoticed sigh.
The garden as evening draws in.
Chairs, in a circle, reclining.
Familiar glances cross: one only evasive.
For the most part calm.

On the reverse of the commonplace,
the vespers bells. Unheeded.
For century after century at this hour
a still warm coil
of blood and sense.
And round about the swallows in their thousands.

I am all of this, the common
place and its reverse
beneath the vault as the last light withdraws.
But nothing can this do against a single
glance of others, self-assured, taking flame
from my own glance

contro gli occhi colpevoli
contro i passi furtivi che ti portano via.

Gli amici

Nell'anno '51 li ricordi
la Giuliana e il Giancarlo
ballerini e acrobati com'erano
con vocazione di poveri
di cui sarà il mondo domani,
salute gioventù fierezza scatto.
E oggi? In una torpida
mattina del '60? O di essi e dei figli
bellissimi e terribili di cui
con intatta vocazione di poveri
ancora può essere il mondo
domani
per la decima estate non si orna
di nuovo la bocca del Magra?
Che tempi—mormori—sempre più confusi
che trambusto di scafi e di motori
che assortita fauna sul mare.
Non lasciatemi qui solo
                        —stai
per gridare—ritornate...
Ma ecco da dietro uno scoglio
sempre forte sui remi
spuntare in soccorso il Giancarlo.

E ti sembra un miracolo.

Appuntamento a ora insolita

La città—mi dico—dove l'ombra
quasi più deliziosa è della luce
come sfavilla tutta nuova al mattino...

against your guilty eyes,
against the furtive steps that are bearing you away.

The Friends

You remember them in '51
Giuliana and Giancarlo
dancers and tumblers as they were
with a calling for poverty
whose like would inherit the earth tomorrow,
health youth spirit zest.
And now? On a dull
morning in '60? With them and their lovely
and terrible children
whose calling for poverty's intact,
their like may still inherit the earth
tomorrow,
isn't the mouth of the Magra
for the tenth summer adorned afresh?
What times—you murmur—always more muddled
what turmoil of boats and engines
what an assortment of fauna on the sea.
Don't leave me alone here
                              —you're about
to cry—come back
But there from behind a rock
always strong on the oars
to the rescue Giancarlo appears.

And to you it seems a miracle.

Appointment at an Unusual Hour

The city—I'm saying—where shade
is all but exquisite as light,
how it sparkles brand new in the morning...

«... asciuga il temporale di stanotte» — ride
la mia gioia tornata accanto a me
dopo un breve distacco.
«Asciuga al sole le sue contraddizioni»
— torvo, già sul punto di cedere, ribatto.
Ma la forma l'immagine il sembiante
— d'angelo avrei detto in altri tempi —
risorto accanto a me nella vetrina:
«Caro — mi dileggia apertamente — caro,
con quella faccia di vacanza. E pensi
alla città socialista?»
Ha vinto. E già mi sciolgo: «Non
arriverò a vederla» le rispondo.
                              (Non saremo
più insieme, dovrei dire). «Ma è giusto,
fai bene a non badarmi se dico queste cose,
se le dico per odio di qualcuno
o rabbia per qualcosa. Ma credi all'altra
cosa che si fa strada in me di tanto in tanto
che in sé le altre include e le fa splendide,
rara come questa mattina di settembre...
giusto di te tra me e me parlavo:
della gioia».
              Mi prende sottobraccio.
«Non è vero che è rara, — mi correggo — c'è,
la si porta come una ferita
per le strade abbaglianti. È
quest'ora di settembre in me repressa
per tutto un anno, è la volpe rubata che il ragazzo
celava sotto i panni e il fianco gli straziava,
un'arma che si reca con abuso, fuori
dal breve sogno di una vacanza.
                              Potrei
con questa uccidere, con la sola gioia...».

Ma dove sei, dove ti sei mai persa?

«È a questo che penso se qualcuno
mi parla di rivoluzione»
dico alla vetrina ritornata deserta.

". . . dries out last night's storm"—laughs my
joy, beside me once more
after a short estrangement.
"Dries out its contradictions in the sun"
—sour, as good as resigned, I come back.
But the shape, image, resemblance
—an angel I'd have said in other times—
reborn beside me in the windowpane:
"Dear"—she openly taunts me—"dear,
with that holiday look of yours.
You're thinking of the socialist city?"
She wins. And already breaking down:
"No, I won't get to see it," I reply.
      (We won't be
together any more, I should say.) "But it's fair,
you're right not to mind me if I say such things,
if I say them from hating somebody
or angered by something. But that other thing
now and then making its way in me,
that includes the others and makes them shine,
believe in it, rare as this September morning . . .
I was fairly talking to myself of you:
of joy."
  She takes my arm.
"Not true it's rare,"—correcting myself—"it is,
you bear it like a wound
through dazzling streets. It's this time
in September repressed in me all year,
it's that fox the boy stole
and hid in his clothes and it ripped his thigh,
a gun you carry recklessly, beyond
the brief dream of a holiday.
      I could
kill with this, with joy alone . . ."

But where are you, where have you gone?

"This is what I think if someone
talks to me of revolution,"
I'm saying to the window empty once more.

IL CENTRO ABITATO

Nel sonno

    I

Tardi, anche tu li hai uditi
quei passi che salivano alla morte
indrappellati
dall'ordine sparso di un settembre
dai suoi già freddi ori, per rientrare nell'ordine
chiuso, coatto, di tante domeniche premilitari
reinventandolo di fierezza e scherno
con tutta la forza del piede, con pudore
di cresimandi della storia,
su spalti, per poligoni di tiro,
comparse alla ribalta che poi vanno nel buio
—e ancora tanta forza da bucare la raffica
spezzare muraglie sorvolare anni,
quei loro passi giunti fino a te.

    II

Per tutta la città, nelle strade
per poco ancora vuote un assiduo raschiare,
manifesti a brandelli, vanno a brani
le promesse di ieri e lungo i marciapiedi
è già il tritume delle cicale scoppiate.
Sceso all'incrocio un manovratore
lavora allo scambio con la sua spranga,
riavvia giorni e rumore.
—Ecco i soli sconfitti, i veri vinti...—
anonima ammonisce una voce.

    III

Di schianto il braccio s'è abbattuto
e passa ad altri, più forti,

THE INHABITED CENTER

In Sleep

I

Late, you too have heard them,
those steps that climbed towards death
squadded together
from a September's scattered ranks
from its golds already chill, re-entering the closed,
compulsory ranks of how many premilitarized Sundays
reinventing them out of pride and scorn
with all the force of feet, with the shame
of those in for history's baptism,
over earthworks, through firing ranges,
extras on the apron stage that then go into darkness
—and plenty of strength still to dash through gunfire,
to smash down walls, fly over years,
those steps of theirs have reached you.

II

All through the city, in the streets
for a while still deserted an assiduous scraping,
manifestos in pieces, the promises of yesterday
in shreds and along the pavements
already the remains of squashed cicadas.
Climbed down at the crossing, a tram driver
operates the points with his bar,
restarts the days and noise.
—These the only losers, the real defeated...—
an anonymous voice admonishes.

III

Abruptly the arm is forced down
and the winner's hand passes

la mano del vincitore.
Dirò che era giusto
e tenterò una compostezza
appena contraddetta dagli occhi folli.
Che presto saranno spenti.
Presto sullo sparato del decoro
il bruco del disonore...

    IV

Abboccherà il demente all'esca
dei ragazzi del bar?
Certo che abboccherà
                    e per un niente
nella sua nebbia si ritroverà
dalla parte del torto.
Lo picchieranno, dopo, più di gusto.
C'era altro da fare delle domeniche?
I giornali attorno ai chioschi
garruli al vento primaverile:
viene un tale, canaglia in panni lindi,
su titoli e immagini avventa un suo cagnaccio.
— La sporca politica
e noi sempre pronti a rifondere il danno,
Pantalone che paga —
e getta soldi all'accorso edicolante.
Approvazioni, intorno, risa.

    V

L'Italia, una sterminata domenica.
Le motorette portano l'estate
il malumore della festa finita.
Sfrecciò vano, ora è poco, l'ultimo pallone
e si perse: ma già
sfavilla la ruota vittoriosa.
E dopo, che fare delle domeniche?
Aizzare il cane, provocare il matto...
Non lo amo il mio tempo, non lo amo.
L'Italia dormirà con me.

to others, more powerful.
I'll declare it was just
and attempt a composure
barely contradicted by the maddened eyes.
That will soon be lifeless.
On dignity's shirt collar
soon dishonor's caterpillar . . .

IV

Will the half-wit take the bait
of the boys in the bar?
Obviously he'll bite
      and for a nothing,
in his fogginess he'll find
he's on the wrong side.
They'll beat him, after, with all the more relish.
Was there ever anything else to do on Sundays?
Newspapers round the kiosks
garrulous in the spring wind:
up comes someone, vermin in fine linen,
sets his hound on the headlines and pictures.
—Filthy politics
and us always ready to settle the damages,
Pantalones that pay—
and tosses coins to the scurrying newsagent.
All around: approvals, laughter.

V

Italy, one endless Sunday.
Scooters bring the summer,
the dejection of the holiday's end.
Vainly the last ball, a while back, flashed by
and it's lost: but already
the winning cycle wheel's glittering.
And after, what to do on Sundays?
Goad the dog, incite the madman . . .
I don't like my times, I don't like them.
Italy will slumber with me.

In un giardino d'Emilia o Lombardia
sempre c'è uno come me
in sospetti e pensieri di colpa
tra il canto di un usignolo
e una spalliera di rose...

VI

oppure
tra cave e marcite una coppia.
Area da costruzioni—con le case
qui giungeremo tra non molto.
E intanto finché dura
abbandoniamoci a questi finti prati.
        Dove sei perduto amore
canta l'uomo alla ragazza
saltata oltre il terrapieno.
«Hai sempre il sole dalla tua» galante
continua a motteggiarla, ritrovandola
di là, capelli al vento gola giovane
anche più bionda a quel ritorno di sole.
Ma poi, divisi dalla folla
separati passando *tra la folla che non sa,*
cosa vive di un giorno? di noi o di noi due?
     Il distacco, l'andarsene
sul filo di una musica che è già d'altro tempo
        guardando in ogni volto
            e non sei tu.
Qui dunque si chiude la giovinezza,
su uno scambio di persona?
Ma sì, quella sfilata di tetti
quei balconi e terrazze
rapido ponte tra noi ogni mattina
e a sera lenta fuga...
già domani potresti abbandonarti
a un'altra onda di traffico, tentare
un diverso versante,
mutare gente e rione
        e me su uno
di questi crolli del cuore, di queste repentine

In a Lombard or Emilian garden
there's always one like me
with suspicions and thoughts of guilt
between a nightingale's song
and espalier of roses . . .

    VI

or else
a couple between quarries and meadows.
Development area—quite soon
we'll reach here with houses.
And meantime while it lasts
let's abandon ourselves to these false fields.
    Where are you lost, love
the man sings to the girl
who's skipped beyond the embankment.
"The sun always shines on yours" blue-eyes
continues to tease her, finding her once more
over there, the wind-blown hair, young throat,
even blonder in that returning sun.
But then, divided by the crowd
walking apart *through the crowd that doesn't know,*
what survives of a day? of us or us two?
    The parting, the going away
on the line of a tune in another time already
    looking into each face
        and it's not you.
Then is youth ended here,
in a mistaken identity?
Of course, that file of roofs
those balconies and terraces
quick link between us each morning
and slow flight every evening . . .
already tomorrow you could give yourself up to
another wave of traffic, attempt
a different slope,
change company and district
        and leave me
on one of these downfalls of the heart, these sudden

radure di città lasciare
con l'amaro di una perdita
con quei passi di loro tardi uditi.
Solitudine, solo orgoglio . . .
       Geme
da loro in noi nascosta una ferita
e le dà voce il vento dalla pianura,
l'impietra nelle lapidi.

I versi

Se ne scrivono ancora.
Si pensa a essi mentendo
ai trepidi occhi che ti fanno gli auguri
l'ultima sera dell'anno.
Se ne scrivono solo in negativo
dentro un nero di anni
come pagando un fastidioso debito
che era vecchio di anni.
No, non è più felice l'esercizio.
Ridono alcuni: tu scrivi per l'Arte.
Nemmeno io volevo questo che volevo ben altro.
Si fanno versi per scrollare un peso
e passare al seguente. Ma c'è sempre
qualche peso di troppo, non c'è mai
alcun verso che basti
se domani tu stesso te ne scordi.

Corso Lodi

E — disse G. sciogliendosi in uno sbadiglio —
e piantale queste cose se ti riesce
nelle fredde gallerie di quadri falsi e di croste,
le zazzere e le zimarre.
Piantala se ti riesce una volta per tutte
la tetra folla che annusa trifola ornamentale,

clearings in the city
with a loss's bitterness
with those late-heard steps of theirs.
Solitude, only pride . . .
                    From them
to us a hidden wound groans
and the wind from the plains gives it voice,
petrifies it on the headstones.

The Lines

They're being written still.
You think of them lying
to anxious eyes that wish you well
on the last night of the year.
They're written in the negative
within a blackness of years
like paying a tiresome
debt that goes back years.
No, the task's no longer happy.
Some laugh: you were writing for Art.
Not even I wanted that who wanted far better.
Lines are made to shrug off a burden
and move on to the next one. But there's always
some burden too many, there's never
any line that's enough
if tomorrow you yourself forget it.

Corso Lodi

So—said G. drifting off into a yawn—
so give up these things if you can
in the cold galleries of false pictures and daubs,
the great coats and grown-out hair.
Once and for all give up if you can
the dismal crowd sniffing for ornamental truffles,

la turba dei baschi marxesistenzialisti
esistenzialmarxisti.
E una volta di più illudendomi
che fosse sul serio per l'ultima volta
sul ponte che scavalca le nebbia della città
dove l'anno si strugge in brace e in cenere
io lo seguii.

L'alibi e il beneficio

Le portiere spalancate a vuoto sulla sera di nebbia
nessuno che salga o scenda se non
una folata di smog la voce dello strillone
—paradossale—il Tempo di Milano l'alibi
e il beneficio della nebbia cose occulte
camminano al coperto muovono verso di me
divergono da me passato come storia passato
come memoria: il venti il tredici il trentatré
anni come cifre tramviarie
o solo indizio ammiccante della radice perduta
una sera di nebbia agli incroci di ogni possibile sera
infatti *è sera qualunque traversata da tram semivuoti*
mi vedi avanzare come sai nei quartieri senza ricordo
mai visto un quartiere così ricco in ricordi
come questi sedicenti «senza» nei versi del giovane Erba
tra due fonde barriere dentro un grigio acre tunnel
con che pena il trasporto buca la nebbia stasera
alibi ma beneficio della nebbia globalità del possibile
che si nasconde ma per fiorire
in alberi e fontane questa polvere d'anni di Milano.

La poesia è una passione?

L'abbraccio che respinge e non unisce—
il mento fermo piantato sulla spalla

the rabble of marx-existentialist
existential-marxist berets.
And deceiving myself once again
it was really for the last time
on the bridge climbing over city fog
where the year's consumed in embers and ashes
I went following him.

The Alibi and the Benefit

The doors flung open for nothing onto evening fog
no one getting on or off but
a gust of smog the newsboy's cry
—paradoxical—il Tempo di Milano the alibi
and benefit of fog things hidden
proceed under cover move towards me
veer away from me gone past like history gone past
like remembrance: the twenty the thirteen the thirty-three
years like trams' numerals
or only winking clue of the root lost
a foggy evening at the intersection of all possible evenings
in fact *it's any evening crossed by half-empty trams*
you see me advance as you know in districts without memory
never seen a district quite so rich in memories
as these supposed to be "without" in the young Erba's lines
between two thick barriers inside an acrid gray tunnel
how painfully the transport pierces fog this evening
alibi but benefit of fog all possible worlds
hiding themselves only to blossom
in trees and fountains this dust from years of Milan.

Poetry Is a Passion?

The embrace that repels and doesn't unite—
firm chin planted on that shoulder

di lei, lo sguardo fisso e torvo:
storia d'altri e, già vecchia, di loro.
Moriva d'apprensione e gelosia
al punto di volersi morto, di volerlo
veramente, lì tra le braccia di lei.
Rabbiosamente non voleva sciogliersi.
Chi cederà per primo? La domenica
d'agosto era, fuori, al suo colmo
e tutta Italia sulle piazze
nei viali e nei bar ferma ai televisori...
Un gesto appena,—si disse—cerca d'essere uomo
e sarai fuori dalla stregata cerchia.
E, la convulsa stretta perdurando
(che lei d'istinto raddoppiava),
alla cieca una mano errò sull'apparecchio, agì
sulla manopola: nella stanza
fu di colpo la gara, si frappose tra loro.

Il campione che dicono finito,
che pareva intoccabile dallo scherno del tempo
e per minimi segni da una stagione all'altra
di sé fa dire che più non ce la fa e invece
nella corsa che per lui è alla morte
ancora ce la fa, è quello il suo campione.
Lo si aspettava all'ultimo chilometro:
«se vedremo spuntare
laggiù una certa maglia...» e qualcosa l'annuncia,
un movimento di gente giù alla curva,
uno stormire di voci che si approssima
un clamore un boato, è incredibile è lui
è solo s'è rialzato ha staccato le mani
ce l'ha fatta... e dunque anch'io
posso ancora riprendermi, stravincere.
S'erano intanto gli occhi raddolciti
e di poco allentandosi la stretta
s'inteneriva, acquistava altro senso, ritornava
altrimenti violenta.
Per una voce irrotta nella stanza...

of hers, the fixed and surly gaze:
others' story and, already old, their own.
He was dying of apprehension and jealousy
so much so he wished himself dead, he wished it
truly, there in her arms.
Angrily, he'd no wish to break free.
Who'll give in first? A Sunday
in August was, outside, at its height
and all of Italy in piazzas, bars,
on the avenues, stuck in front of televisions . . .
The slightest move,—he told himself—try to be a man
and you'll escape the bewitched circle.
And, the convulsive grip persisting
(which on instinct she redoubled),
blindly one hand fumbled with the set,
turned a dial: in the room
at once the race appeared, and came between them.

The champion they say is finished,
who seemed immune to time's derision
and from minute signs, season after season,
they say he just can't make it, but instead
in the race that for him is to the death
he still makes it, he's his champion.
They awaited him at the final stretch:
"if we see a certain
jersey appearing down there . . ." and something relays it,
a shuffle of people down on the corner,
a rustle of voices approaching,
a clamor, a roar, it's incredible, it's him,
he's on his own, has sat up, raised his hands,
he's made it . . . and so I too
can rally, can beat them all hollow.
The eyes meanwhile had softened
and, loosening a little, the grip
grew tender, gained another sense, returned
with different violence.
For a voice irrupted in the room . . .

L'istinto che non la tradisce
scocca esatto sempre al momento giusto
tra i suoi pensieri semplici.
Sa capire il suo uomo: lo sa bene che più
suppone lui di stravincere a sé meglio l'avvince
e fin che vorrà se lo tiene.
«Caro—gli dice all'orecchio—amore mio...».
E la domenica chiara è ancora in cielo,
folto di verde il viale e di uccelli
non ancora spettrali case e grattacieli,
solo un po' più nitidi a quest'ora
di avanzato meriggio dell'ultima domenica
di questa nostra estate. E se a lui pare
che un brivido percettibile appena
s'inoltri nel soffio ancora tiepido che approda
alla terrazza: *anche agosto*
—lei dice d'un tratto ricordandosi—
anche agosto andato è per sempre...

Sì li ho amati anch'io questi versi...
anche troppo per i miei gusti. Ma era
il solo libro uscito dal bagaglio
d'uno di noi. Vollero che li leggessi.
Per tre per quattro
pomeriggi di seguito scendendo
dal verde bottiglia della Drina a Larissa accecante
la tradotta balcanica. Quei versi
li sentivo lontani
molto lontani da noi: ma era quanto restava,
un modo di parlare tra noi—
sorridenti o presaghi fiduciosi o allarmati
credendo nella guerra o non credendoci—
in quell'estate di ferro.
Forse nessuno l'ha colto così bene
questo momento dell'anno. Ma
—e si guardava attorno tra i tetti che abbuiavano
e le prime serpeggianti luci cittadine—
sono andati anche loro *di là dai fiumi sereni*,
è altra roba altro agosto,

The instinct, that never fails her,
strikes always at just the right moment
among her simple thoughts.
She can understand her man: knows well
the more he imagines he beats them
the better she enthralls him
and holds him as long as she wants.
"Dearest"—she whispers in his ear—"my love..."
And the clear Sunday's still in the sky,
the avenue thick with greenery and birds,
houses and skyscrapers still not ghostly,
just a little sharper at this hour
late in the afternoon, the final Sunday
of this our summer. And if it seems to him
a barely perceptible shudder encroaches
on the still-warm breeze that reaches
to the terrace: *August too*
—she suddenly says, remembering—
August too has gone forever...

Yes I too have loved those lines...
too much even for my own liking.
But it was the one book emerged from
anyone's baggage. They wanted me to read them.
For three or four
evenings consecutively, going south
down the Drina's bottle-green to dazzling
Larissa, the Balkan troop train. Those lines
felt far away to me,
very far away from us: but it was what remained,
a manner of speaking between us—
smiling or foreboding, trusting or alarmed,
believing in the war or not believing—
during that summer of iron.
Perhaps no one has caught so well
this moment in the year. Yet still
—and he looked around among the darkening roofs
and the first snaking lights of the city—
even they've gone *over there across serene rivers,*
it's not the same, another August,

non tocca quegli alberi o quei tetti,
vive e muore e sé piange
ma altrove, ma molto molto lontano da qui.
. . . .

APPARIZIONI O INCONTRI

Un sogno

Ero a passare il ponte
su un fiume che poteva essere il Magra
dove vado d'estate o anche il Tresa,
quello delle mie parti tra Germignaga e Luino.
Me lo impediva uno senza volto, una figura plumbea.
«Le carte» ingiunse. «Quali carte» risposi.
«Fuori le carte» ribadì lui ferreo
vedendomi interdetto. Feci per rabbonirlo:
«Ho speranze, un paese che mi aspetta,
certi ricordi, amici ancora vivi,
qualche morto sepolto con onore».
«Sono favole, — disse — non si passa
senza un programma». E soppesò ghignando
i pochi fogli che erano i miei beni.
Volli tentare ancora. «Pagherò
al mio ritorno se mi lasci
passare, se mi lasci lavorare». Non ci fu
modo d'intendersi: «Hai tu fatto
— ringhiava — la tua scelta ideologica?».
Avvinghiati lottammo alla spalletta del ponte
in piena solitudine. La rissa
dura ancora, a mio disdoro.
Non lo so
chi finirà nel fiume.

doesn't touch those trees and roofs,
lives and dies and mourns itself
but elsewhere, but very very far from here.

. . . .

APPARITIONS OR ENCOUNTERS

A Dream

I was crossing a bridge
over a river that could have been the Magra
where I go for the summer or even the Tresa,
in my part of the country between Germignaga and Luino.
A leaden body without face blocked my way.
"Papers," he ordered. "What papers," I answered.
"Out with them," he insisted, firm
on seeing me aghast. I made to appease him:
"I've prospects, a place awaiting me,
certain memories, friends still alive,
a few dead honorably buried."
"Fairy tales," he said, "You can't pass
without a program." And sneering he weighed up
the few papers, my worldly goods.
I wanted one last try. "I'll pay
on the way back if you'll let me
pass, if you'll let me work."
We would never see eye to eye: "Have you made,"
he was snarling, "your ideological choice?"
Grappling we struggled on the bridge's parapet
in utter solitude. The fight
still goes on, to my dishonor.
I don't know
who'll end up in the river.

Ancora sulla strada di Creva

Poteva essere lei la nonna morta
non so da quanti anni.
Uscita a tardo vespro
dalla sua cattolica penombra,
al tempo che detto è dell'estate
di San Martino o dei Morti.
Una vecchia vermiglia del suo riso.
Cantavano gli uccelli dalle rogge
e quante ancora verdi intatte foglie
recava in grembo l'autunno.
Ilare ci fu innanzi
come la richiedemmo della via
nella seta del suo parasole,
nei lustrini dell'abito. E nulla fu
a fronte del riso vermiglio
la cattolica penombra, nulla fu
la gramaglia dell'abito. Né so
che mai vedesse di noi
del giorno e di altro accaldati.
Forse in luogo di noi vide una nube
e lei a quella parlava:
«Ti conosco,—diceva—mascherina,
così brava a nasconderti tra incantevoli fumi.
Già una volta ti ho colta
sulla guancia ancora intatta d'una
che per amore, in cerca
di una quieta corrente, s'era tolta alla vita:
con che fermezza che forza quelle mani
tendevano al sonno gli arbusti
strappati all'ultima riva.
Oggi lo so, non piansi quella fine,
ma quella forza che ti sconfessava
abbandonandosi a te . . . Maschera detta amore,
bella roba che sei.
     Per un po' d'ombra che fa
più vive le acque più battute le siepi più frenetico giugno
quanti anni di vuoto appena dopo, anni
di navata e corsia

On the Creva Road Again

It could have been her, my grandmother
dead I don't know how many years.
Come out at late vespers
from her Catholic twilight,
at the time that's called Saint Martin's Summer
or Commemoration Day.
An old woman scarlet with laughter.
The birds sang from the waterways
and how many still-green leaves intact
autumn bore in her womb.
As we asked her the way
she was merry there before us
in the silk of her parasol,
in her outfit's sequins. And nothing
beside her scarlet laughter
was the catholic twilight, nothing
her mourning weeds. And nor
do I know how much she saw of us
glowing from the day and whatever.
Perhaps in place of us she saw
a cloud and spoke to that:
"Fond disguise,"—she said—"I know you,
so good at hiding in enchanting vapor.
I beheld you once before
on the still whole cheek of one
who for love, in search of
quiet waters, took her life:
with what resolve, what strength those hands
tendered to sleep weeds torn
from the final river margin.
I realize now I didn't grieve at your end,
but for the strength that belied you
abandoning itself in you . . . Disguise called love,
fine thing you are!
             For a little shade that makes
the waters quicker, bushes more fervent, June more lively
how many years of nothing after, years
of hospital ward and nave

di campane smemoranti di
fuligginose sere: c'era sino a poco fa
un così bel sole—e per pigrizia o noia
o distrazione non siamo usciti a goderlo.
Vedi come hai sporcato la mia vita
di tremore e umiltà».

Così delirando di una perduta forza
di una remota gioia, così oltre noi dileguando
scovava, svergognandola, la morte
ancora occulta tra noi. E da quel giorno
e quell'ora
d'amore più non ti parlai amore mio.

Intervista a un suicida

L'anima, quello che diciamo l'anima e non è
che una fitta di rimorso,
lenta deplorazione sull'ombra dell'addio
mi rimbrottò dall'argine.

Ero, come sempre, in ritardo
e il funerale a mezza strada, la sua furia
nera ben dentro il cuore del paese.
Il posto: quello, non cambiato—con memoria
di grilli e rane, di acquitrino e selva
di campane sfatte—
ora in polvere, in secco fango, ricettacolo
di spettri di treni in manovra
il pubblico macello discosto dal paese
di quel tanto . . .

                In che rapporto con l'eterno?
Mi volsi per chiederlo alla detta anima, cosiddetta.
Immobile, uniforme
rispose per lei (per me) una siepe di fuoco
crepitante lieve, come di vetro liquido
indolore con dolore.

of memory-dulling bells
of sun-filled dusks: until just now
there was such fine sun—and from idleness or boredom
or distraction we didn't walk out to enjoy it.
See how you've sullied my life
with humility and trembling."

So railing about a lost strength,
a distant gladness, growing so faint beyond us
she uncovered, disgracing it, death
still hidden within us. And from that day
and that hour
my love I never spoke to you of love.

Interview with a Suicide

The soul, what we call the soul and is nothing
but a pang of remorse,
slow reproof on the shadow of farewell,
upbraided me from the banks.

I was late, as usual,
and the procession halfway there, its black fury
well within the heart of the town.
The place: none other, unchanged—with memories
of crickets and frogs, of marshland and woods,
broken church bells—
now dust and dry mud, repository
of trains' ghosts shunting,
the public abattoir just far
enough to . . .

        With what relation to eternity?
I turned to ask what's called, the so-called, soul.
Motionless, unvarying
a burning bush replied for it (for me)
crackling lightly, like liquid glass,
painless in pain.

Gettai nel riverbero il mio *perché l'hai fatto?*
Ma non svettarono voci lingueggianti in fiamma,
non la storia di un uomo:
                    simulacri,
e nemmeno, figure della vita.

                    La porta
carraia, e là di colpo nasce la cosa atroce,
la carretta degli arsi da lanciafiamme...
rinvenni, pare, anni dopo nel grigiore di qui
tra cassette di gerani, polvere o fango
dove tutto sbiadiva, anche
—potrei giurarlo, sorrideva nel fuoco—
anche... e parlando ornato:
«mia donna venne a me di Val di Pado»
sicché (non quaglia con me—ripetendomi—
non quagliano acque lacustri e commoventi pioppi
non papaveri e fiori di brughiera)
ebbi un cane, anche troppo mi ci ero affezionato,
tanto da distinguere tra i colpi del qui vicino mattatoio
il colpo che me lo aveva finito.
In quanto all'ammanco di cui facevano discorsi
sul sasso o altrove puoi scriverlo, come vuoi:

    NON NELLE CASSE DEL COMUNE
    L'AMMANCO
    ERA NEL SUO CUORE

Decresceva alla vista, spariva per l'eterno.
Era l'eterno stesso
                    puerile, dei terrori
rosso su rosso, famelico sbadiglio
della noia
                    col suono della pioggia sui sagrati...
Ma venti trent'anni
fa lo stesso, il tempo di turbarsi
tornare in pace gli steli
se corre un motore la campagna,
si passano la voce dell'evento

Why did you do it? I hurled at the glare.
But voices tonguing in flame didn't rise,
not the story of a man:
                              simulacra,
and not even those, mere shows of life.

                              The carriage
entrance and suddenly the terrible thing's born,
the cartload of bodies burned by flame-throwers . . .
I came back to life, they say, years later
in the gray of these parts among geranium boxes,
dust and mud where everything fades, not least
—I could swear, he smiled in the fire—
not least . . . and in adorned speech:
"my lady came to me from Val di Pado"
so (they don't fool me—I repeat—
lake waters moving poplars
poppies and moorland flowers)
I had a dog, was too fond of him,
so much I could tell in the abattoir nearby
which was the blow that finished him off.
Regarding the deficit about which they spoke
on the stone or elsewhere you can write, as you wish:

    NOT IN THE TOWN HALL
    FUNDS THE DEFICIT
    WAS IN HIS HEART

He shrank from view, disappeared for eternity.
It was eternity itself
                              childish with terrors
red upon red, the ravenous yawn
of boredom
                    with the sound of rain on churchyards . . .
But twenty, thirty years
make no difference, barely time for
the stalks to be troubled then at peace
should a motor cross the landscape,
they pass on news of the event

ma non se ne curano, la sanno lunga
le acque falsamente ora limpide tra questi
oggi diritti regolari argini,
                          lo spazio
si copre di case popolari, di un altro
segregato squallore dentro le forme del vuoto.
                                       . . . Pensare

cosa può essere—voi che fate
lamenti dal cuore delle città
sulle città senza cuore—
cosa può essere un uomo in un paese,
sotto il pennino dello scriba una pagina frusciante
e dopo
dentro una polvere di archivi
nulla nessuno in nessun luogo mai.

Il piatto piange

Così ridotti a pochi li colse la nuova primavera—
alcuni andati non lontano spostati
non di molto, di qualche dosso o crinale fuor di vista
o di voce, distanti un suono di campane
a seconda del vento sui pianori,
altri persi per sempre murati in un lavoro
dentro scroscianti città.
                       E quelli qui restati?
Qua sotto, venivano qua sotto, nel sottoscala
e per giorni per notti tappati dentro sprangati
gli usci turata ogni fessura: *vedo passo rilancio
come quando fuori piove* al riparo dell'esistere o piuttosto,
fiorisse la magnolia o il glicine svenevole,
dalla ripetizione dell'esistere . . .
                                e no
no il fendente di platino della schiarita sulle acque
no la bella stagione la primavera e i nuovi fidanzati.
Sul torrente del seme chissà non s'avviasse la bella compagnia
ad altri imbarchi altri guadi

but indifferently, the waters know
well enough, falsely limpid now between these
regular embankments today so straight,
                                          the space
is covered with cheap housing, with another
fenced-off squalor in the form of nothingness.
                                        . . .Think
what can he be—you who make
complaints from the heart of the city
about cities with no heart—
what can a man in a small town be
a page rustling under the pen of the scribe
and then
within the archives' dust
nothing no one nowhere never.

Il Piatto Piange

Reduced to so few the early spring gathered them—
some gone not far away, removed
a little, some hills or ridges away beyond sight
or earshot, a ringing bell's distance
depending on the wind across the plains,
others lost forever walled up in some work
within pummeling cities.
                          And those left behind here?
Down here, they come down here, below stairs
and for days and nights shut within barred exits
every crack stopped *I'll see you, pass, I'll raise
when it's raining outside* sheltered from life or rather,
were magnolia or languishing wisteria to bloom,
from life's repetition . . .
                    and no
no platinum cut of brightness on the waters
no fine weather, spring, and the newly betrothed
on the torrent of seed who knows if companions won't set out
for other sailings other fordings

verso selve scurissime vampe di ribes uve nere
ai confini dell'informe?

Io dunque come loro loro dunque come me
come loro come me fuggendo, con parole con musiche
agli orecchi, un frastornante chicchirichì—da che distanza—
un disordine cocente, di deliquio? La solitudine?
E allora dentro il fuoco risorgivo di sé
essere per qualche istante, io noi, solitudine?
Per qualche metro sotto il filo del suolo?
                                O miei prodi...
cadono le picche ai fanti i fiori alle regine—
e la notte muso precario è ai pertugi
stilla un buio tumefatto
                    di palude
rifiuti d'ogni specie. Ma dove c'è rifiuti,
dice uno allarmandosi, c'è vita—e
un colpo di vento tra pareti e porte
con la disperazione che negando assevera
(non è una bisca questa non un bordello questa casa onorata)
spazzerà le carte una voce di vento
e ci buttano fuori.

Sopra un'immagine sepolcrale

Il sorriso balordo che mi fermò tra le lapidi
e le croci, nella piccola selva
dei morti innocenti, delle vite
appena accese e spente nel candore
era la stessa mia stupefazione
che avesse in tanti anni fatto così poca strada.

O dormiente, che cosa è sonno?
                        Il sonno...

E qui egli sta tra i pargoli innocenti
stupefatto nel marmo
come se un Tu dovesse veramente

towards darkest woods, currents blazing, black grapes
at the confines of the formless?

So me like them so them like me
like them like me in flight, with words with music
in the ears, a piercing cock-crow—from what distance—
a burning disorder, of swoons? The solitude?
And then in the flame reborn of itself
to be for some moments, me us, solitude?
And six feet underground?
                              O my brave ones . . .
the spades fall to jacks the clubs to queens—
and the night's poor face is at the gaps
a swamp's tumescent dark
                    is dripping
refuse of every kind. But where there's refuse,
says someone alarmed, there's life—
and a blast of wind between walls and doors
with the desperation that, denying, asserts
(it's no gambling den no bordello this respectable house)
the wind's voice will scatter the cards
and us they throw outside.

On a Cemetery Photograph

The witless smile that halted me between tombstones
and crosses, in the little forest
of the innocent dead, of lives
barely kindled and snuffed out in the whiteness
was my same astonishment
that over years he'd come so little way.

O slumberer, what kind of thing is sleep?
                              Sleep . . .

And here he is amongst the innocent babes
astonished in the marble
as if a Thou should truly

ritornare
a liberare i vivi e i morti.
E quante lagrime e seme vanamente sparso.

A un compagno d'infanzia

I

Non resta più molto da dire
e sempre lo stesso paesaggio si ripete.
Non rimane che aggirarlo
noi due nel vento urlandoci confidenze futili
e crederle riepiloghi, drammatiche
verità sulla vita.
     «Ma tu hai la bellezza...»
      «Chiacchiere
nel vento tenebroso, religione
della morte: gli anni che passano
tali e quali, la collina che riavvampa in autunno,
i campanili
assolati imperterriti,
pietrificate ossa di morti, le nostre
radici troppo simili, da troppo
per non dolersi insieme, che quel vento
fa gemere...».

Un'autostrada presto porterà un altro vento
tra questi nomi estatici: Creva
Germignaga Voldomino la
Trebedora—rivivranno
con altro suono e senso
in una luce d'orgoglio...
Non che sia questo la bellezza,
      ma
la frustata in dirittura, il gesto
perentorio
sul cruccio che scempiamente si rigira in noi,
il saperla sempre a un passo da noi,

come again
to free the quick and dead.
And how much seed, what tears vainly shed.

To a Childhood Companion

    I

Not much remains to be said
and the same landscape's always repeated.
Nothing's left but to move around it,
the two of us shouting futile confidences in the wind
and taking them for summaries, dramatic
              "But you've the beauty..."
                "Claptrap
in the shadowy wind, religion
of death: the passing years
the same, the hill in autumn blazing afresh,
the undaunted
campanili flooded in sunlight,
petrified bones of the dead, our own
too-similar roots, too much so
not to grieve together, that the wind
makes moan..."

Soon an autostrada will bring a different wind
through these rapturous place-names: Creva,
Germignaga, Voldomino, la
Trebedora—they'll live again
with different sound and sense
in a light of self-esteem...
Not that this is beauty,
              but
the final furlong whip, the peremptory
touch at affliction
ruinously turning in us,
knowing it's always one step beyond,

la bellezza, in un'aria frizzante:
questo,
che oscuramente cercano i libertini
e che ho imparato lavorando.

    II

Addio addio ripetono le piante.
Addio anche a me tocca ora di dirti
con la stessa tenerezza
e intensità, con la stessa
umiltà delle piante
che a stormire però continueranno
fuori dallo sguardo immediato.
Non c'è nessuno, sembra, al ponte
che ripasserò tra poco: non figuro mascherato
d'inesistenza non querulo viandante.
Dunque via libera, e basta con le visioni!
Nella domenica confusa
di un fiume alla sua foce si colluttano
salutarmente in me...

Dall'Olanda

AMSTERDAM

A portarmi fu il caso tra le nove
e le dieci d'una domenica mattina
svoltando a un ponte, uno dei tanti, a destra
lungo il semigelo d'un canale. E non
questa è la casa, ma soltanto
—mille volte già vista—
sul cartello dimesso: «Casa di Anna Frank».

Disse più tardi il mio compagno: quella
di Anna Frank non dev'essere, non è
privilegiata memoria. Ce ne furono tanti
che crollarono per sola fame

beauty, in a sparkling air:
this,
which libertines darkly search for
and that work has taught me.

II

Goodbye, goodbye the branches repeat.
Goodbye it's my turn to say to you now
with the same tenderness
and intensity, the same
humility as the branches
that will go on rustling nonetheless
beyond the immediate glance.
There's no one, it seems, on the bridge
I'll recross in a while: no masked figure
of nonexistence, no plaintive traveler.
All clear then, give up those visions!
On the muddled Sunday
of a river's mouth they come to grips
for my own good in me . . .

From Holland

AMSTERDAM

Chance led me there between
nine and ten one Sunday morning,
turning at a bridge, one of many, to the right
along a canal half-iced over. And not
this is the house, but merely
—seen a thousand times before—
"Anne Frank's house," on the simple plaque.

Later my companion said:
Anne Frank's shouldn't be, it isn't
a privileged memory. There were many
who were broken simply out of hunger

senza il tempo di scriverlo.
Lei, è vero, lo scrisse.
Ma a ogni svolta a ogni ponte lungo ogni canale
continuavo a cercarla senza trovarla più
ritrovandola sempre.
Per questo è una e insondabile Amsterdam
nei suoi tre quattro variabili elementi
che fonde in tante unità ricorrenti, nei suoi
tre quattro fradici o acerbi colori
che quanto è grande il suo spazio perpetua,
anima che s'irraggia ferma e limpida
su migliaia d'altri volti, germe
dovunque e germoglio di Anna Frank.
Per questo è sui suoi canali vertiginosa Amsterdam.

L'INTERPRETE

«Adesso tornano. Floridi, chiassosi
pieni zeppi di valuta.
Sono buoni clienti, non si possono respingere.
Informazioni, quante vogliono.
Non una parola di più. Non si tratta
di rappresaglia o rancore.
Ma d'inflessibile memoria».

VOLENDAM

Qui acqua cent'anni fa
— ripeteva la guida Federico —
oggi *polder*.
    Vita
tra *polder* e diga, qui c'è posto
per la procreazione solamente
e la difesa dalla morte. Questo
dicono le facce arrossate dal freddo
fuori dalla messa cattolica
a Volendam, la nenia
del vento volubile tra i terrapieni.

without the time to write.
She, it's true, did write it.
But at every turn, at every bridge, along every canal
I continued to search for her, no longer finding her,
finding her perpetually.
That's why it's one and unfathomable Amsterdam
in its three or four varying elements
which it blends in many recurring wholes,
its three or four rotten or unripe colors
which its space perpetuates far as it stretches,
spirit that irradiates steadfast and clear
on thousands of other faces, everywhere
seed and bud of Anne Frank.
That's why Amsterdam's vertiginous on its canals.

THE INTERPRETER

"Now they're returning. Florid, rowdy
loaded with currency.
They are good clients, can't be turned away.
Information, as much as they want.
Not a word more. It isn't a question
of grudges or retaliation.
But of unflinching memory."

VOLENDAM

Water here a hundred years back
—repeated Federico the guide—
today *polder.*
        Life
between *polder* and dyke, there's room here
for procreation only
and defense against death.
That's what the faces reddened by the cold say
outside the Catholic mass
at Volendam, the dirge
of the varying wind between seawalls.

L'amore è di dopo, è dei figli
ed è più grande. Impara.

La pietà ingiusta

Mi prendono da parte, mi catechizzano:
                              il faut
faire attention, vous savez.
Et surtout si l'affaire
doit marcher jusqu'au bout,
ne causez pas de ces choses bien passées.
Il paraît qu'il en fut un, un SS
qu'il a été même dans l'armée
quoique pas allemand...
                    Ecco in cosa erano
forza e calma sospette
l'abnegazione nel lavoro, la
cura del particolare, la serietà
a ogni costo, fino in fondo...

Intorno c'è aria di niente, mani
sulla tavola, armi (chi le avesse)
al guardaroba: solo adesso
si comincia a capire — e l'affare un pretesto
il pranzo un trucco, una messinscena
benché non esistano dubbi sulle portate
benché non ci siano orripilanti cataste sulla tavola né sotto
— ma in cucina, chi può dirlo?,
ah le dotte manipolazioni di cui furono capaci,
matasse, matassine innocue, oro a scaglie
da coprirne un deserto di sale, nubi d'anime
esalanti-esulanti da camini
con la piena dolcezza degli stormi d'autunno
altre anche meno visibili spazzate da una raffica in un'ora di
    notte —
è una questione d'occhi fermi sul cammello che passa
e ripassa per la cruna in piena libertà —
e con tocchi di porpora una città

Love is for later, it's for the children
and it is greater. Take heed.

The Unjust Pity

They take me aside, they chide me:
                              il faut
faire attention, vous savez.
Et surtout si l'affaire
doit marcher jusqu-au bout,
ne causez pas de ces choses bien passées.
Il paraît qu'il en fut un, un SS
qu'il a été même dans l'armée
quoique pas allemand . . .
                              Here's what made
strength and calm suspect,
self-sacrifice in work,
attention to detail, thoroughness
at all costs, right to the end . . .

Around, an air of nothing, hands
on the table, weapons (those who had them)
in the cloakroom: only now
do we start to comprehend — the deal a pretext,
the meal a trick, a mise-en-scène
despite their being no doubts about the dishes
despite no horrifying charnel heaps on or under the table
— but in the kitchen, who can say?,
ah the expert handling of which they were capable,
skeins, innocuous little skeins, gold in lumps
to cover a desert of salt, clouds of souls
exhaling-exiling from chimneys
with the autumn migrations' full sweetness
others still less visible swept at night by gunfire —
it's a question of eyes fixed on the camel
going back and forth through the needle's eye quite freely —
and a city with touches of purple

d'inverno, una città di cenere si propaga
dentro una lente di mitezza.
Solo adesso si comincia a capire.

Incredibile — dirò più tardi — le visioni
immotivate che si hanno a volte
(e pazienza per queste
ma esserne coinvolti al di là del giudizio
fino al tenero, fino all'indebita pietà...):
le giubbe sbottonate della disfatta, un elmo
ruzzolante tra i crateri, sugli argini maciullati
facce su facce lungo un canale a ridosso di un muro
un reparto in sfacelo che si sbraca, se ne fotte
della resa con dignità, ma su tutte
quella faccia d'infortunio, di gioventù in malora
con la sua vampa di dispetto di bocciato
di espulso dal futuro
nell'ora già densa della campagna
verso l'estate che verrà...

Tra poco sparecchieranno, porteranno
le cartelle per la firma. Si firmerà.
Si firmerà la pace barattandola con la nostra pietà —
e lui rimesso in sesto, risarcito di vent'anni d'amaro
bene potus et pransus arbitro dell'affare.

Non si vede più niente. Se non — per un incauto
pensiero, per quel momento di pietà — quella mano
quel mozzicone di mano sulla parete.
Ci conta ci pesa ci divide. Firma.
E tutti quanti come niente — come la notte
ci dimentica.

Nel vero anno zero

Meno male lui disse, il più festante: che meno male c'erano tutti.
Tutti alle Case dei Sassoni — rifacendo la conta.
Mai stato in Sachsenhausen? Mai stato.

in winter, a city of ash multiplies
within a lens of mildness.
Only now do we start to comprehend.

Incredible—I said later—the motiveless
visions to which we're sometimes prey
(and forbearance for these
but being embroiled in them way beyond judgment
to the point of tenderness, the point of undue pity . . .):
the disaster's unbuttoned battle dress, a helmet
rolling between craters, on torn embankments
face after face down a canal behind a wall
a platoon collapsing, stripping, not giving a damn
about surrender with dignity, but on everyone
that wrecked look, of youth in ruins,
with its flush of resentment, of failure,
of expulsion from the future
at the time when the countryside's already dense
towards the summer coming on . . .

Soon they'll clear the table, bring
the papers to be signed. They'll be signed.
Peace will be signed in short change for our pity—
and fixed up, indemnified for twenty years' bitterness,
bene potus et pransus the deal's mediator.

You don't see a thing anymore. Or just—through a careless
thought, through that moment of pity—that hand,
that stump of hand on a wall.
It counts us, weighs us, separates us. Signs.
And each and everyone as nothing—as the night
disremembers us.

In the True Year Zero

Just as well, he said, the most jovial: just as well all were there.
All at the Saxons' Houses—mentally recounting.
Ever been to Sachsenhausen? Never been.

A mangiare ginocchio di porco? Mai stato.
Ma certo, alle case dei Sassoni.
Alle Case dei Sassoni, in Sachsenhausen, cosa c'è di strano?
Ma quante Sachsenhausen in Germania, quante case.
Dei Sassoni, dice rassicurante
caso mai svicolasse tra le nebbie
un'ombra di recluso nel suo gabbano.
No non c'ero mai stato in Sachsenhausen.

E gli altri allora—mi legge nel pensiero—
quegli altri carponi fuori da Stalingrado
mummie di già soldati
dentro quel sole di sciagura fermo
sui loro anni aquilonari . . . dopo tanti anni
non è la stessa cosa?

Tutto ingoiano le nuove belve, tutto—
si mangiano cuore e memoria queste belve onnivore.
A balzi nel chiaro di luna s'infilano in un night.

La speranza

Non era un sogno, vi dico—
                        se può
non esserlo un paese dove cenano per tempo,
griglie serrande stuoie
nessuno sulle porte (e cosa era, di colpo
sul primo incontestabile giorno di primavera,
quella mesta buriana di piante e siepi?)
un paese che sfila all'infinito
con sagome e targhe straniere
nell'affanno del ritardo
o di un temuto malinteso.
Ma già, primi indizi, ci venivano incontro
sagome e targhe familiari
e facce, a mezzo, a mezz'aria tra certi parapetti
tenere buffe zitte nel po' di luce che restava
finché furono palesi

To eat a knee of pork? No, never.
But of course, at the Saxons' houses.
At the Saxons' Houses, in Sachsenhausen, what's so strange?
But in Germany, how many Sachsenhausens, how many houses.
At the Saxons', reassuringly he says
should a prisoner's shadow in overcoat
slip away amidst the fogs.
No, I'd never been to Sachsenhausen.

And the others then — he reads my thoughts —
those others on all fours round Stalingrad,
mummies of what were soldiers
within that catastrophic sun
fixed in their north wind-bitten years . . . after so many years
doesn't it come to the same?

The lot, the new beasts gobble the lot —
heart and memory these omnivores stuff down.
They skip into a nightclub beneath the clair de lune.

The Hope

It wasn't a dream, I tell you —
                    if a town
where they dine early, grates, shutters, mats
no one on the doors
can be anything but (and what was it, suddenly
on the first incontestable spring day,
that sorry squall of bushes and trees?)
a town marching off to the infinite
with shapes and foreign license plates
breathless from being late
or from a feared misunderstanding.
But already, first signs, coming to meet us
were shapes and familiar license plates
and faces, half seen, suspended between parapets
tender joking silent in the little light remaining
till they were clear

un Carlo qualche Piero alcuni Sergi
e altri che non nomino per ragioni di misura
e per una specialmente, decisiva
se vi dico
che c'era tra loro Maurizio
vecchio argento d'Italia
fuoco calmo e vivo.
Vi dico che non era un sogno.
C'erano tutti, o quasi, i volti della mia vita
compresi quelli degli andati via
e altri che già erano in vista
lì, a due passi dal confine
non ancora nei paraggi della morte.

Metropoli

Altri poi vengono: altri, di altro tipo.
Con frange magari, con lenti spesse e cupe magari
di forte armatura—testa tutta di testa
tutta tecnica, tutto il resto di plastica
dottorini di Oxford.

Guarda invece il vecchio fighter sul quadrato
guardia sinistra o destra, vecchia volpe
abbagliata di città, come muove al massacro:
la sua eleganza, qualità
prettamente animale tra le poche che l'uomo
può prestare alle cose,
la finta saputa a memoria
la danza in scioltezza che gli dura col fiato
purché resti dinamite da spendere

ma sapere che è a vuoto, che ogni volta la posta
non è già più sotto i colpi la stessa
e allora il gioco non ci riguarda più,
le città etichette di valigie fiammelle di necropoli.

one Carlo, a few Pieros, some Sergios
and others I won't name for discretion's sake
and for one more reason, decisive
if I tell you
Maurizio was among them
old silver of Italy
calm and vivid flame.
I tell you it wasn't a dream.
They were all there, or nearly, the faces in my life
including those who'd gone away
and others already in sight
there, a few steps from the border
not yet in the neighborhood of death.

Metropolis

Then others come: others, of another kind.
With fringes perhaps, with thick and dark lenses perhaps
strong framed—head, all head
all technicalities, all the rest of plastic
little doctors of Oxford.

Look instead at the old *fighter* in the ring
southpaw or orthodox, old fox
dazzled by the city, how he moves in for the kill:
his elegance, entirely
animal quality among the few a man
can lend to things,
the feint known by heart
the free and easy dance that's his while he has breath
so long as there's dynamite left to unleash

but to know it's in vain, that each time the stake's
already no longer the same under punches
and therefore the game no longer involves us,
the cities, luggage labels, necropolises' little flames.

Il muro

Sono
quasi in sogno a Luino
lungo il muro dei morti.
Qua i nostri volti ardevano nell'ombra
nella luce rosa che sulle nove di sera
piovevano gli alberi a giugno?
Certo chi muore... ma questi che vivono
invece: giocano in notturna, sei
contro sei, quelli di Porto
e delle Verbanesi nuova gioventù.
Io da loro distolto
sento l'animazione delle foglie
e in questa farsi strada la bufera.
Scagliano polvere e fronde scagliano ira
duelli di là dal muro—
e tra essi il più caro.
                     «Papà—faccio per difendermi
puerilmente—papà...».

Non c'è molto da opporgli, il tuffo
di carità il soprassalto in me quando leggo
di fioriture in pieno inverno sulle alture
che lo cerchiano là nel suo gelo al fondo,
se gli porto notizie delle sue cose
se le sento tarlarsi (la duplice
la subdola fedeltà delle cose:
capaci di resistere oltre una vita d'uomo
e poi si sfaldano trasognandoci anni o momenti dopo)
su qualche mensola
in via Scarlatti 27 a Milano.

Dice che è carità pelosa, di presagio
del mio prossimo ghiaccio, me lo dice come in gloria
rasserenandosi rasserenandomi
mentre riapro gli occhi e lui si ritira ridendo
—e ancora folleggiano quei ragazzi animosi contro bufera e
  notte—

The Wall

I am
almost in a dream in Luino
along the wall of the dead.
Here our faces glowed in the shade,
in the rosy light the trees rained
near nine of an evening in June?
Whoever dies of course . . . but these the living
on the other hand: play nightly,
six a side, the younger generation
of Porto or the Verbanesi.
Turned from them, I sense
the animation of the leaves
and in that the storm making headway.
They cast dust and leafage, cast anger
those on the wall's far side —
and among them my most dear.
                    "Papa" — in childish
self-defense — "papa . . ."

I've not much to resist him, the pang
of love, the start in me when I read
of flowerings in the winter's depth
on upland surrounding him in frost down there,
if I bring him news of his things
if I feel them worm-eaten (the two-faced
insidious fidelity of things:
able to outlast a man's life
and then crumble astonishing us years or moments after)
upon some shelf
in 27 Via Scarlatti, Milan.

He says it's self-interested love, foreseeing
I'll soon be frozen, tells me as if in glory
reassuring himself, reassuring me
while I reopen my eyes and he draws away laughing
—and those spirited lads still fooling against the storm and
   night—

lo dice con polvere e foglie da tutto il muro
che una sera d'estate è una sera d'estate
e adesso avrà più senso
il canto degli ubriachi dalla parte di Creva.

Pantomima terrestre

. . . auprès de margelles dont on a soustrait les puits.
RENÉ CHAR

Ma senti—dice—che meraviglia quel *cip* sulle piante
di ramo in ramo come se il poker continuasse all'aperto:
dimmi se non è stupenda la vita.

Chiaro che cerca di prendermi per il mio verso.
Vorrei rispondergli con un'inezia della mente
un'altra delle mie tra le tante
(gente screziata di luna per porticati
e uno attorno tra loro, dall'uno all'altro:
assaggiate questa fresca delizia).

Certo,—rispondo invece—è stupenda. Vuoi testimoni?
Prove per assurdo? Controprove?
Eccoti di giorno in giorno la mia acredine
la mia insofferenza di gente in gente
(ma queste brezze tra le secche e le rapide
tra i diluvi e le requie dell'essere questi balsami . . .).

Pare bastargli: ma dunque (benedicente, bonario)
ma allora, coraggio!
                Per giravolte di scale
va su col suo coraggio.
                Parli—gli grido dietro—
come un credente di non importa che fede.
E lui per rami di scale, mezza faccia già disfatta
mezza in ombra, canzonandomi con parole d'autore: *¿le gusta
este jardin que es suyo? Evite . . .*

with dust and leaves the length of the wall he says
that a summer's evening is a summer's evening
and there will be more sense now
to the song of the drunks around Creva.

Earthly Pantomime

. . . auprès de margelles dont on a soustrait les puits.
RENÉ CHAR

Just listen—he says—to that wonderful *cheep* in the trees
as if from branch to branch the poker game were going on
    outdoors:
you can't tell me life's not stupendous.

Clearly he's trying to win me through my verse.
I'd like to reply with a trifle of the mind
another of my own amongst the many
(people struck with moonlight through the porticoes
and one among them, moving between them:
taste this fresh delight).

Sure—I reply though—stupendous. Want witnesses?
proofs ad infinitum? Counterproofs?
Here's my bitterness from day to day
my intolerance of one man after another
(but these breezes between the shallows and rapids
between torrents and life's respites these balms. . .).

It seems to suffice: but therefore (blessing, kindly)
well then, take courage!
                      Up twistings of stairs
go he and his courage.
                      You speak—I call behind—
like a believer in no matter what faith.
And from branching stairs, his face half-gone
in shadow, he serenades me with a quote: *¿le gusta
este jardin que es suyo? Evite. . .*

dal basso gli completo la frase: *que sus hijos lo destruyan*
rifacendogli il verso.

Ma se è già guasto, con queste stesse mani:
e tu chi sei tu così avanti sulla scala del giudizio
e del valore, dillo ai tuoi discepoli e seguaci
ai tuoi consoci, vengano a questi bicchieri
di delizia a questi apparati di fresco
ma in comunione ma tutti ma in una volta sola.

È rimasta una chiazza una pozza di luce
non convinta di sé un pozzo di lavoro con attorno
un girotondo di prigionieri (dicono) sulla parola:
sanno di un bagliore che verrà
con dentro, a catena, tutti i colori della vita
—e sarà insostenibile.

Sembra allora di capirlo a che si ostinano
dove puntano che cosa vogliono o non vogliono
che cosa negano che scappatoie infilano
i motori nella giostra serale
con quelli che fingono a ogni giro di andare via per sempre
con quelli che fingono a ogni giro di arrivare
dentro un paese nuovo per cominciare ex novo
—e i primi lampi
                lo scroscio sulle foglie
                              l'insensatezza estiva.

I ricongiunti

A NINETTO

Ti si era dato per disperso

(*si vede che non ce l'ha fatta che non aveva abbastanza ala
per uscirne*—avremmo detto laggiù—
*per togliersi dalle ghiaie del Taro
dalle ultime siepi dalle arie*

I finish the phrase from below *que sus hijos lo distruyan*
mimicking his tone.

As if it weren't already ruined, with our own hands:
and you who are so far ahead on justice's
and value's stairs, tell it to your followers and disciples
to your associates, summon them to these glasses
of delight to these displays of freshness
but in communion all of you and at one time.

What's left is a stain a puddle of light
not convinced of itself a well of work with around it
a dancing ring of prisoners (they say) on parole:
they taste of a flash that will come
and behind it, in a chain, all the colors of life
— and it will be unbearable.

Well he seems to understand what they're insisting
where they're heading what they want and don't want
what they deny what ways out they take
the cars on the evening's roundabout
with those pretending at each turn to go away forever
with those pretending at each turn to arrive
behind a new town to start up from nothing
— and first flares
                rustling leaves
                              the senselessness of summer.

The Reunited
TO NINETTO

They'd said you were lost

(you can see he didn't make it, didn't have wings enough
to leave them — we'd have said below —
to get himself out from the Taro's gravel,
from the last hedges, from the airs

di Calestano: in fondo aveva tralignato
non era più dei nostri)

invece ci siamo tutti proprio tutti
e solo adesso, con te,
la tavolata è perfetta sotto queste pergole.

La spiaggia

Sono andati via tutti—
blaterava la voce dentro il ricevitore.
E poi, saputa:—Non torneranno più—.

Ma oggi
su questo tratto di spiaggia mai prima visitato
quelle toppe solari... Segnali
di loro che partiti non erano affatto?
E zitti quelli al tuo voltarti, come niente fosse.

I morti non è quel che di giorno
in giorno va sprecato, ma quelle
toppe d'inesistenza, calce o cenere
pronte a farsi movimento e luce.
                              Non
dubitare,—m'investe della sua forza il mare—
parleranno.

of Calestano: deep down he'd fallen by the way,
was no longer one of us)

instead we're all here one and all
and only now, with you,
   is the table laid perfect under these pergolas.

The Beach

They've all gone away—
the voice was blathering down the receiver.
Then, knowingly:—They'll not return—.

But today
on this stretch of beach never visited before
those sunlight patches . . . Signals
of theirs, who hadn't left at all?
And when you turn they're quiet, as if nothing.

What's being wasted from day to day
is not the dead, but it's those
patches of the nonexistent, lime or ashes
ready to become light and movement.
                              Don't
be in doubt,—the sea's strength assails me—
speak they will.

da *Stella variabile* / from *Variable Star*

I

Quei tuoi pensieri di calamità

e catastrofe
nella casa dove sei
venuto a stare, già
abitata
dall'idea di essere qui per morirci
venuto
—e questi che ti sorridono amici
questa volta sicuramente
stai morendo lo sanno e perciò
ti sorridono.

In una casa vuota

Si ravvivassero mai. Sembrano ravvivarsi
di stanza in stanza, non si ravvivano
veramente mai in questa aria di pioggia. Si è
ravvivata—io veggente di colpo nella lenta schiarita—
una ressa là fuori di margherite e ranuncoli.
Purché *si avesse*.

Purché si avesse una storia comunque
—e intanto Monaco di prima mattina sui giornali
ah meno male: c'era stato un accordo—
purché si avesse una storia squisita tra le svastiche
sotto la pioggia un settembre.

Oggi *si è*—e si è comunque male,
parte del male tu stesso tornino o no sole e prato coperti.

I

Your Thoughts of Calamity

and catastrophe
in the house where you have
come to live, already
occupied
by the idea of having come
here to die
—and these who smile at you, friends,
surely this time
you're dying, they know it, and that's why
they're smiling.

In an Empty House

If they ever came back to life. They seem to come
back to life from room to room, don't ever really
come back to life in this rainy air. It has
come back to life—me suddenly a seer in the slow brightening—
that host of buttercups and daisies outside.
Provided *there were*.

Provided there were a story anyway
—and meanwhile in the papers Munich at first light
ah thank goodness: there'd been an agreement—
provided there were a story, exquisite among the swastikas
one September in the rain.

Today *we are*—and anyway we're bad,
part of the evil you yourself should sun and lawn turn overcast
    or no.

Toronto sabato sera
A NICCOLÒ

e fosse pure la tromba da poco
—ma con che fiato con che biondo sudore—
ascoltata a Toronto quel sabato sera

ancora una volta nel segno di Tipperary
mescolava abnegazione e innocenza

e fosse pure Toronto non altro che una Varese più grande

con dedizione mercenaria
                        o non mercenaria
in quel dono di sé lacerandosi puntava su un aldilà
non parendo da meno del grande Satchmo
disposto a suonare per gli spazi vuoti
niente meno che con una tromba d'oro una volta sbarcato sulla
    luna

purché resti un'abnegazione capace d'innocenza di là dalla
    mercede

e cosa significa ancora Tipperary
se non tutti i possibili aldilà di dedizione
al niente che di botto può
infiammare una qualunque sera
a Varese a Toronto a...

Posto di lavoro

Quei gradini dove fa gomito la scala, tutta
quella gente passata (e ripassata ogni giorno:
per lavoro) svoltando dalla scala dalla vita.
                                    Logoro
di quei reiteranti il tappeto in quel punto
a un freddo riflesso di luce. Sia inverno sia estate
                                      e là si fredda

Toronto Saturday Night
TO NICCOLÒ

and what if it were the trumpet just now
—but with what breath, what white sweat—
heard in Toronto that Saturday night

one more time in the scar of Tipperary
mixing abnegation and innocence it was

and what if Toronto were just a far bigger Varese

with mercenary devotion
                                    or not mercenary
in that gift of itself, self-lacerating, it bet on a beyond
not to be less than the great Satchmo
willing to play for the empty spaces
no less than with a gold horn once landed on the moon

provided there's still abnegation up to innocence beyond reward

and what does Tipperary mean still
if not all the possible beyonds of devotion
to the nothing that suddenly may
catch flame any evening
in Varese in Toronto in . . .

Place of Work

Those steps at the stairway's elbow, all
those people gone past (and passed again each day:
for work) turning from the stairs, from life.
                                                            Worn bare
by those reiterators, the carpet at that point,
in a cold reflection of light. Be it winter or summer
                                                           and there it grows chill

nell'agguato di un pensiero da sempre simile a sé
sempre previsto per quel punto
sempre pensato uguale
lo sguardo che là invariabilmente cade
a ogni giorno a ogni ora
di anni di lavoro di anni luce
di freddo—come sempre
là comincia un autunno.

Lavori in corso

I

Sarà che esistono vite come foglie morte—
la casa tra le acque
                evidentemente in rovina
quella lebbra repressa dall'acciaio
quei ragnateli di suoni domestici di appena ieri
(*e vuoti i letti umidi i divani le poltrone deserte*)
lasciala nel lampo del suo enigma
espunta dal traffico riproposta a ogni rotazione del Riverside
    Drive

non chiederti dove saranno mai finiti
non dire che la vita è carbonizzazione o divorzio
(ma strano che uno ricordi solo questo di una intera metropoli)

oppure inezie di un viaggio d'inverno nell'immenso—
il palpebrìo del jet nel suo orgasmo di mutante
quando è ancora e non è più
un numero-luce scattato sul tabulatore di New York

o anche quei segni dipinti negli atrii dei formicai—
foglianti epidemie su pareti piastrelle carte da parati
che ci fanno le piccole svastiche qui nel Bronx,
ce n'erano tanti—dicono—ce ne sono tra colombe e falchi
ma puoi anche supporli come emblemi vecchi motivi indiani,
comunque si biforchino in questo mezzo sonno:

in the ambush of a thought forever like itself
ever foreseen for that same point
ever thought just the same
the glance that without fail falls there
on each day at each hour
of years of work, light-years
of cold—as ever
an autumn is beginning there.

Works in Progress

    I

It'll be because lives like dead leaves do exist—
the house amid the waters
                      plainly in ruins
that leprosy repressed by the steel
those cobwebs of barely yesterday's domestic sounds
(*the beds lying empty, the couches damp, the chairs unused*)
leave it in the flash of its enigma
expunged from traffic, reoffered at each curving of Riverside
    Drive

don't ask yourself where they'll have ended
don't say life's incineration or divorce
(but of a whole metropolis strange to recall only this)

or else trifles of a winter's journey in the vastness—
the flicker of the jet in its mutant's spasm
when it is again and is no more
a number-light leaping on the New York data screen

or even those signs daubed in entrance halls of ant hills—
leafy plagues on walls, on tiles, wallpapers,
what are they doing, little swastikas here in the Bronx,
there were many—they say—are plenty among doves and hawks
but you can also think them old emblems, Indian totems
however they fork in this half-sleep:

drappi e stendardi calpestati in Europa
o l'ombra senza speranza dell'indio tra i grattacieli?
Altre sono in cammino nell'agonia o nell'estasi
nuove ombre mi inquietano che intravedendo non vedo.

II

A certi che so non gli basta
di volermi morto. Tale mi sperano:
morto, ma con infamia. Non sanno
che ho fatto di peggio che li ho
miniaturizzati nel ricordo.

Ma questi di qui sono foglie
inezie segni che lavorano in grande
non quei congelati in miniatura quei non addetti
bocche minime vocianti sotto vetro
—e avrebbero ragione se solo sapessero—
rattrappite per sempre nella colata
fossili nel cemento vivo.

III

Inopportuno futile intempestivo
lo spiritello di cui sopra.

Scatta e lo annienta un altro
battente diversa ala da laggiù
dal mare se mare è quel grigio
d'inesistenza attorno a Ellis Island
isolotto già di quarantena
sfumante in nube di memoria:
del giovane Charlie
Chaplin e di quanti con lui
in lista con lui d'attesa
bussarono alle porte degli Stati
con tutta quell'america davanti
presto travolti in quelle
storie sue prime d'ombre
velocissime

drapes and banners trodden down in Europe
or the Indios' shadow without hope amid skyscrapers?
Others are looming in the agony and ecstasy
fresh shadows trouble me that glimpsing I don't see.

II

For some I know it's not enough
to wish me dead. They hope for this:
me dead, with infamy. They little know
that I've done worse, have
miniaturized them in memory.

But these of hereabouts are leaves,
trifles, signs that work full-size,
not those frozen in miniature those incompetent
minute mouths clamoring under glass
—and they'd be right if only they knew—
shrunken forever in the cast,
fossils in live cement.

III

Inopportune futile untimely
the imp of the above.

Another leaps up and annuls him
beating a different wing down there
from the sea if sea it is that gray
of nonexistence round Ellis Island
once quarantine isle
blurring in memory's haze:
of the young Charlie
Chaplin and how many with him,
on the waiting list with him
knocked at the States' doors
with all that America before them
soon overwhelmed in those
first stories of his
about quickest shadows,

di emigranti sguatteri vagabondi
—e vorrebbero oggi rifarsi ricomporsi
con gli sbuffi di fumo del sottosuolo
sempre oro cercando i testardi
contro le vetrate spente
sul gelo sul deserto qui in Wall Street
una domenica.

    New York, 1967

Addio Lugano bella

quando nella notte ce ne andammo
BARTOLO CATTAFI

Dovrò cambiare geografie e topografie.
Non vuole saperne,
mi rinnega in effigie, rifiuta
lo specchio di me (di noi) che le tendo.
Ma io non so che farci se la strada
mi si snoda di sotto
come una donna (come lei?)
con giusta impudicizia.
      E dopo tutto
ho pozzi in me abbastanza profondi
per gettarvi anche questo.
Ecco che adesso nevica...
Ma io, mia signora, non mi appello al candore della neve
alla sua pace di selva
      conclusiva
o al tepore che sottende di ermellini
legni bracieri e cere dove splendono virtù
altrove dilaniate fino al nonsenso
ma vizze qui, per poco che le guardi,
come bandiere flosce.
Sono per questa—notturna, immaginosa—neve di marzo
      plurisensa
di petali e gemme in diluvio tra montagne

about emigrants, kitchen boys, tramps
—and today they'd like to start over, recompose
with the puffs of smoke from underground
always in search of gold, the stubborn heads,
against switched-off shop windows
over the frozen, the deserted here in Wall Street
one Sunday.

New York, 1967

Beautiful Lugano Goodbye

quando nella notte ce ne andammo
BARTOLO CATTAFI

I'll have to change landscapes and places.
She doesn't want to know,
denies me in effigy, refuses
the mirror of me (of us) I offer.
But I don't know what to do if the road
unwinds beneath me
like a woman (like her?)
with proper shamelessness.
                              And after all
I have within me wells deep enough
to throw there even this.
See here now it's snowing . . .
But I, lady mine, make no appeal to snow's whiteness
to its conclusive
                woodland peace
or to the warmth that subtends with ermines
braziers and candles where virtues shine
elsewhere tormented to nonsense
but faded here, for the little you observe them,
like limp flags.
That's why I'm—nocturnal, picturesque—March snow
                    ambiguous
with petals and gems in flood among uncertain

incerte laghi transitori (come me,
ululante di estasi alle colline in fiore?
falso-fiorite, un'ora
di sole le sbrinerà),
per il suo turbine il suo tumulto
che scompone la notte e ricompone
laminandola di peltri   acciai leggeri   argenti.
Ne vanno alteri i gentiluomini nottambuli
scesi con me per strada
                        da un quadro
visto una volta, perso
di vista, rincorso tra altrui reminiscenze
o soltanto sognato.

Interno

Basta con le botte basta. All'aperto
per tutto un pomeriggio ci siamo malmenati.
Finisca in parità.
Le colline si coprono di vento. Altri già
battagliano là fuori, la parola
è alle giovani frasche avventantisi ai vetri
alle eriche alle salvie in ondate
sempre più folte e torbide,
presto una sola deriva.
Questo sarebbe la pace? Stringersi
a un fuoco di legna
al gusto morente del pane alla
trasparenza del vino
dove pensosamente si rinfocola
il giorno da poco andato giù
dalle rupi col grido dei pianori
nel vello dei dirupi nel velluto
delle false distanze fin che ci piglia il sonno?

mountains, transitory lakes (like me,
howling ecstatically at hillsides in bloom?
false-flowering, an hour
of sun will defrost them),
through its whirling, its tumult
that discomposes and recomposes night
layering it with pewters   light steels   silvers.
Sleepwalking gentlemen go stately there
descending by road with me
                              out of a picture
seen just once, lost
sight of, searched for amid others' memories
or dreamed only.

Interior

Enough of the blows enough. In the open
for a whole afternoon we flayed each other.
Let's call it a draw.
The hills are enveloped in wind. Already
others do battle out there, it's the turn
of the young branches hurling themselves at the panes,
of the heather, the sage in waves
ever thicker and more turbid,
soon a single tide.
You call this peace? To draw near
a wood fire,
the dying taste of the bread,
the transparency of wine
where pensively the day
is rekindled, just now gone down
over the cliffs with the cry of plateaus
in the fleece of precipices, the velvet
of false distances, until sleep seizes us?

Crescita

È cresciuta in silenzio come l'erba
come la luce avanti il mezzodì
la figlia che non piange.

I I

Di taglio e cucito

      Il giocattolo,
pecora o agnello che rappezzi
per ingiunzione della piccola,
di testa forte più di quanto non dica
il suo genere ovino
è in famiglia con te. Il tuo profilo
caparbio a ricucire il giocattolo
e quella testa forte: paziente
nell'impazienza—e il tuo cipiglio
che pure non molla la presa
sulla mia vita che va per farfalle
e per baratri... Per ogni
graffio un rammendo, per ogni sbrego
una toppa.
      Quanto vale
il lavoro di una
rammendatrice, quanto
la tua vita?

Marzo, 1961

Growth

She grew in silence like the grass
like the light before midday
la figlia che non piange.

11

Of Cuts and Stitches

          The toy,
sheep or lamb you patch
at the little one's command,
more strong-headed than you'd think
from its ovine genus
is in the family with you. Your profile
obstinate, resewing the toy
and that strong head: patient
with impatience—and your frown
that still doesn't ease its grip
on my life which goes after butterflies
and precipices . . . For every
scratch a stitch, for every tear
a patch.
       How much is
the work of a needle woman
worth, how much
your own life?

March, 1961

Poeta in nero

Nera cintura stivaletti neri
nero il cappelluccio a cencio
tutto bardato di nero se ne sta
ritto sullo sgabello inalbera
un cartello con la scritta: *Ich bin
stolz ein Dichter zu sein*
muovendo le labbra appena.
Sono fiero di essere un poeta.
Ma perché tanto nero?
gli domando con gli occhi.
Vesto il lutto per voi
da dietro vetri neri
con gli occhi mi risponde.

Revival

Bella *L'Opzione* — mi saluta
svelto nel vento il piccolo ebreo
tornato a curare i suoi classici.

Bellissimaaa...
Ripetendolo in echi mi incoraggia
o mi burla
la balconata di cornacchie lassù
issata da quello stesso vento
nel gelido nel bigio.

Tra quanto resta di macerie
e tutta questa costruenda roba
in vetro cemento acciaio
bel posto per riunioni e incontri.
E grinte e sarcasmi da finestre a finestre
che non danno su niente
da facciate minacciate di crollo
da porte che non hanno dietro niente
mi sbalzano

Poet in Black

Black belt black boots
little black hat in tatters
all decked out in black he is
upright on his stool and hoists
a placard with the words: *Ich bin
stoltz ein Dichter zu sein*
barely moving his lips.
I'm proud to be a poet.
But why so much black?
I ask him with my eyes.
I'm in mourning for you all
from behind black glass
with a look he replies.

Revival

Bella *L'Opzione*—the small Jew
greets me, brisk in the wind,
come back to editing his classics.

Bellissimaaa . . .
It's repeated in echoes to encourage
or deride me
by the balcony of crows high above
hoisted up by that same wind
in the freezing, in the gray.

Among what remains of rubble
and all this building gear
in glass, concrete, steel,
fine place for talks and meetings.
And scowls and sarcasm from window to window
that gives onto nothing
from façades threatened with collapse,
from doors that have nothing behind them,
bounce me back

di venti anni all'indietro
in una piazza di Venezia
sull'aria saltellante del Terzo Uomo—
come di attimi a ritroso nel replay
scavalla lo spettro televisivo—...
                              ecco che torna
la pioggia
fredda sulla guerra fredda, la faccia
per pochi istanti allora amata
presto tagliata via
dietro un sipario di lagrime.

Sarà la noia

dei giorni lunghi e torridi
ma oggi la piccola
Laura è fastidiosa proprio.
Smettila—dico—se no...
con repressa ferocia
torcendole piano il braccino.

Non mi fai male non mi fai
male, mi sfida in cantilena
guardandomi da sotto in su
petulante ma già
in punta di lagrime,
non piango nemmeno vedi.

Vedo. Ma è l'angelo
nero dello sterminio
quello che adesso vedo
lucente nelle sue bardature
di morte
e a lui rivolto in estasi
il bambinetto ebreo
invitandolo al gioco
del massacro.

over twenty years
to a Venice piazza
on the jerky air of the Third Man theme—
as from instants reversed in the replay,
the television ghost's rearing— . . .
                                  here it is again

the rain
cold on the cold war, the face
once loved a few moments
quickly cut away
behind a drop curtain of tears.

It Will Be the Boredom

of the long and torrid days
but today little Laura
is really irritating.
Stop it—I say—or else . . .
And with repressed ferocity
slightly twist her tiny arm.

It doesn't hurt it doesn't
hurt, in singsong she defies me
looking up from down below
petulant and yet already
on the point of tears,
I'm not even crying see.

I see. But it's the black
exterminating angel
that thing now I see
agleam in his trappings
of death
and the little Jewish boy
turned to him in ecstasy
inviting him
to the massacre game.

Festival
IN MEMORIA DI L. S.

I tempi da quanto
tempo stanno dandoci torto?
Eccolo sempre più angusto
sempre più stipato di vetrine con
fiale brevetti manichini ortopedici
etichette adesive il corridoio
—e in questo la volata
au ralenti dove i nati per perdere
si contendono
la maglia dei fuori tempo massimo
pedalando all'indietro
lungo un muro di nausea
quelli che erano—o parevano—
arrivati di slancio.

Esterno rivisto in sogno

Mai più—tritume di reggimenti—
saremmo stati tanto uguali.

La spianata. Questa non è la pace.
Sarebbe invece stata
giostra di venti pascolo di echi
nient'altro che il vestibolo del tempo indifferente
comunemente detto fine della gioventù.
E intorno un sòffoco di spelacchiate alture.

Andiamo per gli uadi d'Algeria
a cogliere sassame per muretti a secco
di riparo dalle piogge di quell'autunno.
Saltati i gradi le divise in cenci
ritorna ognuno con un sasso in mano.

Mai più saremmo stati tanto uguali.

Festival
IN MEMORY OF L. S.

How long have the times
been proving us wrong?
More and more cramped here
more and more crowded with shop displays,
with orthopedic mannequins, patents, phials,
sticky labels, arrives the final straight
—and within it the sprint
in slow motion where the born to lose
are vying for the jersey
of riders beyond the disqualifying time
backpedaling along
a wall of nausea
those who had—or seemed to have—
arrived at such a pace.

Exterior Seen Again in Dream

Never again—shreds of regiments—
would we be such equals.

The clearing. This isn't peace.
Rather it would've been
carousel of winds, echoing pasture,
none other than the hallway of indifferent times
commonly called youth's end.
And all around the threadbare plateaus' sultriness.

We go through the wadis of Algeria
to gather some rubble for dry stone walls
as shelter against that autumn's rains.
All rank leveled, the uniforms in rags,
each returns with a stone in his hand.

Never again would we be such equals.

*—Niente pace senza guerra—si sporge
uno tra le file degli andanti e venienti.
Rieccolo l'addetto al fuoco dei mortai
il più gradasso di tutti di tutti il più fanfara
nemmeno fosse il capo
delle artiglierie di tutte le Russie:
certo Campana da Marradi,
esperto in cariche aggiuntive
poeta a tempo perso.*

La pace era lassù. In cresta di collina.

*A una fame di giorni
promette cena un casolare
col suo fumo sperso tra due schiarite.*

*Animo—ammicca quel signore della guerra—
tu coi tuoi fucilieri non lo vorresti
un rinforzo di fuoco?
Saremo a tavola prima che faccia buio.*

Gocce di altra pioggia pungevano la sabbia
della platea predesertica. *La notte
accorre sulla doppia fila
marciante negli opposti sensi.*
Lassù
per poco ancora
un'ultima bontà illuminava le cose.

Giovanna e i Beatles

Nel mutismo domestico nella quiete
pensandosi inascoltata e sola
ridà fiato a quei redivivi.
Lungo una striscia di polvere lasciando
dietro sé schegge di suono
tra pareti stupefatte se ne vanno

*—No peace without war—one leans
from the files of those coming and going.
Here he is again, the mortar-fire man,
the vainest of all, the most blustering,
as if he were the chief
of all the Russias' artillery:
one Campana da Marradi,
additional charges expert,
poet in his spare time.*

Peace was above. On the crest of the hill.

*A cottage with its smoke
dispersed between two brightenings
promises dinner to a days-old hunger.*

*Courage—winks that lord of war—
you and your riflemen, will you not want
some supporting fire?
We'll be at table before it grows dark.*

Drops of other rain prick the sand
of the pre-desert plain. *The night
comes running upon the double file
marching in opposed directions.*
Up above
a little longer
one last goodness illuminated things.

Giovanna and the Beatles

In the home's stubborn silence, in the quiet
thinking herself unheeded and alone
she breathes life into those revenants once more.
Leaving behind them splinters of sound
along a strip of dust,
between astonished walls

in uno sfrigolìo
i beneamati Scarafaggi.

Passato col loro il *suo* momento già?

Più volte agli incroci agli scambi della vita
risalito dal niente sotto specie di musica
a sorpresa rispunta un diavolo sottile
un infiltrato portatore di brividi
—e riavvampa di verde una collina
si movimenta un mare—
seduttore immancabile sin quando
non lo sopraffanno e noi con lui altre musiche.

Ogni volta che quasi

di soppiatto ripasso da Luino
sulla piazza del lago
schizzato fuori da un negozio corre
un tale ad abbracciarmi
farfugliando il nome di mia madre.
Faceva lo stesso anni fa
un suo fratello più grande
e come allora adesso subitanea
sbocciata da una parete d'argilla
a ritroso lungo la trafila
dei morti ci stravolge una mano.

in a crackling they go,
the oh so well-loved Beetles.

Her moment gone with theirs already?

How often at crossroads, at points of life
arisen from nothing under music's guise
unawares, a subtle devil,
a stealthy bringer of shivers reappears
—and once more a hillside blazes with green,
a sea's full of movement —
unfailing seducer until
he's overcome and with him us by other musics.

Each Time That Almost

stealthily I pass through Luino
on the lakeside piazza
spurting from a shop runs
someone to embrace me
mumbling my mother's name.
Years back an elder brother
of his did the same
and like then now suddenly
blossomed from a wall of clay
back along the line
of the dead a hand convulses us.

III

Un posto di vacanza

I

    Un giorno a più livelli, d'alta marea
    —o nella sola sfera del celeste.
    Un giorno concavo che *è* prima di esistere
    sul rovescio dell'estate la chiave dell'estate.
    Di sole spoglie estive ma trionfali.
    Così scompaiono giorno e chiave
    nel fiotto come di fosforo
    della cosa che sprofonda in mare.

Mai la pagina bianca o meno per sé sola invoglia
tanto meno qui tra fiume e mare.
Nel punto, per l'esattezza, dove un fiume entra nel mare.
Venivano spifferi in carta dall'altra riva:
                      Sereni esile mito
filo di fedeltà non sempre giovinezza è verità
               . . .
Strappalo quel foglio bianco che tieni in mano.
Fogli o carte non c'erano da giocare, era vero. A mani vuote
senza messaggio di risposta tornava dall'altra parte il traghettatore.

Un fiume negro—aveva promesso l'amico—
un bel fiume negro d'America.
Questo era il dato invogliante. Opulento a fine corsa
pachidermico
           in certe ore di calma.
                        Era in principio solo canne
polverose e, dalla foce, mare da carboniere . . .
Chissà che di lì traguardando non si allacci nome a cosa
. . . (la poesia sul posto di vacanza).
Invece torna a tentarmi in tanti anni quella voce
(era un disco) di là, dall'altra riva. Nella sere di polvere e sete

III

A Holiday Place

I

A day at various levels, of high tide
—or in the one sphere of the blue.
A concave day that *is* before existing
on the reverse side of summer, summer's key.
Of spoils only, summer's but triumphal.
This way daylight and key disappear
in the flare like phosphorus
of the thing going down in the sea.

Never does the blank or less clean page entice
for itself only, and specially here between river and sea.
At the point, to be precise, where a river flows into the sea.
Airs came on card from the far shore:
                            Sereni slender myth
thread of faith, youth's not always truth
    . . .
Tear up that blank paper you're holding in your hand.
There were no papers or cards to play, true. Empty-handed,
from this side the ferryman returned without word of reply.

A Negro river—the friend had promised—
a fine Negro river of America.
That was the enticing datum. Opulent at its course's end,
elephantine
               in certain hours of calm.
                                   It was only dusty reeds
at the start and, from the mouth, coal-trading sea . . .
Who knows if on arrival over there name's not conjoined to thing
. . . (the poem on the holiday place).
Instead that voice returns to tempt me many years
(a record, it was) from over there, the far shore. Dusty, thirsty
   evenings

quasi la si toccava, gola offerta alla ferita d'amore
sulle acque. Non scriverò questa storia.

Al buio tra canneti e foglie dell'altra riva
facevano discorsi: sulla — è appena un esempio —
retroattività dell'errore. Ma uno di sinistra
di autentica sinistra (mi sorprendevo a domandarmi)
come ci sta come ci vive al mare?
Sebbene fossero (non tutti) più forti rematori nuotatori di me.
Anno: il '51. Tempo del mondo: la Corea.
Certe volte — dissi col favore del buio — a sentire voi parlare
si sveglia in me quel negro che ho tradito:
«*Hai cantato, non parlato, né interrogato il cuore delle
cose: come puoi conoscerle?*» dicono ridendo
gli scribi e gli oratori quando tu...
Ma intanto si disuniva la bella sera sul mare
e sui discorsi sui tavoli sui recinti di canne
dove ballavano scalzi *el pueblo del alma mia*
si dichiarò autunnale il tocco delle foglie
confusione e scompiglio sulla riva sinistra.

Qua sopra c'era la linea, l'estrema destra della Gotica,
si vedono ancora — ancora oggi lo ripeto
ai nuovi arrivi con la monotonia di una guida —
le postazioni dei tedeschi.
Dal Forte gli americani tiravano con l'artiglieria
e nel '51 la lagna di un raro fuoribordo su per il fiume
era ancora sottilmente allarmante,
qualunque cosa andasse sul filo della corrente
passava per una testa mozza di trucidato.
Ancora balordo di guerra, di quella guerra
solo questo mi univa a quei parlanti parlanti
e ancora parlanti sull'onda della libertà...

II

Tornerà il caldo.
Va a zero la bolla di colore estivo, si restringe su un minimo
punto di luce dove due s'imbucano spariscono nel sempreverde

you almost touched it, throat offered to the wound of love
upon the waters. I'll not write this story.

In darkness among reeds and leaves of the far shore
they were debating: — it's just one example —
retroactivity of error. But how does anybody
of the left, the true left (I caught myself wondering)
how can he, how does he live by the sea?
Even if they were (not all) stronger swimmers and oarsmen
    than me.
The year: '51. World climate: Korea.
There are times — I said under cover of darkness —
to hear you speak stirs in me that Negro I translated:
*"Have you sung, not spoken, not put questions
to the heart of things: how can you know them?" laughing say
the scribes and orators when you* . . .
But meanwhile the fine evening fell apart on the sea
and on the debates, on the tables, on reed fences
where they danced barefoot *el pueblo del alma mia*
it was autumnal, the leaves' touch announced
on the left bank confusion, disarray.

Up here the line was, the far right of the Gothic Line,
you can still see — I repeat still today
with a guide's monotony to new arrivals —
the German gun emplacements.
From Forte the Americans fired their artillery
and in '51 a rare outboard's whine upriver
was subtly alarming still,
whatever was floating on the current
passed as a slaughtered man's lopped head.
Still benumbed with war, with that war,
only this made me a part of those talking talking
and still talking on the wave of liberty . . .

    II

The heat will return.
The summer-color bubble goes to zero, is reduced to a minimal
point of light where two take cover, disappear in evergreens

dando di spalle al mio male
—e io al mare—e sull'attimo
di cecità di silenzio si dilata uno sparo.
Chi ha fatto chi fa fuoco nella radura chi
ha sparato nel folto tra campagna e bosco
lungo i filari?
              Di qui non li vedo,
solo adesso ricordo che è il primo giorno di caccia.
Non scriverò questa storia—mi ripeto, se mai
una storia c'era da raccontare.
                    Sentire
cosa ne dicono le rive
(la sfilata delle rive
          le rive
                come proposte fraterne:
ma mi avevano previsto sono mute non inventano niente per me).
Pare non ci sia altro: il mio mutismo è il loro.
Ma il sogno delle canne, le canne in sogno ostinate
a fare musica d'organo col fiume . . .
sono indizi di altre pulsazioni. Vorrei, io solo indiziato,
vorrei che splendessero come prove—io una tra loro.
Una infatti si accende
a ora tarda
          lo scherno della luna ancora intatta
inviolata
          sulla nera deriva sul tramestìo delle acque.
Sul risucchio sul nero scorrimento
altre si accendono sulla riva di là
—lampade o lampioni—anche più inaspettate,
luci umane evocate di colpo—da che mani
su quali terrazze?—Le suppongo segni convenuti
non so più quando o con chi
per nuove presenze o ritorni.
—Facciamo che da anni t'aspettassi—
da un codice disperso è la mia contropàrola.
Non passerà la bandiera di tenebra e di vento.
Non passerà il richiamo già increspato d'inverno
a un introvabile
                traghettatore.
Così lontane immotivate immobili

turning their backs on my anguish
—and I on the sea—at the instant
of blindness, of silence a rifle shot spreads.
Who did it, who's firing in the glade,
who shot in the thicket between countryside and wood
along the rows of trees?
                              From here I don't see them,
only now remember it's the first day of hunting.
I'll not write this story, I repeat myself, if
there ever was a story to be telling.
                                   Listen
to what the banks have to say
(the banks' parade
            the banks
                        like fraternal propositions:
but they were expecting me, are mute, invent nothing for me).
It seems there's nothing else: my muteness is theirs.
But the reeds' dream, the reeds in dream persistent
to be making organ music with the river . . .
they're clues of other urgings. I'd like, alone suspected,
would like them to shine as proofs—myself among them.
One in fact comes alight
at a late hour
                the scornful moon intact still
inviolate
        on the black drift, the scurry of waters.
On the undercurrent, on the flowing blackness
others come alight on the bank over there
—lanterns or street lamps—yet more unexpected,
at a stroke human lights called forth—by which hands,
on what balconies?—I imagine them as signals agreed,
don't know when or with whom anymore
for new presences or returns.
—Let's say I awaited you for years—
my countersign's from a lost code.
It won't pass the barrier of shadows and wind.
It won't pass the call already wrinkled by winter
to an unfindable
                ferryman.
So distant, unmotivated, motionless

di là da questo acheronte
non provano nulla non chiamano me
né altri quelle luci.

Tornerà il caldo.
Guizza frattanto uno stormo di nuove ragazze in fiore
lasciandosi dietro un motivo:
dolcetto con una punta di amaro
tra gli arenili e i moli ritorna, non smette mai,
come ogni cosa qui
si rigira si arrotola su sé. Di là dagli oleandri,
mio riparo dalla vista del mare,
là è la provocazione e la sfida —
un natante col suo eloquio
congetturante:
confabula dietro uno scoglio sale di giri vortica via
triturando lo spazio in un celeste d'altura
con suoni di officina monologa dialoga a distanza —
un'officina liquida, un deliquio
itinerante
di sagra agostana in mortorio di fine estate —
                                                              e l'onda
rutilante, oceanica
con bagliori di freddo sul frangente
obliquo a invetriare sguardi e voci nell'estate tirrenica...
qui si rompe il poema sul posto di vacanza
travolto da tanto mare —
e vinto il naturale spavento
ecco anche me dalla parte del mare
fare con lui tutt'uno
senza zavorra o schermo di parole,
fendere il poco di oro che rimane
sulle piccole isole
postume al giorno tra le scogliere in ombra già:
ancora un poco, ed è daccapo il nero.

over there from this Acheron
they don't prove a thing, don't call me
or call others, those lights.

The heat will return.
Meanwhile a flock of new girls in flower glides by
leaving a motif behind:
sweet-tasting with a bitter trace
among shores and moles it returns, never ceases,
like everything here
it twists, it returns on itself. Beyond oleanders,
my shelter from the vision of the sea,
there's the provocation and challenge —
a craft with its speculative
manner of speaking:
confabulates behind a rock, revs up, spins away
dicing space in a deep-sea blue
with workshop sounds, soliloquizes, converses from a distance —
a fluid workshop, an itinerant
swooning
of August festival in summer-end funeral —
                                    and the wave
resplendent, oceanic
with cold dazzles on oblique breaker
to glaze looks and voices in the Tyrrhenian summer . . .
the poem on the holiday place breaks here,
overwhelmed by so much sea —
and the natural fear overcome
here I am even me on the side of the sea
making a single whole with it
without ballast or screen of words,
to cleave the little gold light remaining
on the tiny islands
posthumous to the day between already shadowed rocks:
a little more, and it's blackness once again.

III

> *«memoria che ancora hai desideri»*
> *dici che non l'intendi — o, se l'intendi, non ami*

I due che vanno lungo il fiume azzurri e bianchi
cosa mai si diranno? Allacciati o disgiunti
da anni li vedo passare
danzanti nel riverbero e nel vento.
Ritta sulla vertigine, estatica indugiando con lo sguardo
sulle colline prossime e più lontane rupi,
a dito segnando in controluce città
che forse furono e non saranno mai —
«Tutto questo,» dice la donna, «ti darò
se prosternandoti mi adorerai».
Ma l'uomo, ìmpari al sogno e alla sopraffazione
si disanima presto, non li solleva una musica più.
          E quasi niuna
di queste cose stata fosse, torna
lei quello che stata era:
un'ombra del sangue e della mente
e verso la marina
in picciola ora si dileguarono.

È il teatro di sempre, è la guerra di sempre.
Fabbrica desideri la memoria,
poi è lasciata sola a dissanguarsi
su questi specchi multipli.
      Ma guarda
— tornano voci dalla foce — guarda da un'ora all'altra
come cambiano i colori: di grigio in verde, di verde
in freschissimo azzurro.
Amalo dunque — da cosa a cosa
è la risposta, da specchiato a specchiante —
amalo dunque il mio rammemorare
per quanto qui attorno s'impenna sfavilla si sfa:
è tutto il possibile, è il mare.

III

> *"memory you still have desires"*
> *you say you don't understand it — or, if you do, don't love*

The two who go along the river, white and azure,
what'll they be saying? Entwined or detached
for years I've seen them pass
dancing in the shimmer and the wind.
Upright above the vertiginous, enraptured with lingering gaze
on close hills and further cliffs,
finger indicating, against the light, cities
that perhaps were and never will be
"All this," the woman says, "I'll give you
if you'll fall down and worship me."
But the man, unequal to the dream and subjugation,
is quickly dispirited, a tune stirs them no more.
                                          And as if not one
of these things had befallen, she returns
to what she'd been before:
a shadow of the blood and mind
and towards the harbor
in earliest morn they disappeared.

It's the same old theater, the same old war.
Memory forges desires
then is left alone to bleed
over these multiple mirrors.
                              But look
—voices come back from the estuary—from one hour
to another look how colors change: from gray
to green, from green to freshest blue.
Then cherish it—from thing to thing
comes the reply, from mirrored to mirroring—
then cherish my remembrance
for as much as it's uplifted here, dazzles, and is done:
it's all the possible, it's the sea.

IV

Mai così — si disse rintanandosi
tra le ripe lo scriba — mai stato
così tautologico il lavoro, ma neppure mai
ostico tanto tra tante meraviglie.
Guardò lo scafo allontanarsi tra due ali di fresco,
sfucinare nell'alto — e già era fuori di vista, nel turchino,
rapsodico dattilico fantasticante
perpetuandosi nell'indistinto di altre estati.
Amò, semmai servissero al disegno,
quei transitanti un attimo come persone vive
e intanto
sull'omissione il mancamento il vuoto che si pose
tra i dileguati e la sogguardante la
farfugliante animula lì
crebbe il mare, si smerigliò il cristallo
di poco prima, si frantumò
e un vetro in corsa di là dalla deriva
raggiò sopravento l'ultimo enigma estivo.
Passano — tornava a dirsi — tutti assieme gli anni
e in un punto s'incendiano, che sono io
custode non di anni ma di attimi
— e più nessuno che giungere doveva e era atteso
più nessuno verrà sulle acque spopolate.

(Che fosse in ansie per Angeliche fuggenti
o per tornanti Elene? Si potrebbe supporlo.
Ma non si creda — benché questo assomigli
a un gran male d'amore e se ne accresca a volte —
non si badi all'implorante dalle rive,
sa essere buon simulatore.
Di fatto si stremava su un colore
o piuttosto sul nome del colore da distendere
sull'omissione, il
mancamento, il vuoto:
 l'amaranto,
luce di stelle spente che nel raggiungerci ci infuoca
o quale si riverbera frangendosi su un viso
infine ravvisato, mentre la barca vira . . .).

IV

Never quite so—the scribe taking shelter
between the banks told himself—never been
quite so tautological, the work, nor ever so
troublesome among so many splendors.
Between two wings of freshness he watched the launch diminish,
forging off into high seas—and already out of sight in the turquoise,
rhapsodic dactylic daydreaming
prolonging itself in the haze of other summers.
He loved them, should they ever suit his design,
those in transit a moment like persons living
and meanwhile
over the absent the missing the nothingness that settled
between the disappeared and peering
the stuttering animula there
sea swelled, the crystal of just before
turned emerald, shattered
and a windshield advancing on the far side of the drift
radiated upwind summer's last enigma.
The years—he was telling himself once more—pass as one
and burst into flame at a point, which is me
custodian not of years but moments
—and nobody else who, expected, should have come,
no one else will come upon abandoned waters.

(Was he anxious about Angelicas in flight
or Helens returning? You might just suppose.
But don't credit it—however much it seems
like a great pain of love and from love at times increases—
take no notice of his pleading from the shore,
he's an experienced pretender.
He wore himself out on a color in fact
or better on the name of a color to extend
over the absent,
the missing, nothingness:
                        the amaranth,
light of dead stars that in reaching us inflame us
or such as reverberate breaking on a face
recognized at last, just as the boat veers . . .).

Tutto salpava, tutto
metteva vela sotto lo sguardo vetrino
tutto diceva addio sull'onda del venti di agosto.
Restava, colto a volo, quel colore
tirrenico, quel nome di radice amara,
la grama preda dello scriba
stillante altra insonnia dai mille soli
d'insonnia luccicante
dei marosi.

v

Del tempo che forse cambia discorrono voci sotto casa,
si estasiano del trascorrente argento
di chioma in chioma dei pioppi pettinati a rovescio,
altre venute dalla piana riferiscono
che l'estate è tuttora fiamma di miraggi,
non ha smesso una cicala o una foglia.
Esplode in più punti e dilaga la sparatoria dei clic-clac.

Pensavo, niente di peggio di una cosa
scritta che abbia lo scrivente per eroe, dico lo scrivente come tale,
e i fatti suoi le cose sue di scrivente come azione.
Non c'è indizio più chiaro di prossima vergogna:
uno osservante sé mentre si scrive
e poi scrivente di questo suo osservarsi.
Sempre l'ho detto e qualche volta scritto:
segno, mi domandavo, che la riserva è quasi a secco,
che non resta, o non c'era, proprio altro?
Che fosse e sia un passaggio obbligato? Mi darebbe coraggio.
Guardo la flottiglia riparare nel fiume spinta dal fortunale.
S'infrascavano un tempo qui i pittori
oggi scomparsi con parte dei canneti: i tempi
hanno ripiegato i cavalletti gettato i pennelli fatto le tele a pezzi.
Sarei io dunque il superstite voyeur, uno scalpore
represso tra le rive, una metastasi fluviale?
uno che sforna copie di ore lungo il fiume,
di stasi e turbolenze del mare?
Viene uno, con modi e accenti di truppa da sbarco
mi si fa davanti avvolto nell'improbabile di chi,

Everyone up-anchored, everyone
under the glazed look hoisted sail,
all said farewell on the wave of August twentieth.
Caught in flight, that Tyrrhenian
color stayed, that name with bitter root,
the scribe's paltry prey dripping
other insomnia from the thousand suns
of glittering insomnia
in the tidal waves.

    V

Of the weather changing perhaps voices talk below the house,
rhapsodize about the lingering silver
in fringe upon fringe of the back-combed poplars,
others come from the plain relate
how the summer's still a blaze of mirages,
not one cicada's gone or one leaf.
It explodes here and there and spreads, the click-clack's gunfire.

Nothing worse, I was thinking, than something written
with the writer for hero, I say the writer as such,
and his own business, his writing life as action.
There's no clearer pointer to imminent shame:
someone observing while he himself writes
and then writing of what he observes.
Always I've said so and now and then written:
sign, I've wondered, of reserves near run dry,
nothing's left, or there wasn't, really any other?
That it were or may be a necessary step? Would encourage me.
I watch the flotilla driven by a storm take shelter in the river.
Painters would nestle amid branches at one time
today disappeared with part of the reeds: the times
have folded easels, tossed away brushes, torn canvasses to shreds.
Then I'm the surviving voyeur, a cry
repressed between river banks, a fluvial metastasis?
Someone turning out copies of riverside hours,
the turbulence and stasis of the sea?
Up comes one with troop-landing manners and tones,
standing before me, wrapped in the unlikelihood

stato a lungo in un luogo in un diverso tempo
e ripudiatolo, si riaffaccia per caso, per un'ora:
«Che ci fai ancora qui in questa bagnarola?».
«Elio!» riavvampo «Elio. Ma l'hai amato
anche tu questo posto se dicevi: una grande cucina,
o una grande sartoria bruegheliana...». Ci pensa un poco su:
«Una cucina, ho detto?». «Una cucina.»
«Con cuochi e fantesche? bruegheliana?». «Bruegheliana».
«Ah,» dice «e anche sartoria? con gente che taglia e cuce?».
«Con gente che taglia e cuce». «Ma» dice «dove ce le vedi adesso?».
«Eh,» dico eludendo «anche oggi ci pescano, al rezzaglio».
«Ma tu» insiste «tu che ci fai in questa bagnarola?».
«Ho un lungo conto aperto» gli rispondo.
«Un conto aperto? di parole?». «Spero non di sole parole».
Oracolare ironico gentile sento che sta per sparire.
Salta fossi fora siepi scavalca muri
e dai belvederi ventosi
non mi risparmia, già lontano, l'irrisione
di paesi gridati come in sonno, irraggiungibili.

Ne echeggia in profondo, nel grigiore,
l'ora del tempo la non più dolce stagione.

   VI

L'ombra si librava appena sotto l'onda:
bellissima, una ràzza, viola nel turchino
sventolante lobi come ali.
Trafitta boccheggiava in pallori, era esanime,
sconciata da una piccola rosa di sangue
dentro la cesta, fuori dal suo elemento.
Mi spiegano che non è sempre così, non sempre
come l'ho vista prima: che questo e altri pesci d'alto mare
si mimetizzano ai fondali, alle secche, alle correnti
colorandosi o trascolorando, a seconda. Non sapevo, non so
niente di queste cose. Vorrebbe
conoscerle l'istinto solo standoci in mezzo,
vivendole, e non per svago: a questo patto solo.
A quegli esperti avrei voluto dire delle altre ombre e colori
di certi attimi in noi, di come ci attraversano nel sonno

of somebody who, after years at one time in a place
and disowning it, for an hour by chance reappears:
"What are you doing here still in this old tub?"
"Elio!" I burst out again, "Elio. But even you
loved this place if you said: a big kitchen,
a big tailor's as in Breughel . . ." He thinks on that a while:
"Did I say kitchen?" "A kitchen."
"With cooks and maidservants? As in Breughel?" "In Breughel."
"Ah," says he, "and tailors too? With those who cut and sew?"
"Who cut and sew." "But," he says, "where'd you see them now?"
"Eh," I say, eluding him, "They fish *al rezzaglio* even today."
"But you," he insists, "What are you doing in this old tub?"
"I've a long account open," I reply.
"An open account? of words?" "Not just words I hope."
Oracular, ironic, kindly, he's about to disappear I sense.
He leaps ditches, pierces hedges, scales walls
and from blustery belvederes
doesn't spare me, already distant, the derision
of places cried out as in sleep, unattainable.

It echoes in the depths, in the grayness,
the weather now, the no longer tender season.

VI

Just beneath the wave the shadow hovered:
beautiful, violet in cobalt, a skate,
fins fluttering like wings.
Transfixed, it pallidly gasped, was lifeless,
spoiled by a little rose of blood,
in the basket, out of its element.
They tell me it's not always so, not always
as I first saw it: this and other deep-sea fish
match themselves to the seabeds, sandbanks, currents
coloring accordingly or changing color. I didn't know,
know nothing of these things. I would like
to understand them by instinct, just being among them,
living them, and not for diversion: on these terms alone.
Those experts I'd have liked to tell of other shadows, colors,
of particular moments in us, of how in sleep they cross

per sprofondare in altri sonni senza tempo,
per quali secche e fondali tra riaccensioni e amnesie,
di quanti vi spende anni l'occhio intento
all'attraversamento e allo sprofondo prima che aggallino
freddati nel nome che non è
la cosa ma la imita soltanto.
                            Ci si sveglia vecchi
con quella cangiante ombra nel capo, sonnambuli
tra esseri vivi discendenti
su un fiume di impercepiti nonnulla recanti in sé la catastrofe
—e non vedono crescere e sbiadire attorno a sé i più cari.
Aveva ragione l'interlocutore, quello
della riva di là, che da un po' non dà più segni.
                                              Ma

—il mare incanutito in un'ora
ritrova in un'ora la sua gioventù—

dicono le voci sopraggiunte in coda al fortunale.

VII

Mai così fitto mai
così fittamente deliberante
appena fuori dalla foce
in tondo il crocchio dei gabbiani. Uno
si stacca a volo, tuffatosi
pesca un alcunché, torna al conciliabolo.

Sei già mare d'inverno:
estraniato, come chiuso in sé.

Amare non sempre è conoscere («non sempre
giovinezza è verità»), lo si impara sul tardi.
                            Un sasso, ci spiegano,
non è così semplice come pare.
Tanto meno un fiore.
L'uno dirama in sé una cattedrale.
L'altro un paradiso in terra.
Svetta su entrambi un Himalaya

through us to sink into other timeless sleeps
by what sandbanks and sea-beds, between flashes and amnesia,
of how many years the intent eye spends
on crossings and sinkings before they surface
frozen in the name that is not
the thing but imitates it only.
                        You awaken old
with that glaring shadow in your head, sleepwalkers
amongst living beings who descend
on a river of unnoticed nothings, bearing in themselves disaster
—and they don't see around them their dearest grow and fade.
He was right, the interlocutor
on the far shore, who for some while hasn't signaled.
                                             But

—the sea gone gray in an hour,
in an hour rediscovers its own youth—

say the voices come over in the tail of the storm.

VII

Never that tight, no, never
that tightly deliberating
just beyond the estuary,
the seagulls screeching in a circle. One
sheers off, diving down,
snatches a something, returns to the cabal.

You're winter sea already:
as if shut in yourself, estranged.

To love's not always to understand
("youth's not always truth"), you learn a little late.
                              A stone, they explain,
is not as simple as it seems.
How much less a flower.
The one branches into its own cathedral.
A paradise on earth, the other.
Above them both a Himalaya

di vite in movimento.
                              Ne fu colto
il disegno profondo
nel punto dove si fa più palese
—non una storia mia o di altri
non un amore nemmeno una poesia
                              ma un progetto
sempre in divenire sempre
«in fieri» di cui essere parte
per una volta senza umiltà né orgoglio
sapendo di non sapere.
Sul rovescio dell'estate.
Nei giorni di sole di un dicembre.

Se non fosse così tardi.

Ma tu specchio ora uniforme e immemore
pronto per nuovi fumi
di sterpaglia nei campi per nuove luci
di notte dalla piana per gente
che sgorghi nuova da Carrara o da Luni

tu davvero dimenticami, non lusingarmi più.

Niccolò

Quattro settembre, muore
oggi un mio caro e con lui cortesia
una volta di più e questa forse per sempre.

Ero con altri un'ultima volta in mare
stupefatto che su tanti spettri chiari non posasse
a pieno cielo una nuvola immensa,
definitiva, ma solo un vago di vapori
si ponesse tra noi, pulviscolo
lasciato indietro dall'estate
(dovunque, si sentiva, in terra e in mare era là
affaticato a raggiungerci, a rompere

of lives in motion soars.
                        At the point
where it became most clear
the deep design was grasped
—not a story of mine or others
nor love nor even a poem
                        but a project
ever in becoming, ever
"in the air" for you to be a part of
for once without humility or pride
knowing that you don't know.
On the reverse of summer.
In one December's sunlit days.

Were it not quite so late.

But you, mirror, uniform now without memory
ready for new smoke plumes
from stubble in fields for new lights
at night from the plain for people
who anew you disgorge from Luni or Carrara

truly disremember me, flatter me no more.

Niccolò

Fourth of September, today
one dear to me dies and with him courtesy
one more time and this perhaps forever.

I was with others a last time in the sea
astonished that over so many clear ghostings
a vast, definitive cloud wouldn't settle
over all the sky, but just a blur of vapor
put itself between us, powder
left behind from the summer
(there he was, we felt, everywhere on earth and sea
straining to reach us, to break

lo sbiancante diaframma).
Non servirà cercarti sulle spiagge ulteriori
lungo tutta la costiera spingendoci a quella
detta dei Morti per sapere che non verrai.

                          Adesso
che di te si svuota il mondo e il *tu*
falsovero dei poeti si ricolma di te
adesso so chi mancava nell'alone amaranto
che cosa e chi disertava le acque
di un dieci giorni fa
già in sospetto di settembre. Sospesa ogni ricerca,
i nomi si ritirano dietro le cose
e dicono no dicono no gli oleandri
mossi dal venticello.

                    E poi rieccoci
alla sfera del celeste, ma non è
la solita endiadi di cielo e mare?
Resta dunque con me, qui ti piace,
e ascoltami, come sai.

        1971

Fissità

Da me a quell'ombra in bilico tra fiume e mare
solo una striscia di esistenza
in controluce dalla foce.
Quell'uomo.
Rammenda reti, ritinteggia uno scafo.
Cose che io non so fare. Nominarle appena.
Da me a lui nient'altro: una fissità.
Ogni eccedenza andata altrove. O spenta.

the whitening diaphragm).
No use searching for you on further beaches
all along the coast pressing on to the one
called the Dead's to know you won't come.

                    So now
the world empties of you and the poets'
false-true *you* replenishes with you
now I know who was missing in the amaranth halo
what and who deserted the waters
of some ten days ago
already with hints of September. All search abandoned,
the names withdraw behind things,
and say no, they say no, the oleanders
stirred by the breeze.

                 And then we're back
to the sphere of the heavens, but isn't it
the usual hendiadys of sky and sea?
So stay with me, you like it here,
and heed me, you know how.

1971

Fixity

From me to that shadow poised between river and sea
only a strip of existence
against the light from the estuary.
That man.
He's mending nets, repainting a boat.
Things I don't know how to do. Can barely name.
From me to him nothing more: a fixity.
All excess gone elsewhere. Or exhausted.

IV

Traducevo Char

I

A modo mio, René Char
con i miei soli mezzi
su materiali vostri.

Nel giorno che splende di sopra la sera
gualcita la sua soglia d'agonia.
O trepidando al seguito di quelle
falcate pulverolente
che una primavera dietro sé sollevano.

Un'acqua corse, una speranza
da berne tutto il verde
sotto la signoria dell'estate.

II
MUEZZÌN

Dalla torre più alta
vuole ci si ravveda
la solfa del malaugurio.
Di quali torti quali colpe ancora?
Dice che Allah è grande
e a quest'ora della notte
in questa ora morta
io ci credo.

Luxor, 1973

IV

Translating Char

I

In my way, René Char,
with my only means
on your materials.

In the day that shines above the crushed
evening its threshold of agony.
Or trembling on the track of those
dust-covered strides
that raise a spring behind them.

Some water flowed, a hope
to drink up all its green
under the lordship of summer.

II
MUEZZIN

From the highest tower
it wants our amendment
the wail of ill omen.
For what wrongs still what blame?
It says Allah is great
and at this hour of night
in this dead hour
I believe it.

Luxor, 1973

III
UN TEMPIO LAICO

Dalla spianata con solennità
tra gradinate e portici
il falsopiano sale
verso i moscerini della morte.

Come si screziano d'oro
come lampeggeranno vuota eternità
dall'una all'altra riva
e così a lungo nella mente
lo strapotere la
destituzione il tradimento.

Valle delle Regine, 1973

IV
VILLAGGIO VERTICALE

Fresco di un passaggio recente
al dubbio di un disguido
risponde il villaggio verticale:
con discorsi di siepi
vaneggianti tra setole e velluti
scricchiolii di porte
appena schiuse rimpalli
d'echi gibigianne cucù.

Sul costone di fronte
un taglio di luce tra le rupi fa
di quattro sassi un'acropoli.
È a un'ora di marcia
al sole dell'altra provincia
la forma desiderata.

III
A LAY TEMPLE

With solemnity from level ground
between flights of steps and porticoes
the false plain rises
towards the gnats of death.

How they shed flecks of gold
how they'll signal empty eternity
from one bank to the other
and for so long in the mind
the overpowering the
dethroning the betrayal.

Valley of the Queens, 1973

IV
VERTICAL VILLAGE

Fresh from a recent journey
to the doubt of a misdirection
the vertical village responds:
with the speech of hedges
raving among brambles and velvets,
creakings of doors
barely open, rebounding
of echoes, mirror gleams, cuckoos.

On the opposite ridge
a slice of light between cliffs makes
of four stones an acropolis.
It's an hour's march away
in the other province's sun,
the desiderated form.

V
MARTELLATA LENTEZZA

A cose fatte pare
di averlo saputo prima
averlo vissuto già
l'evento
mentre ti precipitava addosso
quei tonfi da conto alla rovescia
quei clamori
esplosi nelle caverne del sangue.

A risarcire vecchi danni anni
di prostrazione il bacio
cadde sulla ferita.

Presto persino a me fu chiaro
che mi si premeva contro un giuda
o piuttosto una taide
travestita da boschiva rosa.

VI
NOTTURNO

Confabula di te laggiù qualcuno:
l'ineluttabile a distesa
dei grilli e la stellata
prateria delle tenebre.

Non ti vuole ti espatria
si libera di te
rifiuto dei rifiuti
la maestà della notte.

V
HAMMERED SLOWNESS

Now it's over you appear
to have known beforehand,
to have already lived
the event
as it befell you,
those dull thuds from the countdown,
those clamorings
exploded in the caverns of blood.

To repay old damages, years
of prostration, the kiss
fell onto the wound.

Soon even to me it was clear
that a Judas pressed against me
or rather a Thais
disguised as a rose of the wood.

VI
NOCTURNE

Somebody's plotting against you below:
the crickets' ineluctable
extending and the shades'
star-covered meadow.

It doesn't want you expatriates you
frees itself of you
refusal of refusals
the majesty of night.

VII

MADRIGALE A NEFERTITI

Dove sarà con chi starà il sorriso
che se mi tocca sembra
sapere tutto di me
passato futuro ma ignora il presente
se tento di dirgli quali acque
per me diventa tra palmizi e dune
e sponde smeraldine
— e lo ribalta su uno ieri
di incantamenti scorie fumo
e lo rimanda a un domani
che non m'apparterrà
e di tutt'altro se gli parlo parla?

VIII

Bastava un niente
e scavalcava un anno
una costa splendente
una vallata ariosa
viene a cadere qui
e s'impiglia tra i passi
negli indugi della mente
la foglia che più resiste — voglia
intermittente: Vaucluse.

VII
MADRIGAL TO NEPHERTITI

Where will it be with whom is the smile
which seems if it touches me
to know all about me
past future but unknowing of the present
should I attempt to tell what waters
it becomes for me between palms and dunes
and emerald shores
—and she throws it back onto a yesterday
of enchantments slurry smoke
or postpones it until a tomorrow
which won't belong to me
and of something quite other if I speak speaks?

VIII

A nothing sufficed
and leaped over a year
a resplendent coast
an airy valley
come to fall here
and be ensnared amid steps
in the mind's delays
is the most stubborn leaf—
intermittent desire: Vaucluse.

V

Verano e solstizio

Perché, tu che sai tutto di Roma,
lo chiamate così quel vostro cimitero
con quel nome spagnolo che significa estate?
(così — non lo dissi — per durare
porta la sua radice nell'estate
la primavera, morendovi).

L'estate di Roma ci stava davanti
con la più svaporante
la sua più mortale calcinazione.

Ne prendo nota — sorrise — te lo dico la prossima volta.

Risponde stasera per lui l'invisibile
cicala solista dell'ultima ora di luce
l'abitatrice delle foglie incendiate
di un troppo lungo giorno:
questo è *el verano* e il Verano,
s'infervora l'infaticabile,
questa l'estate di Roma di Spagna di dovunque
questa la primavera nell'estate,
rincara l'univoca la vermiglia voce abbuiandosi
in tutte le Rome di ritorno
di alcune estati prima.

Requiem

Stecchita l'ironia stinto il coraggio
sfatto il coraggio offesa l'allegria.
Ma allora ma dunque sei tu
che mi parli
da sotto la cascata di fogliame e fiori,

V

Verano and the Solstice

Why ever do you, you who know all about Rome,
call that cemetery of yours like this
with that Spanish name whose meaning's summer?
(so as to endure — I didn't say —
primavera bears its root
into summer, dying there).

The Roman summer stood before us
with its own most vaporous,
most deadly calcination.

I'll make a note — he smiled — and let you know next time.

For him this evening the invisible
soloist cicada in the last hour of light
inhabitant of leaves
burnt by an overlong day replies:
this is *el verano* and the Verano,
the tireless one enthuses,
this the Roman summer, the Spanish, everywhere's,
this the spring in summer,
darkling, the unequivocal vermilion voice rises
in all the Romes returned to
of various summers before.

Requiem

Flattened the irony, washed out the courage,
the courage done for, gaiety injured.
So then so therefore it's you
who's speaking to me
from beneath the cascade of leafage and flowers,

proprio tu che rispondi?
                              Oh i paramenti
della bellezza, gli addobbi della morte...
con un sorriso o con un ghigno
con che faccia di sotto a quella maschera?

Paura prima

Ogni angolo o vicolo ogni momento è buono
per il killer che muove alla mia volta
notte e giorno da anni.
Sparami sparami — gli dico
offrendomi alla mira
di fronte di fianco di spalle —
facciamola finita fammi fuori.
E nel dirlo mi avvedo
che a me solo sto parlando.
                              Ma
non serve, non serve. Da solo
non ce la faccio a far giustizia di me.

Paura seconda

Niente ha di spavento
la voce che chiama me
proprio me
dalla strada sotto casa
in un'ora di notte:
è un breve risveglio di vento,
una pioggia fuggiasca.
Nel dire il mio nome non enumera
i miei torti, non mi rinfaccia il passato.
Con dolcezza (Vittorio,
Vittorio) mi disarma, arma
contro me stesso me.

actually you that replies?
                        Oh the vestments
of beauty, the adornments of death . . .
with a smile or a sneer
with what face underneath that mask?

First Fear

Every corner or alley, every moment's good
for the killer who's been stalking me
night and day for years.
Shoot me, shoot me—I tell him
offering myself to his aim
in the front, the side, the back—
let's get it over with, do me in.
And saying it I realize
I'm talking to myself alone.
                        But
it's no use, it's no use. On my own
I cannot bring myself to justice.

Second Fear

There's nothing terrifying
about the voice that beckons me
actually me
from the street below my home
at some hour of night:
it's a wind's brief wakening,
a fleeting shower.
In speaking my name it doesn't list
my misdeeds, rebuke me for my past.
With tenderness (Vittorio,
Vittorio) it disarms me, is arming
me myself against me.

Altro posto di lavoro

Non vorrai dirmi che tu
sei tu o che io sono io.
Siamo passati come passano gli anni.
Altro di noi non c'è qui che lo specimen
anzi l'imago perpetuantesi
a vuoto—
e acque ci contemplano e vetrate,
ci pensano al futuro: capofitti nel poi,
postille sempre più fioche
multipli vaghi di noi quali saremo stati.

Autunno 1975

La malattia dell'olmo

Se ti importa che ancora sia estate
eccoti in riva al fiume l'albero squamarsi
delle foglie più deboli: roseogialli
petali di fiori sconosciuti
—e a futura memoria i sempreverdi
immobili.

Ma più importa che la gente cammini in allegria
che corra al fiume la città e un gabbiano
avventuratosi sin qua si sfogli
in un lampo di candore.

Guidami tu, stella variabile, fin che puoi . . .

—e il giorno fonde le rive in miele e oro
le rifonde in un buio oleoso
fino al pullulare delle luci.
                Scocca
da quel formicolio
un atomo ronzante, a colpo

Other Place of Work

You don't mean to tell me that you
are you or that I am I.
We went by as the years go by.
Here there is nothing of us but the specimen
or rather the imago self-perpetuating
for nothing—
and waters contemplate us and windows,
think of us in the future: headlong into then,
ever fainter postscripts
vague multiples of us as we'll have been.

Autumn 1975

The Disease of the Elm

If it matters to you it's still summer
look here how on the river bank the tree
flakes its more tenuous leaves:
rosy-yellow petals of unknown flowers
—and to future memory the evergreens
motionless.

But it matters more the people step gaily,
the city rush to the river and a seagull,
ventured as far as here, be unleafed
in a flare of brilliant white.

Lead me, variable star, as long as you're able. . .

—and the day casts the banks in honey and gold
and recasts them in an oily dark
until the teeming of lights.
                        It darts
out from that swarm,
the humming atom, hits me

sicuro mi centra
dove più punge e brucia.

Vienmi vicino, parlami, tenerezza,
—dico voltandomi a una
vita fino a ieri a me prossima
oggi così lontana—scaccia
da me questo spino molesto,
la memoria:
non si sfama mai.

È fatto—mormora in risposta
nell'ultimo chiaro
quell'ombra—adesso dormi, riposa.

                        Mi hai
tolto l'aculeo, non
il suo fuoco—sospiro abbandonandomi a lei
in sogno con lei precipitando già.

In salita

«Insomma l'esistenza non esiste»
(l'altro: «leggi certi poeti,
ti diranno
che inesistendo esiste»).
Scollinava quel buffo dialogo più giù
di un viottolo o due
alla volta del mare.
Fanno di questi discorsi
nell'ora che canicola di brutto
i ragazzi Cioè?—mi dicevo
scarpinando per quelle petraie—.
Proprio non ha senso
se non per certi trapassanti amari
quando si stampano per sempre in loro
interi pezzi di natura

with unswerving aim
where it most stings and burns.

Come near to me, speak to me, tenderness,
—I say turning back towards
a life until yesterday close to me
today so remote—drive out
from me the insistent thorn,
the memory:
it is never satisfied.

It's finished—that shadow
murmurs a reply
in the last light—sleep now, rest.

      You've
removed the thorn, but not
its burning—I sigh as I give myself up to her
in dreams with her already falling.

Uphill

"In short, existence doesn't exist"
(the other: "read some poets,
they'll tell you
not existing exists").
That comic dialogue descended
an alleyway or two
downhill towards the sea.
Do they hold such conversations
in the worst heat of the day,
the Y'know boys?—I asked myself
scuffing through those rockfalls—.
It has no sense at all
unless for some bitter passersby
when entire pieces of nature
are stamped in them forever

gelandosi nelle pupille.
                              Ma ero
io il trapassante, ero io,
perplesso non propriamente amaro.

Il poggio

Quel che di qui si vede
—mi sentite?—dal
belvedere di non ritorno
—ombre di campagne scale
naturali e che rigoglio
di acque che lampi che fiammate
di colori che tavole imbandite—
è quanto di voi di qui si vede
e non sapete
quanto più ci state.

Nell'estate padana

Campitello Eremo Sustinente
luoghi di fascini discreti
moltiplicanti l'orizzonte dei borghi
a passeggiate fuori porta
di sguardi e parole all'orecchio
tra gente incappottata ai primi
geli alle prime nebbie
a un sole timido in un passo d'addio

oggi nomi di spettri della calura
per campagne allucinate e afone
dove un amore dorme
acqua sognante acqua
a tutta quella sete.

freezing themselves in the pupils.
                              But I
was the passerby, it was me,
perplexed though not exactly bitter.

The Knoll

What there is to see from here
—you hear me?—from
the belvedere of no return
    shadows of countrysides
natural stairs and what waters'
bubbling, what flashes, what blazes
of colors, what tables well laid—
is how much of you there's to see from here
and none of you know
how much longer you'll remain.

Summer in the Po Valley

Campitello Eremo Sustinente
places of discreet charms
multiplying villages' horizons
for strolls out of doors
with glances and words in the ear
between people wrapped-up for first
frosts for first mists
for a timid sun on a goodbye walk

today naming specters of the heat
through mute and dazzled country
where a love lies sleeping
water dreaming water
for all of that thirst.

A Parma con A. B.

I

Verde vapore albero
al margine di una città.
Un verde vaporoso.
                      Che altro?
Vorrei essere altro. Vorrei essere te.
Per tanto tempo tanto tempo fa
avrei voluto essere come te
il poeta di questa città.
Con infuocate allora ragioni.
Allora incorrisposte (tu
che senza vedermi passi).
Non altro dire oggi sapendo
quel tuffo di verde
dolore fisso si fa.

II

Se dico finestra illuminata
se dico viale inzuppato di pioggia
è niente, nemmeno una canzone.
Avrebbe avuto voce se fossi te
anche per me una mia sera a Parma
e non
accovacciato nella mente
un motivo odoroso di polvere e pioggia
tra primavera e estate.
E se fosse una porta in vista di altre porte
fino a quella là in fondo murata
che prima o poi si aprirà?
Altro dolore. A fitte.

III

In dormiveglia di là da quella porta.
Succede. Qualche volta.
Che a me un altro di me parli

In Parma with A. B.

I

Green vapor tree
at the margins of a city.
A vaporous green.
                What other?
I'd like to be other. Like to be you.
For a long time a long time ago
I'd have liked to be like you
the poet of this city.
With passionate reasons then.
At that time unrequited (you
who pass not seeing me).
No other to say today knowing
that splash of green is
made fixed sorrow.

II

If I say lit window
if I say avenue drenched with rain
it's nothing, not even a song.
Even for me my evening in Parma
would have had voice were I you
and not
crouched over in the mind
a theme of scented dust and rain
between spring and summer.
And were it a door in sight of other doors
as far as that one walled up down there
which sooner or later will open?
Other sorrow. In spasms.

III

Half-asleep beyond that door.
It happens. Sometimes.
That to me another speaks of me

fin dentro di me.
Scendeva la vecchia tranvia
da Marzolara a Parma
fischiava a lungo rasente i Baccanelli
salutando te assente
diceva la certezza l'orrore della fine
ne faceva convinto quel gran cielo d'estate.

Torna a quest'ombra l'orrore di quel vuoto.

   IV

Divino egoista, lo so che non serve
chiedere aiuto a te
so che ti schermiresti.

Abbitela cara—dice—quest'ombra
verde e questo male. Evasivo
scostandosi lo copre con una
sua foglia di gaggìa—
                    biglietto
d'invito a una festa che ci si prepara
vaga come una nuvola
in groppa all'Appennino.

Autostrada della Cisa

Tempo dieci anni, nemmeno
prima che rimuoia in me mio padre
(con malagrazia fu calato giù
e un banco di nebbia ci divise per sempre).

Oggi a un chilometro dal passo
una capelluta scarmigliata erinni
agita un cencio dal ciglio di un dirupo,
spegne un giorno già spento, e addio.

even into me.
The old tramway descended
from Marzolara to Parma
whistled a long time grazing the Baccanelli
greeting you not there
uttered the certainty, horror of the end
and that great summer sky grew convinced.

To this shadow the horror of that emptiness returns.

    IV

Divine egoist, I know that it's futile
asking for help from you,
I know you'd look after yourself.

Hold it dear to you—he says—this
green shadow and this ache. Evasive,
moving aside he covers it
with one of his acacia leaves—
                         invitation
to a feast which is prepared for us
shifting as a cloud
upon the back of the Apennines.

Autostrada della Cisa

Ten years more, not even that,
before my father dies again in me
(rudely he was lowered down
and a bank of fog divided us forever).

Today a kilometer from the pass
a tousled long-haired fury
flaps a rag from the edge of a drop
does for a day already done, and farewell.

Sappi—disse ieri lasciandomi qualcuno—
sappilo che non finisce qui,
di momento in momento credici a quell'altra vita,
di costa in costa aspettala e verrà
come di là dal valico un ritorno d'estate.

Parla così la recidiva speranza, morde
in un'anguria la polpa dell'estate,
vede laggiù quegli alberi perpetuare
ognuno in sé la sua ninfa
e dietro la raggera degli echi e dei miraggi
nella piana assetata il palpito di un lago
fare di Mantova una Tenochtitlán.

Di tunnel in tunnel di abbagliamento in cecità
tendo una mano. Mi ritorna vuota.
Allungo un braccio. Stringo una spalla d'aria.

Ancora non lo sai
—sibila nel frastuono delle volte
la sibilla, quella
che sempre più ha voglia di morire—
non lo sospetti ancora
che di tutti i colori il più forte
il più indelebile
è il colore del vuoto?

Rimbaud

scritto su un muro

Venga per un momento la fitta del suo nome
la goccia stillante dal suo nome
stilato in lettere chiare su quel muro rovente.

Poi mi odierebbe
l'uomo dalle suole di vento
per averci creduto.

Be certain—someone said leaving me yesterday—
be certain it doesn't finish here,
from instant to instant believe in that other life,
from slope to slope await it, it will come
like a summer's return from the far side of the pass.

So the recidivist hope speaks, bites
in a water-melon summer's pulp
sees down there those trees perpetuate
each in itself its own nymph
and behind the halo of mirages and echoes
a lake's tremor in the parched plain
makes of Mantua a Tenochtitlàn.

From tunnel to tunnel, bedazzlement to blindness
I extend a hand. It returns to me empty.
I reach out an arm, embrace a shoulder of air.

And do you still not realize
—she hisses in the curve's roar,
the sybil, the one
who more and more wishes to die—
do you still not suspect
that of all the colors the strongest
the most fast
is the color of nothingness?

Rimbaud

written on a wall

Come for an instant the sting of his name
the trickling drop from his name
inscribed in clear letters on that scorching wall.

Then he would despise me
the man with soles of wind
for having believed it.

Ma l'ombra volpe o topo che sia
frequentatrice di mastabe
sfrecciante via nel nostro sguardo
irrelata ignorandoci nella luce calante...

Anche tu l'hai pensato.

Sparito. Sgusciato nella sua casa
di sassi di sabbia franante
quando il deserto ricomincia a vivere
ci rilancia quel nome in un lungo brivido.

Luxor, 1979

Luino-Luvino

Alla svolta del vento
per valli soleggiate o profonde
stavo giusto chiedendomi se fosse
argento di nuvole o innevata sierra
cose di cui tuttora sfolgora l'inverno
quand'ecco
la frangia su quella faccia spiovere
restituirla a un suo passato d'ombra
di epoche lupesche
e ancora un attimo gli occhi trapelarono
da quella chioma spessa
lampeggiarono i denti
per rinselvarsi poi nella muta
assiepantesi attorno
dei luoghi folti dei nomi rupestri
di suono a volte dolce
di radice aspra
Valtravaglia Runo Dumenza Agra.

But the shadow whether fox or rat
haunter of mastabas
darting away from under our gaze
unrelated, oblivious of us in sinking light . . .

You'd thought of it as well.

Vanished. Slipped off to his home
of stones and sliding sand
when the desert starts to live again
it hurls back at us that name in a lasting shudder.

Luxor, 1979

Luino-Luvino

At the wind's turning
through deep or sun-filled valleys
I was just asking myself if it were
silver of clouds or snowy sierra
things which still set the winter ablaze
when look
the fringe falling over that face
restored her shadowy past
of lupine epochs
and still a moment her eyes leaked
out through those thick locks
the teeth flashed
only to draw back into the woods
into the pack hedged round
with places thick with rocky names
with sweet sounds sometimes
from bitter roots
Valtravaglia Runo Dumenza Agra.

Progresso

Quei suoi occhi morati dorati dall'ultimo sole.
Di botto in fianco a lei s'è accesa
la città s'imporpora
s'intopazia si smeralda.

A tanto sfoggio dalla vecchia foto ride
il sogno del lampionaio
sghembo sul suo biciclo se mai
al solo suo tocco s'irraggiasse
simultanea a un secolo di luci
intera una città
e noi tutti quanti apparituri in lei
—bronco di fiamma ora
smottante giù nella sua cenere.

Altro compleanno

A fine luglio quando
da sotto le pergole di un bar di San Siro
tra cancellate e fornici si intravede
un qualche spicchio dello stadio assolato
quando trasecola il gran catino vuoto
a specchio del tempo sperperato e pare
che proprio lì venga a morire un anno
e non si sa che altro un altro anno prepari
passiamola questa soglia una volta di più
sol che regga a quei marosi di città il tuo cuore
e un'ardesia propaghi il colore dell'estate.

Progress

Those brown eyes of hers gilded in the final sun.
Illumined at a stroke beside her
the city is empurpled,
colored topaz, emerald.

At such ostentation from the old photo laughs
the dream of the lamplighter
askew on his bicycle as though
at just his touch were irradiated
simultaneous with a century's lights
an entire city
and all of us made to appear in her
—stump of flame now
smoldering down in her ashes.

Another Birthday

At the end of July when
from under pergolas of a bar in San Siro
through railings and arches you glimpse
some wedge of the sun-filled stadium
when the great empty bowl amazes
mirroring wasted time and it seems
that exactly there a year comes to die
and no one knows what else another year prepares
let us pass over this threshold once more
so long as your heart withstand those city floodings.

Selected Prose

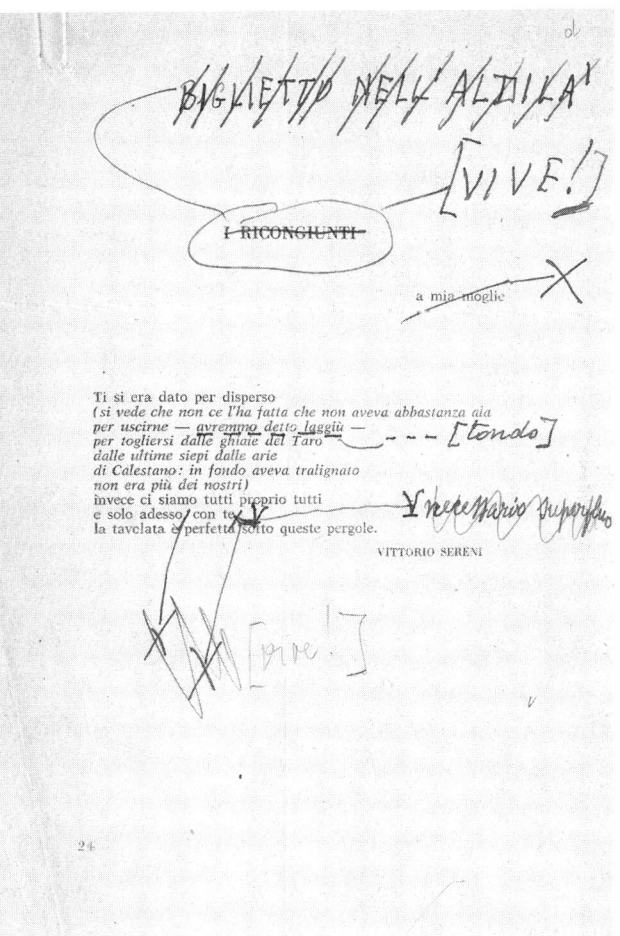

from *The Immediate Surroundings*

Prewar Letter

Parma, May 1938

In fine weather you can see him calmly going around, at the cinema or the café, on a bicycle or walking; somewhat less in winter because his health seems rather delicate (his detractors say in regard to this that he suffers from mild obsessions).

It's good to be drawn into the knowledge and love of a city, previously only a name, through the words of a poet. Recognizing it exactly as I'd imagined from reading *Fuochi in novembre* [Fires in November] (the title of Bertolucci's second slim volume, four years old now) had a certain effect on me. And he, who's probably not lacking in pride, must think of it a bit like Julius Caesar at the time of the prefecture in Spain: better first here than second anywhere else, in some sprawling city. That's another reason why you wouldn't call him a poet of risky evasions. His aura has formed itself among the aspects that surround him: it's as if it were bathed, drenched in the golden light of Parma. His is above all a receptive sensibility: it gathers and restores with extreme fidelity the gift of the air and hours. Certain things you feel here it's useless to try and express in a way different from how he has expressed them: at least that's how it is for me; he's already said it all. Agreed: poetry isn't only this. But in him essentially this is what it is, and enviably so. Perhaps it's also his limit. Is he any less mysterious for this? I wouldn't say so. I think of certain houses in the country where the quiet is instantaneously disturbed by the rustle of a curtain, by the slamming of a door, and the brief animation that follows quickly turns into something faintly obsessive. Bertolucci is spectator and interpreter at one and the same time of an analogous, barely perceptible event. (You want an example? Listen to these very recent, not yet collected, lines:

Once I was a narrow lane.
Invaded by grass,
easeful and rending silence
is my dying, bitter
if even from a high bough
the cicada takes up once more
its own midday song.

To this the author has prefixed these words of Seneca's: "O mors, quam amara est memoria tua homini pacem habenti in substantiis suis" [O death, how bitter the thought of you is to a man at peace in his wealth]. This will perhaps clarify better for you what I was saying with regard to that mystery of his, somewhat domestic, accessible. Think of that pure idea—unmotivated, one might say—of death approaching, at particular times of day perhaps, at the doorstep or a ground-floor window; of the penumbra where for a while the poet throws the mild and serene things among which he lives . . .)

As for me, I think of the summer getting ready to come this way: heavy and blinding. I know I'd be crushed by it, were I to stay. And my poet? He can hardly bear it, I imagine; but bear it he does, as you see . . .

Bologna '42

Bologna in the winter of '42 was a dismal city, virtually a city behind the lines, with a great bustle and variety of uniforms. There were units in formation or in transit for various fronts, but most of all people gazed, with apprehension and pity, at the poor fur-lined overcoats of the Armir. My memory is of many snowstorms and, even more, of the mud and the puddles around a barracks in Pontelungo. Spring blossomed that year with the new blue and amaranth flashes of the Pistoia Division, which was being motorized for North Africa. Without appearing to, the stay in Bologna prepared us for the disaster to come and, aside from the events that precipitated our posting, there was more than a presentiment in the air to sadden Bologna that springtime.

I don't know how always
a desperate murmur oppresses me
in your midday air
so spread out on the hills in sunlight
so crowded and smoke-filled down here.
And there's no flower of yours fails to express
for me the evil quickly gnawing it,
and no music at windows advancing

that doesn't fall bitterly back onto summer.
In vain beneath San Luca every road
voluptuously eases, I'm blind
and defenseless to your joy.
And gilded shadow brims in evening's pyre,
love grows brutal on the faces,
beyond townships the irreparable time of our
cowardice is fleeing.

Ljubliana

August 1942

The troop train is stopped at a station under a ferocious sun. They won't let us get off. A convoy of cattle trucks, sealed with lead, is slowly shunted onto the line parallel to ours and comes to a stop between us and the station building. All the more sinister in the dog days of summer, *carabinieri* in black helmets are escorting it. They are heading for Italy. But it's not the eyes of cattle looking at us from the wagons' gratings: it's the eyes of men and women; surly, burning. Nothing other than human eyes. They multiply and crowd, fixed on us with murderous intensity. Difficult to bear them, so compact, unanimous in their hatred, stronger than their impotence, than their desperation, their hunger and thirst. They were captured in the pacification sweeps. But for us only those staring eyes exist. We make a show of indifference, of softness even . . . But better, better that they take them away. We would end up hating them in turn. Out of self-defense, damn it! Isn't this how the massacres begin? We sense it obscurely, but wouldn't want, we wouldn't want to try the experience.

Cautiously the convoy sets off again with its burden of eyes. When the last truck and the last look have gone by, slowly enough for you to feel yourself branded, we're allowed to go into the station to change our money. I look at the sky and say to myself: Ljubliana. Dubious like its sunny name among the clouds, greenery becoming gray, whiteness becoming ashes. As a boy, hearing its name after Vittorio Veneto, I imagined it like this. Today the Italian flag hangs limply in the heat haze. I was forgetting that Ljubljana has belonged to Italy this past year . . .

Belongs to Italy so much so that when given permission to go into town until 18:00 hours (the troop train won't be leaving for Athens before then), they warn us to stick together, to do nothing that could be taken as provocation, not to trust the women. We wander round the town, buy things, drink enormous mugs of beer. In the street nobody looks at you, everyone avoids you. In the shops, they suffer—that's the word—our orders, put the stuff in front of you with manifest bad grace, take our money with distaste, refuse a tip. Very modern center, with large gleaming cafés in glass and chrome, completely deserted. But the churches, a mix of baroque and rococo, give a foretaste of the Orient. In front of the Military Headquarters are posted, one on each side, two grenadiers armed to the teeth. A lorry goes by loaded with a new burden of eyes, and the gesture of well-meaning mockery from the armed guard escorting them doesn't manage to quell this fresh burst of stares. A heavy atmosphere, in short, whose causes not one of us wants to go into, though everyone vaguely knows. We look around astonished. All the same, each feels human enough to expect to be looked at as himself, irrespective of the grouping he represents. But here that way back is blocked in all directions. We take a walk round the park of the enemy city. Boys stop their game for a moment as we pass. They exchange a few looks. Then they go back to their play. Meanwhile the afternoon declines and the light, gloomy by now, rains from a sky that's growing overcast, above the living green, above the flight of many butterflies.

We head back towards the station. The city closes itself behind us, in its dubious name. But there's nothing dubious about its welcome. We'll have the last beer in a large restaurant, where, strangely obsequious, they emerge, beginning with the red-headed girl who serves us. It's not so strange: we're a few steps from the station, they see us off. Or are some learning the art of collaboration?

Here we are on the troop train. The tracks run a while along avenues on the outskirts of the city. The colonel rubs his hands with satisfaction because he's changed his lire into drachmas at a rate of 1 to 30 instead of the official one of 1 to 8 (he doesn't yet know that at Piraeus you can usually get 250). Lieutenant T. speaks of the eighteen-year-old girl in a blue bathing suit he met at the Ljubliana swimming pool.

The blue of that bathing suit and the tender green of the park in the hostile city will lighten the darkness of a day off you couldn't take.

Sicily '43

The hands stopped at 18:30 on April 6th.

My looking, in defeat, with the eyes of the victor. And there's nothing harder and more tormenting, nothing that annihilates and robs a man of himself more, nothing that makes the defeated feel more defeated, than to place under their eyes the things of before, such as live and pass in others' eyes and for others' stories. Just so a loved woman gone on to another: she moves and speaks, or is silent, and still you know what's behind these motions and silences, but it's not the knowledge that all this is for another that pains you — or not only this — it's the feeling another is taking pleasure in them, reading and discovering there, almost as if he were the first, all you already read and found; or worse, he sees other things than you saw and rubs out your signs, to replace them with his own, on the blackboard that she is. For this is the virile form of jealousy, the offense that comes from the unfolding of others' possibilities for interpretation and action on a still-living, familiar subject.

In every war there must be a moment starting from which not only a light of defeat falls on the uniforms and arms of the side soon to be recognized as the vanquished, but the place itself that's the object of attack or invasion takes on lights and colors through which, in ways moment by moment more evident, it passes to another history from that country's, new accents, new breaths run through it, its skies already match a different flag, even before it's materially unfurled and hoisted into the wind.

Easy to say the others were in the right — besides, many who were supposed to be fighting them, deep down, were convinced of it. As if, so as not to be offended — despite everything — to the root of one's being, it were enough to know who was in the right, and it were not also necessary to bring one's entire physical and moral being to it, enter into it and walk actively with the right, to look with it and not allow it to impose its own eyes. Then came the days of inactivity awaiting orders and finally, all embarkation scrapped because of events across the sea, we were destined for defense of the Nation. It was a period of initiation into the game of death. That came, with no surprises; at regular intervals it flashed from the clouds or delineated itself on the horizon accompanied by a growing roar soon flown across, leaving fresh rubble, almost fleshly and palpitating, on the old and skeletal. Sometimes it was preceded by distant roars or by wailing sirens, hoarse now, as though worn out by too much bellowing, so as soon to be replaced by three dull thuds of antiaircraft fire. Other times, a flurry of white trousers from the direction of the Naval Command was enough to give the signal. But only rarely were fists raised with curses or to swear revenge. To compile the sorrowful, dismayed inventory of new losses, eyes erred here and there, some moistened by a secret instinct—not of disorientation, not of fear—brutally laid bare. With the signal sounding the end of the raid, a voice seemed to linger, more saddened and commiserating than anxious, calling for someone very dear and lost: just a burnt air of sorrow all along the marina, on the gutted houses, the knocked-out wharves, on the tangle of cables . . . Someone very dear and lost. And the evenings, the evenings, and the lamps and ice cream carts between vanished crowds relaxing towards the furthest wharves of Italy, and the chatter in clear weather and the seaside audience outside that theater, now in ruins with its rows of seats and boxes. Now not even the illusory phantoms of love were anymore at hand, and all that shimmered through the gashes was the incredible blue of the summer afternoon.

. . . that evening, when everyone had stayed to smoke into the small hours, in the silence and darkness, behind the battalion command post. Two hours of absolute silence, in the blackness punctuated by the brief glows of cigarettes, and higher up, by the few stars that trickled through the foliage. No one spoke because the news was dismal and everyone was imagining an ugly end for himself, with no alternative but death or capture; from Salemi the pocket was tightening around them over terrain grown definitely hostile, and soon it would close forever. That could have been an evening among friends in the North: people sitting in the garden to enjoy the cool air, tense at heart in actual fact—who hadn't wanted the war—ears to the radio dial left on for a late communiqué. The sense, in all its ambiguity, being absolutely clear, and hence dear to their recalcitrant hearts. And just imagine the coming mornings, for those back there, imagine what they'd be like, with refreshed minds, with joyous spirits, with horizons opened up at last. Perhaps at this thought came a rush of anger: towards that joy of theirs, about to be paid for with lives, or at the very least with humiliation and exile, his, and that of others with him there.

A telephone conversation between one strongpoint and another was cut off suddenly, and it was useless sending out a patrol on the tracks of the unknown saboteurs: the wire was repaired and the conversation could be resumed, unless interrupted yet again at other points along the line. A light flared in the middle of a night raid with the all-too-obvious purpose of offering a point of reference to those above. Rounds were fired off in that direction, men were sent to the location, nothing was ever discovered and so it went on, to the chagrin of all, on the following nights. During the day you bumped into impenetrable faces and if it seemed, at times, that a flash of malice or irony or even hatred was caught there, you immediately thought you'd been mistaken, no longer paid it any attention.

It happened as after certain dreams. A lost love, or another you thought impossible, or grievous, appear. Or else it's the image of someone unknown that suddenly, within the dream, dissolves to gestures and words so you can't help but love her. Not that at waking you run in search of her or anything changes, in life, because of this, but from the dream a piercing sweetness persists the length of the day and through it we're alive, through everything unvanquished that moves within us and is brought to light.

Within the perimeter of Villa Paradiso, in a building attached to the villa where the command post had been set up, a field telephone was manned by four soldiers in whose faces could be read a months' and months' old inertia. Everything between those walls was dusty and torpid and on one of them, as elsewhere in the villa, the words stood out: FORGET ABOUT LEAVE OR DISCHARGE — IT'LL POISON YOUR MIND.

Pin-ups of film stars and dancers hung here and there. Often, day and night, his duties had taken him into that room and each time, waiting for the communications, his glance had played across the cuttings. One, in particular, attracted his attention. An anonymous face appeared there against an uncertain background: intent, either to hold a gaze or because one has been withheld, lips half open, ruffled lively hair. And whether it was the light falling on the picture or an effect of the printing, it gave an impression of wind and sun among burnt stubble. It was—or rather that's how he used to picture it—youth on a hillside, a remnant of years long gone, crept in to witness their passing.

On the day of the attack, while the automatic weapons played at exchanging fire in that sector, having rushed in to report the situation to a superior, he found nothing but disorder and dereliction: the soldiers fled, the wires cut, the equipment smashed. Alone, hanging on the wall, the familiar picture. A breath of air from the open window chillingly animated the pin-up. Speaking as never before, was she complaining once more of being left alone or was she comforting, come running on the wind of those distant years, offering her mouth, the only moist thing in the burning heat of the day? What did it mean, that silent conversation between the man standing there in uniform and helmet and the girl on the hillside? Who won and who lost that day and what was the war's purpose? He didn't know and in truth never had.

Historical diary—They're printed sewn together. Each sheet carries the same headings: Forces reporting for duty in the morning—Sick—Fallen in combat, etcetera. Then, on each sheet, there's a blank space where the most significant episode of the day was to be described, the action . . . Dereliction of duty perhaps by the man responsible, there's nothing written here. Understandable though, given such a war. The men worked for hours in the burning sun digging antitank trenches, outposts, dugouts, worked overtime for this. Likely the day after they had to scrap it all because the calculations were wrong or someone had changed his mind, had to start all over again. And nothing ever happened. Once, a grenade had gone off in a soldier's hands:

Died following the unexpected explosion of a grenade with which he was imprudently playing. Laid to rest in the cemetery of the Marina at T.

This is what was written. Through natural piety.

Or perhaps not. It says "Laid to rest" not "He's buried." The one who filled it in has tried to put a trace of feeling into the bureaucratic prose. Perhaps he would have wished to say something else, to commemorate something else, who can say.

It's useless, we'll have to undertake this task alone. And patiently collect our notes for a work on Sicily during the Second World War.

. . . .
now that not distant cautious
the ambulances draw near the battle
and all of the bridges
have been destroyed
all papers burned
all the cup drained.

Algeria '44

Sainte-Barbe du Thélat, May

Now that the confinement has eased and settled, there's a kind of supervised freedom to enjoy in the immediate vicinity of the camp. The exercise periods take us out to watch regular games of soccer on regular fields, with goal posts, white lines, etcetera. Chanting in the afternoons among low hills and pools. We watch crouched down or half-reclining in the grass. Look at the extraordinary elegance of M., former right-winger for Modena, in his burst of acceleration and dribbling. Extending himself in long swoops with the ball at his feet he moves into the shadowy patch encroaching on the field towards dusk. I can see him hurl himself into the infinite on the heels of the phantom woman who is beginning to obsess us once more in the late Algerian spring.

Camp Hospital 127, June

Under an enormous tent we're laid out just like in a ward. At least once a night the cold or damp inevitably forces us to the latrines. A few nights ago I raised my head to the sky, rather cloudy around a flaccid and ambiguous moon. I was walking half-asleep. The half of me awake thought, "Perhaps tonight they're landing in Europe."

The next day I found it confirmed in the Oran newspaper brought into the camp. More newspapers, with increasingly detailed information, came in over the following days. Among other details I was struck by the Allied organization behind the front which from the very first day allowed them to clear back to England almost immediately, by plane, not only the first seriously wounded but also the bodies of the first fallen.

Postscript very much later

(For this reason, dear Franco, I thought of my "first fallen splayed on the Normandy beaches" as "borne up on wings." It seems he's been identified. A daring cameraman had him in focus. Realizing it proudly, he tried to claim his place in history, and ended up breaking cover. He was caught in the German gunfire. Saba, who'd read it somewhere, related this story to me, many years after, in one of his letters.)

Saint-Cloud, July

A high wooded hill in the shape of a truncated cone, like the Purgatorial Mountain, rises above the new camp. At certain hours of the day we're allowed to walk along the dirt roads that curve around it to the summit. The heat is intense.

"What awful heat," she'd said many years before while sinking into the grass of a quite different hill. "Why go on kissing in this awful heat?"

Saint-Cloud, August

Extraordinary clear nights—someone taught us how to tell the time without the need of a watch, by the position of a few stars.

Meanwhile the places of confinement are changing and with

them the numbers of the camps. 127, 131, 132 . . . The area is always the same, in the outskirts of the same town: a constellation of barbed wire.

Sidi-Chami, October

I am among the few allowed to return, unexpectedly, to a place we were sure we'd left forever. I mean Camp 131, at Sainte-Barbe. I was back there from June to July along with a few convalescents discharged from the camp hospital. I was anxious to be reunited with my tentmates who I knew had been transferred with all the others to 126 Saint-Cloud. The tents were still there at 131, almost deserted by now and half-dismantled. Even the tents remaining were unsteady, some pegs gone, some canvas torn, the drainage canals all but worn away. Now it was a transit camp where—encouraged by the season's uninterrupted fine days—nobody bothered anymore with routine details and scrupulous maintenance fatigues, as they call them on military service.

In evoking those days again later, it's Camp 131 rather than any other theater that is the ideal setting. 131 is where we spent hour after hour each depicting himself a victim of the others, each convinced he had the worst fate of all, and immovable in defense of this supposed preeminence.

There were fine hours too at Sainte-Barbe. That night when a concertina serenade moved through the camp awaking us, and I heard Remo softly crying in the next bunk. Another when the oil lamp lit by Walter, staying in the tent to cultivate his craftsman's fever, guided us back in the dark after a soirée with the amateur but already excellent camp drama group.

The same oil lamp from Sidi-Chami today guides a memory of a memory carrying me back to Sainte-Barbe.

Sidi-Chami, November

Odd how our captivity already has a history within us and we are already able to say: that time at 131 when we discovered how to make a rudimentary shower with a hole in a dustbin attached to a pole and regulated by a makeshift bung...

One year, soon two, let's hope that's enough. Perhaps having some memories of this life when we still can't see an end to it saves us from what the English call "barbed-wire fever." Saves us from it, or is a part of it? I think back to 131 and, seeing it inhabited now by only the memory of us, I wonder if pity for ourselves doesn't by chance go hand in hand with a previously unknown pity for the places that are deserted, now, of us.

Barbed-Wire Fever

In these places of exile and waiting, among this yearning community perpetually used to treading the same few yards of ground (reminiscent of sleepless mill horses), the rare—and for precisely this reason stupefying—appearance of death wasn't restricted this time, as it had been in two or three earlier cases, to a moment's disturbance on the surface of boredom and mutual estrangement. The victim was a person of regard, he was the poet—call him the *vates* even—of the prisoner-of-war camp. And it is no surprise that the dead man is more widely mourned here than any other mortal would have been. Because here the poet, like the philosopher, like the mathematician, seems to have had restored to him the dignity of a communal function, a lost high-priestly splendor. With great effort in fact, day after day, life has regained the upper hand over desolation and over the apathy of the individual who has thrown down his arms and raised his hands in surrender, prompting the formation of a new, rudimentary society.

And, to remain on more disinterested territory, it's curious how here men of the spirit enjoy an honor that is elsewhere reserved for them in much more ambiguous and exterior guises. To this extent the gradual progress of concrete relations and practical organization towards an ever more modern state, tending to reproduce the aspects of so-called civil life, is accompanied by the respect and near-veneration with which the community continues to regard the poet, the philosopher, the mathematician... Perhaps this can be explained by a basic desire to know, to increase one's understandings, or more simply to try and make use of the time forcibly lost. Here everybody reads, writes, makes notes; we have even got so far as to organize a regular pseudo-university course. But there is, there must be, a more subtle, less stated reason: and it is that, the initial period of stupefied animal indifference overcome, everybody feels spiritually refined, ennobled, open to meditation. The distance from home, the few frightening and discomforting pieces of news about what's happening in the world, the total absence of information about how long we will remain in this period of waiting, are our everyday sufferings. Above all, though, what tends to give substance to them contributes to the illusion of a solidity, an inner fullness. Suffering that's not intrinsic, not well-deserved, yet intimately overvalued, exalted: as if it were felt by someone who, arrested by mistake, ends up taking himself for Socrates or Jesus Christ.

From this unconscious presumption the interest is born. And that somebody should say certain things in all our names is socially worthwhile, bringing fame and authority to whoever takes upon himself that function. I remember him, the poet, diligently copying out his verses on the wrapping paper used for the camp's posted up newspaper. There, a brief news summary taken from the *Echo d'Oran* alternated with an article by the chaplain, or a note by my friend R. on the national sickness caused by the infatuation for walls and arches... And let's be clear about it: they were most worthy verses, occasional, granted, but in the best sense; the expert craftsmanship and sense of vocation were evident. Nobody would have expected such an expenditure of fine talent on so humble a sheet. They were all the more worthwhile, therefore. To the extent that they suggested a voluntary expiation on the part of someone who, so long enclosed in a sort of *turris eburnea*, had decided to make contact—intimate contact, ideal and practical at the same time—with the anonymous crowd. Perhaps a more gregarious writer, more prompted by a human interest, would not have been able to achieve it: almost as if imprisonment would last a lifetime and there could be no other public, and this the only possible climate.

Now that his tent companions have put his things in order for the time, whenever it will be, that they can be handed over to his family, out from his rucksack have come notes, annotations, fragments of poems begun, broken off, taken up again. And there's an invaluable notebook containing all his prison camp verse written out in a fair hand—some of which was already known to us, and other pieces that weren't at all.

The latter are not concerned with prison camp life, at least in the sense that they don't seem to have been occasioned by it. They evidently refer to earlier, though always with recognizable place and time.

This man must have been tormented by memories, he had the habit of always putting the date and place name at the foot of every single lyric. Faces, people, bygone landscapes . . . self-pity and pity for his past, for the hours and the meetings that somehow want to survive.

Yes, but these memories are not poetically felicitous: they do not stand out, do not reveal themselves, have no communicative force. And worse: there is an excess of sentimentality, a dangerous abdication to a vulgar poeticality, to the pathetic fallacy, to the emotive theme . . .

Quite, a sickness had crept into these verses. I'll call it barbedwire fever, even if it is inappropriate to use a term that comes from beyond and goes beyond the barbed wire of a prison camp. I can see now, in the light of this overall failure, with what gravity the poet had entrusted himself to the verses he had copied onto the paper from the wall. Earlier it had been possible to give him the benefit of the doubt: to think of a grace applied to slight events, granted to the provisional spirituality of his companions, perhaps slightly inclined to parody. Because everything of the camp was in them; and not just the sigh of longing common to all exiles; but the daylight hours, the confused clamor that routinely welcomed a whirlwind's sudden formation from the stagnant African afternoon air, the long faces above empty plates and cups on the many days of want . . .

An inordinate faith in life (I mean in its ability to transform itself directly into poetry at the point of highest tension) must have presided over this work: and therefore haste, a furious desire to speak, a desperate act of will. The familiar question arises: "What will be clear to those who cannot understand these references, to those who, in other words, have not had the same experience?"

But this time it will not be an accusation of obscurity such as has been formulated so often and so inappropriately in days gone by. If anything, it will be the accusation of obscurity in another, almost diametrically opposed sense: in the sense that the subject matter has remained as it was, inert even if densely concrete; in the sense that this poetry has not created something.

Meaning this: trapped inside here, we do not know what direction poetry is taking, perhaps haven't even wondered about it until now. Or else: hasn't it occurred to us more than once to think of it as a futile and selfish act carried out surreptitiously on the margins of battlefields?

Style, study, syntax . . . what funny words when everything shouts, "It's the big guns doing the talking these days" . . . Perhaps the poets are the first to feel this unease, and, within the more general war, wage their own war against it. Which is fought on two fronts: emphasizing the unease until it is suffocated in the repudiation of past certainties; and overcoming it (but this is much rarer) by defending the certainties.

Certainly, brutal and undiscriminating feelings impose themselves these days. And the dictionary reduces itself to a few words obvious to all. And style is no longer—except for the very few—a problem. It's the time of the anonymous voice, of vulgarizers: a noble, unmistakable cadence can quickly be applied to some immediate object.

Perhaps rhyme is back in fashion, in false popular forms, for the ease it provides once you've got used to using it; or else so-called free verse has lost its rigor and become truly free, if not, actually, uncontrolled.

Because this has taken place: facts have ousted images; four or five basic feelings have superimposed themselves on the imagination. Thus the unfamiliar ways of war—with their horror, their fear, their fury; but also with their courage, their faith in the cause, etcetera—fill, it would seem, many voids; or else they annul forms of fullness and complexity, replacing them with overwhelming realities evident to all.

External events have therefore taken over from men who seem more than ever before the victims of their destinies. And yet, by a curious paradox, it is not rare that they feel greater and more animated, the greater and more brutal the extraneous force that lives them.

Perhaps a centuries-old debate reaches a height of real itchiness during periods like these: and the debate between two opposite terms—classicism and romanticism; pure poetry and surrealism . . .—is conducted on a living and concrete terrain: namely, inspiration in relation to experience. The struggle—we all know—has never produced, nor ever will produce, a decisive victor. This is not, when all's said and done, a truth so certain minute by minute that anyone can take advantage of it when at work. No one can expect, in such a case, to regard things from above; he can only, if anything, mortally fear that one of his raisons d'être can be obscured by it.

But, to come back to our poet, it's clear that the above is said for him, to better define what, with a great deal of uncertainty and with strong reservations, I have called barbed-wire fever. It may simultaneously be a hypothesis (but only that) about work being done by everyone else thrown headlong into other experiences. If the results are aesthetically infelicitous, it won't be us who deny "to the worthy fighter the laurel's shade." Even if our lasting faith resides in the unknown poet who returns home without invaluable notebooks in his rucksack because he still dares to believe in patience and memory.

1945

That Film of Billy Wilder's

... The time has come for me to say something about what *The Lost Weekend* meant to me. I don't think it's an accident, first of all, that the main character is a writer. On the other hand, the general public imagines writers differently. There he is, the actor Ray Milland, part good-looking youth, part handsome man, who gets drunk, sees various forms of Paradise in the bottom of a glass, laughs oddly at the squeak of a mouse, and the laugh becomes a scream as a bat hurls itself upon the mouse and the wall is lined with blood. It's always rather shocking to see something clear and full of life cloud over, start to crack, from delirium, out of something gone astray that escapes from the depths with a violence that suggests long compression. During the film I never once forgot that the main character is a writer, even though the actor's physique, his ways, belied the popular image of the writer... just as it's difficult to imagine an alcoholic with Ray Milland's physique. And, meanwhile, via the actor, an interdependence was being created between the writer and the alcoholic. Am I writing, in another register, what the film had already suggested to me through its own intrinsic force? Pity for the man reached the writer via the alcoholic: a lost illusion, still evident in the healthy young man's face, still innocent in its own way; evidence of a generic taste for life, altered, virtually wrecked by an initial misunderstanding, the force of life misplaced in a chosen vocation, or—if you prefer—displaced into a different vocation, precisely that of the self-styled writer. At no time—in the bar, on the staircase at home, on the dance floor, in the clinic for alcoholics— did people or things not seem to show pity for the waste, the human wreckage; no moment when hands did not seem to be outstretched to help him back onto the road, back into the role of one of "life's elect." The contrast was almost too stark, between the appearance of uncorrupted youth and the inner, intimate corruption of the hero. In the uncontrollable, the shameless vice of drinking—as it happens, alcoholism, but it could have been something else—I felt the presence of another vice, more deeply rooted within him, an even more intractable, ruinous error. In the popular, mocking phrase, people are supposed to "drink to forget"; or else some nonsense is spoken about poets drinking to get inspiration. He, on the other hand, drinks (the actual vice, the form it takes—I say—could have been different, it doesn't matter)—let me put it this way—to make up for something. For what? For the drying up of the flow of vitality within him, which had deceived him, misled him from the very beginning, into choosing the role of writer. Isn't it precisely this that happens every day when someone, mistaken about his own life force, the promptness of his reactions, the acute nature of his feelings, takes upon himself this role? (And perhaps a great deal could be said about the objective conditions of life today, not ones that accommodate or encourage these qualities and gifts, which are exquisitely human qualities and gifts, to grow and prosper in the context of human relations. Philosophers might explain this to us, or perhaps—taking them with the necessary pinch of salt—politicians.)

The film showed the process of decay at an advanced stage, long after the initial phase in which the vitality of the writer is directed into his work or, more generally, towards an art, this energy being enough for both man and writer. Now his self-doubt and doubt about his presumed vocation have become dramatic, and what remains—the artist unable to write and nauseated by creative work—is the stimulus towards those states, emotions, delights, those poisons that are often deadened by the practice, ambition and illusion of art. Drinking is what remains—the outer sign of a psychic cloak, a tension he's unable to renounce because it has become his only way of feeling himself alive. It's the most apparent sign of a most secret vice. It's the metamorphosis of energy into evil, fallen upon the very life of someone who from the outset deceived himself about that energy and how to use it. Towards it, he had pointed exclusively so as to get from it personality and freedom, a human face: to exist and act, with features well individuated, among his fellow creatures. This was the error; this the vice. And this the conclusion: you cannot ask your work (as a writer or artist) to solve life's problems for you; nothing in one's life is summed up or concluded in the work, nothing is absolved or has its full sense there.

This, for goodness sake, is not the story of *The Lost Weekend*. Its action—relating to a failed writer and impenitent drunk—takes place with a different force of persuasion and with different shivers along the spine, with a typewriter that obstinately remains silent and a glass forever full and forever empty, reminiscent of the Danaides' punishment. That doesn't change the fact that the film had this to say to me, in cinematic language, this to bring to mind, or clarify for me. I would call it an allegory, if the term didn't seem to indicate something unduly mechanical, too premeditated for the actual vigor of the film. There is a hint of this intention, if not of the allegory; as for the conclusion, implicit but nonetheless rather arbitrarily arrived at through personal identification, I wouldn't even have thought of it had I not seen it spilling over from somewhere else, I mean from *Sunset Boulevard*. What makes the latest film by Wilder rather sluggish and heavy, if not his fidelity to the original intention, the remote and, before that, rather debatable content of *The Lost Weekend*? Inevitably, his world has shrunk to that of the film studios. His characters are a screenplay writer, an actress past her prime, a former film director, a current film director . . . yesterday the writer, today film artists. And the issue is not so much the sad one of the love affair between the screenwriter and the decayed actress. Rather, it's of that obstinate illusion of hers about giving her life a meaning (and so having the right to love) through the memory of her art: "Stars," Gloria Swanson says, with evident double meaning, "are ageless."

Them too? The filmmakers have reached this point too? So soon? And just think of the completely different direction cinema was taking not so long ago. We were caught between an idea of the cinema as not so different from nature, and the suspicion that the best results are to be had only through a sensibility strongly inflected with technical skills. We went looking for stories told intensely and transparently, restoring the sense of the most direct forms of creativity, a taste for characters, for action. These were characteristics that novels seem all the more to have abandoned. Regretting it, many readers would look for them by going back to nineteenth-century writers with renewed passion, writers such as—let's think—Conrad, Stevenson. At the cinema, it was rare when reflecting about the style of the director to consider anything other than his touch, so to speak, or his eye. I was saying something earlier about coherence, about an intimate continuity, something decidedly spiritual... terms we would previously have used with the greatest care and not a little perplexity in connection with a film director. With Wilder, the cinema has, in this sense, moved terribly quickly. It has reached its own autobiography: the conflict between man and artist, the illusion of art (cinematic or whatever), the problems and interests of the artist as such, which have more or less directly influenced so much creative literature and curtailed its vitality, are now knowingly and not by chance the subject of these films.

Bad sign? Perhaps for Billy Wilder's future work. It's a good sign in general, I dare say. Sign at least that we'll be able to speak more assuredly of content, we who in literature are taken perhaps for formalists. To someone who understands nothing of close-ups, fade-outs, and other such tricks of the trade, the best argument in favor of film today, and against certain suspicious-minded prejudiced friends, is provided by a director who doesn't merely dress up a screenplay, but gives us his whole presence, his human substance. Then the subject of the film is intimately his own—its quality, accent, and the position that those contents acquire in the work. There are not many examples of it yet, not to be confused with the many cases where intentions, self-evident in the contents, barely keep pace with the formal expertise, and vice versa; so that one intention too plainly stands out from the others, has too evidently been superimposed...

1951

Airs of '53–'55

... and it can be said that youth is the only legitimate bridge between the bourgeois world and nature.

THOMAS MANN, *DOCTOR FAUSTUS*

The city could be Milan, were it not for the lights of the funicular railway that, at night, show the height of the hills to the south and east. So it could be Como or Lugano or Lucerne, for example, but it's much bigger. The city is staging a peace conference. Or rather: as everyone knows, even though no one says so, if the conference fails, another war could come. The negotiations have been going on for a few days and nothing has leaked out, but there's no one waiting at the entrance, anonymous and far from the city center, of the conference building. Our country knows almost nothing about wars, except for the refugees and spies to whom it has on many occasions provided hospitality.

These pre-Easter evenings the traffic disappears quite suddenly, leaving the streets almost empty. This evening I have an appointment with G., inside the recently reopened Great Exhibition. It's a rather vague appointment, somewhere near the flaming torches an oil company keeps burning each year high up above its pavilion. I walk around the swimming pool, with the rubber seals, a few dinghies, balls for water games, where, during the day, some men are paid to plunge in, dressed in diving suits, masks and flippers, whatever the weather, as if they were going fishing. In a deserted alleyway I run into O. S., an old comrade from the Conservatory I lost sight of during the war. He introduces me to his son, aged twelve, dressed like a sailor, a throwback, whistle in his pocket, high collar and anchors, hair neatly parted.

"How's the music going?" I was on the point of asking, stopping myself just in time to avoid being exposed to the same question. On the apron of the service station forecourt, no sign of G. That lunatic will be looking at the four huge flames in the darkness from somewhere else in the Exhibition. Soon they'll go out. In fact they go out and that means it's eleven in the evening. I take a few more steps and am about to leave when a neon sign beckons me towards the entrance to the Music Hall.

The suffocated sounds of a nighttime campsite that the Exhibition becomes at this hour are replaced by a subterranean tem-

300

pest of noises in crescendo, soon suffocated by clapping and whistling, but then the silence returns followed by wailing trumpets, a new tune, very slow. I've stumbled into a jazz concert. The seats are all taken, a few spectators standing, along the sides or at the back. As for the music, here or in some glittering ballroom at New Year or during carnival, it's all the same. The sounds spreading among the archways, the echoes and rumbling are those of a crowded ballroom, a huge nighttime gala: they imitate hanging gardens, nights on the sea or the edges of large swimming pools, but they lead back to the ballroom, its atmosphere and circumstances. I follow a handrail to one side of medium height. Here I can begin to see people's faces. I recognize some, lost sight of many years ago, since I moved to the other side of the city, people who went out of my existence more than if they'd died. The orchestra has a famous name but I couldn't distinguish it from a decent ballroom band. I notice people I wouldn't expect to find here. There's a couple already getting on in years, with no children. There's the little German from downstairs I call Wehrmacht, leaving him speechless every time, and there's the girl I used to call New York back when I was reading Dos Passos, making her parents suspicious and perhaps actually offending them. There's the old retired official with a milk bottle in his basket that I'd often meet in Via S. Ecstatic, absorbed, moved to tears, looking at each other, smilingly, knowingly, discrete, like the expressions of believers at mass or during other religious ceremonies. I see inspired, adoring faces. I also see G., but make no move to catch his attention. Now the music changes, no longer evokes dancing and its sanctuaries. It projects a city's hours and events, porticoes under a sudden burst of rain, terraces with flowers on top of skyscrapers, illuminated clock faces, crowds and traffic, traffic and crowds, streets where the summer explodes in feminine garb, a woman's springy step, shops, aquariums, fishmongers. Then there's a tunnel, overhead railway lines cutting the city into segments and then crowds and rain, raincoats and rain, troops on parade, headlights, chimney stacks, stadiums, gasholders, the nine o'clock plane with flashing lights. Then there's a lone man at a piano, playing in candlelight, nodding his head, who knows if to the rhythm of the tune he has in mind while playing, or to someone who's there and not there behind an opaque curtain moved by the wind. And below there's the estuary of a big river with the tugs' desperate horns. Then there are paddle steamers on an even bigger river and the snow on this river or gusting against the windows of a chalet halfway up the mountain. And then there's the fog and rice fields and a train traveling at dawn on the outskirts of the city, triumphing over the embankments between apartment blocks and factories . . .

"Any idea," I say to G., who meanwhile has come over, "any idea what all these people are doing here, at a jazz concert, on the Thursday evening before Good Friday? The sort of people you'd expect to see in church to hear mass and the sermon, if you ever set foot in there?"

G. has other things on his mind, perhaps he's waiting for someone and his eyes are searching round. Or he's taken by the music, like everyone else. No, no, for sure he's waiting for someone, with me. Because, now I realize, I too am waiting for someone, not something, someone, man or woman it doesn't matter, someone very important for me, who has to arrive.

"How," I whisper again in G.'s ear, "can a jazz concert be the meeting place for such different kinds of people? A place with such cohesive force, where everyone's waiting for someone or something? More than the church? More than a party conference? More than a public holiday? More than Labor Day? More than the Conservatory? More . . ."

"More than the cemetery," says G. with a grin. "Give it a break, let's go."

It's late, but neither the orchestra nor the public seems to want to go. There's hardly time anymore for the applause. One tune ends and another starts up, the clapping gets muddled with the music.

Finally G., with a push, manages to get me out of there.

We go up a hill road, under an inoffensive rain, here and there, between the blossoming peaches. With us are two rather plain girls that G. picked up just outside the concert. They pretend, poor souls, poor sex, to fend off G. and his blandishments. Something must have gone down the wrong way for G., an appointment he maybe had in the jazz hall, at the same time as the one with me. But didn't we expect something different, didn't I? G. doesn't pay me any attention. He wants to win back his losses, it doesn't matter how, dragging me into this improvised game of four players.

"I'm tired," I tell him, "dead tired."

"You can have the prettier one," he says, to no effect.

"The less ugly, you mean," I say.

I leave them at the first turning and find myself in bed, clothes off, tucked up, in a room with no windows, with just a slit, high up, very high up, in the wall. Here, I have a dream. The sky in the foreign town fills with clouds. It's going to rain. You say you'll have a bad evening and a worse night after deciding not to stay with them. The separation is intolerable already. So be it. My train is now traveling over the plain. I'm alone. I raise my eyes to the mountain. There's a tiny train struggling upward, it disappears and reappears again after various tunnels halfway up. I've no doubt it all makes sense: it's your train. I follow it with my eyes as far as I can. I'm sure you don't for one moment think of looking down here, of sharing this thought. Don't say you're not an expert in spatial and temporal relations. For me it's mathematical proof that you have already forgotten me.

If waking means this: a city band playing in a square with flowers, while you go looking in the large flower market for someone who won't come, or is there and doesn't recognize you, and the band keeps playing; or some proletarian weddings in an uncertain morning, no less squalid than a bourgeois wedding because proletarian and bourgeois weddings have this in common, there's the bourgeois wedding squalor and the pale face of the bride, the cold light on the bride's dress after the wedding, which rains down memories of many other marriages gone wrong; or there's the leaden sky foreboding a storm that won't arrive and school is over, the grades pinned to the notice board: some passed, some failed, that's that, and it's irremediably summer—if this is waking into the day that enters through the slit, better roll over and go back to sleep.

Later you're outside the house in the hills, it's a sunny day, a silent Good Friday, broken at midday by the noisy rattles kids shake as far as up here—but you didn't hear them. You look down and plainly see the outlines of the players in the stadium. The game's already begun. If you like you could watch it from up here, the action plainly visible. Instead you're falling headlong and someone you bump into teasingly asks if you're running to see the serving girls. You get it when you're already at the match and remember that today your favorite team's playing Servette. You feel a twinge of pity for them, such good players until two months ago, and now resigned in their faded pink jerseys, come all the way from Geneva knowing they'll get hammered . . . There are no barriers round the field because people here don't know what support is. They stand or sit, commenting vaguely on the game. Where the hell are you lot?—you cry out within yourself, furious at the friends you can't find, then hear someone shout: "Referee, you need glasses," an Italian yell in the hardly noticed murmur of the local crowd. You've found them, recognize them, each and every one, you're despairing: "You know how I hate this lack of concern for others, this lack of love, I've been looking for you all over, I've a shoe that's too tight and my foot hurts"—but you're already slapping them on the back, sighing with relief.

In the evening I'm back at the Exhibition, where I run into G. once more. He doesn't mention last night and I'm damned if I'm going to ask how it went. He pushes me towards the Music Hall and says they haven't stopped playing since last night. The orchestra and public, trading on the ecstasy and excitement, stayed where they were. So word got out about this extraordinary concert that shows no sign of ending. People have come from far and wide. The building's packed. Some other orchestras have arrived too—large and small—from nearby towns, some from abroad, they're taking it in turns to play, or forming improvised new combos, musicians from different orchestras. Soon they'll be playing on the staircases, on each floor, they'll be playing in the square, with a rabble looking on, and street vendors . . .

G. and I are waiting, there's no rush in this never-ending concert to find out if someone will come.

In the meantime an embassy servant arrives from the small villa on the outskirts of the city where they're discussing the peace, throws to the cats some leftovers from a snack taken during a break in the talks, and disappears slamming the door.

Then on the night between Good Friday and Saturday I could swear I hear my name pronounced in a normal voice in the street below. I switch on the small light, which flickers and almost goes out, walls and furniture oscillate . . . it didn't last long, was very gentle, and certainly the tremor was felt by two or three neighboring districts, by the other orchestras arriving through the night, by me and you. I say *you* but don't know who I'm talking about, talking to; one thing is sure, I'm speaking in an approximate fashion, just because the earth moved, and we shared that brief moment of trembling half-sleep. Who knows whether you thought the same or whether it's like the time of the two trains, running on parallel tracks. How come it never happens that lightly touching a girl in the street, instead of the usual compliment, anybody says:

a fisherman of sponges
will have this rare pearl

and she comes back with the next two lines:

he'll obtain favor and good luck
because he didn't look for you.

But this long kiss and intimacy that sometimes forms between things, this party frequently coming alight, in its own way deconsecrating and reconsecrating Easter, this meeting that insists on the *you* being here, you'll see, soon it'll break up, come to an end, fall to pieces. Here we are at the dregs, the pretentious solos, dessicated pieces, the cold and lonely sounds, the dry bravura doodles.

There was a last-minute effort to reestablish order around midday, restore the schedule, calling everyone back into the hall where the concert had begun. Here I am with G. and friends from the game, with some of the unexpected spectators of the first evening. We try to stick together against the flashy and fanatical. I notice with horror that O.S.—the former companion at the Conservatory—is among them. He's dragging his sailor boy by the hand, even hoists him onto the stage where the scheduled orchestra is about to burst into life, despite the Resurrection bells, which can be heard just now, over the city. Under a spotlight the Negro singer holds the sailor boy by the hand and asks him to sing a duet. The little lad doesn't hesitate and begins going up the scale with a squeaky, daring, ostentatious voice while the orchestra and Negro singer fall in behind, allowing him long pauses to get out all he can. Give me the shade of a room that retains a little of the day's heat, with a pulsing clock and cup half-empty on the table, a late gleam on the books, and two butterflies that appear for a moment in the window frame.—It's the sense, not in these words exactly, of the song, you know only too well how dated and prewar. Then little sailor boy and Negro singer move off, and the spotlight turns, and an old poet, but I can't be sure in all the confusion of people leaving, an old poet escorting another young lad (or escorted by him) takes the hat round the room, like in a book of our national history, with exiles and goodbyes. It really is over, everyone's going, no one will come. Now do you know what I mean if, on a day that has dared too much, I say there's no remedy for summer?

It's getting late once more. The lights of the Exhibition are already back on and those of the funicular railway again show the height of the hill.

The peace conference has ended too. Without emotion, the spokesman's reading out a communiqué to the journalists. No progress, he says. There won't be war even this time. Or peace.

But those lights, who are all those lights staying on for?—I'm wondering.

The Title of Poet

The title of poet seems to have become an honorific increasingly socially difficult to bear and to maintain even in its normal literary ambit. This is what the smartest and perhaps most vital among the young or those approaching maturity show they feel. The specialized discourse of poetry *as such* irritates the more it tends to place itself on the terrain of comparative or oppositional poetics at the expense of natural reader-writer relations. And it irritates the more it tends, beyond poetry itself, to propose as its ultimate and exclusive aim a more-or-less new idea of itself, one not the less abstract for that. The young I'm speaking of believe less and less in the privilege and primacy of the poetic act as a decisive intervention or as the only possibility for maneuver and adventure. Others, less young, have learned this to their cost. Would it be facile to remark that the discussion—but it's quite another discussion from the one above—has flared up again about a different role assigned to the poetic act: a natural activity, one among many, which people do, this or that person, or else a contribution, using poetry's specific means, to the more general discourse on culture? An old and jealously guarded instinct would lead us to register the inanity of a dilemma formulated in these terms, and to conclude, rather simplistically, that the act, provided it's valid, is always in itself a contribution, and by its own strengths belongs to the cultural horizon—sometimes modifying it profoundly. Actual experience dictates a different language, points to a series of different inanities that starve the artistic outcome on the level of private emotions, and almost reaches the stage of wishing for poetry as object (very different from, even if accidentally congruent with, the "poetry of objects"), anonymous, unsigned... A suspicion of unacknowledged dilettantism doesn't detach itself from the old "faith in poetry," and it's more and more difficult to avoid "this profound repugnance, this need nowadays to reject the sawn-off lines of the poet," as Giansiro Ferrata, a friend of mine, declared some time ago when reaffirming his belief in a book of poetry that has also been important for me.

Solmi's suggestion in relation to "organic thought" is a response to this state of being—for that's what it is; but the suspicion that this is a programmatic formula is fended off by other words of his about the need, without a shadow of rhetoric, to recognize a new calling:

> We'll find it again... purely intuitively in the strength of the grip, like that of an imperious hand, with which we have always been held by the appeal of true poetry. Today once more we expect the poet to tell us what is really important for us, to face crucial questions, to return to giving us, behind its fugitive appearance, the real nature of things. *De re mea agitur*... Can poetry still exercise its grip upon the world?

As we can see, while the first proposition leads to quietism, and untroubled freedom, the second resurrects the terms of an unsatisfied consciousness, grants the necessary interlocutor and cross-examiner the role that the times have assigned to him. What crucial questions and what is it that's really important for us?— you may ask. It was always thought that artistic expression raised questions and at the same time found answers; or that it was in its fortunate nature to coincide almost unconsciously with questionings in the air, clarifying and perhaps even dissolving them. Here those averse to any and every ideology shudder when confronted by the enforced direction, a thick diaphragm of one-way streets and no-entry signs, and are on the point of throwing in the towel.

It seems inevitable these days that creative freedom should be subject not so much to a lengthy "review of reality," as to a preliminary debate on the interpretation of that review. And it is part of the horoscope of immediate destinies that discourse on culture with all its implications be assumed as the object and concrete content of poetry, in particular as the toll that poetry must pay to become a citizen within the circle of culture. We can already notice some all-too-evident signs; and we can also see the twisting, turning, and shifting of which ideological fervor is capable when confronting the risk that it find itself faced with a more complex, but in the end more desolate, form of autobiography. Do we want to see in this an attempt to sabotage the naturalness of the poetic act? Something warns us that in this fear, in this touchiness, lies the irrefutable evidence of weak spirits. Even if, too often we have reason for perplexity when faced with the tendency to make of an artistic outcome, whether specifically poetic or not, a useful "piece" for the development of a broadly demonstrative intervention, or—worse—the training ground for a sort of intellectual acrobatics.

In any case, what we wouldn't wish to see upset, or simply altered, is the natural ability of poetry to communicate and the corresponding inclination to welcome its voice.

1956

You Began

Think of how Milan was, or seemed to you, at the outbreak of the last conflict: a city ready for a new thrust forward, a living refutation of laughable imperial destinies, a definite premise, on the contrary, despite everything and despite its own mistakes, for a European reality.

You began to take stock, concretely, of many things—the

women, the journeys, the books, the city, poetry; you began living fully, once definitively beyond the bewilderment of youth. Came the war, and everything was ruined. That's how you thought to explain the crisis that overcame you and some others of your age after '45, back from the war and imprisonment (and feeling yourself excluded from the Liberation, deprived of its struggle as of an experience you've missed, leaving you forever incomplete).

A realization—it's clear now—would have helped you explain things better. Since you didn't have a political consciousness and not even a political sensibility, it had appeared to you, back then, that you began to live fully beyond the dictatorship and ignoring the dictatorship: looking elsewhere for consciousness, exercising elsewhere a sensibility. Without understanding that it was precisely in this way that the dictatorship carried out its work in you, ignorant of it, so much so that you still bear its mark. You didn't expect the war, didn't believe in it; it took you by surprise. You suffered it like a personal wrong. It's from this that your sporadic political interest, even today—for the most part—derives, of an emotional, an affective, a neurotic character.

1960

On the Back of a Piece of Paper

One would like to add nothing to what one writes. Allow it to speak for itself, if it has the force. Despite this, I must admit that I'm glad to have written "Gli amici," irrespective of the result or what might be thought of it. The people called by name in that poem, by their actual names, are alive and real. I hope they don't feel reduced to a literary pretext. I felt I had a debt towards them and, in this way, I deceive myself that I've partially repaid it. Towards them, towards a place, and a habit of mind that's still alive and fertile in me, and so, in the end, towards myself. I'm less inclined to speak of those lines critically or in terms of aesthetics than I am of other things I've written. If I really had to add a few words, I would say that I hope the poem does not seem merely a homage to friendship or to an uneasy love for a place. Nor a complaint about the progressive mechanization of customs and ways of life, nor nostalgia for simpler forms called—falsely, among other things—the primitive. I, too, am far from being without sin, if sin it is, in this regard and will not cast the first stone. But I'd prefer it to be read as vexation, a feeling of being lost at what changes and becomes confused, without being able to unravel this alteration or muddle. And, as counterweight—miraculous or not—there's the intervention of friends, the sense that friendship can still give, as remedy, an order that, in its own way, it is still able to make of confusion and incommunicability, an instrument suitable for distinguishing and judging the things it manages still to advance.

1960

Two Old Flames

Over there where from tower
to tower agreement
leaps in vain now and is thrown back,
the who-goes-there of the hour,
—just as down here from turret to turret
from the heights of the compound
Moroccan guards call to each other—
who goes in the gloomy midnight's
quick snowflakes, who misses
the final toast on the wind's
black thresholds, sinister
with waiting, who goes . . .
It's an image of ours
distorted, not come
to light. It abandons
a blue vein of oblivion only
between two eras dead in us.

Sainte-Barbe du Thélat, New Year's Day 1944

Valor and grace
are born again.
No matter in what form—a game

of football between prisoners:
                                  especially in him
down there playing on the wing.
O you so light and quick across fields
shadow that extends
in tenacious sunset.
It contorts, flames at length on the end
of a colorless day. And as it blurs
chimerical now your run
grows great within me
bitter in the wake.
                             Sainte-Barbe du Thélat, May 1944

It's not my custom to return to things I've written in the past in order to change or modify them. The consciousness, within me, of what I've written is lost quite soon. I can say so without false modesty; I'm focused on the space between the last thing I wrote and the next thing to be written. I don't give myself credit for what went before, and that survives as a memory of the relationship between the factual circumstance (moment or situation) and a written text. Highly autobiographical, as can be seen.

    This rule applies, of course, to things written and finished—often published—but not to things left off at the beginning or halfway through.

    The two short poems reproduced here are an exception to the rule—or, rather, they confirm it, in the sense that in this case I acted as if they were never finished. In my *Diario d'Algeria* they appeared in even shorter forms:

Over there where from tower
to tower agreement
leaps in vain now and is thrown back,
the *who-goes-there* of the hour,
who goes in the gloomy midnight's
quick snowflakes, who misses
the final toast on the wind's
black thresholds, sinister
with waiting, who goes . . .

It's an image of ours
distorted, not come
to light. It abandons
a blue vein of oblivion only
between two eras dead in us.

    And the other:

And you so light and quick across fields
shadow that extends
in tenacious sunset.
It contorts, flames at length on the end
of a colorless day. And as it blurs
chimerical now your run
grows great within me
bitter in the wake.

    The impression always remained with me that the exact relationship I spoke of earlier, between the circumstance and the text, had been falsified, been in some way sacrificed to purely expressive motives; and the result was, if not an obscure meaning, an abstraction, unusual for me, which I don't like. Was it clear, before, that "Over there where from tower / to tower" referred to the towers and bell towers of Europe, distant towns and cities, felt to be all the more distant the more they were familiar, in the night of the Algerian New Year? I don't think so. Still less, for sure, was it possible to think of the shadow so light and quick across fields as a living person, present in a scene enjoyed and suffered under my gaze. It wasn't a question, I hope it's clear, of improving the texts. On the contrary. Perhaps they're actually worse, less balanced. If that is so, no matter, no matter at all. Perhaps this is an example of how some risks must be taken—or of how you are tempted to take them.

    The fact is that, back then, I wasn't able to clarify this point, but now I can. I don't think this is merely accidental. From this point on, the discussion could become less episodic, could be enlarged . . .

1961

Creative Silence

The humiliation of not being up to it anymore. The humiliation of complaining about it, of the anxiety that it provokes, the shameful spectacle one makes of oneself by confessing this anxiety.

I know a writer who, after reaching a mature age, was no longer able to write a single line. A friend, a little more patient than others, consoled him with reproach: you're too hard on yourself, too much of a perfectionist. The fact that he didn't write a word and didn't even try (except on those rare occasions when he tried as if *in hiding from himself*), was literally true, but his friends didn't believe it. Others perhaps did believe it, but they attributed some exemplary status to this failing and tried to convince him that this silence, although rather longer than normal, was certainly a virtue, proof of coherence and rigor. Closer to the mark came V., violent and bad-mouthed: "Him? He's like someone who can't . . . anymore."

As far as I know this writer did not keep a diary of his impotence—although the temptation is there, with the excuse of writing your way out of the impasse. So what's the problem if someone doesn't write anymore? Where's the shame in that? The only shame is the shame of feeling ashamed about the impotence. You really should be able to put this energy that no longer goes into writing to some good use. But it doesn't happen; you end up feeling incompetent, perhaps socially, a sign that you had thought you were socially valuable as a writer, that this was your identity. The loss of this identity, at worst, comes close to self-contradiction, absurd feeling, a vicious circle: a writer writes if he has something to say, and if he has nothing to say, so what, is that the end of the world? It may happen that the original vice has reached this point, that the writer expects something, some kudos, some human recognition, for his function as writer. On the other hand, there's no doubt that the expression "something to say" is extremely—gravely—approximate. That you had something to say, and precisely what, how often do you find this out only afterwards, after writing it? In all likelihood isn't it very different from what you set out to write? For some this question is senseless unless you first ask: *Why do you write, for whom?* I am not of this opinion, although I stray that way sometimes. Once I had a simpler notion, that what you had to say was, deep down, either a moment or a place in one's experience (existence) *to save*. But this is an idea you cannot hold on to for long, either as a story teller or a writer of poetry. For a writer of poetry (as is my case, but I don't really make a distinction between this and a novelist, or writer in general), this is a big danger, the comic illusion of eternity and everlasting life. How many dispensing machines, how much sleep, how much silence is rooted in them, it hardly matters whether of written silence or of the absence of writing.

If the ice then breaks, you may well look back on that period and want to call it fruitful, necessary. But perhaps what's of interest is less a justification for the former silence as the identification of the psychological burden it represented, the sense of being lost with which it coincided. Was it like losing a form of mediation, as if a vital force had lost contact with reality? This strikes me as having an air of expediency about it, making a period of inertia seem noble, or at least it seems abstract and too convenient. It is at the same time too psychological. I am more persuaded by another idea that—if nothing else—comes more from within the work of the writer, more closely touches the concrete nature of his anxieties, fears, perplexities—but also his hopes and plans for the future. You live for many years with sensations, impressions, feelings, intuitions, memories. The sense of rare or exceptional character, which rightly or wrongly you attribute to them, is due perhaps to the intensity with which life had impressed them upon you. This is the first source of creative dissatisfaction, of reluctance even before the work at hand, which is translated (worse for those who don't feel it) into metrical nausea, into disgust with every form previously tried. You live with your intentions, with ghosts of unwritten poems . . . A poet will always envy a novelist—whether of the conventional type or not—for that kind of sorcery by which he conjures up characters, events, situations that have nothing to do with voice, accent, or immediate lyrical formulation. The dissatisfaction has a great deal to do with this last point. And it is no accident that "lyric" and its corresponding adjective have for some time, at least with some, fallen into disuse. Similarly it is no accident (and I would add it's healthy) that we've stopped wondering what poetry might be, in absolute terms. It makes more sense, I think, to try to understand how emotions develop and lead to representing in a specific way the relation between experience and invention: the search for such a way and such an invention marks the transition from the negative phase of silence I was speaking about to the phase in which the ghosts of dissatisfaction take form. To plan a "figurative," narrative, constructive poem means nothing, especially if in hypothetical literary opposition to an "abstract," lyrical poem of illumination. It does mean something, during a work's development, to feel the need for characters, for narrative elements, for structure: find for yourself a milieu that is socially and historically, as well as geographically and even topographically, identifiable. In it you transpose shreds and stimuli of individual emotional life, as if on a test bench for their secret and final resources, their real vitality, their effective capacity to grip. To create characters and tell stories in poetry as the result of an inner proliferation... Didn't we always think that at the apex poetry and narrative touch, and then, but only then, it makes almost no sense to distinguish between them?

But there are many ways to invent, and inventions don't last forever. On the contrary, you invent one thing at a time, and the invention is tested against your ambitions, feelings, ideas. The invention is always askance, never quite matches any of these elements, and perhaps it strengthens one and weakens another, forces one element forward and another—in other circumstances decisive—back. To be fully aware of this means to prevent one's inventions, one's tried and tested modes of invention, from becoming a formula and a habit. It's to know—at the risk of further silence—that the useful way, the illuminating relation, is never given, but needs to be found; and it also means closer adherence to the variety of feelings in the soul. And that is the price of communication.

1962

The Year '43

The year '43 begins in my memory with an indefinable smile caught on the faces of the people of Athens. It matters little that it was still '42, an October morning in '42, immediately after Montgomery's push to El Alamein. And it finishes with a pair of knickers waved at us Italian prisoners by a German prisoner in a quarry on the outskirts of Oran, Algeria. But before this epilogue, it passes through the carriages of a troop train returning from Athens to Mestre and to the irregular rhythm of the *Rosemunda*. It becomes cowed and saddened in an Empoli cinema-theater for a cabaret girl whose love—no, her love cannot lose itself on the wind with the roses—whose love is dumbfounded and made indignant by a late evening communiqué: those two lunatics had met at the Brenner Pass and decided to continue the struggle in Europe and in Africa, the Axis powers having been reduced to a handkerchief of land in Tunisia. It writhes in fear with misgivings about a journey that was being perpetually postponed and perpetually threatened, at first by air from Castelvetrano and then by sea from the rubble of Trapani. It revivifies and breathes a sigh of relief at news of the fall of Tunisia. It marches on amid the rows of white flags held out by the people of Paceco (Trapani) and the arms of an American airborne platoon. It lays down with another quite different sigh of relief. This one is much deeper and now perhaps only physiological, by now only animal, in the soccer stadium at Trapani that's been turned into a temporary prison camp. I have already written about these things at various times in poetry and in prose. I made myself ridiculous, afflicting friends and family by recounting them. Inside I was seething over them for years. It was almost as if they were a puzzle I couldn't solve—one that memory was constantly reviving, one open to the most various, the greatest number of solutions. It was as if there were a knot inside me, and only after untying it would I have eyes for anything else, ears for anything else. I, who dream rarely (it's not the case, I know), last summer dreamed a kind of allegory of '43, or rather of the Italian surrender in Africa and in Sicily. Some day or other I will write this dream, or else I'll never write it. Today I realize that many things, and not the least important ones, were left out of my brief disquisitions on the people and events of '43. Or perhaps it is truer to repeat that the years or days, memorable in one way or another, are really inexhaustible, nothing is ever truly told, the pit is really bottomless, as you discover each time with feeling. Today, concerning that meeting at the Brenner Pass—it must have been April 10th or 11th '43—I would like to mention certain helmets that never reached Empoli, where we were rearming. So, if the helmets didn't arrive, why on earth would they be sending us to Tunisia where the war was practically over? And in fact I obtained leave to go to Modena for a couple of days and there I listened to the Brenner communiqué, and no sooner had I turned off the radio than a telephone call tore my leave to pieces, for I was to return to Empoli by the earliest means. The orders say Villa San Giovanni—the voice on the phone explained. But I knew that Villa San Giovanni meant Castelvetrano, and that Castelvetrano meant immediate transfer by air to Tunisia, where we would land—if we arrived at all, which was far from certain—only to be shot on sight or taken prisoner. My memory is stuck on that story of the helmets that never arrived, that in our all-too-self-interested reasoning would permit or prohibit our departure. And my image of our absurd destiny lies just there: the lack of congruence between the armed battalion slowly marching, in dead silence, towards the station at Empoli, and those helmets that hadn't arrived.

July 25th is, for me, a camp blanket. We had been taken prisoner not many hours before and were shut into the stadium at Trapani. We officers in a small barrack room next to the sports ground; the soldiers, about ten thousand, in makeshift tents on the field itself. The news, arriving by who-knows-what routes, exploded in a roar from the multitude pressed together there, such an explosion as could never have been heard for past displays of skill, from the stalls and terraces on a Sunday. After the roar, there came a shot. An American sentry, jumpy, frightened maybe, had let off a burst of machine-gun fire. Something over which a blanket had been thrown passed in front of us, borne in people's arms, surrounded by faces of resentment. We looked on in silence, without really taking it in. One of the bearers said to us: "He is dead and you are partly to blame. At least stand to attention, officers."

I was taken prisoner in Sicily, at Paceco (Trapani) by an airborne division of the American army. It was about 13:30 hours on July 24th 1943, the day before the regime collapsed. For virtually two years my division had been trying to reach North Africa, without succeeding. We had been in Athens four months for that purpose with the Axis forces stopped at El Alamein, almost in sight of Alexandria. July '43 was when we finally managed it, as prisoners. We disembarked at Biserta on August 15th amidst the scorn and worse of the French, Gaullists or not, stationed there: colonial-fascists of that particular country as we would say nowadays (though also then). Luckily for us, not even in '43 did the Americans have much of an opinion of them.

It's not necessary to have reached September 8th '63 to discover that one of the most widespread feelings among us, officers of the Italian army, was a kind of guilt towards the ally from whom we were breaking away. The insignia of the regime were removed from the lapels of the Militia officers who had been taken prisoner with us, to be replaced by army stars. Meanwhile, the senior regular officers to whom the Americans had left a ghost of authority because they were held responsible for us rabble, painstakingly sought out the camp's anti-Badoglians, the fascists in other words, in their opinion. So the simplistic mechanism, the only one possible, however, of allegiance to the king—which means allegiance to one's country guaranteed by military honor, which makes wars continue to take place—soon divided the camp into two. There were those who agreed with July 25th and those who didn't but who were already keeping quiet about it.

In whose name, for what reason, did they keep quiet? Let's say, unequivocally: in the name of military honor, of the word given and other undertakings and sworn allegiances. Certainly there will have been some that said nothing even though they saw beyond certain false alternatives. They saw beyond the incompatibility between, on the one hand, the word given, and, on the other, allegiance to the monarch (hornet's nest into which military honor pokes its nose!) But history makes no mention of that swarming prison: namely, Camp 127, Chanzy, Algeria, not far from Sidi-Bel-Abbes, place dear to the Foreign Legion. (*Chanzy, Chanzy*—the voice of a kindly sort of lunatic started up each morning at reveille—*bijou de l'Algérie—eau courante—tous les conforts—visitez-la*). Completing the picture was a considerable number of people captured in civilian clothes, brought here in civilian clothes. They were Sicilians, or people living in Sicily who had sneaked off home from the collapsing division but who had then had to report to the occupying troops. And there was a considerable nucleus of survivors from the African campaign who had not yet been sent to camps on the other side of the ocean. Their abstract witless air ought to be mentioned. For them the war had become nothing more than a personal squabble with the English, months and years back and forth across the desert; and the scorn and scuffles that the presence of those in civilian clothes gave rise to should also be mentioned.

To the shout of "Out with the civilians!" another shout returned across the camp, "Make him a federal!" coined around that time and almost certainly all but incomprehensible to the youth of today.

I barely remember the instructions we received in case of a submarine attack. There was a fine-looking life jacket, red, at the disposal of everyone in the bunks we had been assigned. In its pocket I even found a cigarette packet with two Camels an American had left behind from the voyage over in that fine-looking, comfortable ship which was due to sail, that very September night, apparently, for the United Sates. In the holds we suffocated, it was true. But cheer up, this is nothing, the best is yet to come. When the ship starts rolling, weak as we are, surely they'll now and then let us take a breath of air, up on deck. We'll get to see the sea, the Atlantic. They can't hide it from us, can they? Of course not, why not say we'll have a champagne toast when we cross the Equator, should the route take us that way ... The objection came from Lieutenant Mezzini, from Monghidoro (Bologna), ex-contradictor on principle of the ex-battalion of motorized (on paper) infantry.

He was fairish-haired, pigheaded, a man of few words and of catastrophic predictions. There was never a smile. With one eye perpetually half-closed, an eyelid drooping over his resentment and pessimism, he was destined for the role of Cassandra, and, like all Cassandras, heeded all the less now that he could rely on the unequivocal turn of events. (*Tal saré, muraja*—was the bleak formula for his recurrent foresight, issued unfailingly amidst the euphoric conjecture and light-headedness of others. It literally meant, I believe: —You'll see, dimwit—or something like that, and here I can manage only to reproduce the sound, uncertain as I am of the spelling and exact sense of that pre-Apennine phoneme).

Things now stood like this. We were in the same boat as the Americans on the surface; the Germans beneath us, in the depths of the ocean. It must have been barely more than conjecture or a rumor that they were about to launch a new attack, by submarine. For us it was a fact, or at least it was as much a part of our thinking as the likelihood of suffering seasickness. We speculated about whether the Germans were more interested in sinking the Americans or in saving our skins, the skins of their allies, perfidious to some degree and above all superfluous, yet allies nonetheless. But wasn't it obligatory to notify the enemy which vessels carried prisoners! That way, they don't sink you. Good thinking; you reckon they're so scrupulous. They're interested in the tonnage. That's all. This is a vessel which is going to reach America (if it is going to reach America) and then come back laden with arms and troops. Think of that, and if they get you in their periscope, they send off a torpedo, bet you whatever you like, even if they know that instead of us there are German prisoners on board. Can't argue with that, can't argue. Didn't we hear something about a big vessel sunk off Bona or Bougie by some air-launched Italian torpedoes massacring and shipwrecking hundreds like us? In Sicily, during the decisive last few days, there wasn't a trace of a plane with our markings. You can be sure they'll wake up now, to our misfortune. Or, rather, there are some destinies, the sort that seem to have been written some time ago, where chance and geometry coincide, are there not?

Things did not turn out so badly. We were waiting for the morning refection with the impatience that had been left us after the hungry times at Chanzy when they ordered us on deck for an important announcement. I don't remember if they read us Badoglio's text or just gave us the news. A major from our chiefs of staff exhorted us to make no comment in favor or against ("it is an armistice, and the enemy is still the enemy") and to adopt a proper attitude of impeccable restraint. We had to leave the ship, which was already docking once more, to pack up and return to land. The city of Oran, the gray houses in the still grayer daylight, stood before us. Some shouts of *macaroni* and *chemise noire* greeted us here and there, but subdued, barely convinced, while we filed off, the ship already far behind. As for us, we paid no attention, marched jauntily even, as if about to break into a run, an absurd hope making itself felt in each one of us. How absurd perhaps only Mezzini of Monghidoro knew.

I don't know how long it remained alive. It was the course of the day itself that gradually extinguished it in us, before the events and other news made themselves plain. The Americans who escorted us were more nervous than they had ever been before. It must have been unexpected, an unforeseen duty that disturbed the days of peace and quiet far away from the battle zone.

We finished up in a quarry of stones, fenced with barbed wire and guarded by sentries, on the outskirts of Oran, where, in the absence of precise orders that didn't arrive, they left us. And once more came *macaroni* and *chemise noire* from the windows of the suburb, from the alleyways alongside the quarry where the busy traffic of the warstruck port threaded its way. And with us the boredom, the hunger, the ferocious desire to smoke, no more comments and conjectures. I think each developed a line of thought in their own minds, images of repatriation, and, at the same time, that thin thread rolled itself into a ball, of simultaneity with what was happening elsewhere, on an identical day anywhere, Milan, Naples, Monghidoro, wherever, people fleeing or crowding together with shouts of joy, Germans arriving and Germans leaving....

Here, they were arriving. In lorry loads, in the late afternoon, under a drizzle at first tepid and then increasingly heavy and discomforting. They arrived from Chanzy, from Saint Denis, from Sainte-Barbe, from the various camps in Africa we had heard about, and which we would get to know better. Singing under the ironic gaze of the American posted erect on the cab of each lorry, falling silent when they caught sight of us, the damned Germans grimaced derisively at us, shouted scornfully. But above all they made threatening gestures, of beatings, waving their hands, holding out their fists, flapping their palms, jabbing their fingers, vulgarly. They took our places on the ship we had left that morning. One of them leaned out as the lorry slowed near the perimeter fence, holding up something white; he waved it, rolled it into a ball and held it up again, made a gesture that I won't repeat. Underwear. A woman's. Italian. And as good Italians we began to understand.

The camp at Chanzy, left apparently never to return just three days before, greeted us after a night of pummeling rain in a cattle truck. It had been a particularly uncomfortable journey, the sort when the usual tiresome wit invokes the law of the impenetrability of bodies. Between the toe cap of a boot, an elbow, a knee, back to back, propped up on elbows, half-lying, exhausted, nauseated, famished, there came the exasperated dream of being on the troop train from Mestre to Athens or Athens to Mestre the year before, two memorable journeys for me. Or there came another one, five years before, gentler, more cradle-rocking, as a trainee officer, at the time of Munich, before it all began—everyone electrified by the idea that this same evening war or peace was to be decided. But in the early morning the newspapers persuaded us that peace was better, that the wisdom of the Duce had saved... Here the rain: *tal saré muraja;* and the rails: *tal saré muraja; tal saré muraja*—the train at night—*tal saré...*

At Chanzy the African sun was breaking up the clouds of that September. The signs remained of the tents unpegged three days before, in many places the tents themselves to be set up again after an hour or so of work. But first, food. About time, we haven't eaten since the night before last. It seems the Americans will make amends for so much privation with special rations. Everyone in my tent is out scouting for pegs and poles; me and Remo keep the place by sitting on our rucksacks. We say nothing. At a certain point Remo elbows me in the ribs and nods towards something in front of us. With an air of abject resignation, Lieutenant Mezzini walks past beside Lieutenant Gatta, ex-deputy prefect of the Kingdom and now veteran artillery officer the draft had remembered at the last moment. They're confabulating. Both, despite the fact that the sun's come out once more, are still wearing their greatcoats. Who knows, perhaps they don't want to ruin them! Remo says: "Mezzini is demonstrating to Gatta that contrary to all appearances Gatta is not wearing a greatcoat." Mezzini overhears. For the first time since his call up, he smiles.

An inertia, tinged with anxiety, was beginning.

1963

The Year '45

He was called Kennedy, the man who ruled over our destinies for less than six months, the last in the two years of imprisonment in Africa. He was an American MP, a captain, perhaps the most soldierly of all the military police we encountered. Under him, we passed the most comfortable period of our captivity. We slept in solidly built, well-ventilated huts on what were almost genuine beds; we finally ate properly, almost plentifully—Italian food at last, as suited our tastes. Thank you for those rations of tagliatelle and ice creams on the last Sundays! Let him, Captain Kennedy, be thanked from here, from this distance! For also having got us back into the habit of looking after ourselves, for having fought the tendency in us to let ourselves go in every sense.

I don't know whether one of his duties was to prepare us for repatriation, or whether he had set himself the personal task of supervising our "reeducation." He gave us an example of his pedagogical dash one time when he made a Moroccan woman, a Fatima, the Americans said, march past naked between two armed soldiers after being caught by the MPs sneaking from one of our huts. He had forced us to move aside and make room for the shocking passage of that clandestine Venus arrived as far as here from who knows what "bidonville" in Casablanca. And his comment on the episode was: "So you can see in broad daylight with your own eyes the women you sleep with at night." Before the unusual ceremony came an even more unusual siren and the order to dress in full kit as far as possible, as if on parade, or for an inspection by the Red Cross. Lined up against the huts off Broadway—that was what we always called the main road through the camp, right from the first day—we hoped to hear the announcement that the war was finally over and that soon we would be going home. Not a bit of it, this was only to teach us a lesson, to have us on parade and inspected by our night visitor. Episodes like this made the idea of repatriation recede in us; yesterday's enemy emphasized his superiority as the victor, and by contrast, our inferiority as the vanquished. Strange idea of cobelligerency!

Our role and legal status as cobelligerent prisoners, a direct result of what the Americans willingly termed an ideological war, is, I believe, unprecedented in the history of war and prisoners of war. Almost all of us signed the document of collaboration that the powers above presented to us after September 8th. Those who hadn't signed ended up in special or punishment camps across the Atlantic, whatever the reason (it isn't necessarily the case that only self-confessed or suspected fascists refused). How night visits of that sort—and other daily transactions on the edges of the camp, bread for cigarettes, shirts for other items of comfort—became possible is a long story, and a tedious one. It's enough to say that we were like prisoners on parole, even if being cobelligerent prisoners meant something more complicated, in the sense that as cobelligerents we had only duties, and as prisoners we had only a few, tenuous, rights. What's more, in a certain sense, being co-belligerents signified, among other things, this: the duty not to press our rights as prisoners. Our collective drama, incomparably tiny compared to what was happening in the world at large, was neither more nor less than this.

In all conscience, it must be said that—us having fallen into American hands—no state of detention could have been blander. The various individual dramas that developed in relation to that state are another matter. But our real hardship consisted precisely in that bland, torpid, semi-idyllic imprisonment. I imagined the lot that had befallen others, friends and acquaintances. (One will have ended up in Germany, another interned in Switzerland, yet another will still be floundering in Siberia or the Urals). And thinking back to what they used to say, to how they used to live and behave, I came to the conclusion that everyone gets the imprisonment he deserves. I don't want to say here in what sense I deserved mine. Once, when we were still in tents with canvas full of holes, I said this to my companions: certainly one day we would go into a bar, watch a game of soccer, carry out the most inconsequential act in daily or civilian life when something—a gesture, a way of doing things, a manner of speaking—would reveal our status as ex-prisoners, as *prisoners of war,* from that particular sort of imprisonment. And each of us would unfailingly recognize it in others. This prediction amused my tent mates a good deal because it projected onto an unconfined future the manias, the small foibles and tics in each one of us, made evident and reinforced by each day and each hour of that obligatory cohabitation, like no other cohabitation could.

Here in the camp at Fedala, a few kilometers from Casablanca and a stone's throw from the Atlantic's waves, the period of imprisonment in tents in Algeria had by now become only a memory. But it was already also the memory of a phase in which we'd been more alive, more attentive to the outside world, more bent on an image of the future. It had been a time for examining individual consciences, but also for discussions prompted by snatches of news the Americans, not without reluctance, allowed us to copy from the *Stars and Stripes* newspaper, condensing them into a succinct bulletin; or else by the uncontrolled rumors that penetrated the camp. We knew little of the partisans and of the war of liberation—or rather we knew something very late—, still less of the death camps, and only as a dreadful rumor, but without any kind of detail or facts. We knew, though, about the speech at the Lirico, and about the Nazi hopes for their secret weapons. Someone, I don't know how, had listened to the Salò Republic radio and from this came the image of an almost flourishing Northern Italy, calm and industrious, graced on Sundays with a regular soccer league. Some said they had seen our custodians' faces whiten at the time of Bastogne and some fascist crests were raised once more in the camp.

It didn't last long, as everyone knows. The Soviet offensive of January '45 removed any uncertainty, even in our eyes, about the final outcome of the war. For us there was no real April 25th, or rather it was diluted over a long period between July '44 and May '45—from the news, like a bolt of lightning, of the attempt to assassinate Hitler to the moment when an American officer passed through our camp, wiped from his face the sweat of a particularly torrid day, put something down, almost symbolically his revolver perhaps, on the table of the central hut, and said in a tired, detached voice: "The war is over."

It was a fine moment when they planted the bomb in Hitler's headquarters. The news reached us slowly in the general rumor from one tent to another, in the unfailing echoes of an instantaneous and total surrender of the German army in Italy, of Hitler dead, Mussolini in flight who knows where. The news reached my ears, by now an uproar from the camp, shouts and clamoring to be deciphered before they became news, one morning at waking. The reality, unfortunately, had more modest consequences in the short term. But I would say it was then that the final phase began for us, with our obstinate inertia, the ugly fever of egoism and impatience, no image of the future, no reconstructing a conscience, no returning to responsibility and action. The discussions, the preceding and bitterer state of imprisonment, had divided and united us according to each individual case. We had been united by the common need to organize for ourselves an existence destined to endure no one knew how long, with meetings and debates, training and proper university courses, lending libraries, theater performances. And now, there, within sight of Casablanca and the Atlantic, in the camp at Fedala with its asphalt roads, no longer with towers and sentries, with almost spic and span huts, marvelous showers in working order, reasonably good cooking, under the supervision of Captain Kennedy, that was all over, replaced by insensitivity to any news other than repatriation, mutual intolerance, spying out in each other the symptoms of an insufferable burden and a fever to return, like an ugly sickness we all knew we were suffering from and which we all wanted to hide from the others, the last surviving, by now the only possible, demonstration of virility . . .

Now the one thing we had left in common, the one thing that united us by dividing us, was the wait for repatriation. The interrogations began, duly recorded, about the politics we intended to pursue once back home. Liberals, of course, take a look at all those liberals — said the officer in charge of the interrogations. To be sure, judging by then and there, from our cautious or hypocritical answers, it would have appeared that the transformation of fascism into liberalism was taking place without undue difficulty, quite naturally, almost as if liberalism were the only possible alternative. And what a great party, at least numerically, the Liberal Party would have been if those declarations had been reliable. They weren't, since it was hardly sensible to arouse the American's suspicions, given that when he heard mention of Christian Democrats or Republicans he wondered who they might be. But, to tell it all, those opinions we offered were momentarily reliable, in the sense that only a few imagined, could imagine, after what — for the majority of us — had been years and years of meaninglessness, an alternative to our country's politics. And I have forgotten to say that ours was a camp for officers, not a fact without importance in such an evaluation.

In that stagnant and slightly infected air the news of April 25th fell. *Fell,* I say, not *exploded,* but I should say it crept up on us almost lethargically. The explosion had already taken place, at the time of the failed assassination attempt on Hitler; it had burned itself out then, and since then had worked its way deep into us, as I have said. And now there was Milan, the archbishop's see, Dongo, Piazzale Loreto, Mussolini and Claretta, the fascist leaders. It was merely the macabre part of the story we virtually murmured amongst ourselves in astonishment. Those corpses piled one on top of the other in a close-up of the scene occupied all our attention and some of our sleep, prevented us from seeing the infinite number of other corpses from the war. This, conducted by the same leading players, the same director as before, was the final injustice perpetrated by a story that could not but present itself to us as distorted and abnormal. People came to visit us from the camps in Casablanca. They told us the Italian women there were wearing mourning clothes for the dead Duce. And it is certainly believable if we remember that for many years they too had had to come to terms directly with another fascism, different from ours only because it did not call itself by the same name and spoke a different language. With Mussolini, hadn't their putative natural defender died?

Other names filtered through one at a time, the initials of organizations that were a mystery to us, the C.V.L., C.L.N., Garibaldi Divisions, C.L.N.A.I. And finally, for me and just a few others, for there were not many Milanese in the camp, came the light of some well-known or cherished or familiar names, together with others, less well-known, or until then not known at all: Antonio Banfi, Elio Vittorini, and my namesake Emilio Sereni (to whom I owe a quarter of an hour's popularity in the camp, cautious attention and propitiatory questions about whether and how closely related to him I was . . .). It will appear incredible, but the real demoralization came with those names emerging from the shreds of our former ignorance. And the more familiar or cherished the names were, together with other names we had not heard before or initials we knew nothing of, representing a reality we hadn't shared or lived, the more we were excluded from that moment, relegated to a dead corner of history.

Others came from Casablanca, civilians of Italian origin who had moved there before the war or had got stuck there because of it, distant relatives, or people from the same villages and towns. Here they were on a Sunday visit with philanthropic or medicinal intentions, with the sadness of a meeting in prison or at a sanatorium. "Tell me," said someone, who had remained in the hut, "what would you say, what would you do, if your mother or wife or girlfriend were out there asking to come and visit, to bring you things, news from home, to ask how you are?" "Away with all of them," came the answer, "I would refuse to see them." "Even if they had come from Italy with a special permit from the liberators?" "And you think that would make a difference, do you? Away with them all, out with the lot of them, let them hang, the lot, I don't want to see them." He spoke as if in some way it were possible or imminent. And what's more, aside from this imaginary reaction to friends and relatives, with that part self-satisfied and part perverse imagining, from that moment, our future relations with others, protagonists or otherwise of the events we had failed to live and could not recover, became contaminated. And with them too, the friends from before, people known beforehand, those with whom you might think you could resume the discussions broken off so long before. It wasn't as if you thought you'd find them with the face of an executioner or, at least, of someone who demands that you make proper account of something. There were no scores to be settled, no accounts to render, this no, or perhaps (*perhaps?*) not. But those discussions were simply over, whatever they'd been, these people had moved on to other topics, and we were left with just some useless threads of earlier conversations.

Never had we been such prisoners as at that moment, in spite of what by now were clear signs of our imminent release. Never had we covered ourselves with the slime of defeat so much as now when we were about to emerge from it. An absurd love of habits, the places of our segregation, was developing, withdrawal (spiritual? meditative? aggrieved? lyrical? enraged?) into a solitary spiritual disposition, a prolonged ecstasy bringing on the swell of things and voices from beyond, from the remotest corner of the camp the sight of a vessel toiling its way out of sight in the Atlantic at sunset, the faint whir of the African night beyond the threshold of the hut bathed in the full moon's light. "Lo! 't is a gala night / Within the lonesome latter years!": these two lines from a poem by Poe which I had chanced upon during those days and which I'd translated, summed up those times, that way of feeling. And meanwhile *they,* those others, the people from home, people who'd been one of a kind with me, had transformed themselves into another kind. And always, in the future, in whatever undertaking I was to attempt or to achieve with them I would ask myself, I would have to ask myself, whether, before all else, I should not also make that leap, and when and how. You see it certainly wasn't enough for them, in their own minds, to have accomplished that transformation for me.

So when the lorries arrived to be loaded with us, and our baggage, to take us to Casablanca and the "Liberty" ships, our destination Naples at last, there was very little gaiety in that metallic column of men descending to the sea through the shimmer and ash of an African summer. It was not very different from many another past movement or relocation. This was a wrench and should have been an epilogue; or at least the premise of an evolution, a development. So imprisonment, or that particular state of imprisonment, left its mark, not the one I had jokingly foreseen in the punctured tent, but rather a reluctance, a spasm. I felt it whenever it was necessary to make a choice, in whatever sense and for whatever purpose, even in the most routine and ordinary of circumstances, between solitude and participation. And if only those things had been clearer to me then, if only I had been able to say them then with the clarity of today, if only twenty years had not been necessary to understand them and confess them, in writing, as I am doing now.

1965

The Reunited

They'd said you were lost

(you can see he didn't make it, didn't have wings enough
to leave them—we'd have said below—
to get himself out from the Taro's gravel,
from the last hedges, from the airs
of Calestano: deep down he'd fallen by the way,
was no longer one of us)

instead we're all here one and all
and only now, with you,
is the table laid perfect under these pergolas.

I was just back from a brief trip and he was already telling me a dream he'd had. It was of a secret gathering between the living and the dead who congratulated each other on being there, reunited, unexpectedly, beyond their wildest hopes. He told the story with a dissembling voice used frequently to evoke, virtually imitate, the voice of those talking in their sleep—and all the more if the dream contains people who are dead. I was utterly persuaded. I did something I almost never do. I went out to write down on a piece of paper the very words, or almost, that I'd just heard. So, sometimes, reality provides us readymade, cut out from itself, in the shape of poetic evidence, with a piece which then leaps back at us from the page. But it's an illusory effect: we're not so much provided with a piece of reality, readymade, as an invitation, perhaps even a challenge. A window opens through which we must look.

1966

On the Death of Ungaretti

My father has died a second time. Saying this is his due. I've always known that upon his death I would say this, could say nothing else. I go through his papers (or things, objects, relics) and they already speak differently. Only now does the sorrow outweigh the astonishment; it's here, is next to us, you can touch it in a steady light—here where his words rush to fill the unexpected emptiness. Today it seems they were written, knowingly, for this moment alone. I'll never be able to read them with such clarity again. This moment won't last long. Afterwards, it will come back to shake me, to shake us, off and on, less and less frequently, but no less suddenly, as existence and some books have taught us; and books within existence, among them his own. I spoke to him for the last time on Thursday May 28th just before midday. He had a healthy colorful face and spoke with difficulty, his voice a massive whisper. "I don't go back to Rome willingly," he told me. "Deep down, I've always preferred Milan." This confession didn't fail to surprise me, yet not that much if I recall that those distant "Milanese" lines of his were what drew me, as a youth, to his poetry: they go back to my very earliest years and it's for this reason, among others, that from reading those things I've felt I'm his son and as a son lived and endured his lightning perceptions and his wrath, his peering into the future and his mistakes: rather like Italy itself, because Ungaretti was—and how—also Italy. He carried around with him, in his presence alone, an increasingly rare gift: the memory, as darkened and lacerated as you like, of an original joy. It's perhaps in the unflinching cohabitation with this joy, so immense and taut that it came close to self-destruction, or in his head-on collision with an ever-present sense of catastrophe that the secret of Giuseppe Ungaretti's poetry can be sought—his chiaroscuro, his perpetually replenished energy, his *allegria*.

1970

Self-Portrait

Undoubtedly I'm a meteoropath. The more so now I feel out of sympathy with three of the four seasons: I would be happy if it were always summer and that no atmospheric variation could disturb it. Being out of sympathy with the seasons means being out of sympathy with existence, starting from myself. Writing is part of existence, though I do have a doubt about that. The doubt comes, on the one hand, from the idea that writing represents a slight gain in vitality, and, on the other, from a symptom of incompleteness, an inadequate aptitude for living fully. This too is meteoropathy and also explains why I write at intervals; long, for me extremely long, periods go by in which nothing gets written, although my thoughts are perpetually going in that direction. These periods, I ought to say, are not a matter of abstinence, but of genuine impotence. This is painful to confess, so much so that occasionally I try to convince myself that it's really a slow assimilation eventually bringing things into focus, a silence that has not been imposed but is nonetheless necessary, deriving from something in my own nature. On one occasion I was even moved to call it "creative silence." So the benevolent are mistaken when they attribute to me (some, even more generously, say it's my strength) a kind of perfectionism. The fact is that at my age I still haven't learned how to sit down and work at a desk, and I don't think I ever will. It's a pity, because not only do I tell myself that by now I ought to have learned, but because I'm also convinced it would do me some good, curing me, among other things, of meteoropathy. For example, it would compensate for the unease that shrieks in me on certain sunny, windy winter days, which I sense as a deathly distortion. To sit down at a desk, or, rather, to make experiments, I need a mediator. Then, that way I can and do enjoy it. The mediation may come from a foreign text I'm tempted to, or, perhaps, have been asked to translate. Much more rarely it may be another kind of emissary, something I have written earlier and forgotten. But I don't rewrite it, no, heaven forbid, if anything repair it here and there, applying myself with the benefit of hindsight to the three or four points I remember being dissatisfied with or which had even estranged me, that's the word, from my own text. Could it be a commissioned piece of work? Sometimes, yes, provided it coincides with something I'm interested in at the time, but this is even rarer, and not evidently connected to (how shall I put it?) the intermittent activity of writing poems with which my name is almost exclusively associated.

    I don't know whether it's also true, to give another obvious example, of the informal talk I am giving myself up to here. Probably not, if I think about how I've forced myself to the desk to fill up a few sheets of paper for this purpose. When someone asks if I'm working on something I don't know what to reply. Painful and elusive enough, my response is: "yes, on and off"; or else, less frequently: "yes, I've written some poetry." Work, in this context, for me, means finished work, definitely completed. Much more nebulous and difficult to pinpoint is work in progress: that's to say the phases and progression of the work. For this reason I'll always envy philologists, historians, archeologists, restorers, and, a little less, critics, especially reviewers, as well as full-time novelists with their large canvasses. If the person I'm talking to insists and asks me what "on and off" means, I get embarrassed and become discomforted, as though being asked faithfully to recount, point by point, something extremely personal and private. Such embarrassment is not always modesty or tetchiness, quite the contrary. It's contradicted by the desire to launch myself into a description of how, from the initial sensation, or from an accidental occurrence related to it, the first expressive nucleus was formed, concentrated perhaps in one of those lines that, as they say, is dictated by the gods. And it seems destined for, already mentally placed at, the beginning, the end, halfway or three-quarters through a poem which is yet to be written, but which, from the very first moment, suggests itself in quite precise terms: its outline, width, length, long or short or middling, or whatever. The desire passes quickly because I am aware that never, never could I convey, however involved and interested my listener may be, the intensity with which the imperceptible phenomenon was lived, was welcomed as a little miracle.

    If I am then asked about the origin and general sense or, worse still, the aim of my favorite themes, I get even more embarrassed. But it will never be as grave as the embarrassment of the questioner, who'll certainly be left with the impression of having attempted to sound the depths of emptiness. The fact is I don't have favorite themes; or, if I have them, I'm not conscious of it. For one thing there would be the risk of confusing them with certain spiritual dispositions, in other words, of turning them perpetually into the correspondents of particular states of mind, thus blurring them into psychology. Supposing it's possible to speak in some way of thematics, or themes, this only makes sense to me if related to a specific poem, but even then I'm aware that the poem didn't take shape in order to embody any theme.

Naturally, I am not making of these confidences (what else can they be called?) a rule, for me or still less for anyone else. I'm only seeking, in response to what was asked of me, to account for how I see myself in the face of what I write, or better, have written. My reluctance derives from the discomfort of going about the world with the name "a writer," more specifically, "poet." This title, of which there's nothing to be ashamed, disturbs me when I think of that separated corps, when I think of that inexorably fenced-off zoo. For many reasons and despite many signs to the contrary (which I consider faulty or specious), that's what the writer's and in particular the poet's world has become. To be aware of this and at the same time to have staked too much in the course of a lifetime on the dominating thought of poetry, here is a grave contradiction from which I suffer and which nonetheless I must confess. It doesn't alter the fact that I'd like to see the world of writers and poets—not of writing, or poetry, not the works—dissolve, the bars be removed from the cages of the zoo currently fencing off that separated corps to which, in spite of everything, I belong. Let's suppose it happens. Outside, there's the jungle, no use pretending otherwise. What path will the uncaged creatures follow? Once again I recall some lines by my friend Giorgio Caproni, ones that I often quote with amusement, though fully conscious of their gravity:

Don't ask anymore.
For you nothing's left here.
You're not one of the tribe.
You're in the wrong forest.

Some years ago, in Milan, an exhibition was held entitled *The Search for Identity,* a title disputed by some as a mere pretext, a gratuitous banner under which to bring together a number of more or less worthy, more or less representative works. True or false, the title nonetheless suggested a provisional justification, a reply to otiose questions like why do you write or, in general, work, and for whom. It responds to a recurrent concern in our time, so inescapable nowadays that every piece of work or show founded upon an expressive wish is said to be nothing but a search for identity. Nowadays when no one any longer would feel able even to conceive of a definition of art, or poetry, still less to conceive of it once and for all, it's difficult to imagine that a painting or poem or anything undertaken with artistic intentions has any other significance. It isn't a definition of the fact that signs are put on canvas or words on paper, but certainly a motivation or, frankly, an exculpation for works of this kind: expressing, precisely, the search for identity. One's own naturally, and others' or rather others' with respect to one's own, and vice versa. As far as I'm concerned now—and let me emphasize the now—I wouldn't know what other reasons or justifications to give for what I've written or can imagine writing in the future. This search, at least in my case, cannot yield other than sporadic recognitions, that is, partial and transitory identifications—and self-identifications; it is a hunt that doesn't presuppose a final, comprehensive prey. It lives, if it lives, on a contradiction from which filters, on and off, a primary (call it deluded, call it unfulfilled, call it unrequited) love of life.

1978

Port Stanley Like Trapani

June 1982. I think I know what the men dug into the defensive network of Port Stanley are feeling. We, like them, forty years ago next year, had orders to fight to the last: in the village of Paceco, behind Trapani, at the side of Mount Erice. I have often wondered how things would have turned out if a single inspiration had come to us all; and the Allied troops, arriving on the scene, had found us realigned with them, our weapons aimed at those who, moments before, were to be regarded as our allies. A single inspiration, that's to say, a common resolve—and there's the point. Beyond which my imagination or tardy make believe does not venture, entrusting the consequences to the realms of the improbable.

Today, Sunday June 6th, it seems in the Falklands, where it's winter now, the weather is improving. For some days the newspapers, the radio, and television have been insisting that for Port Stanley it's only a matter of hours. Rather than on the outcome, my mind focuses on those fatal hours hanging suspended and the few armed men confronting each other on a distant island, men who will soon come face-to-face.

The heat was intense that summer in Sicily. "And the dust!" an American reports, "a mixture of cattle droppings and pulverized chalky rock that got into your throat, causing an unbearable thirst. Old desert rats, who'd seen it all, swore it was worse than the sand in Africa."

A military chaplain came to the camp to say mass. He had some peculiar words to say in his sermon. He said a burdened animal goaded on by prods and whippings, brought almost to its knees, what does it do? It kicks back, falls, sinks to the ground, and will not get up. Exactly, he, for one, was not lacking inspiration. Albeit, as later became clear, of Mafia and not divine prompting. The major interrupted him sternly, enjoining him to stick strictly to his priestly duties, and in no time the mass was concluded with a hurried blessing.

Next came some high-ranking officers and a general to raise morale and reassure us, reassuring themselves at a collective banquet: highly unlikely that the landings would take place here; more probably in Sardinia or the Peloponnese. We spent sleepless nights on continuous prealert, illuminated by flares raining down from the reconnaissance planes come to spy on us following the four engine bombers' inevitable daily raid on a port by now unusable and a city that had been in its agony for even longer.

There came a young fascist official too, one recently appointed: how could anybody forget his obstinacy and untarnished faith in those spectral lands, deserted by all other civilian and military authorities?

One night towards the Egadi Islands the sea burst into flames in front of us. A rumbling, as if of running locomotives, passed overhead, crashing to earth somewhere in the night. The camp telephones sprang awake, informing us that some unidentified landing craft were moving towards the coast and that a parachute landing was to be expected, simultaneously, in our sector. It was nothing, or next to nothing: a brief shelling from offshore, a show of force. The landings had been taking place elsewhere for some days. They were to reach us overland and a battle, a brief skirmish rather, lasting less than four hours, was to settle everything, to the relief of the local population, long since hostile, actually menacing, towards us.

The story of those days fluctuates between an anxious questioning of what was about to befall us — how, when, from where — and the horror of its inevitability. A longing to have done with it (but at what price?) and at the same time the rather cowardly resentment that it was us who had to pay.

One afternoon — I had fallen asleep on a bunk bed, exhausted by one of those unavoidably sleepless nights — a Lightning squadron, fearful twin-boomed fighter-bombers, swooped down low over our heads and flew off without making us taste any of its venom or deadly eggs. Never had the bitter truth shown itself so starkly, so terrifyingly, as when, scornfully sparing us, it laid bare our impotence. At that very moment, friends left behind in the North were rejoicing at the turn events were taking, in line with their innermost wishes. Regardless of me, obviously, and my fate. I loathed them from afar. Rather than the accidents of war it was they who were, gleefully, sealing my fate, disposing of me. This was made abundantly clear by one of the last letters that somehow, miraculously, got through, expressing sympathy and wishing me — despite everything — good luck, the only luck that could be hoped for, in saving my skin, my soul being evidently quite beyond discussion.

Who knows, however, if it's true. Leaving aside their natural anxiety about the imminent engagement, who knows whether the men now defending Puerto Argentino — as it is called for them — feel as we did in our defense of Trapani, back in July '43. Everything is different: the situation, the motives, the outlook, above all, the degree of conviction. One thing is certain: they will listen to the rousing speeches of their commanding officers in quite a different spirit from how we listened to ours, officers who did not, or could no longer, believe in their own words.

Everyone agrees about one thing at least: that what is now taking place in the South Atlantic is one of the most absurd spectacles that we have been called upon to witness in recent years, so absurd that it has lent itself to the most vigorous ridicule. Despite this plain fact, people are nonetheless divided less by their opinions than by a sneaking desire to take sides. It has stealthily crept up on us, according to our sympathies, the image we have acquired of the warring parties, and only in distant relation to our political convictions: something not at all unlike support for one soccer team or another, or a taste for betting. As chance would have it, the events that are about to unfold will coincide with—but not necessarily be entirely circumscribed by—the World Cup, due to begin shortly in Spain. I mention this only to register a certain mood among people, the reasons that induce the powerful to take a certain course of action being abstruse for me. I myself, if I am honest, after agreeing with someone about the absurdity of it all, will end up admitting that I hope the British rapidly take Port Stanley. He may feel the opposite, and say so: he'd like to see the British flung back into the sea. We're not about to quarrel over it.

But heavens above, after so much that we have been called upon to witness, after so many declarations and denials, after so many sermons from so many different pulpits, isn't it possible for a more transparent inspiration to make itself felt? One more complete, richer, more unifying and instantaneously grasped than the resolve we failed to grasp and could never have reached in Sicily? Is the time still not ripe? An impulse, I mean, not dictated by military regulations in the face of imminent surrender, but one that might enable both sides, *the people,* the people down there, that's to say the individuals, *the men,* the men sent to their fate by their respective governments, to destroy their weapons simultaneously and to break out of the circle dividing them and run towards each other, to slap each other on the backs or treat themselves to festive kicks up the rear, and embrace: and to hell with those, Argentine or British, who had sent them. They are scarcely a few thousand men. Is it possible that such an idea might not flash into their minds, as one? That they will miss this chance to give an example to the whole world? To offer the possibility of a victory over absurdity by means of the unthinkable become real?

1982

Infatuations

Someone has gone from me, someone who counted for me is rejecting me, breaking free, disappearing. Distancing himself, he grows distant, withdraws the landscape to which he was prelude, bearer, sign. He no longer intends, never intended to be, any of these things, and, spilling over me my own disenchantment, he unmasks the mystification of which he was the object.

The countryside deserted, me deprived of the part that within me held place and person together, if others mention them I pretend not to have heard or have my mind on other things, I change subject. Canceling within me a face, I cancel the town it was inseparable from, such were their dizzying affinities. I change the names on road signs, turn the signposts round, take the opposite direction.

But it's like Cézanne's mountain: abstract in its repeated presence, unspeakably alive in its airy persistence. The womb of one self-same valley opens, new and different, a recognized slope is sun-drenched with the future.

Only now do I understand that just as a face was for me the prelude, carrier, sign of a landscape, so is this with respect to something other I start to glimpse. Far beyond the landscape.

Or at least so it seems.

I can retrace my steps, can start again over there.

1982

VITTORIO SERENI

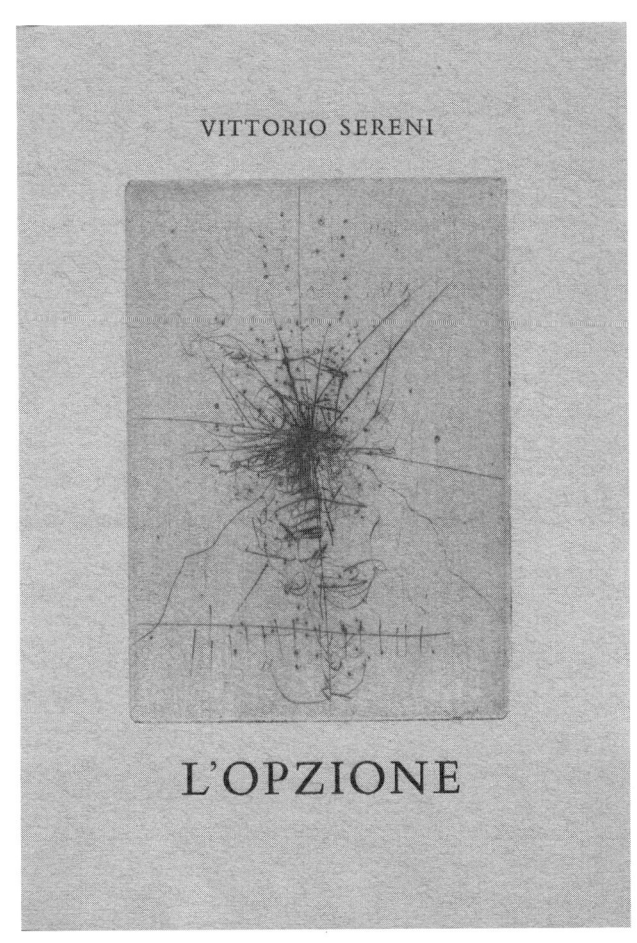

L'OPZIONE

from *Crossing Milan*

The Capture

The landing on the island of M. took place in a perfectly normal manner before a small festive crowd. There was the usual applause for the victors and a shirtless man, barefoot, jumped out in front of them, gripped by a commotion that impressed no one. "Be careful!" he was shouting, "they've got grenades! They won't think twice about shooting, they're shameless!"

It all had the air of a prearranged scene. The *regio maresciallo* standing smugly there on his own, had no idea? A French P. W. B. approached the false madman, telling him to cut it out; the Americans released the safety catches on their rifles and held them like people witnessing a doomed attempt to calm him down. George, the lieutenant, gave the orders. A man from the island was to walk towards the rebels, paving the way, as if by accident, for two officers, Italian prisoners, a lieutenant and a major, suitably behind, who would act as intermediaries, with escorts on either side. The escorts were to move in short sprints, sticking close to the walls, ready to open fire if necessary. The Frenchman was to act as interpreter.

When it came to explaining what the Italians had to do, he felt it his duty to pronounce every syllable clearly and harshly, as if to say: "Follow the instructions to the letter and don't try any funny business. Or you'll find your backs riddled with bullets."

The man at the front of the procession went forward, nose in the air, seemingly distracted. The two Italians kept to the middle of the road under the watchful gaze of the Frenchman who followed about twenty meters back; on either side, the escorts went cautiously past the houses and at every turning or crossing sprinted over the open ground between them, keeping as low as possible.

On a nod from the guide, the two Italians went forward alone, without cover, followed by the suspicious gaze of the Frenchman, immobile under a huge vault, while two armed men took up positions at the corners of the road. The garrison refusing to surrender was stationed in a house on the main road through town, no different from any of the others. The garrison, with such hostile intentions according to the *maresciallo,* had so far shown no sign of life. When the two Italian prisoners called, a head appeared from a window on the top floor and withdrew, with an exclamation of surprise. Hurried steps were heard going down the staircase and, a few moment later, a youngster, tall and smiling, astonished and at the same time happy to find two countrymen still fairly well kitted-out before him, appeared on the threshold of the ground-floor doorway. Very young, not much more than twenty years old. And really, if what had been said about his behavior was to be believed, one would need to imagine that a fierce, unyielding force could steal into the clothes of a good-natured, smiling Milanese accounts clerk, one of those soldiers whose uniforms are evidently just a shell to shuffle off, confined by fate to a distant shore as an advanced sentry for Italy.

It was true that for some days, following the destruction of the equipment during a night bombing raid, it had been impossible to receive or transmit, by heliograph or radio, from the island to Sicily: perfectly true that he knew nothing of what had happened to the city or the Admiralty; he suspected, certainly, that both had fallen permanently to the Americans, but what was he supposed to do? You mean to say that now it was a soldier's duty to shout *come and get me, come and get me,* to tie oneself up and lie down on a rock, and wait . . . When informed of the surrender, briefly by the major, he did not waste time on the oddity of the procedure. He surrendered. He only wished he could get his hands on the ineffable *maresciallo,* an old acquaintance, for a quarter of an hour. In brief, everything was clear, just as Franchi, on the basis of his own experience, had foreseen. When they'd got wind of what was happening, the people from the village had tried to make off with the provisions intended for the garrison. The young soldier and his men, all too obviously, had stopped them: more or less the opposite of what the *maresciallo,* concerned about his future position with the conquering powers and the islanders, had reported. That's how the strange expedition had ended. Franchi took part in it, despite himself, and not without a certain relish for the unexpected. And another story finished too: of a handful of men for months, perhaps years, posted as lookouts on a rock, scrutinizing the sea. Or listening to it, rather, the sea, and conversing with it, conversations that no history of the country will ever recount? It ended. There, as elsewhere. Without a desperate defense, without holding out to the last man, with applause for the victors and a sigh of relief from many; with a bitter sigh, and nothing more, from a few.

The Frenchman stepped forward and with his evidently customary arrogance, at the beginning of such contacts, insisted that the new prisoner respect the rules of surrender: hands raised, he pushed him into the house for interrogation and an inventory of the arms and materials available on that tiny island. The picture was complete when the two men who until then had been posted at the corners of the road took up positions in front of the command post, to defend it, rifles at the ready and with affable faces, beneath the gaze of the curious.

George arrived with the news that the collection point for everyone during the hours before reembarkation would be the Finance Police barracks, placed at his disposal by the *maresciallo* who had momentarily disappeared.

An old couple who could probably make little of the jumble of different uniforms timidly approached Franchi and the major, placing themselves and the population of the island in their good hands, and beseeching . . . everybody would die of hunger in the next few days if nobody took care of them. Upon which the two prisoners didn't have the heart to confess their own present state and, not so much in words, but in a reassuring gesture, held out the prospect of immediate plentiful provisions. In whispers at doorways, in faint glimmers of light from cracks, day ended on that stretch of land that seemed such easy prey to storm waves, so open was it at every point to the impact and sigh of the waters. Uncertain figures darted out of alleyways and after depositing their whispers in far from neutral ears, disappeared once more.

"These Italians, they're all the same," said Di Maggio, when the last nocturnal informer had gone away. "They think of nothing but stabbing each other in the back."

Di Maggio, it should be said, was the name of the Frenchman. But he spoke Italian well enough.

The Italo-French-American dinner with which the day ended had come off exquisitely, creating an atmosphere of fraternal euphoria. The local innkeeper had not spared himself and laid his hands on certain secret reserves, whose existence hardly tallied well with the desperate plight claimed for the island. He had only asked for absolute secrecy, and so everything had taken place behind hermetically sealed windows, when the island was deep in sleep. An American guard, one Donnart, who, Di Maggio told Franchi, had been connected with the cinema during peacetime, did an entertaining number portraying the different behaviors of a Frenchman, an Italian, and an American during an air attack and bombing. George's ways and his warm voice became more and more winning in Franchi's eyes, so much so that they stifled the scruple he felt about being treated so differently from the new prisoners, under lock and key in the Finance barracks like mischievous children; while Di Maggio, whom the Americans were pleased to ignore, had made a truce between the Latin peoples, whispering into Franchi's ear *To hell with the Anglo-Saxons, the lot of them.* If he were to be believed, without French generals and French intelligence, no American would ever have set foot on a European beach. And at this point he let fall, as a generous concession, and between clenched teeth, a eulogy for the Italian counter-intelligence service. As for the Italian major, he had no reason to regret the evening despite certain mournful presentiments that he would be the defenseless object of the victors' scorn.

Everything, in short, had taken place in the best possible way, so much so that the image was conjured of a peaceful group of friends seated at a banquet. Every distinction of nationality lapsed, every ideological distance bridged, the war reduced to a pallid memory. Towards the end, even the dusk of a dear melancholy had wrapped itself around the heads of the fellow diners, who now lay half-asleep, or already fast asleep, in the beds and bunks of their improvised billet.

He saw that the escorting troops were not the same as the day before: now it was a squad or little more, with an officer as well. From the day before, only George remained. He was glad. He watched them straggling themselves over the bridge as the fishing boat pushed off. Exactly, it would have been sufficient to glance meaningfully at the soldiers captured with him, to make a circle around the crates of grenades the enemy had imprudently put aboard as trophies of war. He was himself sitting on one of those crates. It wouldn't have been difficult to lift the latch, get up swiftly, open the lid...

Then they would have forced the pilot to change course, perhaps towards Sardinia, avoiding the ships cruising on the open sea.

Almost a delightful story of pirates with sails raised in the morning of the world. This time his glance stopped at the American officer. He too was seated, face half-hidden in the shadow thrown by his heavy helmet, the rest illuminated by a reflection as if of running water. "Austere and enchanting," he had said one day of a woman's face, which George's without any loss of virility now resembled.

The island dissolved into the blue. A daring intent dropped into the void. Not because a farcical tenderness had intervened; no, his very way of looking at that face made it clear that he, personally, was not made for such deeds of daring-do. Many months' feelings pouring back into that last pretext, but immediately they flooded over it.

So he didn't know whether, in the months gone, things and events had been decked with phantasms of love and other mirages, or whether, on the other hand, the force of life in him had rotted and corrupted so as to reconcile the irreconcilable on a road fraught with snares, shadows, imminent misunderstandings, nights with no moon . . .

He went back to those months, and their course—zigzagging and broken in more than one place if looked at as a sequence of real events—it straightened and became unambiguous in that sort of drifting, that excess of heart they'd been in him. The voice that ran through the marina and the old and recent rubble, the abandoned hotel and the disorder of requisitioned rooms—and the imagination intent on pretending for itself a story of love in that southern city—, the night fire of the antiaircraft guns, sometimes too far over the horizon for the chilling crashes to reach, easy to take them for fireworks at some distant celebration. Sure, he had not been without ardor. But as for converting it into reasons and acts of war . . . He had got caught in the labyrinth, and inexplicable things had happened. The threat of death in combat hung over him, of imprisonment in a foreign land. He suffered it as an injustice, as an outcome at odds with the thoughts he'd had, the actions he had performed.

Between the brief and not particularly bloody exchange of fire and his capture, a night had gone by. The men remained in the dugouts or lying in the grass; fires blazed here and there; a depot was burning like a calm and desolate flame towards the port. Horses and mules belonging to the crumbling divisions took to the fields, some found their way into the ground floor. It was a cloudy, unsettled night, fleecy and undulating, with hilltops and crevices, with a faint breathing and rustling. Somewhere they were shooting, madly, for one last time against the shadows, against their own fear, against the war; or, more simply, they were using up their ammunition, uselessly stockpiled during those months, to such an extent that the sector was full of it, beyond all need. Unable to sleep, he had strayed for hours along the villa's fencing. The whole village was awake, in its turn, and seemed to be busy with feverish preparations.

Franchi had lain down in the grass right between Villa Paradiso and Villa Sigma. Perhaps he ended up nodding off there, at the point where, one night during an inspection, he had felt a fervent gaze fixed upon him from the branches and leaves. Amid the sound of twigs trodden underfoot, somebody strayed breathlessly, struggling to get out of the tangle. The plants came alive. It seemed he would manage to get out in the end. Franchi wanted to stand up but stayed rooted to the spot. He expected suddenly to see rifle barrels trained on him from all around—but then the half-dream had taken a different turn. The disquiet was suddenly interrupted, and, finally, out from the rooms where she'd been kept for months and months, pushing aside the fronds, the Villa Sigma owner's daughter came up to him, head bowed. Then, looking him bluntly in the face, with a vague gesture at the tireless village, at the countryside, and all the darkness on the sea, she said: "Forgive me, for Sicily."

The shadow of an airplane darkened for a moment the surrounding water. From the bridge someone waved a handkerchief in salute, an act that had fallen for some time into disuse, which appeared strange, bitter perhaps, to some of the voyagers. Franchi breathed a sigh of relief. Those things had happened, but the backwash did not return them in the form of debris, unclarified, which would trouble him still. They had happened. That is, he had had them. And now one of them, he did not know exactly which, perhaps that last memory, superimposed itself upon the others. He no longer saw them. He sensed, instead, the single long wave, that sea which bore him now—energy, exaltation, whatever, or blue inebriation—which bore him and the others on an indefinite voyage, and the large fishing boat and those seagulls that, in a confiding circle, abandoned themselves to the quiet, barely perceptible motion.

He stole a glance at George and went over to sit by him. (*How many things we could do, you and I, George. Disembark at Marseilles and walk along the avenues and wide boulevards of France or look up at the mountains of Austria where the sky grows deeper, with a touch of gloom, a genuine sky of Central Europe, go into a town nearby around midday, with the sense of taking it all in style, everything, shop windows, squares, gardens. You could be the style, George, and I could be the knowledge. Or vice versa, if you like. . . . But George was talking about the Germans, of the indiscriminate bombing in which they cared little if some ancient wonder of Europe were destroyed. It's in these things, he innocently said, that you can recognize how civilized a people are . . . But by now the Stukas were a thing of the past.*)

He listened, as one listens to a fellow traveler, when it hardly matters what is said, provided you talk or are silent in a certain way, and in the meantime you're on the road or out at sea on a morning like this.

"Would you like one?" George offered, holding out his case.

"Thank you, thank you very much," he replied, taking one, and he immediately added in a style that must have seemed exaggerated at least to the other: "But how very, very good . . ." He couldn't see the coast that was already fading into the mute white city, the soccer ground, the villas along the seafront, the mountain in the background.

"Here we are," someone said. The motorized fishing boat dropped anchor at the entrance to the harbor. The prisoners, dutifully escorted, would reach the shore in boats that were drawing alongside. Everybody on board stood up, and he lost sight of George, who he expected to find again on shore.

Looked at from the boat, the water of the port was ashen. It was taking on the color of the heat haze, midday being close. The color of the rubble coming back into view. And the water was as if infected by the swollen and corroded bodies borne many times over the last months almost everywhere onto the coast.

Trucks were waiting on the shore. And armed men around them and others in civilian clothes speaking confidentially to them. Ironically, when he and the others were on land.

He looked around for George. Who wasn't there. He turned

his eyes towards the motorized fishing boat, stationary at the entrance to the harbor. He thought he saw him moving in the shadow of the quarter deck.

"Goodbye, George!" he shouted, with a voice that began to crack.

The trucks were waiting with their engines on already.

The Option

He's quite a character—says Marcel, and I agree. But what is it about him, is it those eyes that seem to see everything, through at least 180 degrees, if not more, simultaneously, as they settle on some point or other? The voice deep, insistent: the bistrot, là on est tout à fait bien, inexpensive, excellent cuisine, genuine, central, yet out of the way, away from the traffic. The voice insinuating, inviting us to a prohibited, a subtle pleasure—incomprehensible to most. The consideration of a first-class waiter. Tender, rather pained eyes behind the glasses. To the extent that later, after advising us what to order, so well that at the first taste of each dish everyone looks at him approvingly and with gratitude, after settling up, us outside talking about where to go now, he mentions a party he really can't miss. (It'll be so tedious compared to your charming company, but if you, at least, will agree to come, it would be a pleasure and an honor). He doesn't insist on inviting anyone else, but who knows if it's from discretion or desire or the need to drop us? Fact is he disappeared, vanished at the corner of the street and the big man didn't notice. Some interesting people, after five years coming here I'm getting to like it . . . Maybe you haven't noticed but we're all, more or less, in couples. He was on his own, so he left. Granted we're improvised couples, interchangeable what's more . . . no, I didn't mean, I wasn't implying . . . You go ahead with him, that way I can find out more about the woman who was next to me at dinner. So, as I was saying, he went off, slipped away in the manner of a stylish benefactor, I told you, there's something I just don't get. As if he'd no other obligation or wish than this: to send us out roving, in twos and threes, in couples along the riverside, at such an hour, fine evening, limpid, the bridges in full view, that flaring skyscraper on the far bank where

I have never been, the neat outline of the houses, the cathedral, the antennae with an intermittent flake of light at its summit, perfect visibility, celestial blue.

There, I knew it, at Sammy's Bar, such novices. Not really though, a bit better this evening, some of the elite . . . See the one with the monocle just now, see him make such a meal of me? First time since we've known each other, the great Seeler deigns to acknowledge that we've met, knows my name and who I work for, rattling away in French. You'll say he's had a few, but he's always had a few, which makes us even. His present interest's worth the same as his previous indifference, exactly as if he never touched the stuff, he says he's had me wrong up to now, this coming year will get to know me better—and for now, to prove it, he slips a flower into my buttonhole. Fine, this coming year, but look at them, please, those two nearby, she so splendid, him likely a jerk who doesn't deserve her, but the fact is I find them delicious, ah youth, the splendor of youth, for a quarter of an hour I've been admiring you. So, the blonde that's in with Taylor. You were saying? No, it's not one of my usual mess-ups. Sadly not, better if it were. Well I'll tell you. The first year I find myself with her at a dinner and start giving her meaningful looks across the table. Then at the bar I manage to get up close to her, or rather it just so happens that we find ourselves sitting by chance at a small table in that seraglio of sorts which is the bar with its little orchestra at the Excelsior Hotel . . .

Take it easy, I'll tell you another time why some things keep happening to me in the same way. Fine, if I were to tell you then how I started talking to her and how, at a certain point, she seemed to be listening, I really don't know, can't remember. I know that the next evening I rather fancied my chances. I maneuver her once more towards the bar, but she declines. It seems she's dropping on her feet, barely tolerates me, says she's got a bad cold, has brought her departure forward, tomorrow morning at nine. (As I've said, I find those two next to us utterly enviable, but let me say it again, sweet bird of youth, fits them like a glove, even if it's the title of a dreadful film). So now she's actually going to bed, it's clear, it means nothing to her if my company's not enough to overcome her cold and tiredness. This is definitive and desperate proof that she cares nothing for me. I say so and she shrugs. She doesn't care at all if I think and feel and say this is proof of her not caring for me at all. She allows me to accompany her along the corridors where she'd like to take a last look at the tapestries that, she says, are her real love—she'd go so far as to steal them, she loves them that much. But at the door to her room she barely extends me a hand, with her other on the key already in the lock, she shrugs definitively when I ask whether I may telephone the next morning to wish her a bon voyage. Now, as it happens, that night I sleep badly, get to sleep very late, wake up, then fall asleep again I don't know how many times. And when I telephone it's well after daybreak. The phone rings in vain a while. She must have left already. The phone rings in vain, but not upon her empty room, upon a clearing in the Black Forest or the banks of the Rhine, upon her journey in the sun, upon a still summery day, more than summer—it's so full of sun. Whatever, I'm in a room, in the dark, still in bed, the receiver in my hand, and in vain the phone's ringing, in a vast, dazzling emptiness; I'm a prisoner in a hotel room, separated from a stunning day of sunshine I will never live. I know what you're thinking. The blonde's got nothing to do with any of this, and it's nothing to do with missing my chance with her. Situations of this kind, thoughts of this kind, descend upon me anyhow. Maybe you're right, but let's not talk about it now. (That said, I hope I never find myself alone with this girl standing next to me). Let's pretend Taylor's blonde does matter to me. That takes me to yesterday evening and the dinner in honor of that Sitwell character. You'll have noticed she was at the end of the table, on my side. After the dinner I stand up, allow the lady on my right to pass, the gentleman on her right to pass. Meanwhile she's coming towards me, purposeful, with her steely eyes that don't look at me and don't see me, and she's about to go by when I hazard:—Je vous admire toujours de loin. L'autre soir encore je vous ai vue, pardon, rencontrée chez . . . —Please, don't laugh. And don't laugh if I add that Bernardoni, that fool, butted in just then and ruined the effect. "Mais celle-ci c'est de près qu'il faut la regarder, quoi . . ." I knew it, you're sniggering, sniggering shamelessly. It takes away the pleasure in telling it—on top of this racket and idiot music. Well, you need to know I've had a fetish about glances since I was a boy, such that I consider it impossible, worse, unjust that a glance, the commitment of a glance, should not be repaid with a returning glance. It was just as though she'd never set eyes on me, never met me before. Maybe she doesn't like me because I'm Italian. That happens between Italians and Germans. It wouldn't be the first time, whatever they say. But that's not it, as I discovered shortly after seeing her at the bar with, of all people, Gastone. Maybe she doesn't think I'm sufficiently important for her work, whereas he . . . You see him over there on the bar stool, with his torso emerging from shadow, like that time at the seaside when he was up to his waist and, side on, he looked like a centaur, with rump and thighs like a horse's below the water's surface? And the blonde bestowing upon him, as he smiles with all teeth showing, not the steely look of before, but her most beautiful aquamarines, allowing me, looking at her from behind, to see only the iridescent white layering of her more or less blonde blondeness . . . Changeable, quite, from steel to acquamarine, but I expect on occasions she's all incandescence, with the incandescence of cats or some blue-blonde children . . . What do you reckon, she likes centaurs, the blonde?

And now look at her there before us, sitting next to that Taylor fellow. Both relaxed, at their ease, leaning back on the sofa without losing their composure, superior and detached from all else, with the air of two old acquaintances, or better, of two who've had an understanding for quite some time: they don't so much as look at each other, they talk side by side with eyes on the emptiness, barely moving their lips like two people trying to make a date or say something in the presence of others so as not to be overheard, as if nothing were happening.

But you know, I'm really beginning to like this autumn date with people you don't see for the rest of the year, or hardly ever, but meet here for a rendezvous—and it looks as if they feel out of place should you happen to meet them in Paris, London, or Milan, even if it's their home—, these familiar faces that swim before your eyes right on cue, one year later, with the look of old acquaintances standing out from the opaque and silent flow of visitors; or you're drawn towards them, their fluid presence, behind that corner or in the adjacent corridor under the signs for the Olympic Village, Italia, France, España, etc., acting as points of the compass if you don't care to stop and look at the guidebook, or they light up suddenly just when you thought you'd lost the thread of the maze and are about to throw yourself down, hot, legs aching, on the first chair you can find, only to bump into ubiquitous Gastone, just as tired and, what's more, furious for some reason of his own, like this morning at the table of the Fair's main bar. I'm the foolish one—he was railing—persisting in seeing the world split into the intelligent and the idiots. Brilliant, but where do you put the criminals? Yes, sir, the criminals. Because you and I imagine we're moving among the intelligent, or at least that we're more intelligent than the next man, and the next man is up to your tricks, allows you to believe it . . . he knows you play by the rules and respect them, that's just what he's counting on, your being law-abiding and him above the law, on breaking the rules you follow but not him, oh, no; you speak and make moves hoping to beat him to it within the limits of what's fair and he, hot-foot—wham—he arrives, with his latest crime, just when you thought you'd beaten him to it, but you've not yet learned that there's no getting there first, not if he's ready, two or three seconds after you, two or three hours after, with his lawlessness, when there are other criminals like him waiting only for this to take his side . . . Ah, but he'll pay, he'll pay—and it won't be me that makes him pay, it'll be one of those other criminals who's right now on his side . . . God knows who he was railing about, and I certainly didn't ask, specially since from not far off there came the metallic and slightly forced snigger with which Guglielmo admits, and at the same time confirms, some underhand maneuver of his when the deal's been done and there's no getting it back. I left him to his rage, and the funny thing is I felt embarrassed as if it was me who'd done him wrong, imagine that, and walked away leaving him on his chair, wounded centaur or dying cock, whichever, at an intersection in the Fair.

Guess what, I got a note from my Colombian friend. I went to his stand; he wasn't there. I left him a note in turn. See if he doesn't get here any moment. Yes, the books have arrived for him, this time, his wife and son, I don't know, maybe this year he's left them at home. We must ask him round for lunch, one of these days, with what little time the Fair leaves for being together. Him and Sternheim, they know each other, actually me and Sternheim became friends over there in part thanks to him . . . But you see, I don't know, with Sternheim it'll be work, the most precise and frequent occasions for being together, I always touch ground, you're on firm ground, while with Alvarez . . . no, it's not his fault, actually he gets to the point, he doesn't waste time on memories of our meeting over there, talks about the new plant, his plans . . .

understandable, it's hard to connect, the areas too different, really tricky to integrate, noncommunicating in actual fact, but he does all he can to integrate and communicate, no, it's not his fault if at this point I don't feel I've anything else in common with him except flowery and melodious rambles, clouds swollen with light and rain over a city that's a little bit Milan and a little bit Genoa, some pieces of lunatic architecture like nothing I've ever seen before, blown up from the encounter of a sculptor's and a stage designer's dreams, the more complete the more they've been left interrupted, breached, open to the invasion of light and air, not far from the place where their designer and builder ended up with brain fever, mind swarming with these or other designs, and still others yet to be constructed—below a clattering suburban tram . . . Such is Alvarez more than one year later, certainly it's my fault, and I already have to make an effort, to crash through a palisade of clouds at the banquet table to find under the full moon anyone who resembles him, Colombian by choice, former Spanish refugee, who laughing in the moonlike light commemorates a Spanish-born self who's already lived there, fought in those places during the civil war and from there, from that same city, escaped some time after, who knows how, political refugee, who knows how, to Colombia . . . And what else is Alvarez more than one year later? He's someone who has set in motion inside me rambles, clouds, architecture, little more than that, and if you really want to undo, unroll the mummy's bandages still further . . . here's the congress room, completely crowded that morning, everyone hushed, listening to his speech against censorship—and the pandemonium, at the end, the standing ovation, a few with watery eyes, and everyone with a desire for warmth, strength, ardor, sacrifice. Well, I've already told you about it. So, at last year's Fair, for a moment he was like he'd been that morning: the stand empty, and that funny writing in French with which the publisher Rafael Alvarez apologized to his illustrious colleagues, from the world over, for the fact that the books had, mysteriously, failed to arrive. The first thought was of reprisal or sabotage, hard to say on whose part, given that he'd been Colombian for some time, no longer Spanish; and thus he, beyond the rambles, clouds, and outrageous architecture, was momentarily turning back into the hero of that morning . . . but hang on, don't get me wrong, I'm not regretting the eclipse of the hero in this jovial man who, to get his idea across, repeats the sentence he wants you to attend to, twice, comically pronouncing each syllable—all the time giving his listener a cunning little jab in the stomach or the arm—, no, it's not that at all, it's that I'm mortified to no longer have anything to share with him but rambles, clouds, and mad architecture, the mortification of having to fall back on the solidity of Sternheim as witness for Alvarez's reality . . . Rather, the other evening, Dolores, at that Babel of a lunch with hundreds of invitees, told me something fabulous. You know Suarez, Castillo's colleague? For a month or more after we left, Dolores says, every evening he went back to the Florida and stood there like a lonely dog repeating to himself that the congress wasn't over, that his friends would be coming down soon—French, Italian, English—for confabulations with Luisito, to hatch some plots . . . I can't tell you what those on our side thought of him, but one year on all that remains is the embarrassment of having fallen into easy boasting, trips back and forth from Montjuïc by taxi or rented car, a holiday mistaken for a secret mission, emotion for dedication, a throwback to twenty years ago . . . the embarrassment and slight shame of getting trapped in your own veiled emphasis and your own bad conscience maybe, emoting tourists, sensation seekers: those afternoons already summery, heavy, often stormy, a nerve-torn wait for the sirens of alarm, of shutters clattering down on streets suddenly deserted, the first shots, a clamor started two streets away, barricading yourself into the hotel become a fort, hoarding the water that would soon run out, standing firm, remaining loyal to others you can't see but you know they're there, and they know that you are, strangers there by chance or not chance at just the right moment, till the first patrol of avengers shows up on the fringe of Mount Tibidabo and . . . *Aquí estoy—frente a ti Tibidabo—hablando viendo—la tierra que me faltaba para escribir "mi patria—es tambien europa y poderosa"* . . .[1] it renders very well what Dolores's friend and ours was perhaps churning through his mind for hours over a whisky at the bar in the Florida after we'd left. I don't say all, but some Spaniards, some Portuguese, who come here, they come here, yes,

1. These lines are from the poem "Ca ni guer" (that's to say, "Guernica") by the recently dead Blas de Otero. [They read: "I'm here—in front of you, Tibidabo—talking seeing—the land that I missed so as to write 'my homeland—is both Europe and strong'"—*trans*.]

to sell their books and to buy others within (and beyond) the authority given them, but they also come for something else, above all for something else, to stand like the poet and like Suarez in front of Mount Tibidabo. In general they mix with us Italians, and for obvious reasons. But since yesterday evening—you were there too and I knew from your glances that you understood me—I've found myself in difficulties over this. The dismantling of Rafael has begun—you seemed to be saying when the man I'd not met before, what's he called, that Portuguese guy, anyway the one who was staring at me and said *je n'aime pas qu'on fasse des affaires en y mêlant la politique,* you know perfectly well who he was talking about . . . Yes, I confess I'd begun to suspect it a little, since last year if you want to know, but that's no reason to feel rancor, to hold it against him, it's his way of getting by, another lesson for my veiled emphasis, superficiality, lack of preparation . . . Poor me, poor me not at all, I'm not feeling sorry for myself, this is a serious matter, every now and then I bang my nose against it, much more serious than it seems. Because it's true that today failures are collective failures, the most painful disappointment is a collective one, no, not the most painful, but the one that most leaves its mark, I mean the illusion that's followed by the disappointment, in group terms, of a meeting, of a failed assembly is a hope you can't get back to, an experience you can't take another stab at, but it hurts just the same, it's no less painful that somebody younger than you, a youngster, coldly, rationally shows you in no time at all how you've understood nothing, that your implements no longer work for anything, that you're a man of feeling, that you can't help the Spanish or Portuguese or anyone else that's in need with sentiments, that mixing with these or those, apart from being the easy thing to do, makes no sense and for them it's actually harmful, you only help them stay stuck with you, in remorse, the mourning, for lost opportunities, for youth flown by, for self-commemoration . . . Oh, here's our man himself. How's it going, how's it going, mon cher ami?

Really I just don't get it. At the Schmidt lunch, out of courtesy, I say a few words to someone at my table, out of courtesy alone. Actually, he wants me to give an opinion and since the thing's a bit complicated and I don't have a piece of paper with me, he gets up and brings me pencil and paper. Meanwhile from your table—

you're a woman, you'll have noticed, won't you? — Hilde's sending alarm signals in my direction, with her hazel eyes and gestures, increasingly frantic, she begs me to wait, not to commit myself. How come, you'll be wondering, weren't they, aren't they still friends? Sure, close ones, tender even in public, but the trouble is they work for rival houses; bed's one thing, but business is business. Well and good, I told myself, it must mean Hilde's suffering from competitive anxieties. I tried to reassure her, the information my neighbor was seeking was entirely marginal — no need to worry. She was only partly reassured, made me promise if anything interesting came my way I'd tell her first. We've become friends for a reason, no? She almost made me swear an oath. I was taken aback, looked at her with genuine concern. In fact her alarm wasn't about what I might have written on that piece of paper, but my seeming to initiate confidential relations in a sphere of work outside her own. Just imagine! With what we have to go through to get them interested in our things, how when they take a book from you it's like they descend from on high after months or maybe years of wavering, of ifs and buts. But hang on, the good part comes next. I was in the cloakroom and the guy from Luxembourg came up, you know, the faithful bistrot guide, transfixing me with a flash from his semi-all-seeing, sad eyes set in an inscrutable face: — Monsieur. — He looks me over once more and says, rapid and decisive, in a style reminding me of the strange talk between the blonde and Taylor at Sammy's Bar, that I'm wasting my time. An explanation, please. Not here, pas ici, he'll phone me at the hotel in an hour. Funny thing is that at lunch he hadn't turned to me once, a slight bow at the start and that's all. He was at Guglielmo's table; he works for him in Paris, which explains a lot. (You've no idea to what heights of suspicion Guglielmo will arrive. Once, at a cocktail party, he saw me chatting with a writer, not even a very important one, and with his usual heavy-handedness he barged in and insisted in a tone supposed to be jokey but actually ridiculously solemn that I shouldn't try to steal his authors... God knows it was the last thing on my mind at that moment). Fact is an hour later, on the dot, the man phones, and asks can he come up to my room. I almost felt like passing him on to you, but you'd gone to have a lie down and I spared you. Monsieur, you are wasting your time. Why did I want to see you here? But it's obvious, in the hall there's always so much confusion...

too many eyes watching, too many ears listening, and I'm about to give you some absolutely precious news, de tout premier ordre. How come to you, the competition? Don't ask questions, je vous en supplie, trust me . . . let's say I'm doing it because I like you. Yes, it's true I work for someone else, but I might change one day, you never know, on ne sait jamais . . . And here he spells out the name and room number of the person in possession of this marvel. Quick, don't waste time, on vous attend, it's the Fair's only real big deal, the rest c'est des bricoles. Don't insist on asking questions, don't thank me either . . . he leaves. I phone the number, already knew the person, and head for his suite on the floor above. As I expected, his partner's here too, also known to me for some time. The guy, I'm sure I've already described him to you, the man with the cruel thin cigar, Dutch, a face full of teeth, more, when he walks he seems hung by his teeth on some invisible hook. On other occasions I've seen him fairly merry, extremely gallant with the ladies, a perfect drunk, of the kind you rarely see, the type who never lose their figure—and at the same time he reminds you of those respectable gentlemen in old French farces who cross the stage in their underwear and steal out of the Commune on tiptoe—he speaks French, English, and German, prefers German; who knows why I got the idea that when the Dutch speak a language not theirs, and all the more the less familiar the language they're speaking, they give themselves a hand by wobbling their heads with every sound they emit, as if jabbing at the person listening, to cut right through the pronunciation problem. So the man with the thin and cruel cigar, not the least bit drunk at that moment, sets about showing me the outline or mock-up book, let's say the maquette. You need to know, and I remembered it only then, that other mock-up books used to circulate among us in the days of an association of European publishers with its headquarters or contact address in Geneva whose civic aim was, of course, the joint publishing of works testifying to the persistence over time of a self-proclaimed European spirit—and other pleasantries. Result: an eminently elegant and eminently useless tome dedicated to the fountains of Europe. You get the picture? After gatherings, journeys, exhausting get togethers, piles of correspondence, you need something more than fountains to freshen the urge to meet up again and make a deal at all. Hence my perplexed look, but he doesn't appear to recall the precedent; I flick over the pages of the maquette, shift my eyes to his partner, who smiles at me. I go back to examining the maquette, while those two start talking about design criteria, quality and number of illustrations etc. etc. In so far as I could tell the projected book wasn't bad. It's done—they explain—as a reply to one question, namely: what will take place in the world over the next ten years? And that's to say, what directions will politics, science, town planning, transport, literature, the arts, behavior take? A book to do quickly, of course. The texts, from the pens of certain illustrious professors of various nationalities, were 80 percent ready, as were the illustrations. I ask if they're thinking of a joint edition and, if so, with how many publishers and which ones. Not necessarily, they reply. Are they already talking to Italian houses? French, American? They keep it vague. I try to buy time. My boss wasn't able to be here, I should at least give him a call. What about a schedule, a descriptive outline, une table des matières, une synopsis with all the details to discuss in Milan after the Fair? They could have our reply in a week. Here they let the killer phrase drop, which after all I was expecting, about the keen interest of another Italian publisher. In short, they give me till tomorrow; but they retain the right to act freely should anyone else meanwhile show a concrete interest in the book . . . But of course, granted, the war of nerves is always granted, in these cases. Now, the idea wasn't so unusual, they'd discovered nothing new. Television back home, the glossy magazines have already done something similar. If I were more expert in these things, I could even say to what extent our readers take an interest in stuff like this. My guess would be: not much. And besides, the sorts of cases in which I'm inclined to take a risk without asking for instructions are different, not these. One thing was evident here and could be stated honestly: that the project's interest didn't lie in the what but in the how. Nobody ever discovers, really discovers, anything alone—as we all know. So what happens is that a tepid initial interest in the what becomes a passion for the how. It's a matter of seeing from where the how begins . . . I'll have to keep my eyes open during these three days remaining until the end. As often happens, there'll be another three or four ideas like this one going the rounds. In what lounge, what room, at what stand? Fine, I bought myself twenty-four hours, at my own risk, of course. You, what would you have done in my place? And, here's the point, why was our bistrot guide so kindly playing the intermediary? Because he likes me, as he says, nothing else? If you like; but in that case you've got to admit Guglielmo's not interested in the book. A good enough reason—one of just how many?—for not going further ourselves. Let's say: a useful guide given my lack of expertise in this "type of thing." Either that or the Dutchman's tired of Guglielmo and wants to come over to our side, so he does something to build up his position, to prompt our gratitude? Or else: Guglielmo and the Dutchman already have an agreement, but Guglielmo knows there's another "how" doing the rounds. The man with the cigar knows it too; but he doesn't know that Guglielmo knows. Now Guglielmo wants someone, let's say us or Gastone, to be thrown off this other "how." So up steps Luxembourg, to whet our appetites, spread rumors and get Gastone to follow the Dutch trail... One last theory, for the time being: Luxembourg works in Paris for the Dutchman too but Guglielmo doesn't know that, or he's thinking of ditching Guglielmo and going over to the Dutchman alone; in either case he's defending the interests of the Dutchman who wants to get as much as he can from the deal, he already has an agreement with Guglielmo and in the end the book will be his, but he needs to jack the price up, and ergo... Ah, yes, I forgot to tell you the man from Luxembourg asked me specifically not to mention him to the Dutchman... But then how to explain the fact that the Dutchman finds it entirely natural that I go to his room with the air of someone who doesn't know precisely what's happening but knows it's important? The only important deal at the Fair... Eh? what do you think? Well then... the other evening, the evening at the bistrot, what was Luxembourg trying to hide by sending us for a walk along the river? A coincidence? Yes? No? You could speculate differently about it, after all...

But this huge hotel that wasn't here last year, have you ever seen anything like it... As you say, the lobby like the airport at Fiumicino or Orly, the man for the taxis down there, a cross between a general and Hitler's chauffeur, all decked out in a beret, gabardine, boots; and then, once they know the destination, they shoot us—literally shoot us—up to the top floor in an elevator, which ignores, won't allow intermediate stops, until you feel gently sucked in like a feather and deposited among a cheerful racket of Italian voices, but not only Italian because the Italian reception now includes other voices and accents; it never happens that someone grows tender anymore, as they did still just two or three years back, about this "strip of Italy in the leaden heart of Central Europe," oh here's your friend from the other evening, your and our Marcel ... But of course, I know, only did it to make you laugh, believe me, absolutely no insinuation, it's dead right, I'd almost sort of prefer it if between you two there were some tenderness, rather than ... No, nothing, rather than, oh, in short, what I meant to say is that when he was being ironic about having suddenly turned into a number, room 1518, from the actually famous writer he is—as he usually thinks himself, it's not that now and then he fails to give himself some airs, oh, no, not at bottom unpleasantly, he's rather good at putting up a smokescreen of pleasantries for us, human, all too human, absolutely tolerable your beloved, get away with you—as I say, when he was ironic about his number and, exaggerating his terror at the very idea of Sunday afternoon, he begged us to meet and keep him company ... well, I was thinking about that face of yours (*do stop thinking you're alive by chance, slipped by chance out of the horrifying charnel heap ...*), your face just after you stepped down from the plane, at passport control, at baggage reclaim, with the taxi man sent by the hotel. Because two like you, well actually I want to say for you Jews (you see, one hesitates still, stupidly, before pronouncing this word as if it were impolite or improper or offensive to those it designates; as if one took a stealthy look around before pronouncing the word, lowering one's voice a little—and the reality is that in this calm designation there's the shame, a shadow of shame which is none other than a memory of when it was a brutal discrimination and one tolerated being protected by it, in alliance with it) I mean it must make an impression on you to walk freely in a country where for many years you weren't able to take a step without being in mortal peril—and so without even a sign, without so much as a word spoken between you, I understand very well that something quickly brought you together, I didn't say the one drawn to the other or vice versa, wouldn't dream of it, simply for a walk, arm in arm, talking perhaps of nothing much, along the river, with the rest of us straggling behind ... But a few days were enough, you see, even you no longer think of it, the thought's remote, abstract even, and is no longer accompanied by a shiver or start—a little wellbeing was enough, the hotels' warmth, the shimmer of laid tables, these frenetic gatherings, cocktail parties and banquets, up by elevator, in and out of a taxi, the clatter of ice in glasses, the tinkling of a toast . . . And this city, where until a short time ago there were still ruins; but they were still human ruins, made of flesh and blood, certainly more human and pulsating than these skyscrapers and shop windows . . . And the people from here, above all on Sunday afternoon, when they walk along the Zeil . . . could even not be here, never have been born, be other people, with other faces—and it'd be the same—be another city, at another time—as if they'd no roots anywhere, no history, no past—or been moved here, immigrants from who knows where, to repopulate, to start again: with behind, in the background, the by now imperceptible crackling of combustion, the rustling time of the furnaces . . . Excuse me one moment, Hilde's sending me her usual signals.

She's like that. Hilde, in a state of agitation, practically accuses me, she's heard about the Dutchman, I don't know how, and wants to know, she says I'm no friend of hers because I didn't put her in the picture. She says her publisher could come in for the Germans . . . "unless you prefer a competitor . . ." and from the slight sign of doubtful tenderness I understand she's referring to her friend-rival of the other day, blowing him kisses from afar—meine Liebe!—to obtain his forgiveness, and then back to me: "Coward, tell me the truth, tell me what you wrote on that piece of paper." Oh for goodness sake, my dear girl, I've no idea what to do about any of this, the twenty-four hours are nearly up and I haven't decided, but I'm inclined to let it go. Besides, I've got the impression she's trying to keep me on side, accusing me from excessive scruple, so as to leave no stone unturned. Maybe I'm wrong, but she knows more than I do, has other information, she knows the inside track leads elsewhere . . . but where? And to what? Ten years, the book about the next ten years? Not a chance, so much trafficking for something of the sort, much ado about not very much, the idea's by no means as original as it seems . . . I've come to the conclusion that the real "thing," the real delicacy, is elsewhere, if anywhere at all, somewhere between the plutocrats and aristocrats—pay no attention, it's just an expression of mine, we'll get to it later. You've got to think it out by process of elimination, from one taxi to another, one lobby to another, one cocktail party to another, from lunch to lunch, in the kermesse that the Fair's become . . . Once upon a time this was a place of business, among other things, endless negotiations everywhere, in the lobby, in hotel bars, in the reserved or public hotel lounges, in the rooms, the beds unmade still, leftovers of breakfast going stale on a side table, and men in shirtsleeves or dressing gowns passing each other documents, studying projects, drawing aside to add up the figures, paper, customs duties, binding, number of copies, the cheap edition—and generally the figures didn't add up, France 30,000, Germany 45,000, Italy 15,000 no it won't work, we've left out reproductions and typesetting in this or that language, we have to add these in to the total, excluding royalties, please open the window, this isn't a room, it's a gas chamber (why are you elbowing me, I've not said anything untoward, oh, I see, alright, the worse for him, I didn't invent them, did I! What? What's he saying? The other? Oh, I'm truly sorry, but who knows, perhaps he doesn't mind if someone shows he's got a memory where that ugly mug making difficulties is concerned), now it's quite different, three or four parties going on at once every day, meaning, to put it mildly, if you want to be friendly you can't do anything else, negotiations replaced by public relations . . . except that they seem designed to throw you off the scent of the one deal worth making, the *unicum,* the book in one or more volumes, secret, unidentifiable; so you just grope around in the dark, sounding people out, deflecting people, till you run out of time, there's only three days left, two, and you want to surrender to the temptation of staying out of it, letting others tear themselves to pieces over it, much good it'll do them in this—what else call it?—treasure hunt, which the Fair's become in the last few years . . . You know, I'm now of the opinion that the Dutchman's idea could be quite a publishing coup, but it's a false target. Sure, if you forget the idea of the book about the next ten years, you have to conclude that it's the ambiguous sign of a far deeper interest. But in what? How can it be identified, or even just guessed? Ten years, ten . . . This is what I'll do: out of extreme scruple—for no other reason, note—I'll lay my cards on the table with someone who's almost certainly not interested in the Dutchman's book. One of the aristocrats, of course. I'll try to phone him now.

Well, I don't know what I was hoping he'd say . . . He looked at me just long enough to square up and freeze someone out, make someone squirm under his gaze, as if he'd not heard or hardly, but more with an air that takes it for granted I've nothing of interest to say. He quickly found a way of steering the subject to "what are you up to this evening, since there's nothing important left to do" giving me the unpleasant sensation that he'd concluded who knows what deal, and now was having fun drawing me in and making sure I miss any last chances of getting back lost time, the last few useful turns of the public relations merry-go-round (we're late, late, all we need now is for the zipper to go neither up nor down and the chambermaid not to arrive and give you a hand, but remind me to tell you of a thing that happened in the lobby as I was waiting for you, try to get the taxi driver to understand he has to wait exactly ten minutes, time to put in an appearance with the French, and then he can take us to the other place, it's vital) you know what he's like, embroiling you in blandishments, false modesty, making his interlocutor seem the discourteous, the stubborn one, while it's him dominating you, with that indolent drawl of his . . . Since this time I don't give in, don't want to accompany him to one of those improbable restaurants he likes so much, he throws out a phrase as if to spite me:— Come on, come on, you know perfectly well it's a vulgar copy.— So you tell me if he's not wicked. A copy of what? And tell me while you're at it if that isn't talking in enigmas, I could think anything, that he wants to distance me from the Dutchman so he can then fall on the prey, or encourage me to buy so he can bank on a sort of inverse auction as the price tumbles; or that there's really something else he's already secured, so we're to go and celebrate his triumph, we're to eat, drink, and toast something only he knows, which makes him smile while I'm smiling idiotically at the pleasure of being in company . . . Well, yes, you can say I'm complicated, or that I have complicated thoughts, it's all the same, I don't see any great difference . . . Fact is that this time at least there's one thing he's not made me do, made me traipse round with him and his court, and if I had to think about it calmly, or trust to what little intuition I've got left, do you know what I'd conclude? That he doesn't give a damn about the Dutchman, which is what I foresaw given his aristocratic nature—one moment, I'm getting there. And you know what above all I'd conclude? That he's got an idea, not very precise, but further advanced than mine, that there's still something doing the rounds that's worth the trouble, but it's hard to find, the clues are faint and contradictory, and who knows if he's given up for good or is just waiting for more information, quietly, ready to pounce? And yet and yet, I may be wrong, but this time I've put a doubt into his body, this time he's accusing me of diversionary tactics... Only that he anyway seemed pessimistic, a shade tired, the voice feeble, not feeble in a possible contest with us of course, let's call it a collective, an objective pessimism about whether anyone, he or us, can bring it off. So ask the taxi driver if he can try and wait for us those ten minutes, the time to shake some hands, be noticed, snatch a glass from a passing tray, and then off to that other place...

You'll certainly have noticed. Those faces inside calm lights, the throng on the parquetry in one room after another inside the old building, and among the smiles a few cutting looks or others who watch you without appearing to, you even wink as if to people who've just struck it rich, it can't be this week that's starting to go to my head—us vaguely targeted... for once at center stage—it was almost worth staying just to find out more, understand more. Ah, you've noticed, it's not only my imagination. So, let's see, in that other place, so much so that... don't forget to remind me to tell you when I've a moment about what happened earlier, yes, when I was waiting for you in the lobby. You should understand that these aristocrats stick together, they're an elite, as is natural. Not that they neglect business; but, unlike the plutocrats (relatively speaking, you understand, where only books are concerned), they don't have an air of doing any. It's not just a question of style, though, needless to say. They only do a certain type of business, and this does in some way confer honor on them. They have their groups or teams, for destructive or constructive purposes, of course, with varying degrees of complexity, many-colored, with secret memberships. For real business they use these operatives, never do things personally, or only rarely, to add a measured, an elegant, final touch. While they're in some restaurant or nightclub with a woman or girl, usually one of the crowd, I mean, in the publishing business, someone who buys and sells books, and an operative just off-duty; meanwhile, those on duty are negotiating the deal, there they are before your very eyes, eating and laughing or getting bored, you relax in their company, away from the lists, and that's precisely when you let the deal slip through your fingers, having witlessly failed to make the key appointment . . . But this is tactics, a form of involuntary tactics, not what really matters. For them business is nothing but a transit area, a way of acquiring knowledge. If they've got sympathies for a popular political party it's only because it gives them a good vantage point, a loftiness allowing them to see far ahead, nodding this way and that at their peers, the others in the elite, and it hardly matters that at the same time they're trying to fleece each other over real business matters . . . They have a vocation for the future, sometimes it looks like snobbism, the snobbism of the future . . . A little like, on airplanes, those noises, voices, signals from the cockpit that the passengers can't understand and which may worry or reassure them according to their mood, while someone else is calmly turning them into the remaining flight time, data in space time, material ETA, weather, ground conditions below, the ground that replaces the air, elements coming together, reintegration with the earth . . . Here, it's like that: they, the aristocrats, always one step ahead, always one moment or some years ahead, they plot with a network of understanding looks, with divination, under the noses of the plutocrats (in a manner of speaking) who are perpetually alarmed, whatever business they're doing, suspecting that some bigger deal has escaped them, big fish and little fish swimming together in the net of all-seeing looks, Dutchmen who show you a draft volume, Spaniards and Portuguese waiting for some news, which is always about just one thing, while for them, the aristocrats, rather demagogically benevolent towards Spaniards and Portuguese, towards their brothers, confreres, naively looking into the future, the news is complex and unstable, heterogeneous, multifaceted . . . but they have no other bait than this to catch it, one day or another, their books, their deals, moving with anxiety among shrapnel of the *entre deux guerres,* fragments of old Europe, customs barriers, evening train to Paris, night train to Amsterdam, morning train to Vienna, dazzling toasts, other shreds of old Europe, repeated in the subhuman world, heaped up in the dead time of the furnaces . . . The option, the twenty-four hour option is expiring. Let it expire, by now clearly it's not the option that matters . . . Ten years, the book of the next ten years, not a chance. I'm amused by the idea that they'll think of us briefly as the holders, the enviable holders, of the option that counts — the plutocrats at least, not the others, the elite, barely disgruntled by the fact that through sheer chance someone stumbled onto the right clue, interfered with their plans . . . Ahah—they enjoy themselves, hovering above the lists, the elite (and among them, always a few notes above, anguished as the plutocrats who can't pass as aristocrats, barn owls dressed as hawks, there's always an intrusive bird, an abusive flutter)—ahah. Faites vos jeux, Messieurs Dames. Faites donc vos jeux . . .

Well, I don't believe it. Just wait and see, these days anything you do gets interpreted in that way, open to conjecture. But what spoiling operation, fine state of mind, fine detective-novel psychosis we've got ourselves into over just a few days with this story of the option . . . It certainly looked like a chase—from one hotel to another, from one gathering to another . . . More or less the same faces everywhere, you manage to get rid of three or four and find them a few moments later exactly where you were heading, calm, relaxed, smiling—and deep down out of breath . . . so if by chance you bumped into someone you've never seen before you suspected they were made up, in disguise . . . No, I don't believe they'd go that far. Just wait and see if someone will manage to get a woman into his room by taking advantage of the pandemonium, and immediately the others are thinking he wanted to reveal all and take out . . . an option! Yes, it's not a bad one that, you liked it, call it an option . . . Quite a laugh, though . . . ahah, he's there on the point of, come to the point of, or almost, and—no sir—just then the others downstairs phone to tell him his boss needs him urgently. He's got enough nerve to come back that his boss may have all the extreme desires in the world to see him but he's got something else to do, other extreme desires, and those down below they start again, all over—and so on, I don't know how many times, so that in the end . . . well, let's drop it—just a joke, nothing more than a cheap and nasty joke . . . Tell me, rather, what are we to think, and here's what I wanted to tell you, what are we to think of the blonde, of her sudden interest in me . . . I'm in the lobby, already dressed for the French cocktail party, messenger boys and customers to-ing and fro-ing, the phone ringing and ringing, I sit down at a free table, throw my raincoat on the only armchair left vacant, light up, order something to drink . . . and the blonde appears in front of me, moves my raincoat, sits down, lights a cigarette and . . . I couldn't believe my eyes, yet after the evening of the centaur she'd suddenly lost all interest, fair enough, buyers lower the price you'll say, but believe it or not this sudden return didn't get the blood coursing through my veins . . . I hear her make some ironic comment half in English, half in Italian, about how good I am at hunting, she lets fall a phrase I didn't get at the time, though it was clear enough, about my new specialization in prophetic books . . . And here, finally! Not the steel but the acquamarines . . . This time I was the ice block, I swear, at least at the start, but I do try to keep my end up, vaguely complain of her usual coldness, especially the other evening after the dinner, don't mention the affairs four years back, didn't even think of them, I wasn't in the mood, or was already unknowingly caught in the option psychosis, and the blonde had nothing to do with it, don't ask me how come she did have something to do with things four years back or some evenings ago but now no more, it's a question of a definitive sign in a given context, of a symptomatic knot, of a harmony, but now the context's changed, it forms other knots, tends towards other heights . . . yes, yes, I get it, but I'm not playing the intellectual, if that's how it seems then it just means I don't have a clear idea on this one, I'll explain this to you too some time . . . Fact is that to my complaints she responds unexpectedly, says the other evening she was just testing me and that, when I didn't insist, I disappointed, deeply disappointed her—just imagine, after four years of ignoring each other. Precisely for that reason, she says, she wanted to put me to the test, see whether it was just a fancy of mine returning, a whim . . . And though she's looking at me steadily now from the bottom of the sea, I feel she's trying her futile best to be alluring, I say futile because a woman like her, when she decides to look at you from the bottom of the sea, only a regal indignation or a regal benevolence will do . . . But this woman, I'm wondering, who sent her here? Mr. Luxembourg, the Dutchman, his friend from Sammy's Bar? Who else? Sure, the prophetic books, that wretched book about the next ten years . . . I don't have proof, you understand, but this is no time to bring out your female solidarity, believe me, that woman wanted to get me to sing, or at least to verify for herself whether I was or wasn't interesting prey . . . far as I'm concerned she was on the warpath the evening of the centaur and then at Sammy's Bar when speaking from the side of her mouth to that other fellow . . . So I went on the counter-attack and pretending to play the same game, I try to make a date for later... I must have been clumsy, didn't put enough conviction into it, she keeps it vague, says she'll telephone, can't say when, perhaps tomorrow evening, this evening that's to say, even in my room? Even in my room, even if it's late? Even late, well, perhaps she went away because you were approaching, perhaps not, the impression she gave was of doing (but for whom?) the rounds of all the useful points or those considered to be, and that I was one of them.

There you see, my Colombian friend's gone by, he even made a shy gesture, then carried on walking, perhaps he was expecting me to encourage him to stay, but I didn't... no, it's not that I don't want to know anything more about him, I was worried he'd notice something different in me, some embarrassment, I don't resent him, he's still got all or nearly all my gratitude, I'm not even disappointed, really... it's a fact that... that I wasn't taking anymore interest in him or what he represented for a few days, the picture's changed, the relationship's changed, a link in the chain has broken, I no longer spring down those steps surrounded by the greenery on an exquisite morning to look for a taxi I'll find more easily here ... same thing can be said for the blonde of the other evening, no longer hotel corridors and taking leave of the tapestries, the phone ringing uselessly within the sunshine of her journey... these things have a value in the connection with which they present themselves, if just one element disappears, one link breaks, one pearl falls from the necklace, and you're in a different connection, or no connection, and if an element of the past connection returns, it's simply in the way, an intruder, a nuisance, an unpleasant diversion, you either take it on again or get rid of it... That other man's also gone by, the young Portuguese from the other evening. He turned a mocking smile towards my friend who this time, on the stand at the end, brushed past and, not looking at me, sarcastically said: *Ah! votre héros, quelle blague, regardez-le, pas un jour de prison, pas un jour de sa vie,* pas un jour *je vous dis,* maybe he's a loyalist, an agent provocateur, you never can tell... By the way, did you notice the Dutchman, the man with the cruel thin cigar, waiting for me at the corner, hanging by his teeth from his invisible hook, and when I went past he turned the other way, murmuring something, him too, something ironic, I think, something like "Science fiction, nothing more than science fiction," yes, I realize, he's probably found out I'm negotiating with someone else, yes, the Englishman of yesterday evening, the fake aristocrat, I haven't told you about that . . . I went up to his room, after midnight, the only authentic thing was the robe, splendid, covering the tango of his languid movements— . . . the rest: ectoplasms of the future with a few lines sprinkled here and there, a mediocre text, was my impression, but with more illustrations than the Dutch book . . . Another phony, another diversion, the last, on the next ten years, I've had enough of this rummaging among fakes for a prototype that doesn't exist, or is just the idea of some superbrain, a way of measuring how moods change, how the wind of success is blowing elsewhere. So why not invent something, take the bother of the last few days for exactly what it is, a sign of change . . . Because something is changing, don't you think? I'll tell my boss, he'll know how to handle it, come up with a new formula . . . and from now on stick to what's concrete, go back to ideas and negotiations, with passion, humility, dedication . . . without this idée fixe, this obsession . . . maybe it's got nothing to do with it, or maybe it has . . . never seen so many people on the last day of the Fair . . . No no, I'm not mistaken, can recall the other years very well, could tell you who was returning to Paris at this precise moment, who was driving back to Italy, no hurry, a stop in Basle . . . But this year. The biggest names on parade, all of them, the last day, a hesitation, a lack of satisfaction, a reluctance to go, this last-minute fashion parade, this unexpected sunshine filtering through the windows, invasive, adding heat to the heat, a stifling air to a stifling atmosphere . . . from one stand to another, from one pavilion to another, a charge, retracing your steps, walking lazily—and slowly the knot loosens, the tension is released, the anonymous sea that churns and covers everything, those in the know or think they are, those who get things wrong and then the small fry, the minimum, the obscure, who have no other tension than the small, minimum, obscure deals to be done, perfectly blind at the nerve centers of the game, yet involved, Portuguese and Spaniards inhaling an illusory air of freedom from the remains of old Europe, everyone, everyone covered by the crowded sea of Central Europe, the living who could as yet be unborn, pink flesh, milky epidermis, tame pupils of woodland cattle easy to alarm . . . now it seems everyone's rushing towards a new anxiety, in one-way corridors, towards an exit you don't see . . . surrounded by unbreakable glass. Curtains.

What do you reckon? It's not bad as a form of farewell: "I'm thinking of my rabbit"—said in Italian. First time I've ever heard her try not just a few words but one whole sentence in Italian . . . Who, who. Who do you think? The blonde, die Blonde. Well, I'll explain. The other evening, after the visit to the man in the dressing gown, I go to my room, throw myself on the bed without undressing, lie there in the dark, dead tired, undecided. I hear someone knock, or rather scratch at the door. I switch on the light, am about to say, "Come in," but she's already in. I didn't even have time to sit up in bed. A surprise, however you look at it, because first I wasn't thinking anymore of the half-arranged date from a few evenings back, second, because I wasn't sure she was staying in the same hotel, third because I thought I'd locked the door. The move surprises me less, I don't know why, however unexpected. Hey, don't jump to conclusions, not like that at all. She'd the air of a neighbor who comes round to smoke a cigarette before bed. Tells me to stay where I am, pushes an armchair towards the bed, but not too close, and does, in fact, light one. Let's see what she's up to, I think. I can just see her eyes in that penumbra, and her dazzling gold, that too. She smokes, says nothing. So I try to get her talking, ask her where she was during the war, if she has brothers or sisters, her parents still alive. No, her father died on the Russian front, lost without trace, a brother, too, not long after. She barely replies, doesn't seem touched by these memories. Yes, she experienced the bombing, but gives no details. She was only nine or ten, after all. And so? So nothing. She smokes. I would very much like to ask her what she's doing here, but don't want to speak too soon. The option, ten years, prophetic books . . . you wait, she'll be the first to bring up the subject, perhaps she wants to know if I'll be leaving with empty hands or not. But not in the least, it's as if we'd never spoken of such things. Who knows, maybe she felt guilty for a few days ago, I could turn out to be useful, sooner or later . . . and me, lying there, as if dead, nothing to do with her, unable to bring any warmth to the situation or interest in any of the situations gone by, not a dazzling blonde, not steel or aquamarine . . . That's the way it happens, it's sometimes enough to get near the heart of the matter, the central possibility, the raw flesh, and it all comes into focus, all your energies pour into it, organically, according to certain connections; you try at other times, but one false piece of information's enough, one clumsy move, or the lack of a single element from before, a trifle, and the buzzers remain silent, the lights don't come on . . . This person, what makes her do things? I'm beginning to suspect it's business, no, not business, her work, pride in her work, the . . . "sense of personality achieved through work" and so she's capable of anything, capable of giving anything . . . but outside that, she struggles to get by, to speak to anyone, forgetful even that people like her. It's a theory. And here she starts talking about a household myth, of birds, cats, rabbits, and herself ruling the roost, a heroine, looking after them . . . no, not a spinster's tale, for heaven's sake, all you have to do is look at her. I remember I just vaguely wondered how it was so different—because it certainly was different—from a spinster's tale, what emptiness, what sterility she tried to compensate for, with that talk, if it was a way of keeping me definitively at a distance by feigning to admit me finally into her intimate circle, when . . . now don't laugh, I fell asleep like a child, I don't know how or when she left, later I woke up half-terrified, just as I'd fallen asleep, still fully dressed—but she'd been kind, she'd taken my shoes off, something you don't usually do with a stranger . . . The bedside light was still on, she'll have left it so as not to bump into things when leaving or so I would immediately see the maquette . . . yes, she'd left a maquette there, at the foot of the bed, but it was completely blank, apart from the imitation leather cover, but with no title, let alone text or illustrations, blank, nothing but white sheets of paper, a blinding whiteness, not the slightest clue or indication . . . What's more, she must have gone to get it after I'd fallen asleep, because she certainly didn't have anything of the sort with her when she came in . . . If I were a writer, say Marcel or someone like that, or she were aware of such a fond ambition in me, all this might have some sense, a positive sense, a friendly gesture, open, a challenge if you like—or even an affectionate exhortation, a kind wish . . . but seeing as I am—you know what I mean—nothing more than a literary-publishing man, I leave the interpretation to you. This was just last night, and certainly I wouldn't have spoken to you about it if I hadn't phoned her, don't know why, partly out of foolish tact, partly out of curiosity, this morning before leaving the room vacant—rather early in the morning, to tell the truth, but I could afford that, couldn't I? And she responded as I told you, and that was her farewell because she'd not added anything else and I felt no desire to add anything either, let's not talk about it anymore.

I couldn't bear the sight of the room, was anyhow leaving in two hours; I just tidied up a little, asked the maid to pack for me, went down to the lobby, which they were still cleaning, the vacuum cleaners working, the rugs rolled up, armchairs and chairs shifted or stacked; but a few people were already leaving, and the mulatto lady, who must get up very early, *une si bonne dame!* says the Algerian, on the night shift, he'd already walked her dog . . . Like every other day, but probably she and her husband, the man I like to think of as Anglo-Turk, are staying till tomorrow or later, to rest from the labors of the Fair, like every year! Look at the other one, absolutely fascinating, blond, bald, in his impeccable gray suit, he's only lacking a monocle and spiked helmet, and there you are on the Marne, forty years back nearly, among the Boches and poilus, that fellow, you understand, pays no attention to the fact I exist till the last-but-one day and then stops me anywhere, here in the hotel or at the Fair, to offer me some most reputable most tedious writer no one wants, this year for the fifth year running . . . there must be a conference of industrial chemists or doctors, I don't know, I've already seen a lot of new faces going by, just arrived, you can tell immediately they're not in our business, in the lobby there's almost no one left sitting at the tables, but the bureau is busy, one last look around, Aldo's scrutinizing Jean's face but is trying to look unmoved, actually he looks rather satisfied, Jean notices, beams at Max trying to pass on Aldo's glance, who now feels stared at by Max and Jean and turns to looking at the tiny details on the bill . . . Another wave of new faces, in this town you go from Fair to congress, from congress to exhibition, every goddamn week, the hotel never has a moment's peace.

What a magnificent day—worthy of the departure of the blonde four years ago, but why talk about it again, go over the bridges and you're already in the woods, on asphalted roads, they're more farsighted than us, have guard rails everywhere to keep the lanes separate, I saw a driver lose the tread of his tire and go into a spin, at Monza, years back and emerge unscathed thanks to the guard rail, it's true though he died not long after in a much more banal fashion . . . but what did I have to say, ah yes, I'll tell you and then I won't mention it again, you know how I could still give my interest in the blonde a go, stay on here after everyone's left and instead of the sunshine there's fog on the Zeil, like a few evenings back, and there's a nip in the air, as in the first cold days of the season, but high up, much higher than the fog, the phosphorescence of an illuminated dial, prisms, triangles, circles of light reprojected from below, reproduces a fairground, a cathedral, a huge Christmas tree to the north, in the winter, and then there'll be an unexpected meeting, everything begin again, dazzlingly, I mean by "everything" what you know, the scraps and pieces of what you know, which in itself is nothing or just the cold disorder of indifferent, disassociated things, it could take on a new, a stimulating life, oh, not for long . . . because, you see, these things have nothing to do with affection, what's affection if not a more or less tenacious memory you try to hang on to, of those who were kind to you or you tried to be kind to, you can no longer live from these things, no you live by creating and destroying fortuitous circumstances and situations, according to your energies in this or that moment, I don't say it bitterly, I'm trying to describe a new biological state, in a manner of speaking . . .

But before we get to the airport I want to tell you of another piece of imagining, or theory I've come to at the end of this week. No one managed to lay hands on the book, the projected work that some, by process of elimination or approximation, had managed to establish the existence of, whilst others had guessed its qualities. Needless to say these few, these optimized, Aldo looking at Jean who tries to pass on the attention to Max, who's dying of rage, without showing it, suspecting George who acts out his role better than anyone else (a process already described in part and which you were able to see from one hotel to another, one gathering to another etcetera), came nowhere near locating the prey. This didn't happen without creating some confusion and upset in those who, coarser and more . . . practical, more . . . concrete, that emerging in the form of business, an important deal, the rather chimerical trace of the former ended up complicating the negotiating game, throwing the entire Fair off its stride. Not to mention the smallest of all, those who work in the margins: they stumbled about blindly, without seeing the enormous difference between the disquiet of this year and of former years. Perhaps at this very minute they are counting the lost time and money, complaining about this mania for public relations, without even suspecting they'd been tricked, played as pawns in someone else's game. But now for the good part: the book exists, doesn't matter where, we left it behind in some stand they're right now dismantling, forgotten in some drawer, left on a table in one of the lounges of a hotel, the curtains blowing through the windows that opened onto rooms where radiators are boiling senselessly in the beautiful sunshine. The book exists, from first to last page, it perfectly describes what *really* will happen over the next ten years. Or else, in this city or one not far away, this hour, or this minute, someone, unbeknown to us, someone who has been tense for days, or years, radiating to us without wanting to—drawing us into his force field, at this time someone . . .

A squadron of leaves tumbled along Friedrichstrasse, picking up squads of the like, whirled a moment at the crossroads, turned at the first corner. At that moment the old Chancellor was getting ready to give up his post to the new Chancellor while a cyclist hurled insults at a distracted pedestrian, probably an outsider, wandering down the cycle lane with his nose in the air. The first plane in Operation Big Lift had appeared in the sky above the city at the very moment the customary airline Caravelle was taking off from the airport.

—Who knows! one passenger deep in thought began in that mixture of engine noise, kerosene, hissing and other lesser noises, sunshine.

The writer stopped a moment. Ah, if he'd only had a special punch, and in addition a welding tool. Intent on forming, rather than expressing or representing, obsessed as he was by the circularity and simultaneity of the acts, large and small, that make up existence, he needed to avoid those second thoughts, suspensions, emotional wanderings, intrusions that, faster than pen or keys of a typewriter, instantaneously fall and create the stickiness of the moment and the mold of the present—which, as everyone knows by now, as soon as you notice and name, passes, especially these days, even more so. Ah, the past perfect, the great enemy, much more so than the past historic. Besides, having abolished any presumption to or pretense of foreshadowing the future, he needed to concentrate on a competitive but at the same time collaborative tension in relation to time, which manipulates reality and how this manipulation occurs ... He went back to his work, trying to avoid even a crumb of comfort in the idea that the city's finally empty, at least without the—for him—tiresome bores brought in by the Fair. For him the countdown finished that morning, at the moment the first plane in Operation Big Lift appeared above the horizon. From that moment on, a staggering series of images of life was to be set in motion, each lasting one minute, no longer, since a moment's really not enough. A pity, there was so much sunlight to distract him, he didn't know that the fog would arrive in the early afternoon, autumn already come. Now the implement was beating regularly, and so it went on, for hours, days ... But it's like this with machines too, with engines: the time comes when their regularity indicates their precarious state, so it is when you grow fond of a car: you're moved by the labored breathing and within that its being junk—and you suffer for it, as for a sick child struggling, panting, against a disease, too strong for him. It beats out its rhythm, joyous, it seems everything's going fine, and suddenly then you're pained by it, you hear it like a spluttering coffee pot, a rattling old heap. If only it sufficed to weld one moment to the next, but it's not enough, if you want to create, it's not enough to avoid stickiness and mold, the next moment must come from you, not from the one you're in ... Or at least writing's not enough, the implement available is nothing if it's got no part, and you with it, in the next moment ... By now the rhythm was a death rattle, and snow, storm over the Zeil. *Cecidere manus.*

Twenty-Six

twenty-six years
your phantom's crossed over
now to remain in these lines
C. P. CAVAFY

It was so easy. Starting from this April weather, but like so many days between that April and July. The hour has come, just as it was, it's come back as before, with sallies in puzzling showers, majestic clouds, approaching heat balanced on the oppressiveness. We were instantly spotted.

"German?" asks the elder of two who'd come running up, probably the father, not surprised.

"No, no, Italian: Milanese," I apologize repeatedly, beg leave to see once more, try to explain.

"No trouble at all," and he shows me the way.

Mediation is my wife's affair; a kind of Enlightenment traveler, I call her. It turns out he vaguely knows what occurred here then, but quite, it's a perfunctory notion presumably derived from other occasional visitors who've passed through (he thinks, mistakenly, he's seen me before). At that time he was working in Germany. Conscripted or prisoner? No difference, hell in any case. Wouldn't go back dead. Bombers came, so many they blotted out the sun. Giovanna, my daughter, too young a spectator, is thinking maybe—things sinking in a moment—that even the Persians' arrows, if the history book's anything to go by . . . But no, she skips over the ruins of this other, already old history. In her military-style coat (as chance would have it), two clips in her hair—that certain something her schoolmate falls in love with, like her not yet awoken to sex. Will she record on some secret page, in her own way, not with words: with colored pencils, as usual, moments of this journey? For a second I'm bent on contemplating things of the dead twice over.

I have no eyes for this nothing come of nothing, look through its diurnal apparition at the walls, the ceiling where cracks have lengthened and multiplied (up there, from a perilous balcony one night we saw *the sea burst intermittently into flames, entire stretches revealed, ablaze*), this room the command post, this other my office where I also slept, floors covered with plaster, in heaps, in avalanches, but also odd slippers, tin cans, nameless materials, not datable, without inventory, and not even rubbish: ruins. Preservers of ruins we were, *the villa on the point of decaying into farm and country residence, but with evident memories of better days, of guests' carriages on the gravel drive.* And now this man, diurnal apparition, preserver of the ruins of us preservers of ruins, considers it "a good thing" to have wanted to return here. I too—he says, speaking only to Luisa now—would go back if I could. To Germany, he means. But—didn't he say: not even dead? It isn't clear to him, or more likely he can't make it clear to himself. Perhaps it's just a question of syntax that can't bind two different impulses running in parallel. And me? Overwhelmed, silent. Everything indicated, illustrated, reawakened. All legible on my face—not even if I were God or the others were. All-seeing, all-remembering, all-speaking in a circle. But the owners? Who are they? What's become of them? Do they ever return? And this man—his family? Why here? On whose permission or without it? Farm managers? Leaseholders? Can't possibly be here just to bear witness and preserve . . . But Luisa—she'd like to know these things—has given up this time. Out of regard for me I'm afraid, who wake up, become aware of the guide just to apologize once more, say thank you, ask permission to leave by a pathway and side gate. Over here the terrain slopes gently, the car slides smoothly towards the pilasters of a nonexistent gate, like the main one for that matter, to a road that intrigues me. A boy dozes stretched out on a flower bed, which in those days still had flowers, but today, amid the withering grass, just the shape remains.

"He's northernizing in his dreams," I observe half out loud. He raises himself on an elbow and watches us go by.

Asphalt's been laid on a fair stretch of the road I'm intrigued by. Down there, along a ridge I can't quite single out, two fighters hedge-hopping had caught us one afternoon. The lorry, terrifyingly slow . . . Oh, the light from the salt works (women who worked there one morning and another fighter—with Italian markings! but what's it doing?—dived to machine gun, no one ever knew). I ask Luisa, "What does P.'s book say?" "Heralded by reflections from the salt works," she reads, "which give them the shimmer of a mirage, Trapani appears; dominated by Mount Erice; facing the Egadi Islands . . ."

Further, further on. Here it is: "The salt works . . . give Trapani's air an ever-present pellucid glitter."

I know it, I know it: *everything like that April afternoon when, from the train, the city first appeared before his eyes, in a semicircle low on the sea horizon, irradiated by an ambiguous splendor from the salt works.* I'm not in search of a road, or a village, but a name. The name is Torre Nubia and has always been linked with that ambiguous splendor (the "shimmer of a mirage"—the "pellucid glitter," the brief triumph and finality of the train on that stretch where all Italy's railways lines end, the marina's nearness, its lowest limit, almost indistinguishable between land and water, indicated by some dry grasses or stalks rather, brackish). I go back to the name, forgotten and suddenly remembered, to its sound denser than the things to which it's connected, from the marina on the scent of other names. In the countryside, interlinking them, there's bound to be a network of roads and alleyways, accessible with patience, a patience for which there's neither time nor means of rapid movement. The car sniffs at crossroads, tries routes, desists. It seemed an advantage, mobility, compared to the fixity imposed back then. On the contrary it represents, inverted, the same impossibility. It doesn't penetrate, above all doesn't spread. The land front, so-called, some fifteen to twenty kilometers between Mount Erice and the sea, was made up of deployments grouped together in strongpoints. They formed a defensive system such that surveillance was maintained in all directions, and an arc of fire could be unleashed without interruption through 360 degrees, a form—come to think of it—of all-seeing, purely tactical, however, entrusted to a telephone line from camp (*a conversation between one strongpoint and another was cut off suddenly and it was useless sending out a patrol on the tracks of the unknown saboteurs—later unfamiliar voices, with conspicuous island accents, came on the wires, ironic, with false gentility and persuasiveness, suggesting we surrender*).

But what do you expect, says Luisa with her silence, to squeeze everything into one single time? What are you searching for? With my silence I answer that I'm following a hypothesis. What hypothesis? It isn't clear to me. Have a go. A fellowship, a human fellowship. Because that's what it was? No, it could have become one. I see: an idyll, *a living event of your life in the space of few crowded kilometers . . . The countryside and, within it, those same fortification works . . . the camouflage of leaves . . . the ambiguity of forms, of the bodies' outlines, which the veil of water from makeshift showers shattered and recomposed at whim; faces transfigured by the wisteria's reflection along the walls.* Your supposing, sensing a life together drawn from nothing, patterns of consensus and agreement that at the first setback you cast aside like empty forms, to disown with complete indifference, should it ever begin to seem they no longer correspond to you, deny they ever inspired you, if over some nothing they disappoint you. The fact is I'm here, after so many years, how many years, I wanted it with all my strength. But it's something different. No, that I don't believe. It isn't a pilgrimage, if anything a reconnoiter. I'd like to transfuse myself into those names, Timpone Mosca, il Torrazzo, Torre Bianca, Timpone Sole, for them to open, to open myself to them. Confirmation doesn't interest me. I'm not disappointed. Everything's in its place, I thought as much, a little asphalt changes nothing; at least one existence I've substantiated, Torre Nubia, the level-crossing under a spray of rain at the eruption of the locomotive with the few empty carriages, and the boy in the flower bed looking from the gateway to see us return, and quiet, upright, kneeling on the back seat, apparition in transit, Giovanna... Of course a handful of unaltered names isn't much, without substantiating those barely touched here back then, without inspecting those remaining, impossible to make the two journeys coincide, tourism superimposes itself on every other impulse. But deep down I wanted projections onto unknown spaces and not simple returns, always a good sign this. Giovanna, with increasing impatience: E-ri-ce / E-ri-ce / E-ri-ce, by way of remonstration.

Indeed, Erice. We must get there before sunset. What does your book say? "... at the summit of a sheer cliff, in the corner of Sicily, it is swept by a mountain wind that brings fog or exceptional limpidity."

First, however, Milo, the airfield that woke us every morning with its engines. One started, and after a while it was a chorus, swelling as far as here one summer morning in Versilia with the cicadas. Stretched out on the camp bed, in darkness (Milo was a name too, a rotating dizziness against the sun already high), I asked myself what volition presided "still" over that inescapable operation—because *in every war there must be a moment starting from which not only a light of defeat falls on the uniforms and arms of the side soon to be recognized as the vanquished, but the place itself that's the object of attack or invasion takes on lights and colors* etcetera *new accents, new breaths run through it, its skies already match a different flag* etcetera etcetera.

"Milo? Let's see, turn round, go right, then straight on just over a kilometer and you're there. But you know, the field no longer exists, these days the airport is nowhere near, it was only a base. Yes, they're building. A few hangars must still be there as warehouses for something or other, a little over a kilometer, you can't miss it."

"Just look how he's sweating," Luisa remarks.

He reminds me of someone I came across back then. Only because of the sweat, perhaps. He'd come before me to request a signature and stamp to gain exemption from the work in town. We were already on full alert. He understood immediately there was nothing I could do. He began to sweat. Distraught, caught between the risk of throwing himself into those storm waves and the horror of making a false move, between physical fear and anticipated demotion. I saw myself in him, I was on his side in the very act ("and us, us, what are we doing here?") of harshly refusing him the chit. Other days would go by, suffocating, and we'd begun to know, he and I, reduced to mere functionaries of war, that we were already in the aftermath. In his sweat, behind the fear, our common degradation. After, when the state of alert had moved elsewhere, to him and other functionaries of the South no relief would come, they would wriggle under other frustrations, fresh little irritations, fresh little hardships, stirring the evening in the breeze of the walk along the shore.

But Erice. I'm going there today with you both, for the first time. So, an everyday sight, I'd never climbed it in the course of duty. It interests me less, understandably, remains out of the pattern. Or it's only a background. Important, of course: the air-raid burst through up there between its contour and the clouds, or grew visible on the horizon *preceded by distant roars or by wailing sirens, hoarse now, as though worn out by too much bellowing, so as soon to be replaced by three dull thuds of antiaircraft fire*. It's not part of that story. At the last strongpoint our stretch of the front touched the slopes of the mountain, ended here. Between here and the sea the fellowship was established, the community. I know it's only a manner of illustrating the hypothesis, an unreal hypothesis. It conceals the desire to imagine what would have become of us had more seasons passed, the exchange of visits from one strongpoint to another, the one who burst out singing without fail each evening an "o mama mia mi sun luntan senti la nustalgia del mè Milan," the fortification work whose point we gradually forgot (... *the men worked for hours in the burning sun digging antitank trenches, outposts, dug-outs, worked overtime for this . . . likely the day after they had to scrap it all because the calculations were wrong or someone had changed his mind, had to start all over again*). You mean to say? You were turning yourselves into something else? Settlers? Pioneers? Ready for a different order, a new condition? Or more simply for an undertaking that, finally, had a sense, a value? I wouldn't know. Every time I try telling this story to someone I beat my head against this wall. The external pointers, certain stable atmospheric data, certain permanent signs absorb the facts, count for more than the facts. They fade, empty themselves as soon as I try to cast them into a meaning. Did we seriously believe, albeit only for a moment, that we'd found some cohesion? But it was a cohesion without object, as became obvious when the first shots were fired. Some had already put on civilian clothes, perhaps they'd had them ready for a while, scattered, vanished, nothing more heard of them. That's to say they'd understood before the others. Nobody today would speak of betrayal or desertion, it would be laughable. At least among things left to ferment in the salt-works' light, it would be good to know the fate of those who fled; or what ours would have been, if, for one hour longer, we'd believed in that cohesion of only negative origin, and without regard for allies or enemies, as one man we'd opened a road to the strait. An hour more, it would have been enough, for a different design from the one which, with hindsight, it seems others had reserved for us (fate, we say, or else chance; on the contrary, it's the point at which a lengthy inertia unconscious of itself is released and becomes a precipitous slide): to dissolve the parley on the for and against, whether or not to try to save face (for whom? in whose name?) by fighting to the last, to break and throw down our arms, more damaging than useful even for personal defense once it's decided not to get involved in skirmishes and to consider the least engagement a mishap, to slip away through the opposing ranks no longer men in arms but swarms of pilgrims—by dry fords, skirting riverbeds, within sight of metropolises which are rubble against the light—scattered, reunited by prearranged routes and rendezvous, filtering, breaking through: overflowing finally, motley and bare, but already rich in other resources, deftness and craft, unanimous in the furrow of one of the possible futures—which is what I was in search of down there, I seem to realize now, among those few revisited kilometers. I see the captain make a stick from a branch, set off with his indolent movements towards temples empty like mirages. The glimpse reaches no further, no further than these beginnings of an unrealized future.

The extraneous splendor of Erice gone by, black angels pursue us down the opposite slope to the one we'd come up (*dressed in black from head to foot, as for a village festival, men who, from the edges of roads, the day of the attack, had set about sending intelligence signals to whoever, invisible, between rows of trees, hedges, wheat fields*) they want to overtake, repeatedly sound the horn, it's no good, for a while I hold out, then give in to an old uneasiness that the solitary place reinforces, they go by scornfully.

At Trapani the clocks say 6:30 in the afternoon, they're about an hour slow; can it be they've stopped at the same time as before, that there is no other time at Trapani (*on the wristwatch's face the hands hadn't moved from 18:30 on April 6th, from that day he'd said, the city, apart from some stray dogs, had practically ceased to exist*). On this side the seafront's crowded with houses and buildings, but deserted. With feigned assurance I ask where the old sports ground is. You can still see the notices: stands, terraces, players entrance (*the clamor of faraway Sunday crowds*), but the turnstiles and gates have been walled up. This—I say to my women—was the first, provisional prison camp, we were here for a fortnight before crossing the sea (*the days overflowed with ill-feeling woven by the continuous passage of bombers heading North . . . there was the usual emptiness of the months before the surrender and the usual silence, had it not been for the ill-feeling of the echoes spread by the planes . . . the roar that broke from above and then rose swelling in the sky*).

Trapani, I would like to add, is a repressed cry sustaining its old ruins and new buildings that respect the vanished skyline; *and of course towards evening, a slight breeze rising from the sea . . . between vanished crowds relaxing towards the furthest wharves of Italy . . . a voice seemed to linger, more saddened and commiserating than anxious, calling for someone very dear and lost: just a burnt air of sorrow all along the marina.* That cry is, now and still, mine also, it expires between the naval offices and customs houses in the mild air of the port in our senseless comings-and-goings along the edge of the sea.

What fury he must feel, the stocky hunchback, powerfully built with striking head and profile, but hunchbacked. A notice announces that the café and bar's up for sale, the management is moving to a "bathing spot." His tongue splutters its fierce rage into the receiver, about to die down it flares up afresh at the objections of an invisible other, at once pitiful and frightening. Will he crack? The reason must be futile, but underneath there's utter desperation. It draws us all in: regulars, staff, interlocutor—and everyone and every story files towards the last escape, to the sea, the sea, which is rather the last emptiness, known for centuries, the absenteeism, abstention of the sea.

Evaporating in a light already summer's, where along wharves the flapping of white uniforms attempts a note of gaiety, thus Trapani bids us farewell.

The route to Palermo forks into two roads, inland and coastal, much the same number of kilometers. I take the inland one, keeping the coast for later if need be. From here, a little to the right and low down, I can clearly see the village and the countryside, can make out the dense trees around the villa and everything else as far as the beach at Torre Nubia.

Certainly Timpone Sole, the strongest of the strongpoints, was well chosen as the heart of the defensive system: a pronounced spur, in a dominant position for shelling fields and plateaus, whose alleyways I make out now, as never before, forming shaded supply lines by which, if necessary, reinforcements could have arrived under cover. Pointing it out, I omit to say it was from there that the few useful shells were fired during the opening skirmishes of the attack.

Goodbye forever? That remains to be seen. Luisa knows where I am as the car accelerates. She talks about the man who yesterday led us through the ruins. Not a sign of surprise or diffidence, you noticed, when we were before him. He spoke with propriety, precision, despite those unforeseen, uncoordinated sentences. But later, at the moment of departure: as if the encounter had never taken place, as if he'd never even seen us, an unexpected reserve, a blind dropped suddenly down across a window. The fact is I'd returned, for a while I was again beneath the trees of Villa Paradiso (but Luisa and Giovanna, I'm not excluding you, bewildered to see you making your debut on this ground, to see you being, the two of you, the never-supposed future of my being there then) more intensely than yesterday when I was actually there. In the meantime his figure had taken on other proportions and lineaments, had grown beyond measure. Now, in the changing countryside, I see him whiten on the horizon in a funereal resignation. How long it is since yesterday. I'd arrived there very apprehensive and unsettled. About not even finding the village, the place, that everything would be changed, that, ashamed, I'd have to ask old witnesses of our shame perhaps (*disarmed and in columns under the goad of the enemy platoon . . . shamefully weeping*), that, under their again ironic eyes, I would find myself in difficulties on the narrowing left and right that descends from the village to the villa, that the main gate might be barred, I might have to request a special permit—supposing the villa still existed—to visit an entirely rebuilt edifice, unrecognizable, converted for different use. Already at Selinunte, not to let myself be distracted by its African light, or that Marinella varying on the left, consoling quarters for someone confronting its beauty and placing himself within its surroundings; at Marsala, moving away from there, and then onto the main road more and more crowded with houses—not sure if it's Marsala spreading out or Trapani reaching it—rolling forward on a line of gas under the vast thick cloud bank, speeding along with windows open to the old poem's reluctantly cancelled lines *now that not distant cautious, / the ambulances draw near the battle,* kilometer after kilometer on the reminders of the white lines, but it was all so easy, too much so, a glance at the other villa halfway round the corner, dominated then by a particular presence (*the white linen outfit in certain dazzling hours of summer, the shadow of the Panama hat on the dark and olive green face, the walking stick made to roll gently round the fingers*) and now all freedom and relief, air circulating from wide-open doors and windows—and finally the gate removed, pilasters in full view, the tree-lined avenue still tree-lined: the hour has come, just as it was, it's come back as before.

I didn't go there with writing intentions, I swear. If anything to free myself from them. But it happens to those who write or have written at some time in their lives: that they go round with the consciousness or memory of this fact. Usually, not always, always in my case, we are bad traveling companions—which doesn't entirely mean bad travelers. Why besides having a body, a gaze, and a voice, are we not endowed with a special transparency allowing those close to us to live with us fully, without recourse to that distorted emanation of ourselves which writing is, and to which we regularly refer them? This being the case, means and writing implements abolished, the writer would cease to exist, wouldn't go about as such. Certainly one day we will have to reach that undistorted emanation, not hesitating, but direct and instantaneous, in a strict correlation between acts and words. I don't mean to say that writing corresponds to a defect in vitality, quite the contrary, but rather that it carries with it the hint of an imperfection. I have instinctively sought my friends among people who bear witness to this unconsciously yet visibly through the demon that goes with them—half-men half-artists who most of the time have forgotten this second half or not yet discovered it within themselves. They go from outing to outing, from place to place. They arrive like instantaneous bringers of joy, even to the point of sadness. Some would crown them with flowers at first sight, when they arrive, but others would erase them at a stroke.

In the space between my anxiety to arrive and the wrench of departure it was as if I had got jammed. The first brushes with what I'd have wished to avoid, with what at the outset I was sure would not happen, poured down on me. Reinforcements flooded in, uncalled for, actual and true intrusions in the form of intermittent recollections of things written by me at various times related to that place and to events occurring there, illusory pegs for reliving them when, if anything, I'd have liked to live them afresh, setting out from a particular moment only, as if that had been the moment at which they had actually come to an end. So I wasn't a revisitor only, not one who'd been here and returned, but one who, more than that, had written about it and knew only too well that he had. At this level—of affections, of memories—the inadequacies, bitterness, failures of writing do not at all differ from other human unfulfillment, bitterness and failure: on the contrary, they're added to them, are squadded together. Already beforehand, from Selinunte onwards, and from Marsala growing louder, a murmur, a mumble, a torment had infiltrated me until it scanned the journey's progress. Presumably it was the same road, at least from a particular stretch, down which the enemy's vanguard had fallen upon us. Frightening to conceive of it, to put yourself for a second in *their* place. Precarious, characteristic of the strain of giving a name to certain states and moments. Later, I understood what it was, a tremor, a sustained vibration, Cavafy's lines come to my aid, rumbling far off, reinforcement for other reinforcements uncalled for. Twenty-six years . . . your phantom . . .

But how many years is it, now I come to think of it? I wrench myself away from the rumble, count up: twenty-six exactly since I first set foot here.

Twenty-six years.

They're bending over us, these great afflicted trees.

In reality those few lines had played out the conflict in my name, it hardly mattered they weren't mine (they were mine, though, weren't they? more and better than if I'd been their author). Together they'd made me double between myself and the villa, myself and the man of the ruins—and established a reciprocity by which we found ourselves over and over again imploring forgiveness of each other for the time that had passed unopposed by us. This, if nothing else, was released by the voice come to my aid and not by chance. The premises would have existed from which to recount that story point by point, clearly, simply, over again—not as I had attempted long before in that narrative, *The Capture,* nonsensically told in the third person and before that in a more extended version left in the drawer. Everything had been tidied away, but not because of this, not to this end, had the slate been wiped clean by those lines. I found it superfluous if not actually dishonest to return to writing, to produce the written double of those facts that I'd have preferred to leave in the hands of a historiographer of a deeper history, appropriately told. Or else extract from it anecdotes for someone who, with me on a later journey, might show some interest in them, sitting in the shade, fortified by the panoramic vantage point, on the natural platform of Timpone Sole where the imagination sites an unlikely hostelry.

For the rest, particular unchangeable elements of those lived circumstances—which previously barely furrowed them: the wisteria's reflection that will soon spread over the walls, the ambiguous splendor between the salt works—contradict and annul them, no more nor less than at that time fireworks from a distant party, represented by batteries too remote on the horizon for alarm or noise to carry, removed themselves, dissociated themselves from the state of war. They drew themselves away, they passed over it. Fermenting this long in the sun, they've formed a clot of ashes and light—the guardian of the ruins, my-his diurnal apparition—that condenses them into a human figure and refracts them from itself. I should in turn pass over him, now, and the circle of supplication and tenderness (dearly beloved, we are gathered together, forgiveness for the time past, for questions not asked in time, for replies not given, for the trees we'll leave to die), the inevitable falsetto for which we're all preparing ourselves: custodian of the ruins, sleeper in the flower bed, breathless passerby, stocky hunchback who pushes on towards the sea, Luisa, Giovanna, me. The reality that inspires us is always born to one side, oblique to the realities we stumble upon, wisteria's reflection, mirage of the salt works, preserver of the ruins, whoever.

But why at the moment in which, with the help of Cavafy's lines, peace was established, has there arisen, or better, has there returned to me—first in the form of a repressed cry and before that as a murmur, mumble, sustained vibration—the desire to write? How has the report of a journey transformed itself into the diagram of that wish? One thing only is clear: I am standing at the limit where I've always stopped myself whenever I put pen to paper. The point at which the true adventure, the true undertaking begins. From somewhere an anxiety rises resembling the one that urged me along the obliterated defensive system of twenty-six years ago so as to be everywhere, not in any specific place. And at the same time a repugnance. There stands before me a wood, the words, to travel through following a line that gradually forms as you walk, forwards (or back) towards the transparency, if that is the right word for the future.

COMMENTARY

For these translations from the authorized poems collected by Vittorio Sereni we used the text edited by the poet's eldest daughter, Maria Teresa Sereni, published by Mondadori in 1986. In substantial respects this text was reproduced in the critical edition, *Poesie,* edited with an apparatus by Dante Isella, published by Mondadori in 1995. Isella's text introduced a few minor errors that were almost all corrected in the 2004 edition, and we have cross-checked our texts against this later one too. In a small number of cases where there are minor textual issues, we have described our choices in the following notes. Revising the translations and writing the commentary, we used the most recent editions of Sereni's works; for the poems, *Poesie,* ed. D. Isella (Milan: Mondadori, 2004); for the prose, *La tentazione della prosa,* ed. G. Raboni (Milan: Mondadori, 1998). Commentaries and notes by Dante Isella in *Poesie,* by Luca Lenzini on the poems selected for *Il grande amico: Poesie 1935–1981* (Milan: Rizzoli, 1990), those by Dante Isella and Clelia Martignoni for *Poesie: Un'antologia per la scuola* (Luino: Nastro & Nastro, 1993), by Maria Teresa Sereni in *Gli immediati dintorni, primi e secondi* (Milan: il Saggiatore, 1983), and by Giulia Raboni in *La tentazione della prosa* have been indispensable. Readers who would like to take further their knowledge of Sereni's work and its cultural contexts are recommended to begin there.

SELECTED POEMS

from *Frontier*

AUTHOR'S NOTE (1966)

The first edition of *Frontiera* is from 1941: it was published in a print run of three hundred numbered copies, and twenty not intended for sale, appearing under the *Corrente* imprint, directed by Ernesto Treccani in the poetry series edited by Luciano Anceschi, with a small drawing by Renato Birolli on the cover. The book was issued in a second edition from Vallecchi just over a year later, with the title *Poesie* and the following preface.

> It is best simply to say that this second collection is little more than a reprint with a few additions, with no revisions or surprises. Readers of *Frontiera* in the "Corrente" edition will find the entire book reproduced in these pages including the weaker pieces which one would like to suppress, if it were not for having so meager a vein, and moreover, for a tenacious, perhaps obsessive, all-too-human fidelity to the times and the circumstances lived.
>
> The author's intention in publishing this second collection is not to force his name upon the public's attention, nor to consolidate his reputation; and the title itself—generic and suitable for a collection, compared to the previous one, cherished yet too specific—demonstrates a clear awareness of how distant this book is from the ideal one, which it only vaguely represents.
>
> But the author also knows that this is his one book, the book which, good luck and circumstances permitting, he will always continue to write: it was necessary to give it a more lasting form, one that might—in the event—be definitive.
>
> This is why, at the moment that he leaves for remote parts and his fate as a living creature is placed in the balance, he wishes to entrust his book once more to the heartfelt memory of his friends.

This was followed by the forwarding address, P.M. (Posta Militare) 76 and the date August 1942.

The mirage, or myth, of the "one book" should be viewed in the context of that year and that particular psychological (and public) moment; today I would certainly not endorse it.

This reprinting of the book makes it once again available to readers after many years. Some unpublished verses have been included, some of the titles have been revised; the internal organization of the book is rather different, including for the first time "Lines to Proserpina," two sections of which had previously been included in *Diario d'Algeria*. The dates in parenthesis given on the contents page [here in the commentary] are, this time, dates of actual composition. This, then, is my prewar book, but with one foot already in the war, as can be seen, I believe, not only from the dates.

I dedicate this edition to the memory of Giovanni Scheiwiller, the friend who every young poet would have wished for as his publisher in those years.

WINTER

The poem is dated December 1934 in a manuscript draft where it is entitled "Lontananze" [Distances]. The poem is set in Luino. The lyric, which opens the definitive edition of his poetry, begins with a line of dots and a lowercase "but if," indicating a suppressed passage to which this remnant responds. Sereni wrote in "Dovuto a Montale" [Owed to Montale] (*Gli immediati dintorni* p. 159) of his distinct preference, early in life, for winter.

GARDEN CONCERT

The poem is dated June 1935 in the manuscript materials. First published in *Il Frontespizio* in November 1937, with an introductory note by Carlo Betocchi, it was the first work of Sereni's to make his name known to the literary world. This was the opening piece in the first edition of *Frontiera* (1941). The "red and white torpedoes" are Italian and German racing cars. "Avus" is a motor racing circuit in Berlin. Isella notes that the poem is built around the pun on "trumpet" in the Lombard dialect—a word used for hydraulic pumps—but, of course, with military associations.

SPORT ON SUNDAY

Also written in June 1935 but not collected in *Frontiera* until the 1966 third edition, this poem was originally entitled "Inter-Juve." Internazionale, the team Sereni supported, had blue-and-black jerseys. Here they are playing against Juventus, the Turin team from Piedmont, whose colors are black and white—"the zebras." The "realm" can also signify Piedmont, the historic territory of the House of Savoy, the Italian royal family.

RECALLING AMERICA

Dated 1935. The poem paints an imaginary scene drawn from the poet's interest in American films. Sereni had not visited the United States at the time.

LOMBARD SONG

Dated January–February 1936. The original of "and us, we feel we're from Lombardy" borrows a Florentine form of speech. The phrase in italics is revised from the first lines of an uncollected poem called "Periferia" [Outskirts], written at Easter 1935.

BIRTHDAY

Dated 1936. This poem was originally dedicated to Salvatore Quasimodo (1901–1968). For the reason why the dedication may have been cut, see the note to "Storm at Salsomaggiore." For "smiling," cf. Leopardi "A Silvia," l.4.

FOG

Dated 13 January 1937. The poem is set in Milan.

STORM AT SALSOMAGGIORE

Though dated 1938 in the index to *Frontiera,* a draft existed in the late summer of 1936. Salsomaggiore is a spa town in Emilia-Romagna, not far from Parma. Sereni visited the town with his mother. The critic Giosue Bonfanti speculates that the poem may have arisen out of difficulties in the poet's courtship of his future wife. It was first published in *Corrente* in April 1938, and was the cause of a rift between the poet and Salvatore Quasimodo, who accused Sereni of plagiarizing a number of details. Sereni offered a sustained defense of his poem in a letter to Quasimodo on 26 April.

TO M. L. PASSING ABOVE HER TOWN
IN AN EXPRESS TRAIN

Dated 1938–40 in the index to *Frontiera.* M. L.: is Maria Luisa Bonfanti, whom Sereni met at university in Milan and married in 1940. The title of the poem was suggested by Attilio Bertolucci with the example of Wordsworth's "Tintern Abbey" in mind. The town is Parma. Sereni passed through on a train to Rome in 1938—as indicated in letters of the following year to his future wife. Sereni's original of "the beaming lands" alludes to the myth of Phaeton, son of Helios, who was thrown into the river Po by Apollo. Lenzini suggests Vincenzo Cardarelli's "Passaggio notturno" (1934), also set in a train passing through a town dear to the poet, as a possible model.

DIANA

Dated 1938. The Navigli are a series of canals connecting the river Ticino with Milan. Originally entitled "June," this poem is also implicitly addressed to Sereni's future wife. The woman in the poem, though, has been described by the poet as a composite made up of three figures—his wife-to-be, an unnamed girl met in Milan, and even the actress Jean Harlow, who had died in Los Angeles in 1937. "It depends," Sereni adds, "on the extremely laborious and difficult gestation of this lyric. And the death may be moral or physical, distance or forgetting, as you like. Meaning, as far as I am concerned, something which is irredeemably lost, with a sense heightened by this actual imminent departure and by the nostalgia for what has not been lived" (Sereni to Giancarlo Vigorelli, letter dated 8 July 1938, cited in the latter's *Carte d'identità* [Milan, 1984]). "Torni anche tu, Diana," imitates Montale's opening to the third verse ("Torni anche tu, pastora senza greggi") of "Corrispondenze" first published in January 1937.

SOLDIERS IN URBINO

Dated 10 February 1939. The poem was occasioned by Sereni's military training as a junior infantry officer. See the chronology for details.

3 DECEMBER

Dated 1940. The poem remembers Antonia Pozzi, a poet Sereni met at university in Milan. She committed suicide, and her body was discovered in fields on the outskirts of Milan towards Chiaravalle on 3 December

1938. She was twenty-six. A manuscript copy of "Diana" (see above) was found on her body with the following lines scribbled at the bottom: "Addio Vittorio, caro—mio caro fratello. Ti ricorderai di me insieme con Maria" [Goodbye, Vittorio dear—my dear brother. Remember me together with Maria]. "3 dicembre" alludes to Pozzi's poem "La porta che si chiude" [The closing door], whose last stanza reads in our translation:

> And then, with lips sealed,
> with eyes open
> on the mysterious sky of shadow,
> there will be
> —you know it—
> peace.

Antonia Pozzi's father, with whom she had a complex relationship, was a keen huntsman. The associations between hunting and love are implicit in "Diana." For "tumult" see line 7 of Pozzi's "Fine di una domenica" [End of a Sunday]. The word indicates both the noise of trains and psychological crisis.

MILITARY POEM

From 1940. The poem is occasioned by Sereni's posting to the French front after Mussolini brought Italy into the war in June 1940. Garessio is in Piedmont, near to the coast, a town (as Sereni reported in a letter to Vigorelli on 20 November 1940) full of churches.

PIAZZA

From 1941.

TO YOUTH

Dated 1941. The sunflowers allude to Montale's lyric from *Ossi di seppia* (1925), "Portami il girasole . . ." [Bring me the sunflower].

WINTER IN LUINO

Dated 1937. Luino, Sereni's birthplace, is on Lake Maggiore close to the Swiss frontier. The "coal heaps jagged in the sun" were to fuel steam engines on the railway line crossing the border. Originally Luino was intended to be on the main line, but Chiasso subsequently became the main frontier station.

TERRACE

From 1938. The torpedo boat is a customs vessel on Lago Maggiore searching for contraband and, as Sereni notes in *Gli immediati dintorni* (p.164), "possibly not only doing that." In a postcard to a Luino friend, Sereni refers to the poem as "La menta" [Mint], the drink they commonly enjoyed on the terrace suspended above the lake. In chapters 36 and 37 of Hemingway's *A Farewell to Arms,* a novel the poet read in French translation in late 1938 or 1939, the hero and Catherine Barkley make an escape to Switzerland by rowing boat: "The lake widened and across it on the shore at the foot of the mountains on the other side we saw a few lights that should be Luino."

ZENNA ROAD

Dated 1938. Originally entitled "Zenna," the name of a town on the Swiss frontier a few kilometers from Luino. In his poem "Rincorrendo Vittorio S. sulla strada di Zenna," Luciano Erba notes that the whistle of a train combined with a cloud passing across the sun was believed by old people to be a sign of bad weather: "*ecco,* dicevano, *s'annuvola il Signore*" [*look,* they'd say, *the Lord clouds over.*] Isella believes this poem to be inspired by Bianca B., a young girl Sereni met in Luino in summer 1938.

SEPTEMBER

Dated 1938–40. The poem (which grew out of the previous one) was also inspired by the poet's friendship with a young girl, Bianca B. in Luino. However, the title and the fact that the poem was not completed until 1940 suggest that it may also allude to the Munich crisis at the end of September 1938 and the attempt to avoid war in Europe.

ANOTHER SUMMER

From 1940. The river Tresa flows into Lago Maggiore.

IMAGE

Dated 1940. "Garessio, Val d'Inferno," as in "Poesia militare," is in Piedmont near the French border. Sereni was posted there as part of the Italian forces invading southern France after the German forces had ensured victory in the north. A ceasefire was called before his regiment saw active service on this front. "*Santa, santa mia*" is from a popular song in the Mexican movie *Santa* (1931).

YOUR MEMORY IN ME

Dated 1938–40.

CREVA ROAD

Dated 1941. The Creva road goes past the cemetery on the outskirts of Luino. The poem refers to a number of saint's days (15, 17 and 21 January), frequently a time of rather mild weather, and cites a Lombard proverb that the poet echoes in the phrase "lucerte vanno per siepi."

"SEE HOW THE VOICES FALL AND FRIENDS..."

Dated 1940.

Algerian Diary

AUTHOR'S NOTE (1965)

The first edition of *Diario d'Algeria* was published by Vallecchi in Florence in 1947. This edition, which partially restructures the book, has omitted "Vecchi versi a Proserpina," which belong to the period of *Frontiera* (in an ideal new edition of that book), and "Via Scarlatti" which I have preferred to move to the opening of *Gli strumenti umani* (Turin: Einaudi, 1965). A third poem, "Pin-up Girl," returns in a greatly reduced form (though some of the suppressed lines have been recast under the title "Villa Paradiso"); finally, two other poems are included in the versions used in *Gli immediati dintorni* (Milan: il Saggiatore, 1962). All the poems appearing in the first two sections ("The Athenian Girl" and "Algerian Diary") were written during my two years of captivity during the last war (Algeria and French Morocco, 1943–45). Likewise "Bolognese Diary," which had previously only appeared in *Gli immediati dintorni,* and is now included for the first time. "The African Sickness" was composed after 1947 and the Vallecchi edition. This poem, which gives its name to a whole section here, has already appeared in *Gli strumenti umani.* It was also brought out in a limited edition in 1957 by Franco Riva and Vanni Scheiwiller, as well as in the book already mentioned published by il Saggiatore. The individual dates, where they appear, refer not to the composition but to the occasions of the poems.

It seems hardly necessary to remind the reader that in "The Athenian Girl" *despinís* in modern Greek means "girl" or "Miss" and that Kaidari is a suburb of Athens where, in the summer of 1942 some regiments of the Pistoia Division, intended for the Egyptian front, were encamped.

OUTSKIRTS 1940

Written in that year. The book begins with two poems occasioned by Mussolini's declaration of war in June 1940.

CITY AT NIGHT

Inspired by passing through Milan on a troop train heading for the French border in the summer of 1940. The poet's parents lived in Via Scarlatti, near Milan's central station.

BOLOGNESE DIARY

The Pistoia Division spent the winter of 1941–42 stationed in Bologna. This poem, written during Sereni's POW years, did not appear in the 1947 edition of *Diario d'Algeria*. It is illuminated by the short prose memoir "Bologna '42" included in this edition.

BELGRADE

Though inspired by Sereni's journey from Mestre to Athens during August 1942, the poem was composed in North Africa during his imprisonment and first published in July 1946. "—the Danube! the Sava!—" is a late addition, first introduced in the 1979 printing, and included (Sereni explained) because of critical confusion about the two "chimeras" in the poem. Ungaretti's famous poem of the Great War, "I fiumi" [The rivers], may lie behind the lines. Giosue Bonfanti, no relation of Sereni's wife, was a literary critic and friend he had met during his university days.

ITALIAN IN GREECE

The phrase "slender myth" from this poem is cited in Franco Fortini's epigram "Sereni esile mito" (1954), which the poet himself cites in the opening section of "Un posto di vacanza" [A Holiday Place], see pp. 226–27 of this edition and the notes to the poem at p. 414.

DIMITRIOS

The poem is dedicated to Maria Teresa Sereni (b. 24 July 1941), the poet's eldest daughter and his literary executor until her death in October 1991.

THE ATHENIAN GIRL

"despinís" is Sereni's transliteration of the Greek for "miss"; "Kaidari" is a suburb of Athens where part of the Pistoia Division was encamped during the summer of 1942, waiting to reinforce the Axis armies in North Africa. As the note of places and times at the end of this poem indicates, the first two sections refer to Sereni's situation before his capture and the following parts are from afterwards. Lenzini suggests that the "prey" must be civilians trying to escape across the border being hunted by Axis forces. The "friendly fleet" refers to the British invasion of Greece in October 1944. Sereni has explained that the entire section from "Whoever sleeps" to "of hope of mercy of fear" are words attributed exclusively to the girl, and the dead refer only to *her* dead. The "defeated" (Sereni noted) refers to the "little enemy," Dimitrios, who here has his "revenge."

UP THE ARNO FROM PISA

The Pistoia Division was transported back from Greece in the autumn of 1942, and spent the winter encamped in the vicinity of Empoli before being once again posted, this time to Sicily, in April 1943.

VILLA PARADISO

This fragmentary poem is made up of lines salvaged from the first stanza of the first published version of "Pin-up Girl" (translated below). Villa Paradiso was the command post for Sereni's regiment during the spring and early summer of 1943 as they prepared to defend Sicily against invasion.

PIN-UP GIRL

This poem is composed of the final two verses from the original version given below, a poem of the same title that was published in the 1947 edition of *Diario d'Algeria*.

. . . .
Now far too tender

your war's become.
You too a shred of disheartened
delights, no better than the thread
of breeze that in the morning
of wisteria
moves on the bombarded coastline,

you're outmoded among the vulgar idols
and I can barely recognize you
in the clippings' easy divas
who from walls through long winters
offered themselves to soldiers and watched over
insomnia and homesickness.

Sister of baseness, from there too
you can come down to men who turn
and look at you no longer
now that not distant cautious
ambulances draw near the battle
and *all of the bridges*
have been destroyed
all papers burned
all the cup drained . . .
                        You
suffer? There's no suffering for who
was once crazed by you, by sky.
He doesn't suffer from the war of men.

Look at the sorry cutting grown limp
in the dazzling air:
the July afternoon
has hints of bad weather,
stray voices of alarm.

And for a while the thirst
is quenched on your lips
still moistened in the wind.

                Trapani front, July 1943

ALGERIAN DIARY

The section's dedicatee, Remo Valianti, was one of Sereni's fellow prisoners. He had something of a reputation as a man who could get things done in the camp and, with Walter (named in part 8), would steal out of the compound to barter for food from nearby houses. "Algeria '44," Sereni's commentary on some of the poems in the sequence, is included in this edition.

Over there where from tower...
The three lines between dashes in this poem were composed at some point between 1947 and 1961. The text given here is from the 1965 edition. In "Two Old Flames," included in this edition, Sereni discusses his revisions of parts one and three of the sequence.

Valor and grace...
The first six lines of this poem were composed at some point between 1947 and 1961. The text given here is from the 1965 second edition. See "Two Old Flames" in this edition. This poem is discussed by Sereni in the first part of "Algeria '44."

He knows nothing anymore, is borne up on wings...
This poem is discussed by Sereni in the second part of "Algeria '44."

Alas how what returns...
The poem recalls a high school romance from the poet's years in Brescia. It is discussed by Sereni in part 3 of "Algeria '44."

They don't know they're dead...
This poem is discussed by Sereni in the fourth part of "Algeria '44."

Only the summer is true and this...
The "frail hedgerow" is a reminiscence of Leopardi's "L'infinito" and the "German crowd" an allusion to *Inferno* XVI, l. 5.

And again in a dream the tent's edge...
This poem is discussed by Sereni in the fifth part of "Algeria '44."

Often through tortuous alleys...
This poem is discussed by Sereni in the sixth part of "Algeria '44."

FRAGMENTS OF A DEFEAT

The prose sections are excerpted from "La sconfitta" [The Defeat] written in 1951, and also appear in "Sicily '43" in this edition.

THE AFRICAN SICKNESS

First published in 1962. Commenting on the title, Sereni told the translators that "African sickness" is an expression for a persistent feeling of nostalgic attraction and repulsion, said to afflict anyone who visits that continent. An earlier title for the poem appeared in a draft table of contents for the poet's third book as "Vecchio conto con l'Africa" [An old score with Africa].

The first thirty-two lines of the poem remember the train journey "west-southwest" from the last of the prison camps in Algeria to Fedala in Morocco, before the end of the war. The next part includes descriptions from the voyage of repatriation in the summer of 1945, from Morocco, via Gibraltar and Sardinia, to the Italian mainland.

Giansiro Ferrata, the poem's dedicatee, was a literary critic and friend of Sereni's, whose 1958 visit to Algeria occasions the poem. In 1954 the National Liberation Front led by Ben Bella turned to armed insurrection against the French colonial government. The battle of Algiers was fought in 1957 and in 1959 De Gaulle recognized the right of self-determination for the Algerian people. These events had strong echoes in Italy.

"Bidonville" is a French word meaning "shanty town." "Barracans" are a type of Arab clothing. The "Isle of Sards" is Sardinia, alluded to in this form because the original adapts *Inferno* VI, the Ulysses Canto, l. 104.

In the collected editions of Sereni's poetry, this poem appears twice: here in *Diario d'Algeria* and also in the fourth part of *Gli strumenti umani* between "Corso Lodi" and "L'alibi e il beneficio." We have followed the example of Maria Teresa Sereni's and all subsequent collected editions, giving the poem in full where it first appears.

NOTES FROM A DREAM

This is a transcription of a dream the poet had during the summer of 1962 about the Italian capitulation in North Africa and Sicily. The text was first published on 18 February 1964.

SEPTEMBER THE EIGHTH

On 8 September 1943, General Badoglio, head of Italy's government after the fall of Mussolini on 25 July, signed a separate armistice with the Allies. *"Sale macaroni"* [Dirty Italians] is a taunt hurled by French-speaking Algerians at Sereni and his fellow prisoners of war as they were marched through the port of Oran after being sent back on shore from ships that were to take them to POW camps in the USA. Instead, now that Italy was no longer at war with the Allies, they were to remain in North Africa.

from *The Human Implements*

AUTHOR'S NOTE (1965)

All the texts in the volume belong to the period 1945–1965. Only some groups of poems are given a more precise date. For example, the poems in "A Backward Glance" belong, in principle, to the period 1945–57, while those of "Appointment at an Unusual Hour" and "Apparitions or Encounters" should be thought of as belonging to the periods of 1958–60 and 1961–65, respectively. All things considered, rigorous dating would be merely arbitrary for individual pieces. For each one it would be possible, perhaps, to establish starting and completion dates: in that case, however, probably some beginnings could actually be placed prior to 1945. Such a long period between starting and finishing a poem in no way indicates protracted work upon it due to dissatisfaction or to stylistic fussiness, but rather to a series of revisions and additions, variants and rephrasing, expansions or contractions, prompted or suggested, if not actually imposed, by life, chance, or the mood of the moment (a typical case in point being "Poetry Is a Passion?" published here although unfinished, a "work in progress" destined perhaps for a future book, and with partly unforeseeable developments; an exception to the rule, on the other hand, is "A Factory Visit," considerably revised since its first publication in a magazine): I felt the need to make this point and hope its meaning is clear. Where a date appears in the text it indicates, without exception, a starting point or phase and never a date of composition.

One more comment should be made, this time concerning the lines or phrases by living or dead authors inserted here and there in the text without quotation marks or italics. They should be recognizable as and when they occur, and it is therefore unnecessary to state either where or why they have been adopted.

VIA SCARLATTI

The Serenis lived at 27 Via Scarlatti, Milan, from 1946 to 1952. The "opera duet" is an evident reference to the composer after whom the street is named. The poem was first collected in the 1947 edition of *Diario d'Algeria*. Its form is modeled on poems by Umberto Saba such as "Città vecchia" from *Trieste e una donna* (1912).

INTERRUPTED COMMUNICATION

This and the following two poems emerged as a single draft and were then separated. The poem refers to the abolition of the monarchy by referendum and the consequent exile of the House of Savoy in 1946.

THE PROVISIONAL TIME

Milan had suffered serious bomb damage during the war, one of the heaviest raids being in August 1943.

JOURNEY AT DAWN

Dated 1947. Voldomino is a group of houses near Luino. The poet is responding to Vasco Pratolini's suggestion that the name derives from "Volto di Dio" [Face of God]. The last two lines of the poem are adapted from the Roman Catholic Mass.

THE RETURN

Dated 1947–48. Originally entitled "Cartolina Luinese" [Postcard from Luino].

IN THE SNOW

Mendrisio is in Switzerland. In 1946, at the time of the referendum, the Republican Party symbol was a sprig of ivy. This poem continues Sereni's meditation on his place, or lack of one, in the direction taken by postwar Italian poetry, culture, and politics.

JOURNEY THERE AND BACK

Written between 20 and 22 May 1958 but conceived some eight years before. The "screech" in the penultimate line of the poem comes from the sound of a steam locomotive.

THE MISAPPREHENSION

The poem recalls Baudelaire's sonnet "A une passante" [To a Passerby] from *Les Fleurs du Mal*. In a 7 May 1958 letter to Franco Fortini, Sereni explains "in povertà" as relating to Proust's portrayal of love and obsession in *À la recherche du temps perdu*.

ON THE ZENNA ROAD AGAIN

The poem is set in the Luino area. The opening lines were prompted by Sereni's memory of similar phrases in an Italian version of Chekhov's *Uncle Vania*.

WINDOW

Written either 1953–54 or 1954.

THE SHARKS

The first poem set in Bocca di Magra, once a fishing port on the Ligurian coast south of Lerici. Sereni and his family began taking annual holidays there in 1951.

MILLE MIGLIA

The poem was written in 1956. "Mille Miglia" was a thousand-mile sports car rally that started and finished in Brescia. It took place annually on open roads until 1957 when an accident killed spectators. Orlando and Angelica are two of the main protagonists, separated lovers, in Ariosto's *Orlando Furioso*. The Angelica that Sereni has in mind here, though, is the figure in a fragment by Leopardi that begins "Angelica, tornata al patrio lito / Dopo i casi e gli amori" [Angelica, returned to home shores / After incidents and loves.]

YEARS AFTER

Like the previous one, this poem is set in Brescia. Its inspiration can be dated to 1954, though the writing probably took place in March 1956 and 3–11 May 1958. The title echoes a phrase of Antonia Pozzi's.

THE ASHES

Originally entitled "Mercoledì delle Ceneri" [Ash Wednesday] and composed 3–9 March 1957.

SIX IN THE MORNING

Dante Isella describes the occasion of this poem:

> One evening, at the time of local elections, in spring 1956, Sereni went with friends to an important meeting of "Unità Popolare," in Via Cerva, and came back, unusually for him, only at dawn. His wife, in the depths of the night, stretched out an arm to reassure herself of his presence and felt only the cold of the empty bed. Anxious, she got up, wandered around the empty rooms, opened the door and left it ajar . . . All as if he were in fact dead. The next morning she described this to her husband.
>
> The poet, estranged from himself, imagines *his own* death in a vision of dismay, as if it had just happened in his own home, the door being left open for visitors to the deceased and the house therefore stirred, symbolically, by the wind.

An earlier version of the final line read "di Milano ancorata nel suo vento." [of Milan, anchored in its wind.]

A FACTORY VISIT

The poem was finished, according to a manuscript note of Sereni's, on 16 April 1961. It was first published in Elio Vittorini's magazine *Menabò* 4, September 1961, with a note indicating that the dates "1952–1958" do not refer to drafts of the poem but to the poet's own personal experience— namely, his period working for Pirelli in their publishing and publicity department. The factory is their "Bicocca" works just outside Milan.

"E di me si spendea la miglior parte" [And the best part of me has been squandered] is line 18 of Giacomo Leopardi's famous poem "A Silvia."

THE GREAT FRIEND

Written in Luino in 1958. Influenced by Alain Fournier's novel *Le grand meaulnes,* a work much admired by Sereni, who read it in the 1930s. The poem's name is the Italian title for Fournier's novel. The final lines were inspired by his second daughter Silvia's anxieties when being taken to school by her father in the 1950s.

DISCOVERY OF HATRED

Also written in 1958. Some phrases from this poem date back to an early draft of "Diana" written in 1938.

A NIGHTMARE

First published in 1960.

THOSE CHILDREN PLAYING

First published in "Nuova Corrente" (April–June 1960). The poem's draft title was "Imperdonabile" [Unforgivable]. Sereni frequently heard Umberto Saba (a poet whose work is often concerned with children) repeat the aphorism quoted in italics, which is not to be found in any of his poems. Lenzini suggests G. Pintor's Italian translation of Rilke's *Sonnets to Orpheus* II, 1–8 as a source for Sereni's title and occasion.

SABA

Written some years after the death of its subject, the poem was first published in *Paragone* in 1960. Umberto Saba (1883–1957) was a Triestine poet and friend of Sereni. They had first met in 1939, but became better acquainted when Saba spent much of his time in Milan between 1946 and 1948. On 18 April 1948 the Communists and Socialists of the *Fronte popolare* were defeated by the Christian Democrats in the first elections for the new Italian Republic. Saba, who, as the poem makes clear, was a supporter of the Popular Front, expressed his own view of this period in the poem "Opicina 1947": "Dopo il nero fascista il nero prete; / questa è l'Italia, e lo sai" [After the black of the fascists the black of the priests; this is Italy, and you know it]. The opening lines of "Saba" were inspired by a large photograph of the poet owned by the Sereni family.

PASSING

This is the first of a group of three poems set in Bocca di Magra.

SITUATION

Attempting to clarify this enigmatic poem, Sereni told the translators that it might be entitled "Jealousy."

THE FRIENDS

For Sereni's comments on this poem see "On the Back of a Piece of Paper," in this edition.

APPOINTMENT AT AN UNUSUAL HOUR

"the stolen fox . . ." alludes to the story related by Montaigne in *Essays* I.XIV derived from Plutarch's *Life of Lycurgus,* 18.

IN SLEEP

Sereni dated this sequence 1948–1953 to indicate the period in which it was experienced and conceived; it was not in fact completed until the Christmas holiday of 1962–63. In the body of the poem, Sereni alludes to 25 April 1945, the end of the Second World War, to the postwar reconstruction of Italy, and again to 8 September 1943, when General Badoglio signed a separate peace with the Allies. The Popular Front was defeated in the elections of 1948, a result that many saw as a betrayal of the ideals of the Resistance, whose leaders had formed Italy's first postwar provisional government.

The "compulsory ranks of how many premilitarized Sundays" in part I refers to what was called the Fascist Sunday when citizens were required to take part in para-military sports activities.

"Pantalones" in part IV refers to the figure from the *Commedia dell'arte,* Harlequin's greedy and mean master, perpetually tricked into paying by his cunning and resourceful servant.

The italicized lines in part VI are from a song called "In cerca di te" [In search of you] written in 1945 by Eros Sciorilli and Giancarlo Testoni. The quoted part of the song lyric would read in English:

> I go through the city alone
> I go through the crowd that doesn't know
> that doesn't see my sorrow
> searching for you, dreaming of you, no longer mine.
> Each face I look into and it's not you
> each voice I listen to and it's not you
> Where are you lost love?
> I'll see you once more, I'll find you, I'll follow you.

THE LINES

Written in about 1960. The poem's cut opening lines, which help to contextualize its anguish and resentment, translate as follows:

> Populists and Poundians
> have ruined the art,
> wordsmiths have done the rest,

the super-anapaestics, the top
of the class, vitalists, you
yourself who variously fail to be
wordsmith, Poundian, populist,
Horace to their Curiatii.

CORSO LODI

First published in 1965. Corso Lodi is in Milan. "G" is Gansiro Ferrata, a friend of the poet.

THE ALIBI AND THE BENEFIT

Luciano Erba (1922–) is a Milanese poet. Sereni cites lines from his poem "Tabula rasa?" first published in *Linea K* (1951):

It's any evening
crossed by half-empty trams
moving to quench their thirst for wind.
You see me advance as you know
in districts without memory?
I have a cream necktie, an old
weight of desires
I await only the death
of every thing that had to touch me.

The phrase "Il Tempo di Milano," a newspaper, could also mean "the weather in Milan."

POETRY IS A PASSION?

The Drina is a river, and Larissa a town in the Balkans. The "summer of iron" is 1942. The lines in italics are from Gabriele d'Annunzio (1863–1939), citing ll. 131–32 and 194 of "Il novilunio" from *Alcyone* (1903).

A DREAM

First published in June 1960.

ON THE CREVA ROAD AGAIN

The Creva road leads past the municipal cemetery at Luino. The poem alludes to Leopardi's "Amore e morte."

INTERVIEW WITH A SUICIDE

Also set in Luino, this is the most Dantescan encounter, borrowing in particular from *Purgatorio* XXVI, among this section of poems all influenced by the *Commedia* and its ghostly interviews. *"my lady came to me from Val di Pado"* cites *Paradiso* XVII, 137.

IL PIATTO PIANGE

"Il piatto piange" [the plate is crying] is an idiomatic phrase in poker requesting players who have not yet matched the stake to do so. *"when it's raining outside"* (*come quando fuori piove*) is a mnemonic for the suits of cards in Italian: cuori, quadri, fiori, picche [hearts, diamonds, clubs, spades]. Sereni's poem shares its title with Piero Chiara's first novel that features the lives of card players in Luino, their native town, during the fascist era. One evening during the winter of 1956–57 Chiara told his stories of gambling in Luino, and it was partly at Sereni's insistence that Chiara wrote the novel, which was then published by Mondadori in 1962.

ON A CEMETERY PHOTOGRAPH

The original of the italicized line, *"O dormiente, che cosa è sonno?"* is from the *Codice Atlantico* by Leonardo da Vinci and continues "Il sonno ha similitudine colla morte" [Sleep has a likeness to death].

TO A CHILDHOOD COMPANION

Another poem set in the Luino area. It concludes with an allusion to "A Dream," pp. 166–67.

FROM HOLLAND

All three parts were composed on 3 April 1961, and owe their existence to a brief visit to the country for work and then a short stay there. *The Diary of Anne Frank* was published in Italy by Mondadori.

THE UNJUST PITY

"il faut . . . allemand" [one must be careful, you realize. And above all if the deal is to go through, don't talk about these things all over and done with. It seemed there was one of them, an SS, who was in the army too, although he wasn't German . . .].

IN THE TRUE YEAR ZERO

Author's note: "*Sachsenhausen* is the name of a district in Frankfurt, but also of a place about twenty kilometers from Berlin where, as early as 1933, the first Nazi concentration camp was established." The poem alludes to Roberto Rossellini's neorealist film *Germania: Anno Zero* (1947) set in Berlin in an immediately postwar 1945.

THE HOPE

Author's note: "*Maurizio* was Ferruccio Parri's combat name during the resistance." Ferruccio Parri became the first postwar prime minister of Italy. The poem was written between June and 11 November 1962.

METROPOLIS

The poem was written on 17–18 March 1965 and comments on the literary scene in Italy at that time.

THE WALL

The poem's original title was "I morti" [The Dead], then "Il muro dei morti" [The Wall of the Dead]. One draft contains a handwritten note in pencil that describes the poem as finished on 24 April 1965.

EARTHLY PANTOMIME

The epigraph ["near the rims from which the wells have been removed"] cites *Fueillets d'Hypnos* no. 91; *cheep* ("*cip*") is also the sound made by poker players to signify "I pass"; "*¿le gusta . . . destruyan*" [It pleases you, this garden which is yours? Prevent . . . your children from destroying it] appears in this form at the end of Malcolm Lowry's *Under the Volcano*.

THE REUNITED

"Ninetto" is Ninetto Bonfanti (1927–1967), the poet's brother-in-law. Calestano is a village on the river Taro near Parma. The poem was added to the second (1974) edition of *Gli strumenti umani*. For Sereni's brief comment on the poem see the piece from *The Immediate Surroundings* included in this edition. The alternative title added and deleted on a proof (see p. 279 above) reads "Biglietto nell'aldilà" [Note in the Beyond].

THE BEACH
Another poem set in Bocca di Magra.

from *Variable Star*

On the front inside flap of the first edition, there were four lines of help for the reader by Sereni himself: "Nature that invites and dissuades. Omnipresent and fugitive beauty. The world of men that offers itself to, and withdraws from, judgment, and can never be fully judged." These lines introduced the following quotation translated from Montaigne: "La vita fluttuante e mutevole" [Fluctuating and mutable life]. A note by Maria Teresa Sereni for the first collected edition reads: "It was the author's intention to alter the inside front flap retaining the quotation from Montaigne, but replacing the few lines before in which he had intended to give the reader 'some help' [see above] with the definition of *Variable Star* taken from the book by Ferdinando Flora, *Astronomia nautica*, Hoepli, Milan 1964, p. 122: 'The light of most stars is not constant; it varies from time to time. That is to say, the stars do not always appear to have the same size; but, over various periods which may be long or short, sometimes a day and sometimes more than a year, their size changes: these stars are called *variable*.'"

YOUR THOUGHTS OF CALAMITY
The piece was occasioned by a surprise housewarming party organized when the Serenis moved into their apartment in Via P. A. Paravia 37, Milan, in September–October 1967. The poem was first published in 1972.

IN AN EMPTY HOUSE
Dated 1–16 May 1967. The poem recalls the Munich agreement of 29 September 1938. An earlier published draft of the poem cites the title of the jazz standard "September in the Rain" by Al Dubin and Harry Warren.

TORONTO SATURDAY NIGHT
"Niccolò" is Niccolò Gallo, a literary critic and friend of the poet. "Tipperary" is the popular song of the Great War. "Satchmo" is, of course, Louis Armstrong. The poem's final lines refer to the fact that Toronto has a large population of Italian extraction.

PLACE OF WORK

The poem is set in the old Mondadori offices in central Milan.

WORKS IN PROGRESS

Author's note: "I: "the beds lying empty etc" reproduces two lines from the poem "These" by William Carlos Williams. III: Ellis Island was the quarantine island for immigrants, the symbolic and official door for millions of future citizens of the USA, from 1892 to 1954, when it was closed. The little island has now become a historical monument, joining the not distant Statue of Liberty." First published in 1969. As well as being the Italian phrase for "Road Works" or "Men at Work," *Lavori in corso* was the title used for a cultural television program on the Swiss service of RAI hosted by Sereni during the 1960s.

BEAUTIFUL LUGANO GOODBYE

"Addio Lugano bella" is the title of an Anarchist song; the epigraph ["when in the night we went away"] cites "Dalla fiamma" in Bartolo Cattafi, *L'aria secca del fuoco* (1972).

INTERIOR

Written before 18 October 1970, and first published in 1972. This poem relates to the atmosphere of student unrest in 1968 and to the poet's senses of exclusion and aging.

GROWTH

The poem is about the Serenis' second daughter, Sylvia. It adapts the title of T. S. Eliot's "La Figlia che Piange" [The daughter who cries] and we have left it in Italian to allow the allusion to function. The lines were excerpted from a much longer piece of writing about his daughter that has now been published in Isella's edition, pp. 699–701.

OF CUTS AND STITCHES

The poem was held over, unfinished, from the period of *Gli strumenti umani*.

POET IN BLACK

Dated 7–14 September 1975.

REVIVAL

Author's note: "*L'Opzione* [The Option] is a story of mine written at the beginning of the Sixties, published by Scheiwiller in '64 and eventually reissued as the first half of *Il sabato tedesco* [The German Saturday] (il Saggiatore, 1980). It is set in Frankfurt am Main, as are the lines that allude to it." The final image is a memory of the closing sequence in *The Third Man* when Harry Lime's girlfriend Anna Schmidt walks past Holly Martins on the avenue leading to the cemetery in Vienna.

IT WILL BE THE BOREDOM

"Laura" is Laura Chiari, daughter of Maria Teresa Sereni and Nico Chiari, the poet's granddaughter.

FESTIVAL

Written in May 1978. "L. S." is the poet Leonardo Sinisgalli (1908–1981). The dedication was added to the poem after 31 January 1981, the date of his death.

EXTERIOR SEEN AGAIN IN DREAM

"Campana da Marradi" is the poet Dino Campana (1885–1932). The author of *Canti orfici* is talking posthumously to Sereni during his POW years (1943–45). Campana's relevance to this poem recollecting wartime may derive from the fact that the older poet kept trying to enlist in the Italian army during the First World War and was regularly refused on the grounds of mental instability. Campana, on occasion, accused himself of causing the outbreak of war. For Sereni's thoughts on Campana, see *Sentieri di Gloria,* pp. 123–126.

GIOVANNA AND THE BEATLES

Written on 26 August 1981. Giovanna is the Serenis' third daughter, born in 1956. The Beatles were humorously known in Italy by the mistranslation "Gli Scarafaggi" [The Beetles]. The first line of the last verse may also allude to "Tempo e Tempi" (*Satura,* 1971), Montale's reflections on music and the passing of time, themes discussed by Sereni himself in "Il sabato tedesco," *La tentazione della prosa,* p. 218.

EACH TIME THAT ALMOST
Written between 13 and 27 June 1981.

A HOLIDAY PLACE

The author's note to this poem in seven sections first collected in *Stella variabile* (Milan: Garzanti, 1981) begins: "It appeared for the first time in *Almanacco dello Specchio* 1 (Mondadori, 1971), and was reprinting as a booklet in the "Pesce d'Oro" series (Scheiwiller, 1973) accompanied by a long note of which I reproduce here only the part dealing with the explication of various details..."

The "Holiday Place" in question is Bocca di Magra on the Ligurian coast just a few miles below Lerici.

"*Sereni slender myth...*" is an epigram on the poet composed by Franco Fortini who had a holiday house on the opposite bank of the Magra at Fiumaretta. The earlier version dates from 1953 or 1954, and was collected in a revised text in *L'ospite ingrato* (Bari: De Donato, 1966). This text (used by Sereni for his poem) reads in translation:

Sereni slender myth
thread of faith
youth's not always truth
another generation arrives with the years,
there's a sequel for your perplexed music...

You beg pardon from the "ranks of brutes"
if you want to leave them. Give up the tired
and bloody game, of modesty and pride.
Endanger your soul. Tear it up, that blank paper
you're holding in your hand.

These lines, in turn, allude to Sereni's "Italiano in Grecia" of August 1942. See above, pp. 80–81.

The "Negro I translated" is the Malagascan Jean-Joseph Rabéarivelo. The words following are taken from his poem "Ton Oeuvre" in *Presque songes* (1934). Sereni's Italian version is from *Gli immediati dintorni,* collected in *La tentazione della prosa* ed. G. Raboni (Milan: Mondadori, 1998), p. 32–33. An English rendering of it would read:

Your Works

"You've done nothing but listen to songs, you yourself have
    done nothing but sing; you've not listened to men speak,
    you yourself haven't spoken.
What books have you ever read other than those that preserve
    the voice of women and of unreal things?
Have you sung, not spoken, not put questions to the heart of
    things: how can you know them?" laughing say
    the scribes and orators when you magnify
    the everyday miracle of sea and sky.

But always you sing and astonish
thinking of the prow which tries
a furrowed road on the still water
towards unknown gulfs. It astonishes you,
the bird that stands fast in the desert of blue,
but rediscovers paths
of its forest homeland in the wind.

And of unreal things a murmur
will be contained in the books you write—like dreams,
through too much life, unreal.

"*el pueblo del alma mia*" is a popular song from the Spanish Civil War period. "The Gothic Line" was a German defensive system established across the Italian peninsular from Rimini to Pisa with the aim of stopping the Allied advance during 1944–45.

"Forte" is an abbreviation of Forte dei Marmi, a seaside resort in Versilia.

Sereni pointed out that the "slaughtered man's lopped head" means to recall the closing shots of dead partisans floating down the river Po in Roberto Rossellini's movie *Paisà* (1946).

The last lines of part one appear to be a memory of Jacques Prévert's "L'Orgue du Barbarie" from *Paroles*.

III

Author's Note: "The lines in italics at the head of this part are mine from a poem left uncompleted a number of years ago. This, in its turn, recalled another old poem of mine, 'Gli squali' (in *Gli strumenti umani*)."

"All these things . . . if you'll fall down and worship me" is from the Devil's temptation of Jesus in Matthew 4:9.

"And as if nearly none . . . they disappear": the two quotations are from Boccaccio's tale of Nastagio degli Onesti in the *Decameron*. In the tale Onesti, shunned by his beloved, is walking through a wood, contemplating suicide, when he has a vision in which a woman, terrified and naked, is pursued by two dogs and a man on horseback. Nastagio tries to defend her but the knight justifies her punishment by saying that he took his own life for love of the coldhearted lady who remained forever indifferent to his fate. Nastagio steps aside and the knight tears out her heart, then feeds it to the dogs. To the horror of the local townspeople, the scene is repeated every Friday and ends with the figures disappearing into the mist in the early morning. To avoid such a fate, Nastagio's beloved agrees to marry him.

V

Author's Note: "Elio, needless to say, is Elio Vittorini, reappearing in one of our haunts." Elio Vittorini (1908–1966) was a novelist, literary critic, editorialist, translator (E. A. Poe, D. H. Lawrence, W. Faulkner) and leftwing intellectual at the forefront of cultural life in Italy before and after the Second World War.

NICCOLÒ

The poem is an elegy to the literary critic Niccolò Gallo. "The poets' false-true *you*" alludes to Montale's "Il tu," the first poem in Satura (1971).

FIXITY

Though the theme is related to the closing sections of *Un posto di vacanza* completed in 1972, this poem was composed during September and up to 18 October 1981. It is one of the very last poems Sereni completed.

TRANSLATING CHAR

The author's note in *Stella variabile* (Milan: Garzanti, 1981) reads: "they are moments of life, or better, recoveries (not exercises, not 'studies') related to the time I was occupied with that work."

Sereni's most sustained translation work is devoted to the oeuvre of René Char, a poet with whose writings he felt a complex affinity, expressed in the magazine *Il bimestre* (1969): "I read Char not as similar, but as a salutary antagonist." He translated the entire *Feuillets d'Hypnos* during 1958. It was published first in 1962 in a selection from Char, edited by Giorgio Caproni, then alone as *I fogli d'Ipnos* (Turin: Einaudi, 1968). His second phase of translating Char occurred during the early 1970s and resulted in the volume *Ritorno sopramonte e altre poesie* (Milan: Mondadori, 1974). The "moments of life" derive from this later period.

René Char is the French poet of the Vaucluse. He was a leading member of the French Resistance during the Second World War and revisited the landscapes and themes of that period from his life in work translated by Sereni in the 1974 collection. Char's poetry charges the natural world with metaphors of the conflict between European barbarism and humanism, a subject which is also central to Sereni's life and work.

Petrarch, the Italian poet of the Vaucluse, is an emblem of fidelity to the pains of attachment and experience. Sereni's essay, "Petrarca, nella sua finzione la sua verità" [Petrarch, his truth in his fiction], published in 1983, is a fusion and revision of a number of articles on the poet published in the same year as *Ritorno sopramonte*.

I. *In my way, René Char...*
For ll. 4–5, see "Au jour brillant au-dessus du soir" and "froissé son seuil d'agonie" in Char, "Le gaucher"; for ll. 6–8, "la réalité de ces poudreuses enjambées qui lèvent un printemps derrière elles," "Vétérance"; and for ll. 9–11, "[je bus] sa verdeur sous l'empire de l'été," "Éprouvante simplicité," with translations by Sereni in *Ritorno sopramonte*, pp. 106, 190, 196.

II. *Muezzin*
Though referring to an occasion from the poet's visit to Egypt in 1973, the poem appears to have been written, or completed, on 9 January 1981.

III. *A Lay Temple*
Final work on the poem, also related to the Egyptian visit of 1973, took place during late January 1981.

IV. *Vertical village*
Sereni's title derives from Char's "Le village vertical" translated in *Ritorno sopramonte*, p. 86, which the translator's note suggests may itself be a portrait of the hill village Le Beaucet (Vaucluse).

V. *Hammered slowness*
The title is derived from the following phrases in Char's poem "Le baiser": "Massive lenteur, lenteur martelée," translated by Sereni in *Ritorno sopramonte*, p. 160.

VI. *Nocturne*

Written at various moments between December 1975 and February 1978, it was conceived as a separate poem, first called "Insonnia" then "Paura terza," before finding its place in the sequence.

VII. *Madrigal to Nephertiti*

This poem, at first called just "Madrigal," seems also to have been conceived as a separate work before being included in the sequence. It was written between July and September 1978.

Nephertiti is the name of a queen from ancient Egypt. Sereni saw the most famous of the portraits of the queen in Berlin. Her name means "beauty made flesh." Sereni addresses a female character in the prose piece *Il sabato tedesco* as Nephertiti.

VIII. *A nothing was enough* . . .

Written between August 1980 and January 1981. For lines 3–4, see Char's "Ballo alle Baronie" in *Ritorno sopramonte*, p. 68: "une vallée ouverte / une côte qui brille."

VERANO AND THE SOLSTICE

Author's note: "the association of Verano, the cemetery in Rome, with *el verano*, summer in Spanish, is entirely arbitrary; a little less, the noticing of the Latin name for spring (*ver*) in the root of the Spanish name for summer."

Written between July 1974 and July 1975, the poem is associated with the death of Niccolò Gallo, who is buried in the Verano cemetery.

REQUIEM

Written in July 1975, it was first entitled "Ma allora" [So then], and was dedicated upon first publication to Pietro Salati, although composed a little before his death.

FIRST FEAR

Written in September and October 1975.

SECOND FEAR

Written in September and October 1975.

OTHER PLACE OF WORK

Written in October 1975 and originally entitled "A Segrate" [In Segrate], the poem is set in the new Mondadori offices, a modern complex of buildings purpose built in the countryside beyond the suburbs of Milan.

THE DISEASE OF THE ELM

Set in Bocca di Magra. Composed between November 1975 and July 1976. It was first published in a volume of tributes to Eugenio Montale.

UPHILL

First published on 6 August 1977. "The Y'know boys" is an equivalent for "i ragazzi Cioè." The original refers to the use of the word "cioè" [that's to say] compulsively, like a verbal tic, in the talk of young people at that time.

THE KNOLL

Written between 3 and 6 July 1977.

SUMMER IN THE PO VALLEY

Written on 26 and 27 August 1978. Campitello and Eremo are villages on the road from Parma to Mantua, which crosses the Po; Sustinente is in Sicily near where Sereni was captured by American forces in July 1943. The poem alludes to the characters taking a walk in the country that punctuates Luis Buñuel's film *The Discreet Charm of the Bourgeoisie* (1972).

IN PARMA WITH A. B.

The poem was begun on 25 May and completed on 13 August 1978. The bracketed lines in part I are a late addition made between its appearance in *Stella variabile* (1981) and *Tutte le poesie* (1986). A. B. is Attilio Bertolucci (1911–2000). The Baccanelli is an area on the outskirts of Parma in the direction of Felino where the Bertolucci family owned a small holding, a farm they sold after moving to Rome in the 1950s. Sereni had cycled from Felino to visit Bertolucci there before the war. The poem was first read by Sereni in public at a conference in Parma on 21 September 1979. Bertolucci, who was in the audience, responded years after with a late lyric "A Vittorio Sereni dopo molti anni" [To Vittorio Sereni, after many years].

AUTOSTRADA DELLA CISA

Author's note: "The stretch in question is La Spezia-Parma in the direction of the Po valley. "Tenochtitlán," today Mexico City. In its time blessed by a lake, it was the capital of the Aztec empire before the Spanish conquest: a city fond to memory, as always since the catastrophe."

The poem was begun in September 1977 and completed in August 1979.

RIMBAUD

Author's note: "anyone who has visited the temple of Luxor would have been able to see that writing. As far as I know, no evidence has been found or documents discovered about a journey there by the 'Homme aux semelles de vent' [Man with soles of wind], and in any case it is improbable that he wrote it. *Mastaba* is the modern name given to ancient pyramid-shaped Egyptian burial chambers in stone."

The poem was completed between 18 and 22 March 1981.

LUINO-LUVINO

Author's note: "in the last century Luvino was the name for Luino, my birthplace."

Completed over 23 and 24 September 1978.

PROGRESS

Two lines in this poem, the first and sixth, date from the first half of the 1960s. It was completed between August and October 1980. The concluding lines refer to the suicides transformed into trees in *Inferno* XIII, l. 26.

ANOTHER BIRTHDAY

Composed from August to early October 1980. San Siro is the common name for the Meazza Football Stadium in Milan where Milan and Internazionale, Sereni's favorite team, both play.

SELECTED PROSE

from *The Immediate Surroundings*

PREWAR LETTER

Author's note: "I think it is clear that the portrait of Attilio Bertolucci and his poetry refer to the prewar years, as does the letter. Today, something more could be said about him, and, indeed, more has been said and written." Note by Maria Teresa Sereni: "This and other remarks about the letter 'to a presumed recipient' can be found in the official documents of the historical and literary conference entitled 'Poetry of the Thirties (and Beyond),' which took place in Parma on 21 September 1979 during celebrations dedicated to Attilio Bertolucci. 'During the Fifties I had been asked by someone in Parma to give something to an almanac that some friends were getting together: *La luna sul Parma*. So I wrote an imaginary letter, with many of the things I had wanted to say for some time, and dated it back to 1938, the time I first met Attilio and his city. I should say, because it is important, that I had loved both, before and from afar, through another person and from reading *Fuochi in Novembre* [Fires in November].'"

BOLOGNA '42

Author's note: "I had already published the lines of poetry elsewhere. I wrote them in Africa, during my imprisonment but had not included them in the book that arose from that experience. At that time the last line was: 'fugge oltre i borghi un tempo irreparabile' [beyond the townships an irreparable time is fleeing]. The reference to cowardice was added much later."

This piece introduced "Fragments of a Defeat." The Armir is the *Armata Italiana in Russia*—the second army sent to the Eastern front, after the destruction of the first.

LJUBLIANA

From an uncollected piece entitled "Ricordi di una guerra non combattuta" [Memoirs of a War Not Fought] eventually published in *La tentazione della prosa*. Ljubliana, then part of Yugoslavia annexed by Italy in 1941, is now in Slovenia. The battle of Vittorio Veneto (24 October–3 November 1918) was the decisive Italian counterattack against Austro-Hungarian forces in the closing days of the First World War.

SICILY '43

From an unpublished piece entitled "La Sconfitta" [The Defeat]. An excerpt was published with the title "Il ritaglio" [The Clipping] in *La Situazione,* November 1958, with the following note by the author: "The excerpt comes from an unpublished story written seven years ago. It is, so to speak, the narrative version of the lyric 'Pin-up Girl' in *Diario d'Algeria* . . ."

ALGERIA '44

The text is a series of commentaries on poems from "Diario d'Algeria" (see pp. 88–101 above). It was composed in December 1956. "Franco" is Franco Fortini (1917–1995), the cultural critic and poet.

BARBED-WIRE FEVER

First published in *La Rassegna d'Italia* in May 1946. A *turris eburnea* is an "ivory tower." The original of "to the worthy fighter the laurel's shade" is line 5 from "La tregua" [The Truce] in *Alcyone* (1903) by Gabriele d'Annunzio.

THAT FILM OF BILLY WILDER'S

Sereni's piece refers extensively to *The Lost Weekend* (1945) and, glancingly, to *Sunset Boulevard* (1950). We have translated the text of the longer version that appears in the 1983 edition of *Gli immediati dintorni.* In *La tentazione della prosa,* the piece ends at "This was the error, this the vice." The remainder is given in the notes. Though this cut, on the 1971 proof of a never-published second edition, may accord with the poet's latest impulse, for the purposes of this edition it seems more practical to keep the two parts in one place.

AIRS OF '53–'55

The lines quoted in the text are from "Adolescente" by Vincenzo Cardarelli. In a letter to Niccolò Gallo of 5 June 1962, Sereni discusses the possibility that this text might be used as the basis for a film script. Nothing came of the project.

THE TITLE OF POET

The text in *Gli immediati dintorni* is a passage excerpted from Sereni's afterword to Sergio Solmi's *Levania e altre poesie* (1956). It was added to the book in 1961. The entire afterword appears under the title "Levania" in *Letture preliminari* (1973). *"De re mea agitur"* means "these things concern me."

YOU BEGAN

Completed by January 1962.

ON THE BACK OF A PIECE OF PAPER

Added to the text of the first edition between December 1961 and March 1962. It is dated "1960" so as to connect it with the poem "Gli amici" [The Friends] (on pp. 148–49 above), dated on one manuscript draft: 20–26 September 1960.

TWO OLD FLAMES

First published in *Vetrina di poesie e arte* in 1961.

CREATIVE SILENCE

Drafted at intervals during the 1950s.

THE YEAR '43

"The Year '43" and "The Year '45" were the second and third of five pieces of prose collected in *Senza l'onore delle armi* [Without the Honor of Arms], published in 1986 by Scheiwiller. The first piece was "The Capture" and the fourth "Twenty-Six." The book included an appendix, "The Sands of Algeria," a title chosen by *Storia Illustrata*. Sereni made his selection in January 1980. The book opened with a quotation from Giorgio Seferis: "La giornata era fosca. Nessuno prendeva decisioni./ Soffiava un vento lieve. 'Non è greco, è scirocco' disse qualcuno." [The day was dismal. No one took any decisions. / There was a mild breeze. "Not from Greece, from the southeast," someone said.]

At the beginning of the second paragraph in the third section, we have preferred to translate "Non c'è bisogno di arrivare all'8 settembre '63" (the reading in the 1983 *Gli immediati dintorni* and *Senza l'onore delle armi*) to "all'8 settembre '43" (as it appears in *La tentazione della prosa*).

"bijou de l'Algérie — eau courante — tous les conforts — visitez-la": jewel of Algeria — running water — all the comforts — visit it.

"Make him a federal!": the "federale" was a political appointment, the highest member of the fascist party in any particular province. The two groups are exchanging insults that have become all but meaningless with the fall of the regime.

THE YEAR '45

Mussolini's appearance at the Lirico Theater in Milan on 16 December 1944 was the last speech he gave before his death. In it he concentrated most of his words on the issue of who had betrayed him. The references later in this piece to "Milan, the Archbishop's see, Dongo, Piazzale Loreto, Mussolini and Claretta, the fascist leaders" refer to the last days of the Salò Republic. The Archbishop of Milan arranged a meeting between Mussolini and the partisans; he was killed along with his mistress Claretta Petacci at Dongo while fleeing towards Switzerland; their bodies and those of other fascist leaders where displayed and mistreated in Piazzale Loreto, Milan.

Bastogne is a town in Belgium associated with the Battle of the Bulge — the last threatening counterattack made by the German Army on the western front during the winter of 1944–45. The "Garibaldi Divisions" and the initials refer to partisans in the Italian campaign of 1943–45.

"Lo, 'tis a gala night . . ." is the opening of E. A. Poe's poem "The Conqueror Worm." Sereni made a now-lost Italian version of it for one of his fellow prisoners in 1945.

ON THE DEATH OF UNGARETTI

Published in *Il dramma* XLVI, 6 June 1970 and in *Panorama*, 18 June 1970 (under a different title). "Chiaroscuro" is the name of a poem from the opening section of Ungaretti's *L'allegria*. The early Milanese poems that Sereni refers to are in that same section.

SELF-PORTRAIT

The manuscript bears the date 18 January 1978. It was broadcast on a RAI transmission in March of the same year. Sereni cites in its entirety Giorgio Caproni's "Cabaletta dello stregone benevolo" [Cabaletta of the benevolent sorcerer] from *Il Muro della terra* (1975). *La ricerca dell'identità* [The Search for Identity] was an extremely heterogeneous art exhibition held in Milan during 1974.

PORT STANLEY LIKE TRAPANI

Completed by 3 July 1982, and first published the same autumn.

INFATUATIONS

First published posthumously in the magazine *Sul Porto* in 1983. Subsequently included in the edition of *Un posto di vacanza e altre poesie,* ed. Z. Birolli (Milan: Scheiwiller, 1994). Added to *Gli immediati dintorni* at the suggestion of Ferrucio Benzoni and Stefano Simoncelli. This prose poem is connected with the end of Sereni's work translating René Char.

from *Crossing Milan*

THE CAPTURE

This piece was quarried and then developed from the unpublished "La Sconfitta" (The Defeat), which also supplied material for "Sicily '43," "The Year '43," and "Twenty-Six." It was first published in the magazine *Pirelli* vol. 16 no. 1, February 1963. Sereni provisionally included it in *Gli immediati dintorni* after "That Film of Billy Wilder's," but then removed it. It was eventually collected in *Senza l'onore delle armi,* the gathering of Sereni's prose writings connected with his war experiences.

A *maresciallo* is a senior noncommisioned officer. A French PWB is a member of the Psychological Warfare Branch. The "Stuka" was the Junkers Ju 87 dive-bomber used especially in the 1939–40 Blitzkrieg. By 1943 it was already obsolete.

THE OPTION

First published in *Questo e altro* no. 8, 1964 and separately as *L'Opzione e allegati* in the same year—with a note on the meaning of the term "option" in publishing, and a citation in French from the brochure of the Savigny Hotel, Frankfurt. Sereni explained in a letter to the publisher Vanni Scheiwiller that he did not mention the city by name in the story because he wanted to distance himself and others from its narrator and its various characters. It was collected in *Il sabato tedesco* (1980).

English renderings for the passages of French, German, and Latin are as follows: "là on est tout à fait bien": there everyone's looked after; Je vous admire toujours de loin. L'autre soir encore je vous ai vue, pardon, rencontrée chez . . .: I always admire you from afar. The other evening I saw you, pardon me, met you at . . . ; "Mais celle-ci c'est de près qu'il faut la regarder, quoi . . .": But you have to look at her here from close up, what . . . ; "*je n'aime pas qu'on fasse des affaires en y mêlant la politique*": I don't like mixing business with politics; "de tout premier ordre": of first importance; "je vous en supplie": I'm appealing to you; "on ne sait jamais": one never knows; "on vous attend": they're waiting for you; "c'est des bricoles": they're small fry; "une table des matières": a contents list; "meine Liebe": my love; "*entre deux guerres*": between the two wars (i.e., 1918–1939); "Faites vos jeux, Messieurs Dames. Faites donc vos jeux": Place your bets, Ladies and Gentlemen. So place your bets; "*Ah! votre héros, quelle blage, regardez-le, pas un jour de prison, pas un jour de sa vie,* pas un jour *je vous dis*": Ah! Your hero, what a windbag, look at him, not a day in prison, not a single day of his life, *not a day* I tell you; "*une dame si bonne*": such a fine lady; *Cecidere manus:* the hands subsided.

Montjuïc is not far from Barcelona. The architect being referred to appears to be Gaudi. Monza is the motor racing circuit near Milan where the Italian Grand Prix is held. The Zeil is a pedestrian area in Frankfurt am Main. There is a Friedrichstrasse in both Frankfurt and Berlin. The "Big Lift" refers to the Berlin Airlift of 1948–49, when the Russian blockade of the city was neutralized by round-the-clock air transport flights. It marked the clear ending of the uneasy wartime East-West alliance and the beginning of the overt Cold War.

TWENTY-SIX

Written in 1969, twenty-six years after Vittorio Sereni's capture on 24 July 1943, by the Allies landing in Sicily. First published in *Forum Italicum* IV (1970), it is a final piece of prose by Sereni devoted to the events leading up to his capture. The first, written in 1951, and entitled "La sconfitta" [The Defeat], was not published during Sereni's lifetime, although parts of it appeared in the section "Sicilia '43") and in "La cattura" [The Capture]. "Ventisei" was included in the limited edition of *Stella variabile* (1979), but withdrawn for the 1981 trade edition. The italicized passages are quotations from "Sicily '43" and "The Capture" with the sole exception of two lines revised out of the poem "Pin-up Girl" (see pp. 398–99), lines also cited in "Sicily '43." The epigraph is from the poem translated in English as "Comes to Rest" in C. P. Cavafy, *Collected Poems,* trans. E. Keeley and P. Sherrard (Princeton: Princeton University Press, 1975), p. 183.

BIBLIOGRAPHY

Works by Vittorio Sereni

POETRY

Frontiera. Milan: Corrente, 1941.
Poesie. Florence: Vallecchi, 1942.
Diario d'Algeria. Florence: Vallecchi, 1947.
Frammenti di una sconfitta. Milan: Scheiwiller, 1957.
Gli strumenti umani. Turin: Einaudi, 1965; 1974.
Diario d'Algeria. New edition. Milan: Mondadori, 1965, 1979.
Frontiera. New edition. Milan: Scheiwiller, 1966.
Poesie scelte 1935–1965. Edited by L. Caretti. Milan: Mondadori, 1973.
Un posto di vacanza. Milan: Scheiwiller, 1973.
Stella variabile. Limited edition. Verona: Amici dei libri, 1979.
Stella variabile. Milan: Garzanti, 1981.
Tutte le poesie. Edited by M. T. Sereni. Milan: Mondadori, 1986.
Il grande amico: Poesie 1935–1981. Introduction by G. Lonardi, commentary by L. Lenzini. Milan: Rizzoli, 1990.
Frontiera and *Giornale di 'Frontiera'* (Dante Isella). Milan: Rosellina Archinto, 1991.
Poesie: Un'antologia per la scuola. Edited by D. Isella and C. Martignoni. Luino, 1993. Second edition, Turin: Einaudi, 2002.
Un posto di vacanza e altre poesie. Edited by Z. Birolli. Milan: Scheiwiller, 1994.
Poesie. Edited by D. Isella. Milan: Mondadori, 1995. Revised edition. 2004.
Diario d'Algeria. With a preface by G. Raboni. Turin: Einaudi, 1998.

PROSE

Gli immediati dintorni. Milan: il Saggiatore, 1962.
L'Opzione e allegati. Milan: Scheiwiller, 1964.

Ninetto Bonfanti. Milan: privately printed by the author, 1970.
Letture preliminari. Padua: Liviana Editrice, 1973.
Il sabato tedesco. Milan: il Saggiatore, 1980.
Gli immediati dintorni: primi e secondi. Milan: il Saggiatore, 1983.
Senza l'onore delle armi. With a note by Dante Isella. Milan: Scheiwiller, 1986.
Sentieri di gloria: Note e ragionamenti sulla letteratura. Edited by G. Strazzeri Milan: Mondadori, 1996.
La tentazione della prosa. Edited by G. Raboni. Milan: Mondadori, 1998.
Taccuino d'Algeria (1944). Edited by D. Isella. Pistoia: Edizioni Via del Vento, 2000.
Le carte di Vittorio Sereni. Edited by B. Colli. Luino: Nastro & Nastro, 2000.
Poeti francesi letti da Vittorio Sereni. Edited by B. Bianchi. Luino: Nastro & Nastro, 2002.
Amici pittori: I libri d'arte di Vittorio Sereni. Edited by D. Isella and B. Colli. Luino: Nastro & Nastro, 2002.
Viaggio in Cina. Edited by E. Sartorelli. Pistoia: Edizioni Via del Vento, 2004.
La casa nella poesia. Preface by P. V. Mengaldo. Parma: Monte Università Parma, 2006.

TRANSLATIONS

Char, René. *Fogli d'Ipnos.* Turin: Einaudi, 1968.
———. *Ritorno sopramonte.* Milan: Mondadori, 1974, 2002.
Green, Julien. *Leviatan.* Milan: Mondadori, 1947; Milan: Tascabili degli Editori Associati, 1991, 2002.
Il musicante di Saint-Merry e altri versi tradotti. Turin: Einaudi, 1981. With a preface by P. V. Mengaldo, 2001.
Valéry, Paul. *Eupalinos. L'anima e la danza. Dialogo dell'albero.* Milan: Mondadori, 1947.
Williams, William Carlos. *Poesie.* Edited and translated by C. Campo and V. Sereni. Turin: Einaudi, 1961, 1967.

LETTERS

Bertolucci, Attilio, and Vittorio Sereni. *Una lunga amicizia: Lettere 1938–1982.* Edited by G. Palli Baroni. Milan: Garzanti, 1994.
Chiara, Piero, and Vittorio Sereni. *Lettere (1946–1980).* Edited by F. Roncoroni. Rome: Edizioni Benincasa, 1993.
Miei cari tutti quanti . . .: Carteggio di Vittorio Sereni con Ferruccio Benzoni e gli amici di Cesenatico. Edited by D. Isella. Genoa: Edizioni San Marco Giustiniani, 2004.

Pozzi, Antonia, and Vittorio Sereni. *La giovinezza che non trova scampo: Poesie e lettere degli anni trenta.* Edited by A. Cenni. Milan: Scheiwiller, 1995.

Scritture private: Con Fortini e con Giudici. Bocca di Magra: Edizioni Capannina, 1995.

Un tacito mistero: Il carteggio Vittorio Sereni-Alessandro Parronchi (1941–1982). Edited by B. Colli and G. Raboni. Milan: Feltrinelli, 2004.

UNCOLLECTED WORKS

For a full bibliography of Sereni's prose compiled by B. Colli, see *La tentazione della prosa,* ed. G. Raboni, pp. 479–511.

"A Letter from Vittorio Sereni." In *PN Review* 5, vol. 2. no. 1 (1977): 42.

"A partire dal vissuto." In Giovanni Raboni, *Il più freddo anno di grazia.* Genoa, 1978: 7–11.

"Il lavoro del poeta." In *Poetiche* 3 (1999): 331–51.

Note for the cover of Fernanda Romagnoli, *Il tredicesimo invitato.* Milan: Garzanti, 1980.

Note for the cover of Paolo Bertolani, *Incertezza dei bersagli.* Milan: Guanda, 1976.

Note for the cover of Umberto Saba, *Trieste e una donna.* 4th edition. Milan: Mondadori, 1980. Interview in Ferdinando Camon, *Il Mestiere di poeta.* Milan: Garzanti, 1982: 121–28.

"Per Banfi." In Francesca D'Alessandro, *L'opera poetica di Vittorio Sereni,* 213–26. Milan: Vita e Pensiero, 2001.

"Sergio Solmi, Poeta." In Francesca D'Alessandro, *L'opera poetica di Vittorio Sereni,* 227–47. Milan: Vita e Pensiero, 2001.

"Testimonianza di Vittorio Sereni." Atti della Tavola rotonda "D'Annunzio e la lingua letteraria del Novecento." *Quaderni dannunziani* 40–41 (July 1972): 14–16.

TRANSLATIONS OF VITTORIO SERENI

The Disease of the Elm and Other Poems. Translated by M. Perryman and P. Robinson. London: Many Press, 1983.

Étoile variable. Translated by P. Renard and B. Simeone. Lagrasse: Éditions Verdier, 1987.

Selected Poems of Vittorio Sereni. Translated by M. Perryman and P. Robinson. London: Anvil Press, 1990.

Sixteen Poems. Translated by P. Vangelisti. Fairfax, CA.: Red Hill Press, 1971.

Variable Star. Translated by Luigi Bonaffini. Toronto: Guernica Editions, 1999.

Critical Writings on Vittorio Sereni

For a full, although not complete, secondary bibliography of writings in Italian during 1937–2000 compiled by B. Colli, see *Poesie,* 5th edition, ed. D. Isella, pp. 891–942.

BOOKS AND MAGAZINES

Agosti, Stefano, et al. *La Poesia di Vittorio Sereni.* Atti del Convegno. Milan: Librex, 1985.
Baffoni Licata, Maria Laura. *La Poesia di Vittorio Sereni.* Ravenna, 1986.
Barile, Laura. *Sereni.* Palermo: Palumbo, 1994.
Bartoloni, Paolo. *Interstitial Writing: Calvino, Caproni, Sereni and Svevo.* Market Harborough: Troubador, 2003.
D'Alessandro, Francesca. *L'opera poetica di Vittorio Sereni.* Milan: Vita e Pensiero, 2001.
Di Bernardi, Alessandro. *Gli 'specchi multipli' di Vittorio Sereni.* Palermo: Flacciovo Editore, 1978.
Ferretti, Gian Carlo. *Poeta e di poeti funzionario: Il lavoro editoriale di Vittorio Sereni.* Milan: il Saggiatore, 1999.
Grillandi, Massimo. *Vittorio Sereni.* Florence: Il Castoro, 1972.
Isella, Dante, ed. *Per Vittorio Sereni: Convegno di poeti.* Milan: Scheiwiller, 1992.
Memmo, Francesco Paolo. *Vittorio Sereni.* Milan: Mursia, 1973.
"Omaggio a Vittorio Sereni." *Poesia* no. 59 (February 1993): 2–21.
Pagnarelli, Remo. *La ripetizione dell'esistere: Lettura dell'opera poetica di Vittorio Sereni.* Milan: Scheiwiller, 1980.
Ricci, Francesca. *Il prisma di Arsenio: Montale tra Sereni e Luzi.* Bologna: Gedit Edizioni, 2002.
"Vittorio Sereni." Edited by Giovanni Giovannetti. *Poesia* 76 (September 1994): 37–44.
Vittorio Sereni. Special edition of *Poetiche* 3 (1999).

ARTICLES, REVIEWS, MEMOIRS, POEMS

Cucchi, Maurizio. "Poeta, scaccia da me la memoria." *Rinascita* 32 (27 August 1982): 22–23.
Debenedetti, Giacomo. "Il poeta da giovane." In *Poesie.* Edited by D. Isella, xix–xxvii. Milan: Mondadori, 1995.
Dego, Giuliano. "A Poet of Frontiers." *London Magazine* 9, no. 7 (October 1969): 28–38.
Fortini, Franco. "Sereni esile mito." *L'ospite ingrato.* Second edition. Casale Monferrato: Marietti, 1985.
———. *Saggi italiani* and *Nuovi saggi italiani.* 2 vols. Milan: Garzanti, 1987.

Isella, Dante. "Per Vittorio Sereni." In *L'idillio di Meulan: da Manzoni a Sereni*. Turin: Einaudi, 1994.
Mengaldo, Pier Vincenzo. "Ricordo di Vittorio Sereni." *Sei poeti all'insegna del pesce d'oro*. Milan, 1987.
———. "Caproni e Sereni: due versioni," "Tempo e memoria in Sereni," "*La spiaggia* di Vittorio Sereni." In *La tradizione del Novecento*. Turin: Bollati Boringheri, 2000.
Merry, Bruce. "The Poetry of Vittorio Sereni." In *Italian Studies* 39 (1974): 88–102.
Montale, Eugenio. "Vittorio Sereni." In *Sulla poesia*. Ed. G. Zampa. Milan: Mondadori, 1976.
Muscetta, Carlo. "Vittorio Sereni: *Diaro d'Algeria*." In *Rinascita* 4, nos. 11–12 (Nov.–Dec. 1947): 351–52.
Raboni, Giovanni. "Vittorio Sereni." In *Poesia italiana: il Novecento*, vol. 2. Edited by P. Gelli and G. Lagorio. Milan: Garzanti, 1980.
———. "Sereni a Milano." *Per Vittorio Sereni: Convegno di Poeti*. Edited by D. Isella. Milan: Scheiwiller, 1992.
———. "Prefazione." *Diario d'Algeria*. Milan: Einaudi, 1998.
Ramat, Silvio. "*Frontiera* di Vittorio Sereni." In *Poesie* 76 (Sept. 1994): 46–56.
Robinson, Peter. "Vittorio Sereni (27 July 1913–10 February 1983)." In *PN Review 32,* 9 no. 6 (1983): 12.
———. "A Note on Vittorio Sereni." *Siting Fires* 2 (1983): 35–37.
———. "A Thread of Faith." *London Magazine* 27, nos. 1–2 (1987): 124–28.
———. "Introduction." In *Selected Poems of Vittorio Sereni*. Trans. M. Perryman and P. Robinson. London: Anvil Press, 1990.
———. "Envy, Gratitude, and Translation." In *In the Circumstances: About Poems and Poets*. Oxford: Oxford University Press, 1992.
———. "The Music of Milan." In *Times Literary Supplement* 4868 (19 July 1996): 11.
———. "'Una fitta di rimorso': Dante in Sereni." In *Dante's Modern Afterlife: Reception and Response from Blake to Heaney*. Edited by N. Havely. London: Macmillan, 1998.
———. "Translating Sereni: A Discussion." In *Modernism and Translation*. A special issue of *Literature and Translation*. Edited by A. Piette. Edinburgh: Edinburgh University Press, 2003.
———. "Vittorio Sereni's Escape from Capture." In *Poetry Ireland Review* 80 (August 2004): 70–75.
———. "Translation and Self-Accusation: Vittorio Sereni's 'momento psicologico.'" In *Agenda* 41, nos. 3–4 (2005): 125–34.
Sciascia, Leonardo, Interview cited by Marco Forti on the cover of *Diario d'Algeria*. Milan: Mondadori, 1965.
Welle, John P. "*Forza accomunante:* Popular Culture in the Poetry of Vittorio Sereni." In *Rivista di studi italiani* 7, nos. 1–2 (1989): 28–34.

INDEX OF TITLES AND FIRST LINES

Absorbed in shadow that nears and makes vain, 59
A cose fatte pare, 252
A day at various levels, of high tide, 227
Addio Lugano bella, 210
A Dream, 167
A Factory Visit, 135
A fine luglio quando, 274
A great friend towering above me, 141
Ahimè come ritorna, 92
A Holiday Place, 227
Airs of '53–'55, 300
Alas how what returns, 93
A Lay Temple, 251
Algeria, 100
Algeria, 101
Algeria '44, 289
Algerian Diary, 89
Alla giovinezza, 58
Alla svolta del vento, 272
Alla tenda s'accosta, 80
All'ultimo tumulto dei binari, 56
A lone motorcycle, 107
Already in the gardens the fragrant olea, 65
Altri poi vengono: altri, di altro tipo, 190

Altro compleanno, 274
Altro posto di lavoro, 260
A modo mio, René Char, 284
A M. L. sorvolando in rapido la sua città, 52
Among the hills a raucous song, 59
Ancora sulla strada di Creva, 168
Ancora sulla strada di Zenna, 124
And again in a dream the tent's edge, 95
and catastrophe, 203
Andrò a ritroso della nostra corsa, 122
and what if it were the trumpet just now, 205
A Nightmare, 143
Another Birthday, 275
Another bridge, 49
Another Summer, 67
A nothing sufficed, 255
Anni dopo, 130
An unexpected vacancy of heart, 89
A Parma con A. B., 266
A portarmi fu il caso tra le nove, 180
Appointment at an Unusual Hour, 149

Appuntamento a ora insolita, 148
Appunti da un sogno, 112
A quest'ora, 42
A Return, 123
A single day, not that. An hour or two, 147
Assorto nell'ombra che approssima e fa vana, 58
At the final tumult of the lines, 57
At the end of July when, 275
At the wind's turning, 273
At this hour, 43
A un compagno d'infanzia, 178
Autostrada della Cisa, 268
Autostrada della Cisa, 269
Avvilite delizie, non meglio del filo, 86

Barbed-Wire Fever, 292
Basta con le botte basta. All'aperto, 212
Bastava un niente, 254
Beautiful Lugano Goodbye, 211
Belgrade, 79
Belgrado, 78
Bella *L'Opzione*—mi saluta, 216
Bella *L'Opzione*—the small Jew, 217
Beret pipe stick, the lifeless, 145
Berretto pipa bastone, gli spenti, 144
Be untroubled by the roar, 53
Birthday, 49
Black belt black boots, 217
Bologna '42, 282
Bolognese Diary, 77
but if you turn and watch, 43

Campitello Eremo Sustinente, 264
Campitello Eremo Sustinente, 265

Canzone lombarda, 46
Certo si piacciono, certo, 142
Chance led me there between, 181
Che aspetto io qui girandomi per casa, 132
Ci desteremo sul lago a un'infinita, 62
Città di notte, 76
City at Night, 77
Come for an instant the sting of his name, 271
Comunicazione interrotta, 118
Compleanno, 48
Concerto in giardino, 42
Confabula di te laggiù qualcuno, 252
Con non altri che te, 118
Corso Lodi, 158
Corso Lodi, 159
Così ridotti a pochi li colse la nuova primavera, 174
Creative Silence, 313
Creva Road, 69

Dalla spianata con solennità, 250
Dalla torre più alta, 148
Dall'Olanda, 180
Da me a quell'ombra in bilico tra fiume e mare, 246
Death breaks the seal, just so, of everything, 133
dei giorni lunghi e torridi, 218
Diana, 54
Diana, 55
Diario bolognese, 76
Diario d'Algeria, 88
Di colpo—osservi—è venuta, 126
Di là da garrulo schermo di bambini, 124
Dimitrios, 80

Dimitrios, 81
Di noi che cosa fugge sul filo della corrente?, 128
Di passaggio, 146
di soppiatto ripasso da Luino, 224
Di taglio e cucito, 214
Discovery of Hatred, 143
Disheartened delights, no better than the thread, 87
Domenica sportiva, 44
Donau?, 78
Donau?, 79
Dove sarà con chi starà il sorriso, 254
Dovrò cambiare geografie e topografie, 210

Each Time That Almost, 225
E ancora in sogno d'una tenda s'agita, 94
Earthly Pantomime, 195
e catastrofe, 202
Ecco le voci cadono e gli amici, 72
È cominciata una canzone losca, 58
È cresciuta in silenzio come l'erba, 214
Edere? stelle imperfette? cuori obliqui?, 122
E—disse G. sciogliendosi in uno sbadiglio, 158
e fosse pure la tromba da poco, 204
Enough of the blows enough. In the open, 213
Eri prima una pena, 100
Ero a passare il ponte, 166
Esterno rivisto in sogno, 220
Every corner or alley, every moment's good, 259
Exterior Seen Again in Dream, 221

Festival, 220
Festival, 221
Finestra, 126
First Athens evening, drawn-out goodbye, 81
First Fear, 259
Fissità, 246
Fixity, 247
Flattened the irony, washed out the courage, 257
Fog, 49
For sure they please each other, for sure, 143
Fourth of September, today, 245
Fragments of a Defeat, 103
Frammenti di una sconfitta, 102
Fresco di un passaggio recente, 250
Fresh from a recent journey, 251
From beyond a chattering barrier of children, 125
From Holland, 181
From me to that shadow poised between river and sea, 247
From the highest tower, 249

Garden Concert, 43
Già l'òlea fragrante nei giardini, 64
Giovanna and the Beatles, 223
Giovanna e i Beatles, 222
Gli amici, 148
Gli squali, 128
Green vapor tree, 267
Growth, 215
Guarda il ritaglio triste che s'affloscia, 86

Hammered slowness, 253
He knows nothinganymore, is borne up on wings, 91
Here the moth in the timber, 121

Here the traffic wavers, 49
Here was the wrong, here the inveterate error, 143
How long have the times, 221
How many years, what months, what seasons, 121

I am, 193
I don't know how always, 77
I due cunicoli, con feritoie, 112
If fever for you no more sustains me, 99
If it matters to you it's still summer, 261
If they ever came back to life. They seem to come, 203
Il giocattolo, 214
Il grande amico, 140
I'll go back down the way we came, 123
I'll have to change landscapes and places, 211
Il male d'Africa, 106
Il muro, 192
Il piatto piange, 174
Il Piatto Piange, 175
Il poggio, 264
Il sorriso balordo che mi fermò tra le lapidi, 176
Il telefono, 118
Il tempo provvisorio, 120
Il verde è sommerso in neroazzurri, 44
Image, 67
Immagine, 66
Improvvisa ci coglie la sera, 62
In an Empty House, 203
Infatuations, 338
In me il tuo ricordo è un fruscìo, 68
In my way, René Char, 249
In Parma with A. B., 267
Inquieto nella tradotta, 76

In salita, 262
In Sleep, 153
"In short, existence doesn't exist," 263
«Insomma l'esistenza non esiste», 262
Interior, 213
Interno, 212
Interrupted Communication, 119
Interview with a Suicide, 171
Intervista a un suicida, 170
In the home's stubborn silence, in the quiet, 223
In the smuggled glass, 101
In the Snow, 123
In the True Year Zero, 187
In una casa vuota, 202
Inverno, 42
Inverno a Luino, 60
Io non so come sempre, 76
I ricongiunti, 196
Italian in Greece, 81
Italiano in Grecia, 80
It could have been her, my grandmother, 169
I tempi da quanto, 220
It'll be because lives like dead leaves do exist, 207
It wasn't a dream, I tell you, 189
It Will Be the Boredom, 219
I versi, 158
Ivy? imperfect stars? oblique hearts?, 123
I was crossing a bridge, 167

Journey at Dawn, 121
Journey There and Back, 123
Just as well, he said, the most jovial: just as well all were there, 187
Just listen — he says — to that wonderful *cheep* in the trees, 195

L'abbraccio che respinge e non unisce, 160
L'alibi e il beneficio, 160
L'anima, quello che diciamo l'anima e non è, 170
La finestra ti reggeva nella sera, 66
La forza del luogo comune, 146
La giovinezza è tutta nella luce, 76
La malattia dell'olmo, 260
La pietà ingiusta, 184
La poesia è una passione?, 160
La ragazza d'Atene, 82
La speranza, 188
La spiaggia, 198
La splendida la delirante pioggia s'è quietata, 130
Lassù dove di torre, 88
Late, you too have heard them, 153
Lavori in corso, 206
Le ceneri, 132
L'equivoco, 124
Le portiere spalancate a vuoto sulla sera di nebbia, 160
Le sei del mattino, 132
Lietamente nell'aria di settembre più sibilo che grido, 134
Ljubliana, 283
Lombard Song, 47
Long raging summer, 67
Look at the sorry cutting grown limp, 87
L'otto settembre, 114
Luino-Luvino, 272
Luino-Luvino, 273
Lunga furente estate, 66

Madrigale a Nefertiti, 254
Madrigal to Nephertiti, 255
Mai più—tritume di reggimenti, 220

Martellata lentezza, 252
ma se ti volgi e guardi, 42
Ma senti—dice—che meraviglia quel *cip* sulle piante, 194
Memoria d'America, 46
Meno male lui disse, il più festante: che meno male c'erano tutti, 186
Metropoli, 190
Metropolis, 191
Mezzanotte fu sui cancelli, 58
Midnight on the gates was, 59
Military Poem, 59
Mille Miglia, 128
Mille Miglia, 129
Mi prendono da parte, mi catechizzano, 184
Muezzìn, 248
Muezzin, 249

Nebbia, 48
Nel bicchiere di frodo, 100
Nella neve, 122
Nell'anno '51 li ricordi, 148
Nell'estate padana, 264
Nel mutismo domestico nella quiete, 222
Nel sonno, 152
Nel vero anno zero, 186
Nera cintura stivaletti neri, 216
Never again—shreds of regiments, 221
Niccolò, 244
Niccolò, 245
Niente ha di spavento, 258
Nocturne, 253
Non era un sogno, vi dico, 188
Non resta più molto da dire, 178
Non sanno d'essere morti, 92
Non sa più nulla, è alto sulle ali, 90
Non ti turbi il frastuono, 52
Non vorrai dirmi che tu, 260

Notes from a Dream, 113
Not much remains to be said, 179
Notturno, 252
Now it's over you appear, 253
Now the day's a sigh, 83

Of Cuts and Stitches, 215
Often through tortuous alleys, 97
of the long and torrid days, 219
Ogni angolo o vicolo ogni momento è buono, 258
Ogni volta che quasi, 224
O mia vita mia vita ancora ansiosa, 86
O my life my life still anxious, 87
On a Cemetery Photograph, 177
Only the summer is true and this, 95
On the Back of a Piece of Paper, 309
On the Creva Road Again, 169
On the Death of Ungaretti, 330
On the lake the sails made a white and compact poem, 123
On the tables the drinks grow clearer, 47
On the Zenna Road Again, 125
Ora il giorno è un sospiro, 82
Other Place of Work, 261
Outskirts 1940, 77
Over there where from tower, 89

Pantomima terrestre, 194
Passing, 147
Paura prima, 258
Paura seconda, 258
Perché quelle piante turbate m'inteneriscono?, 124
Perché, tu che sai tutto di Roma, 256
Per fare il bacio che oggi era nell'aria, 128

Periferia 1940, 76
Piazza, 58
Piazza, 59
Pin-up Girl, 86
Pin-up Girl, 87
Place of Work, 205
Pleasingly in September air, more hiss than howl, 135
Poesia militare, 58
Poeta in nero, 216
Poet in Black, 217
Poetry Is a Passion?, 161
Port Stanley like Trapani, 334
Posto di lavoro, 204
Poteva essere lei la nonna morta, 168
Presto la vela freschissima di maggio, 68
Prewar Letter, 281
Prima sera d'Atene, esteso addio, 80
Progress, 275
Progresso, 274

Quanti anni che mesi che stagioni, 120
Quattro settembre, muore, 244
Quei bambini che giocano, 144
Quei gradini dove fa gomito la scale, tutta, 204
Quei suoi occhi morati dorati dall'ultimo sole, 274
Quei tuoi pensieri di calamità, 202
Quel che di qui si vede, 264
Questa notte sei densa e minacciosa, 50
Queste torri alte sulla memoria, 54
Qui il tarlo nei legni, 120
Qui il traffico oscilla, 48
Qui stava il torto, qui l'inveterato errore, 142

Recalling America, 47
Reduced to so few the early
　spring gathered them, 175
Requiem, 256
Requiem, 257
Revival, 216
Revival, 217
Rimbaud, 270
Rimbaud, 271
Rinascono la valentia, 90
Risalendo l'Arno da Pisa, 86

Saba, 144
Saba, 145
Sale macaroni piove sulla memo-
　ria, 114
Sale macaroni rains on the mem-
　ory, 115
Sarà che esistono vite come
　foglie morte, 206
Sarà la noia, 218
Scoperta dell'odio, 142
Second Fear, 259
See how the voices fall and
　friends, 73
Se la febbre di te più non mi
　porta, 98
Self-Portrait, 331
Se ne scrivono ancora, 158
September, 65
September the Eighth, 115
Settembre, 64
Se ti importa che ancora sia es-
　tate, 260
She grew in silence like the grass,
　215
Sicily '43, 285
Si ravvivassero mai. Sembrano
　ravvivarsi, 202
Situation, 147
Situazione, 146
Six in the Morning, 133
Soldati a Urbino, 54

Soldiers in Urbino, 55
Solo vera è l'estate e questa sua,
　94
Somebody's plotting against you
　below, 253
Sono, 192
Sono andati via tutti, 198
Soon May's freshest sail, 69
Sopra un immagine sepolcrale, 176
So—said G. drifting off into a
　yawn, 159
Spesso per viottoli tortuosi, 96
Sport on Sunday, 45
Starmene solo nel ranch, 46
Stay by myself on the ranch, 47
stealthily I pass through Luino,
　225
Stecchita l'ironia stinto il corag-
　gio, 256
Storm at Salsomaggiore, 51
Strada di Creva, 68
Strada di Zenna, 62
Suddenly the evening seizes us,
　63
Suddenly—you notice—it's
　come, 127
Sui tavoli le bevande si fanno più
　chiare, 46
Sul lago le vele facevano un bianco
　e compatto poema, 122
Summer in the Po Valley, 265

Tardi, anche tu li hai uditi, 152
Tempo dieci anni, nemmeno,
　268
Temporale a Salsomaggiore, 50
Ten years more, not even that,
　269
Terrace, 63
Terrazza, 62
That Film of Billy Wilder's, 296
The African Sickness, 107
The Alibi and the Benefit, 161

439

The Ashes, 133
The Athenian Girl, 83
The Beach, 199
The Capture, 341
The city—I'm saying—where shade, 149
The Disease of the Elm, 261
The doors flung open for nothing onto evening fog, 161
The embrace that repels and doesn't unite, 161
The force of the commonplace, 147
The Friends, 149
The Great Friend, 141
The green's submerged in blue-and-blacks, 45
The Hope, 189
The Knoll, 265
The Lines, 159
The Misapprehension, 125
Then others come: others, of another kind, 191
The Option, 348
The Provisional Time, 121
There's nothing terrifying, 259
The Reunited, 197
The Reunited [prose], 329
The Sharks, 129
The soul, what we call the soul and is nothing, 171
The splendid the delirious rain has eased, 131
These towers high in the memory, 55
The telephone, 119
The Title of Poet, 306
The toy, 215
The two tunnels, with gratings, 113
The Wall, 193
The window lifted you one evening, 67

The witless smile that halted me between tombstones, 177
They don't know they're dead, 93
They'd said you were lost, 197
The Year '45, 322
The Year '43, 315
They're being written still, 159
They've all gone away, 199
They take me aside, they chide me, 185
Those brown eyes of hers gilded in the final sun, 275
Those Children Playing, 145
Those steps at the stairway's elbow, all, 205
3 dicembre, 56
3 December, 57
Ti distendi e respiri nei colori, 60
Ti si era dato per disperso, 196
The Unjust Pity, 185
To a Childhood Companion, 179
To M. L. Passing above her Town in an Express Train, 53
Tonight you are close and threatening, 51
To make the kiss that was in the air today, 129
Too late has the time come, 97
Torna il tuo cielo d'un tempo, 54
Toronto sabato sera, 204
Toronto Saturday Night, 205
To the tent approaches, 81
To Youth, 59
Traducevo Char, 248
Tra il brusio di una folla, 102
Translating Char, 249
Troppo il tempo ha tardato, 96
Tutto, si sa, la morte dissigilla, 132
Twenty-Six, 375
Two Old Flames, 310

440

Un'altra estate, 66
Un altro ponte, 48
Una motocicletta solitaria, 106
Una visita in fabbrica, 134
Uneasy in the troop train, 77
Un giorno a più livelli, d'alta marea, 226
un giorno perdoneranno, 144
Un grande amico che sorga alto su me, 140
Un improvviso vuoto del cuore, 88
Un incubo, 142
Uphill, 263
Un posto di vacanza, 226
Un ritorno, 122
Un sogno, 166
Un solo giorno, nemmeno. Poche ore, 146
Un tempio laico, 250
Up the Arno from Pisa, 87

Valor and grace, 91
Venga per un momento la fitta del suo nome, 270
Verano and the Solstice, 257
Verano e solstizio, 256
Verde vapore albero, 266
Vertical village, 251
Viaggio all'alba, 120
Viaggio di andata e ritorno, 122
Via Scarlatti, 118
Via Scarlatti, 119
Villaggio verticale, 250
Villa Paradiso, 86
Villa Paradiso, 87

We will arise on the lakeside, 63
What am I waiting for turning round the house, 133
What escapes of us on the line of the current?, 129
What there is to see from here, 265
Where will it be with whom is the smile, 255
Why do these troubled branches touch me?, 125
Why ever do you, you who know all about Rome, 257
will one day forgive, 145
Window, 127
Winter, 43
Winter in Luino, 61
With none other than you, 119
With the rustling of a crowd, 103
With solemnity from level ground, 251
Works in Progress, 207

Years After, 131
You Began, 308
You don't mean to tell me that you, 261
You remember them in '51, 149
Your Memory in Me, 69
Your memory in me is a solitary, 69
Your sky of those days returns, 55
Your Thoughts of Calamity, 203
You stretch out and breathe in the colors, 61
Youth is all in the light, 77
You were first a hurt, 101

Zenna Road, 63